Molly.

Dambuster-in-Chief

Dambuster-in-Chief

The Life of Air Chief Marshal Sir Ralph Cochrane GBE, KCB, AFC

Richard Mead

Pen & Sword
AVIATION

First published in Great Britain in 2020 by
Pen & Sword Aviation
An imprint of
Pen & Sword Books Ltd
Yorkshire – Philadelphia

Copyright © Richard Mead 2020

ISBN 978 1 52676 507 9

The right of Richard Mead to be identified as Author of this work has been asserted by him in accordance with the Copyright, Designs and Patents Act 1988.

A CIP catalogue record for this book is
available from the British Library.

All rights reserved. No part of this book may be reproduced or transmitted in any form or by any means, electronic or mechanical including photocopying, recording or by any information storage and retrieval system, without permission from the Publisher in writing.

Typeset by Mac Style
Printed and bound in the UK by TJ Books Limited,
Padstow, Cornwall.

Pen & Sword Books Limited incorporates the imprints of Atlas, Archaeology, Aviation, Discovery, Family History, Fiction, History, Maritime, Military, Military Classics, Politics, Select, Transport, True Crime, Air World, Frontline Publishing, Leo Cooper, Remember When, Seaforth Publishing, The Praetorian Press, Wharncliffe Local History, Wharncliffe Transport, Wharncliffe True Crime and White Owl.

For a complete list of Pen & Sword titles please contact

PEN & SWORD BOOKS LIMITED
47 Church Street, Barnsley, South Yorkshire, S70 2AS, England
E-mail: enquiries@pen-and-sword.co.uk
Website: www.pen-and-sword.co.uk

Or

PEN AND SWORD BOOKS
1950 Lawrence Rd, Havertown, PA 19083, USA
E-mail: Uspen-and-sword@casematepublishers.com
Website: www.penandswordbooks.com

Contents

Introduction		vii
Prologue		x
Chapter 1	The Cochranes of Dundonald	1
Chapter 2	From Fife to Scapa	11
Chapter 3	Lighter than Air	21
Chapter 4	Heavier than Air	32
Chapter 5	Moving Up	45
Chapter 6	Squadron Commander	57
Chapter 7	Staff Officer	63
Chapter 8	New Zealand	77
Chapter 9	Training	90
Chapter 10	3 Group	103
Chapter 11	5 Group	115
Chapter 12	UPKEEP	124
Chapter 13	617 Squadron	131
Chapter 14	Operation CHASTISE	144
Chapter 15	Time and Distance	155
Chapter 16	Cheshire	164
Chapter 17	The Big City	177

Chapter 18	The Independent Air Force	186
Chapter 19	Germany and the Tirpitz	199
Chapter 20	Transport Command	211
Chapter 21	The Air Council	223
Chapter 22	Into Industry	236
Chapter 23	Family Business	249
Chapter 24	Reflections	261

Abbreviations	269
Acknowledgements	272
Notes	274
Sources and Bibliography	283
Index I & II	288

Introduction

On the morning of 17 January 1991, I arrived at Charing Cross station in London on the way to my office. As I passed through the ticket barrier on to the concourse I became aware that the announcements of arrivals and departures had been temporarily suspended, replaced instead by loud music. The tune was very familiar to me, a busy introduction giving way to a swelling melody, both repeated later on their way to the climax. It was *The Dam Busters March*, the theme to the film of 1955, and it was being played for good reason. Much earlier that day and thousands of miles away, Operation Desert Storm had just been launched and would in due course result in the liberation of Kuwait from the rule of the Iraqi dictator, Saddam Hussein. The initial attack had been made by the air forces of the US-led coalition, and the RAF was playing a prominent part. British Rail had clearly decided to generate patriotic support by a direct allusion to a much earlier and dramatically successful operation. I have no doubt that I was one of many who made the connection, and I left the station with a lump in my throat.

As a young boy in the 1950s and a teenager in the 1960s, Paul Brickhill's book *The Dam Busters* was high on my reading list, as was Guy Gibson's *Enemy Coast Ahead*, and I saw the film on multiple occasions on television. If you were to ask anyone of my generation to name some of the wartime exploits of the RAF, the destruction of the Möhne and Eder Dams by 617 Squadron would probably be eclipsed only by the Battle of Britain. For those of all generations who have any interest in the air war of 1939–45, this almost certainly remains the case today.

Unlike the Battle of Britain, with its cast of thousands, the Dams Raid was conducted on a relatively modest scale. There was no pantheon of fighter aces, but instead two heroes, the brilliant scientist and the fearless bomber pilot. The former produced the weapon, encountering numerous obstacles on the way, the latter delivered it on target, but not without incurring a high rate of loss amongst his crews. Although some may question the value of the operation, there is no doubt that these two men, Barnes Wallis and Guy Gibson, fully deserved the plaudits they received at the time and thereafter. However, overall responsibility for delivering success lay with another, Air Vice-Marshal the Hon. Ralph Cochrane, the Air Officer Commanding 5 Group, by whom 617 Squadron was raised and under whose personal control it went on to serve with great distinction for the remainder of the war.

I have known about Ralph, whom I will call by his given name from here on to distinguish him from other members of his family, for over sixty years. I had an opportunity to learn much more about him recently, whilst I was undertaking the research for a biography of Marshal of the Royal Air Force the Lord Elworthy. Sam Elworthy had a relatively short involvement with the Dams Raid himself whilst working as Group Captain Operations at Bomber Command HQ but, more pertinently, he served under Ralph on three occasions, the first briefly whilst Chief Instructor of an Operational Training Unit in a group commanded by Ralph, the second as one of his station commanders in 5 Group and the third, during the last year of the war, as his Senior Air Staff Officer. He admired Ralph more than any other officer he encountered in his long RAF career.

I found that the Elworthy and Cochrane families had become friends and was delighted when Air Commodore Sir Timothy Elworthy, Sam's eldest son, gave me an introduction to John Cochrane, who was at the time in the course of sorting out his father's papers. John very kindly allowed me to look at them, which helped considerably with Elworthy's story. Moreover, in the course of my research, I came to realize that Ralph was much more than just the man behind the Dams Raid, which had in fact occupied only two months of his thirty-seven year service career. He seemed to be an obvious candidate for a biography himself.

When I suggested this tentatively to John Cochrane I encountered a problem which I had come across on two earlier occasions, which was that my proposed subject, an inherently modest man, had himself not wanted any biography to be written, although he was always immensely helpful to other authors writing about his former colleagues. Quite understandably, his children were initially reluctant to go against his wishes, but they were persuaded that their father fully deserved to be better known and were thereafter highly supportive.

I had already seen a number of valuable documents during my research on Elworthy, but I was astonished by the amount of material which Ralph had accumulated. It included diaries, flying log books, essays and articles which he had written and the transcript of an interview which he had given to the Air Historical Branch of the RAF in 1975. The family also produced letters from him to his wife, Hilda, which added much to my knowledge of his private life. Most excitingly of all, I discovered that towards the end of his life Ralph had written his memoirs for the benefit of his family. Covering some eighty pages of typescript, these provided an invaluable framework to his story, as well as contributing to my understanding of the man himself and the events with which he was associated.

Ralph had an intriguing start as an aviator when he joined the airship branch of the Royal Naval Air Service during the Great War. This was followed by a highly successful career in the RAF between the two world wars, during which he developed two particular specializations, bombing and flying training. The recognition of his high intellect resulted in his selection, as a relatively junior officer, to advise the Government of New Zealand on the country's air defences, and he was asked to stay on to become the first Chief of the Air Staff of the Royal New Zealand Air Force. As for his activities during the Second World War, the success of his squadrons in applying new techniques of target marking and precision bombing was arguably greater than that of the Pathfinders, and was spectacularly demonstrated by the sinking of the German battleship *Tirpitz*. Following his wartime exploits he went on to achieve much for the post-war RAF, notably in forging the peacetime Transport Command, and he rose to become the Vice-Chief of the Air Staff. He was, in short, an exceptional officer, and telling his full story has been long overdue.

It is, however, Ralph's role in the raising, training and deployment of 617 Squadron and, in particular, in the planning of its most audacious operation on the night of 16/17 May 1943, for which he will continue to be best remembered. He took an unusually close interest in all the squadron's activities, personally chose its four commanding officers after Gibson and remained in contact with its members for the rest of his life. There is every reason to believe that they thought of him not only as their overall commander but as one of themselves, and that is why he fully deserves to be known as the 'Dambuster-in-Chief'.

Prologue

The mood in the Operations Room was sombre, the atmosphere on the brink of oppressive. Whilst quiet conversations were taking place elsewhere, the three most important people in the room were now silent, their thoughts focused on events taking place hundreds of miles away. The scientist was the most agitated of the three, pacing up and down, going over and over in his mind the implications of what he, more than any other person, had set in train. The Air Chief Marshal and the Air Vice-Marshal stood still as the minutes ticked by.

Four times the telephone had rung, and each time the signals officer had reported the codeword for no result. Now the telephone rang again. The officer asked for confirmation and, when it came, his face lit up as he shouted out, 'It's Nigger!' A wave of relief swept through the room. The scientist began to pump his arms up and down as the Air Chief Marshal went over to shake him vigorously by the hand. On the face of the Air Vice-Marshal, a man not given to extravagant displays of emotion, a rare smile appeared as he realised that his plan for the most extraordinary operation in his service's history had at last come to fruition.

Chapter 1

The Cochranes of Dundonald

Both the roots and the name of Clan Cochrane have long been matters of debate. As to the former, some say that the clan was of Scandinavian ancestry, others that it was descended from the Strathclyde Britons. Like those of many great Scottish families the name is most probably territorial, deriving from the Barony of Cochrane – not a peerage, but a territory held as a tenancy-in-chief from the crown – which in the Middle Ages was situated near Paisley in Renfrewshire. However, it has also been suggested that it derives from the Gaelic words pronounced as 'coch ran', meaning 'roar of battle', bestowed as a result of some deed of valour. Whatever the case, the Cochranes were firmly established in the Paisley area by the late thirteenth century.

The members of the clan were loyal supporters of the early Stewart kings, not always to their advantage, as Robert Cochrane, a favourite of James III, who created him the Earl of Mar, discovered to his cost when he was seized by rebellious nobles in 1482 and hanged without trial. In spite of such setbacks the family prospered overall, and in 1592 the then chief, William Cochrane, was wealthy enough to be able to attach a high tower to his manor house, which became known as Cochrane Tower or Cochrane Castle. It was subsequently demolished, although its site is still marked by a stone. William was the last of the direct male line of the senior branch of the family, but he entailed his estate to one of his daughters, Elizabeth, and arranged for her to marry Alexander Blair, on condition that Blair assumed the name and the arms of Cochrane.

Alexander and Elizabeth had seven sons, all of whom became soldiers. The oldest, John Cochrane, found himself torn in his allegiance. On the one hand, he was a supporter of Charles I; on the other, he was sympathetic to the National Covenant, whereby the Episcopacy, the bishop-led and essentially Anglican church which Charles tried to impose on Scotland, was abolished by the Scottish Parliament in 1638 in favour of the Presbyterian faith, which abjured bishops. John, who had been serving in Ireland, returned to join the Covenanter army. He was, however, then implicated in 'The Incident', a plot to kidnap the Marquis of Argyll, the leader of the Covenanters, and other Scottish nobles of the same persuasion. The plot failed and, indeed, hastened the end of Charles's efforts to impose the Episcopacy. John Cochrane avoided execution, but he lost his commission in the Scottish army and part of his estates, only avoiding confiscation of the rest by making over the Barony of Cochrane to his next brother, William. He then joined the King's army and was partially compensated for his losses with a knighthood. He subsequently acted for the King as one of his representatives on the Continent and later joined the future Charles II in exile, but he probably did not live to see the Restoration.

William Cochrane not only took over much of John's property but also developed a large estate of his own, which included Dundonald Castle and the land around it. The castle, which lies in Ayrshire between Troon and Kilmarnock, is a 'Peel Tower' constructed in the fourteenth century, but by the time of its acquisition it was no longer habitable, so William and his family lived at the nearby Auchans House. Like his brother John, William was a staunch supporter of Charles I, was similarly knighted by the King and, in 1647, created Lord Cochrane of Dundonald. He raised a regiment in support of Charles II's forlorn attempt to regain his throne after his father's execution, which came to nothing at the Battle of Worcester, and continued to back Charles during his years of exile. In 1653 William acquired the Place, or Palace, of Paisley, lying just next to Paisley Abbey in the heart of the old clan territory, and he and his family moved to live there subsequently. His support for the Stewart kings resulted in a severe financial penalty from the government of Oliver Cromwell, but he retained his estates and, for his longstanding loyalty, was created Earl of Dundonald by the restored king in 1669.

The Cochranes have, throughout their history, had an extraordinary record of service in the armed forces of first Scotland and then Great Britain, and this was certainly true of the descendants of the 1st Earl of Dundonald, although few of them achieved high rank over the next century. Archibald Cochrane, who succeeded as 9th Earl in 1778, managed to serve both as a cornet in the Army and as a midshipman and acting lieutenant in the Royal Navy, although it is as a scientist and inventor, who amongst his other achievements discovered a simple way of extracting tar from coal, that he is best known. The properties in Paisley and Dundonald, including the Barony of Cochrane, had by this time been sold, and Archibald lived on a large estate at Culross, brought into the family by his grandmother. Culross was a major coal-mining area, and Archibald was able to build kilns on his own land for the extraction of the tar. He also discovered coal gas, but failed to realize its potential as a source of fuel, the exploitation of which would have made a considerable difference to the family fortunes. In the event, he was to die a pauper.

The first Cochrane to achieve flag rank in the Royal Navy was the 9th Earl's younger brother, Alexander Cochrane, who joined as a midshipman in 1775, in time to serve in the American War of Independence. In 1779 he was promoted to lieutenant and in 1780 he acted as signal officer to Admiral Sir George (later Lord) Rodney, taking part in the indecisive action against a French fleet off Martinique, in which he was wounded. Rodney's patronage saw Alexander's swift promotion to commander and appointment to the command of a 14-gun American-built sloop, HMS *Pacahunter*. He was promoted to post captain only two years later, but this coincided with the end of hostilities with France, resulting in his having to go on half-pay. In 1790, however, he was given command of the 24-gun frigate HMS *Hind* and was still captaining the ship when France declared war on Great Britain in 1793, going on to capture no fewer than eight enemy privateers. He was then appointed to the 38-gun HMS *Thetis*, in which he was equally successful, taking two French frigates returning from the West Indies, for which he was presented with a sword by the Lloyd's Patriotic Fund. In 1799 he took command of his first ship-of-the-line, the newly built 74-gun HMS *Ajax*.

Ajax joined the Mediterranean Fleet under Admiral Lord Keith, who delegated to Alexander Cochrane the responsibility for directing the British landings at Aboukir Bay on 2 March 1801. Alexander's barge, whose passengers included the British military commander, Major General Sir John Moore, was the first to touch ground in a successful operation which spelled the end of the French occupation of Egypt. Alexander's relationship with Keith deteriorated, however, and it was perhaps no surprise that, when peace was declared in 1802, the *Ajax* was paid off and he was placed on half-pay. On the resumption of hostilities in 1803 he was given command of the 74-gun HMS *Northumberland*.[1] In the following year he became a rear admiral, hoisting his flag in the same ship, and in 1805 he was appointed Commander-in-Chief of the Leeward Islands Station. In 1806 he was second-in-command to Admiral Sir John Duckworth at the victory over the French fleet off San Domingo, for which he was awarded a Large Gold Medal by the Admiralty and a Sword of Honour by the Corporation of the City of London and was created a Knight of the Bath. After toying with support for the growing rebellion against Spain by its South American colonies, for which he earned the disapproval of the British Government, he redeemed himself by capturing the French islands of Martinique and Guadeloupe, becoming Governor General of the latter before being appointed to command of the North American Station on 1 April 1814, by which date Great Britain had been at war with the United States of America for nearly two years

Alexander Cochrane's appointment coincided with the abdication of Napoleon, which freed up naval resources to carry out a strict blockade of American ports. He was not, however, prepared to conduct this reactively, preferring to take the fight to the enemy. He sailed into Chesapeake Bay in August 1814 and orchestrated an attack on the US capital city, Washington, which was carried out by Major General Robert Ross, with the enthusiastic participation on the ground of Rear Admiral George Cockburn, Alexander's second-in-command. As a response to the burning of Toronto (known at the time as York), the attackers set light to a number of key government buildings, including the Capitol, and also to the President's house, only the walls of which were left standing. When the house was rebuilt, its walls were painted white to hide the marks of the fire, giving rise to the name by which the building became known. Alexander was subsequently unsuccessful at Baltimore, although his attack on the city was later immortalized in the words of the 'Star Spangled Banner'. His Army colleagues, conveyed in Alexander's ships, were even less successful at New Orleans on 8 January 1815, a disastrous battle from a British perspective, even though the war had actually been concluded by the time it was fought.

New Orleans marked the end of Alexander's active service, although he was subsequently appointed C-in-C at Plymouth. He had established a strong naval tradition in the family, and two of his sons joined the Royal Navy. The oldest, Thomas John Cochrane, served under his father, whose patronage ensured his rapid promotion. He became a post captain at the extraordinarily young age of seventeen and fought at Martinique and in the War of 1812, in which he captured an American privateer. He was Governor of Newfoundland from 1825 to 1834 and eventually hoisted his flag as a rear admiral and second-in-command of the East India Station in 1841. Much of the latter part of his career was spent in the Far East, and his final command was as C-in-C Portsmouth from 1852 to 1855. He lived long enough to become an admiral of the fleet in 1865 and died in 1872.

By some way the most famous member of the Cochrane family, and a remarkable man by any standard, was Alexander's nephew and the eldest son of the 9th Earl of Dundonald. Thomas Cochrane was born on 14 December 1775 but did not succeed to the earldom until 1832, by which time he had concluded his most noteworthy exploits, and so he is generally known to history by his courtesy title, Lord Cochrane. He was the beneficiary of an outrageous and, indeed, unlawful system known as 'false muster', by which his name was placed by his uncle Alexander on the books of a number of the warships which he commanded. The purpose of this was to give the boy vastly accelerated seniority when he actually joined the Royal Navy on 23 July 1893 at the age of seventeen as a midshipman in Alexander's then ship, HMS *Hind*. This enabled him to achieve fast promotion to acting lieutenant in 1795 and, having passed the necessary exam, to lieutenant in the following year. When Alexander was appointed to the *Thetis* he took his nephew with him, but Lord Cochrane subsequently served on other ships before joining Lord Keith's flagship, HMS *Barfleur*, in the Mediterranean. Having transferred his flag to HMS *Queen Charlotte*, Keith ordered Cochrane, who had accompanied him, to sail a large French prize, the *Généreux*, from Palermo to Mahon in Minorca, at that time a major British base. The voyage, with a crew whose numbers were not really sufficient for the task, proved to be a difficult one, and the ship was very nearly lost in a storm, but the prize was brought in safely and, by way of reward, Cochrane was given command of the brig *Speedy*, with promotion to commander. After a short period on convoy duty, he was given a roving commission by Keith to wreak the greatest possible damage on shipping along the Spanish coast, Spain being at this time allied to France. During a period of thirteen months he sank numerous ships and took many others as prizes.

On 6 May 1801, Cochrane carried out what many believe to have been the most extraordinary ship-on-ship engagement in naval history.[2] The *Speedy*, whose armament consisted of fourteen 4-pounder guns, encountered the Spanish 32-gun frigate *El Gamo*, with a crew nearly five times the size of Cochrane's own. Closing right up, the brig grappled with its opponent, whose guns were unable to depress sufficiently to cause any damage, whilst the *Speedy* could deploy its own light armament at point-blank range. After breaking off and grappling again, Cochrane ordered the doctor to take the helm, whilst the whole crew, which now included his younger brother, Midshipman Archibald Cochrane, stormed the *El Gamo*. One of the *Speedy*'s crew managed to haul down the enemy's colours, the Spanish surrendered and their ship, with the crew as prisoners in the hold, was sailed to Mahon. Three months after this great success, however, the career of the *Speedy* came to an abrupt end when she was overcome by three French line-of-battle ships and Cochrane was made prisoner, although he was exchanged for a French officer shortly afterwards.

Lord Cochrane was promoted to post captain on 8 August 1801, his appointment having been delayed by the adverse reaction of the First Lord of the Admiralty, the Earl of St Vincent, to his uncle Alexander pressing his case somewhat intemperately and to Cochrane himself seeking promotion for his own first lieutenant in similar vein. He was not appointed to a ship before the Treaty of Amiens brought the war to a temporary end, and it was only by dint of persistence that he obtained the command of the 22-gun HMS *Arab*, formerly a French privateer. The task he was allotted was unspectacular, convoy escort and fishery protection in the North Sea. It was only when St Vincent was replaced by Cochrane's fellow Scot, Viscount Melville, that he was given command of a new 32-gun frigate, HMS *Pallas*, in which he conducted a highly successful cruise off the Azores which brought in some valuable prizes. In August 1806 he was transferred to a larger ship, the 38-gun HMS *Impérieuse*, with orders to harry the Mediterranean coast of France and Spain, frequently working in conjunction with Spanish guerrillas on land. This led to his receiving the plaudits of his superior, Admiral Lord Collingwood, but also provoked the disfavour of the Admiralty for what they considered to be his profligate use of gunpowder and shot.

In March 1809 Cochrane returned to England, only to be summoned to the Admiralty and ordered to produce a plan for the destruction of a large part of the French Atlantic fleet, which at that time lay in the Basque Roads, a sheltered anchorage between the Isle of Oléron and the French mainland. The French were being blockaded by a British fleet under Admiral Lord Gambier, who had shown a strong disinclination to use fireships to destroy the enemy as the Admiralty proposed. Cochrane delivered his plan and was instructed to put it into effect. He reported to Gambier, to whom he made it clear that he had been personally ordered to carry it out, and this caused a great deal of jealousy amongst far more senior captains. Cochrane took his small force of fireships and a few other vessels in across the boom which had been erected to protect the French ships and, although they did little direct damage, they forced the French to weigh anchor, following which many of them ran aground. Gambier, however, failed to support him and, although a large number of enemy ships were destroyed, many escaped to fight again.[3]

Cochrane was made a Knight of the Bath by a Government badly needing good news at this stage of the war and treating the Basque Roads as a great victory, while it was proposed that Gambier should receive a vote of thanks in the House of Commons. Like many serving officers, Cochrane had by this time entered politics, in his case as a Member of Parliament for the constituency of Westminster, and he made it known that he would oppose the motion to thank Gambier. In response, the admiral demanded to submit himself to a court martial, the result of which was that he was not only acquitted of dereliction of duty but congratulated on his achievement.

Lord Cochrane's fortunes now went from bad to worse. The Admiralty was exasperated with his stance on Gambier, but became even more so when he began a campaign in the House of Commons to expose corruption in the Admiralty Prize Courts, and particularly the Court in Malta, whose officials he claimed, with considerable justification, had retained large sums due to the officers and crews of ships which had taken prizes. He even travelled to Malta at his own cost, only to be sent to prison, from which he managed to escape with the aid of his many sympathizers.

His fortunes dipped even further when in 1814 he became involved, naively but quite innocently, in a major Stock Exchange fraud. His trial was presided over by Lord Ellenborough, who was not only Lord Chief Justice but also a Cabinet Minister, at a time when Cochrane was causing great embarrassment to the Government. The verdict went against him and his sentence was a fine of £1,000, a year in jail and an hour in the pillory. The last of these was dropped in the face of public indignation, but he was imprisoned in the Marshalsea, from which he escaped, only to be recaptured. He was also expelled from the House of Commons, but immediately re-elected by the voters of Westminster. Worst of all, he was struck off the Navy List and his knighthood was forfeited.

It was thus unsurprising that when in May 1817 an invitation was extended to him to become C-in-C of the Chilean Navy, Cochrane readily accepted it. He oversaw the building of a new warship for the Chileans, the *Rising Star*, before leaving with his wife and two children for what was effectively exile from the United Kingdom. Spain's South American colonies were by this time in open revolt. Argentina had already fallen to the nationalists, and in 1817 the Army of the Andes, led by José de San Martin and Bernardo O'Higgins, crossed into Chile, seizing Santiago and Valparaiso. The centre of Spanish resistance was to the south in Valdivia, which Cochrane, in his flagship *O'Higgins*, took from the sea in a stunning attack. The seizure of the last Spanish stronghold in Chile freed him to accompany San Martin in an assault on Peru. Cochrane's contribution was again immense, the centrepiece being the cutting-out of the Spanish flagship, the *Esmeralda*, in Callao harbour.

Cochrane's relationship with the liberators, especially San Martin, was not always an easy one, largely due to their failure to honour their obligations to pay him and his crews. Undaunted, he sailed north to Ancon, where he seized the treasure which had been confiscated from the Spanish and paid his crews the arrears they were owed, before handing back the balance. This, however, was the final nail in the coffin of his relationship with San Martin, which had by that time deteriorated considerably. In any event, Cochrane believed that his work in Chile and Peru was now over, so accepted an invitation to command the Brazilian Navy

Brazil was at this time still ruled by the Portuguese royal family, who had escaped there when the French occupied their country in 1807, but the King's son, Don Pedro, had announced the country's independence when his father returned to Portugal, and had declared himself Emperor. The Portuguese still held much of northern Brazil, but within four months of his arrival in March 1823, Cochrane had defeated their much larger fleet, thereby effectively liberating the rest of the country. He was made Marquess of Maranhão in recognition of his service.

His work in Brazil at an end, in 1825 he accepted an offer to command the Greek fleet in the country's war of independence from the Ottoman Empire. His achievements there were not as spectacular as those in South America, and it was an Anglo-French-Russian fleet under Admiral Sir Edward Codrington which destroyed the Turkish fleet at the Battle of Navarino in 1827. Cochrane now returned to England to carry on the campaign to clear his name. It was the accession to the throne in 1830 of William IV, himself a former serving naval officer and broadly sympathetic to Cochrane, which provided the stimulus to remedy the injustices done to him and, having succeeded as the 10th Earl of Dundonald in 1831, he was restored to the Navy List with the rank of rear admiral. It was not until 1847 that he was reinstated in the Order of the Bath and, in the following year, he was appointed C-in-C of the West Indian and North American Station for three years, his last service at sea. He died on 31 October 1860 and was buried in Westminster Abbey at the request of Queen Victoria.

There were no later Cochranes able to emulate the feats of the 10th Earl of Dundonald, at least partly because of lack of opportunity, but many were highly distinguished in their own way. Lord Cochrane's second son, Arthur, also joined the Royal Navy, serving in the Baltic during the Crimean War, commissioning in 1861 HMS *Warrior*, the Royal Navy's first iron-hulled and armour-plated ship, and hoisting his flag as C-in-C of the Pacific Squadron in 1873. The eldest son, also Thomas, later the 11th Earl, served in the Army but failed to progress beyond captain in rank. The 12th Earl, Douglas, on the other hand, had a successful military career, whose high point was the command of the Mounted Brigade in Natal during the Boer War, in which role he relieved Ladysmith. In due course he achieved promotion to lieutenant general.

The second son of the 11th Earl, Thomas Horatio Arthur Ernest Cochrane, was born in 1857. He began a military career in the Argyll and Sutherland Highlanders, later serving for some years in the Scots Guards before returning to his former regiment. In 1892, however, he entered politics with his election as the Liberal Unionist Member of Parliament for North Ayrshire. He served in government, initially from 1895 to 1901 as Parliamentary Private Secretary to Joseph Chamberlain, the Secretary of State for the Colonies. He then took leave of absence from Westminster to take part in the Boer War as a staff officer, before returning to serve as Under-Secretary of State for the Home Department in the Government of Arthur Balfour from 1902 to 1906. He was narrowly defeated by the Liberal candidate in the General Election of January 1910 and subsequently focused on his business interests, although he commanded the 2nd/7th (Fife) Battalion of the Black Watch, which saw no service overseas, from 1914 to 1917. In 1919 he was raised to the peerage as Lord Cochrane of Cults.

In 1880 the future Lord Cochrane of Cults married Lady Gertrude Boyle, the elder of the two daughters of George Boyle, 6th Earl of Glasgow. They had eight children, four girls, one of whom died in infancy, and four boys, the third of whom and the seventh child, Ralph Alexander Cochrane, was born on 24 February 1895.

Chapter 2

From Fife to Scapa

Ralph Cochrane was born in the family home, Crawford Priory, situated about two miles south-west of Cupar in Fife. The greater part of the house was built by the eccentric Lady Mary Lindsay Crawford in the early nineteenth century, on the site of a modest hunting lodge erected by her father, the 21st Earl of Crawford. The architectural style of the main building was a strange mixture of Scottish Baronial and Gothic and was said to resemble a priory, although there was no religious connection. Following Lady Mary's death the estate passed to the Earls of Glasgow, and in the 1870s the 6th Earl attached a tall tower and a chapel. Whilst not as large as many country houses, its indoor staff nevertheless numbered about twelve, with two gardeners, two gamekeepers and two foresters outside.

The grounds of Crawford Priory extended to some 4,000 acres and included a substantial lime works of medieval origin, which was said to have provided material for the building of the Palace of Holyroodhouse in the seventeenth century. The agricultural land was substantially worked by tenants until well after the Great War, when Ralph's father decided to farm it himself.

The house and estate formed the dowry of Ralph's mother, Lady Gertrude Boyle, whom his father married, doubtless out of love, but also in the belief that she was a great heiress. He was therefore taken aback to find out after the event that the property was burdened by a substantial mortgage. Moreover, his new father-in-law invited him for a meeting shortly afterwards at which he was asked to lend the Earl, who was effectively bankrupt, a substantial sum of money! The 'old rogue', as he called his father-in-law, left him with debt from which he only extracted himself in due course through his own good management.

Notwithstanding this setback, Ralph's parents went on to produce a large family. The oldest of their offspring, Louisa, was already grown up when Ralph was born, but was unmarried; she was frequently unwell and was to die of tuberculosis in 1916. Tom, the eldest son and the heir to the title, was ten years older than Ralph, and Archie, the second son, eight years older, so during his childhood they were away a great deal, Tom at university, after which he was called to the Bar, and Archie training for and then commissioned in the Royal Navy. Another daughter, Marjorie, died in infancy long before Ralph was born. This left Katherine, always known as Kitty and born in 1890, and Dorothy, born in 1893, as the two nearest to Ralph and thus his regular playmates. A fourth son, Roger, was to be born in 1898, but was an invalid from his early days and died at the age of ten.

As with all children of this era born into the nobility or landed gentry, Ralph's early childhood was spent in a nursery, which was ruled over by the children's nurse, Alie. Alie, always called Atta by Ralph, had begun service as a nursemaid but had been promoted at the age of eighteen when her superior was sacked by Ralph's father for some misdemeanour; she was to remain in service with the family for sixty years. Ralph's recollection of his early years in the nursery was dominated by the cold in the house during the winter months, possibly because his father was unable to afford effective heating,

As Ralph grew up, the estate became increasingly attractive as his playground, with many mature trees for climbing, including one magnificent beech whose lower branches were ideal for swings. At the age of ten he was given an airgun, with which he used to terrorize the local rabbit population. On one occasion he shot a pheasant through the eye, his father's subsequent outrage at this feat having been performed in the close season being somewhat moderated by appreciation of his son's marksmanship! Ralph and his sisters also made friends with the driver of 'Puffing Billy', the old tank engine which drew the empty wagons up to the lime works and brought them back again filled with the product. They were even, on occasion, allowed to work the regulator and the brakes.

In the early years of the twentieth century the motor car was becoming an established means of conveyance, and Ralph's father's first such vehicle was an Arrol Johnston 'Dogcart'. This extraordinary wooden-bodied conveyance had two rows of seats facing forward, one for the driver and one passenger, situated behind and above that for two other passengers, with a third row facing backwards behind the driver. Ralph was invariably consigned to the last of these, and suffered accordingly from all the dust kicked up by the solid tyres. The car was far from comfortable and no faster than a horse-drawn carriage, but, as his father used to say, no gentleman would ever want to travel at more than 12mph!

By the time that Ralph was born, his father was well established in his political career, which required him to stay for much of the time at his London house in Eaton Square; he was sometimes accompanied by the family, and one of Ralph's earliest memories was being lifted up by Kitty to watch Queen Victoria driving past in Hyde Park. The constituency was a long way from Fife, and general elections were therefore fought from The Pavilion in Ardrossan, a large house which was the summer residence of the Earl of Eglinton and Winton. During Ralph's childhood, elections were held in 1900 and 1906, the latter resulting in the fall of Balfour's Conservative/Liberal Unionist coalition in a landslide defeat to the Liberals, although Ralph's father was able to hold North Ayrshire. The children were frequently employed in distributing election addresses and other tasks.

In the summer holidays of Ralph's childhood and schooldays, the family, or at least those still living at Crawford Priory, went to stay every year at Shane's Castle on Lough Neagh in Ireland, the home of Ralph's Aunt Louisa, who was married to Lord O'Neill. This they always greatly enjoyed, especially as two of the O'Neill daughters were reasonably close in age to Ralph, Kitty and Dorothy.

At the age of ten, Ralph was packed off to board at Ardvreck, a prep school which was and still is situated outside Crieff in Perthshire. It had been founded in 1883 by Mr W. E. Frost, who was the headmaster when Ralph arrived, although Ralph himself always believed that the school was really run by his wife, Katie. Ralph very much enjoyed being able to explore the local woods and moors, although on one occasion he and another boy, separated from the school party, became lost in fog. They decided to place a stick on its end and follow the direction in which it fell. By the sheerest good luck, this led them back to the party and not to a cold night out on the moor.

Academically, Ralph was a late developer, starting near the bottom of his first class but gradually working his way up the order, helped in some measure by extra coaching laid on by his parents during the holidays. By his last year his reports were showing 'good', 'very good' or 'excellent' for all his subjects, and although he was by no means top of the class, he was more than holding his own in the end of term examinations.

In January 1908, at the age of nearly thirteen and having passed the entrance exam and undergone a none too rigorous interview at the Admiralty, Ralph entered the Royal Naval College, Osborne in the Drake Term. He appears to have played no part in the choice of the Royal Navy for his future career, but neither did he object. His brother Archie had by that time been in the service for some years and was doing well, and there was, of course, an immense family tradition in the service. It may be that the decision was occasioned by his father's continuing to pay off the debts incurred by his father-in-law. Service in the Royal Navy required no private means, unlike the Army, in which the son of a noble family would have been expected to join a 'good' regiment, where the cost of living would have significantly exceeded his pay and required a sizeable allowance to make up the difference.

Osborne had been opened only five years earlier, as the result of a decision by the Admiralty that all officer cadets for the Royal Navy should spend their first two years there before moving on to Dartmouth. The Navy insisted on the recruitment of its officers at an early age, in the belief that there was no other way in which they could gain adequate technical knowledge before being commissioned. Ralph came to consider this absurd and was proved right when a large number of public-school boys were commissioned in the early years of the Great War on the back of only six months training and proved to be just as good as those who had spent four years at the two colleges.

At the time of his entry to Osborne, Ralph was impressed by a sign which greeted the cadets on their arrival at the college and read, 'There is nothing the Navy cannot do', although he was to realize very quickly that this was nonsense; he was in no way a nonconformist, but it is evident that he was already starting to question conventional wisdom. This assertion of the Navy's omnipotence was, in any event, spoilt shortly afterwards by a mathematics master who, incensed by the indolence of his students, banged his desk and shouted at them, 'I know you think that you are the salt of the earth, but let me tell you, you are nothing more than a lot of grubby little schoolboys!'

Ralph found Osborne strange and, at times, unpleasant. The accommodation, built around the stable block of Queen Victoria's former residence on the Isle of Wight, was spartan and very cold in winter, and the discipline was tough, exercised in part by cadet captains who used knotted lanyards on the bare bodies of their juniors. Boys in his term would accompany him on to Dartmouth in due course, so he came to know them well. One who did not stay the course was George Archer-Shee, who was accused of stealing a postal order from another cadet and expelled in disgrace. His father took the case to court, for which he retained as counsel Sir Edward Carson, one of the finest barristers of the day. The case resulted in a victory for the Archer-Shees and payment of damages and costs by the Admiralty, and was later immortalized in Terence Rattigan's play 'The Winslow Boy'.

Other near contemporaries included Prince Edward, later Prince of Wales and briefly King Edward VIII, who was two terms Ralph's senior, and Prince Albert, later Duke of York and King George VI, who was two terms his junior. The former was by far the more popular, outgoing and charismatic, unlike his shy and stammering brother, but as Ralph was to recognize many years later, the right man got the job in the end.

It was with some relief that Ralph moved with his class to Dartmouth in January 1910. The college building was magnificent, the dormitories were light and airy and the plunge baths, which had been freezing cold at Osborne, were actually heated. When it came to extra-curricular activities, Ralph was neither a fast runner nor a heavyweight, so did not excel at rugby, but he did enjoy sailing on the Dart in the College's cutters. Academically, he began to edge his way up the class. Having settled about a third of the way down the sixty cadets by the time he left Osborne, by the end of his fifth and penultimate term at Dartmouth he had edged into the top ten, his tutor reporting, 'He has done an excellent term's work and is well reported on by all masters who like him. His examination results in Mathematics, Navigation and Science are excellent.'[1]

The last six months of the course were spent at sea on the armoured training cruiser HMS *Cornwall*. The cadets joined the ship at Plymouth, where, lying at anchor in the Sound in a swell, Ralph experienced seasickness for the first time, a disability which he was never able fully to overcome. The ship crossed the Atlantic to St Lucia, where it was coaled, before sailing on to Barbados. There Ralph met his father, who was on his way to Trinidad to inspect the family oil and asphalt concession. This had been acquired by the 10th Earl of Dundonald whilst he was C-in-C there in the mid-nineteenth century, but the title deeds for most of the concession had been destroyed by a fire in the records office, allegedly inspired by Standard Oil, which wanted it for itself. However, the title to some sections remained, and Ralph's father formed Trinidad Oilfields to exploit them.[2]

From Barbados HMS *Cornwall* made its way to Bermuda and from there sailed to Quebec, where it anchored in the St Lawrence opposite the site of General Wolfe's famous victory. The next port of call was Halifax in order to coal ship, following which the cruiser re-crossed the Atlantic, encountering some ice and passing close to the spot where RMS *Titanic* had sunk only weeks earlier.

The final examinations saw Ralph placed sixth out of the remaining fifty-nine cadets, with first class passes in Part I (general academic subjects), Part IIA (Navigation and Science) and Part IIB (Seamanship and Engineering) and winning the second prize for both Navigation and Seamanship. He was later to say that none of the other top cadets reached high rank and, indeed, that the only one who became an admiral in due course was well down the order. He was referring to Cadet A. C. G. (later Admiral Sir Alexander) Madden, who was placed thirty-eighth, with two seconds and a third in the three parts of the exam. Ralph was, however, mistaken, as two more highly placed cadets would reach flag rank in due course: Cadet (later Vice Admiral) R. D. Oliver was placed second overall and Cadet T. H. (later Admiral Sir Thomas) Troubridge was placed eleventh. Nevertheless, Ralph was correct in that success at Dartmouth was not a particularly good guide to a cadet's future career.

On 15 September 1912 Ralph was appointed a midshipman in the Royal Navy. Just under a month later, in company with three others, he joined his first and, as it would turn out, his last ship, HMS *Colossus*, which was moored at Devonport. *Colossus* was a 20,000-ton dreadnought battleship, which had only been commissioned a year earlier and was thus at the cutting edge of naval technology. As her main armament she carried ten 12-inch guns in five turrets, one forward, two aft, and one each on the port and starboard wings. As secondary armament she mounted sixteen 4-inch guns and three 21-inch torpedo tubes. With a crew of 751, she was a significant component of the

Second Battle Squadron, which was at the time under the command of one of the country's great sailors, Vice Admiral Sir John Jellicoe. Jellicoe was, however, to become Second Sea Lord in December 1912 and was succeeded by Vice Admiral Sir George Warrender.

Ralph's arrival coincided with coaling, a tiring and dirty job which was inevitably followed by intensive cleaning and painting. The *Colossus* then sailed to Spithead to pick up Jellicoe, who hoisted his flag in the ship, before retracing her course as far as Weymouth, where the rest of the squadron had assembled, for two days of exercises. The combined squadron then sailed to Berehaven[3] on the north shore of Bantry Bay, where there was a naval dockyard. Here Jellicoe struck his flag on the ship, which shortly afterwards sailed to Portland to join the First Battle Squadron under the command of Vice Admiral Sir Stanley Colville.

The next few months were spent in shuttling backwards and forwards between the south coast of England and the south-west coast of Ireland, carrying out gunnery and torpedo exercises and general drills with the squadron, culminating in February 1913 in major manoeuvres with the whole Home Fleet of three battle squadrons, one battle-cruiser squadron, a cruiser squadron and a destroyer flotilla

Apart from his susceptibility to seasickness, Ralph was happy enough in his new profession. The gunroom, where the sub-lieutenants and midshipmen messed, saw a strange mixture of bullying and friendliness. A number of games were devised by the senior members: 'Crawl for Jesus' was the signal for the junior midshipmen to crawl under the table of the seniors where they received a number of kicks to smarten them up, whilst 'Froggie would a-wooing go' required them to hop round the gunroom with knees bent. With alcoholic liquor heavily subsidized, a great deal of drinking took place.

Ralph's initial post was in the forward transmitting station, where the readings from five range finders were transmitted on to a moving paper. His job was to strike an average and pass it to the main control room, where it was used to calculate the range of the opening salvo. His superior officer was Major 'Skintight' White, a large and friendly Royal Marine who was inebriated more often than not, which meant that Ralph was often effectively running the station.

In the late spring of 1913 there was a change of scenery when the squadron sailed up to the west coast of Scotland, conducting operations largely in and off the Firth of Clyde from an anchorage in Lamlash Bay, but venturing north as far as Oban and Mull, before sailing across to Ireland, where the ships were open to the public both in Bangor and in Dublin. In mid-July the fleet entered Scapa Flow, the first time Ralph had visited what would be its main base in the event of hostilities with Germany. This was followed by a series of major war exercises in the North Sea off the coasts of both Scotland and England, the likely setting for any major confrontation with the German High Seas Fleet.

One episode in the summer of 1913 always stuck in Ralph's mind. The *Colossus* and a number of other vessels had entered Loch Ewe, on the west coast of Scotland, with a view to establishing whether it could be used as a substitute for Scapa Flow. Ralph was on the bridge, acting as assistant to the Navigator, Lieutenant Commander Geoffrey Freyberg, his role being to time the run between two marks ashore and the moment of dropping the anchor, which needed to be measured accurately in seconds. He had spent a shore leave in London, during which he had attended the White City Exhibition, where he won no fewer than three wristwatches, one of which he was using. To his horror it stopped at the critical moment, a fact which became rapidly clear to both Freyberg and Captain Goodenough. Once the confusion had cleared, the captain's voice rang right across the bridge: 'And how much, young man, did you pay for that watch?'

On one of the squadron's occasional visits to Bantry Bay, Ralph was detailed to take charge of the Roman Catholic church party going ashore for a service. He had by that time learned to handle the ship's cutters, but the pinnace in which he was ordered to take the party had quite different sailing characteristics. By the time that the service ended, the wind had come up significantly and the small vessel had to be close-reefed. As Ralph neared the vast battleship, he saw the Commander (the ship's second-in-command) pacing up and down on the quarterdeck. Basing his approach on his experience with the cutter, Ralph tried to bring the pinnace smartly alongside, but to his dismay the vessel failed to respond and its bow ran straight into the gangway with a loud rending noise. Ralph went up to the Commander to report the party's return, to be met with the words: 'Go below, I have told the senior midshipman to beat you.'!

In February 1914 there was a welcome change from routine when the First Battle Squadron visited Portugal, sailing initially for Arosa Bay. The weather en route was so bad that a man was washed overboard, and in spite of a life belt being dropped immediately and the ship itself heaving to and reversing its course, he was never found. At Arosa Bay the squadron met up with other elements of the Home Fleet for exercises there, in Pontevedra Bay and off Vigo. There was some opportunity for relaxation, with races between the ships' whalers, crewed by their midshipmen, but no shore leave. However, on the return journey there was a formal visit to Cherbourg, which included a trip to a carnival ashore, whilst the ships were illuminated at night and at times open to visitors.

With war looming, the Home Fleet assembled at Spithead, anchoring in two long columns, and on 19 July King George V carried out a review from the Royal Yacht *Alexandria*. As the crisis deepened, the fleet was ordered north to Scapa Flow on 29 July. *Colossus* was at Portland when the order came through and weighed anchor with the rest of the First Battle Squadron to leave harbour through a narrow entrance known as 'the hole in the wall'. For some reason the helm was showing the wrong way on the main bridge, and the captain ordered Ralph to stand by the helmsman on the lower bridge and to acknowledge and reverse each order as it came down, thereby allowing the tight gap to be satisfactorily negotiated.

The last months of 1914 and the early part of 1915 were a miserable time for the sailors, although, as Ralph was to concede readily, much preferable to Flanders. Scapa was isolated from the rest of the country, there was no leave and little in the way of diversion ashore. The units of what had by now been renamed the Grand Fleet conducted frequent sweeps in the North Sea, but saw no sign of the enemy. Ralph, who had been made an acting sub-lieutenant in September 1914, was quartered in the midshipman's flat near the bow of the ship, where the rise and fall in rough weather could be as much as 80ft, and the sea coming over the fo'c'sle penetrated down the cables, saturating clothes and bedding.

On one day in early March 1915, Ralph was on watch on the bridge of *Colossus* during a sweep off the Norwegian coast in a Force 10 gale. Her five turrets of heavy guns instead of the more normal four meant that the ship was inherently top heavy, and she seemed to roll almost to the horizontal when the sea was on the beam, so he was feeling the effects of serous seasickness. A signal arrived which he was ordered to take to the Captain, the Hon. Edward Fitzherbert. Seeing that it came from the Admiralty and was addressed to all captains, asking for thirty midshipmen or acting sub-lieutenants to volunteer for special duty in the south, and in spite of having no idea as to what was involved, Ralph requested permission to do so as he handed over the signal. On the ship's return to Scapa Flow, he was duly selected and shortly afterwards found himself in a train, on his way to London with twenty-nine others.

Chapter 3

Lighter than Air

On their arrival in London, Ralph and the other volunteers reported to the Admiralty, where they were received by none other than the First Sea Lord, Admiral of the Fleet Lord Fisher. Jackie Fisher gave them a talk on the menace of German submarines, which had carried out a number of successful attacks on Allied shipping in the English Channel and the North Sea. He then went on to explain that the Admiralty believed the threat could be significantly reduced by the use of airships to escort the convoys, that it was proposed to deploy many more than were currently in service and that they were now to learn how to fly them, beginning with a course on unpowered balloons. That he also said that most of them would probably either be dead or have won VCs within a year did nothing to deter his audience, all of whom were delighted to have left Scapa Flow.

Ralph was promoted to substantive sub-lieutenant on 15 March 1915 and re-designated as a flight sub-lieutenant in the Royal Naval Air Service two days later. He and his fellow would-be pilots were ordered to report to a large house in Roehampton, which was the home of No. 1 Balloon Training Wing RNAS. Here they came under the command of, in Ralph's words, 'two charming and elderly gentlemen who had ballooned as a hobby before the war and were now only too delighted to return to their pastime'.[1] In fact, the two were Lieutenants John Dunville and Charles Pollock, both of whom had established considerable reputations as balloonists, winning international prizes, and who had been granted temporary commissions as instructors. Neither man had yet reached his fiftieth birthday.

Four students at a time were taken up by one or other of their instructors in a large basket slung under a balloon filled with coal gas. Once the bag was full of gas, ballast was thrown out and the balloon rose into the air. With no power, it was now at the mercy of the wind. The height could be adjusted, either by throwing more ballast overboard to rise or by venting gas from a valve to fall. Before landing, 400ft of heavy rope was lowered over the side, down which could be slid a grapnel to slow the balloon or even to stop it, if it held on to a hedge. Then, in combination with letting out more gas and if necessary ripping open a panel in the envelope, the balloon was brought back to terra firma.

As the direction of flight was entirely at the whim of the wind, three aids were required. One was a map, the second an ABC rail timetable and the third a copy of *Debrett's Landed Gentry*. The last of these was essential for the identification of a suitable landing site in a large estate, with the likelihood of retainers who might be employed in packing up the balloon to take to the nearest station, whilst the crew took tea with the owners of the property, hopefully including the young ladies of the family. This worked well, except on one of Ralph's flights when a large building in parkland surrounded by a wall was spotted and a successful landing made, only for the party to discover that they were in the grounds of the Broadmoor Criminal Lunatic Asylum!

In order to pass out, the trainee pilot had to undertake a solo flight in a small balloon, this time filled with hydrogen, although the general principles remained the same. Ralph's flight took place in gusty conditions and was initially hampered by a blockage in the release valve which required him to climb on to the side of the basket and free the obstruction; not only that, but whilst he was attempting to land, the panel in the envelope failed to rip and the grapnel to hold, so he was dragged across some fields. Nevertheless, he did pass out and, with the other graduates, was posted initially to the RNAS station at Kingsnorth for initial training on airships.

Kingsnorth, situated in Kent on the Hoo Peninsula, close to the north bank of the Medway, served as the main centre for testing new airships, which were usually assembled for the first time on the site. The history of airships in the armed forces of Great Britain was a short one, going back only as far as 1907 in the Army and 1909 in the Royal Navy, the latter service taking over full responsibility for their development, construction and employment in 1914. There were three types of airship, rigid, semi-rigid and non-rigid, but the semi-rigid were, at least for the moment, not being used. The rigid airships, of which there were none operational at this time but which would in due course play a major role, consisted of a lightweight metal or wooden frame, which was covered overall by the envelope and within which were containers of lighter-than-air hydrogen gas.

The non-rigid airships lacked a framework and were thus much cheaper and quicker to build, for which reason they were produced during the Great War in very much larger numbers. The gas was contained within the envelope, but because hydrogen expands as the airship rises and contracts as it descends, fabric compartments called ballonets were placed inside the envelopes into which air was blown by the engine, enabling the envelope to keep its shape. Control was exercised by a small crew seated in a 'car' slung below the airship.

Although there had been many experimental and development models, the first type of non-rigid to come into general service, developed at Kingsnorth under a team led by the talented Commander T. R. Cave-Brown-Cave, was the Submarine Scout, the initial model of which comprised a 60,000cu.ft. envelope, with a car, consisting of the fuselage of a Royal Aircraft Factory BE2 reconnaissance aircraft, attached to the envelope by wires and patches. The car was powered by a 75hp Renault engine and had two cockpits, which contained the controls for the rudder and elevator. It was on the Submarine Scout that Ralph received his training, and in only a very short time he was informed that he had qualified as a pilot and ordered to pick up a ship straight off the production line to take to his first active posting. This was at the RNAS station at Capel-le-Ferne, near Folkestone, under the command of Flight Commander A. D. Cunningham.

The role of the Submarine Scouts at Capel was to escort the ships taking the men of the British Expeditionary Force to and from France and to patrol the English Channel as far west as Dungeness. The patrols were uneventful, possibly because the very presence of the airships, carrying 160lbs of bombs, acted as a deterrent to the submarines, which as a result were seldom seen. The officers lived in a large house on the cliffs and were able to go to the theatre in Folkestone once or twice a week.

In September 1915 Ralph was posted back to Kingsnorth to act as understudy to the chief test pilot, whom he was in due course to succeed. By this time, alternative models of the Submarine Scout were coming into service, with larger envelopes of 70,000cu.ft. and different cars, including one using a Maurice Farman body, which was popular because it used a 'pusher' rather than a 'tractor' engine, whose exhaust did not blow into the crew's faces. It was suggested that it should be determined whether or not it was possible to restart an engine in the air, and Ralph was ordered to try.

This involved climbing out of the car on to 2½ inch wooden rails under the side of the fuselage and edging along until he was able to grasp the prop with one hand, whilst the other hung tightly on to the car, and then swinging it as vigorously as possibly. As the engine on this occasion was warm, it started without much trouble, but failure would have meant no air being blown into the ballonets, potentially causing the envelope to collapse. Moreover, Ralph was carrying out the exercise without a parachute!

In early 1916 a new class of airship, the Coastal, made its first appearance, and Ralph spent much time on the early production models, ironing out the snags. This was a much larger ship with a 170,000 cu.ft. envelope which was tri-lobed, copying an earlier French Astra-Torres design, and a car created out of the fuselages of two Avro 510 seaplanes, with an engine at each end. The availability of a ship of this size prompted Ralph to develop some ideas for shooting down German Zeppelins, which had carried out their first successful raid on British soil on the night of 19/20 January 1915 and by 1916 were attacking London and other towns and cities in the south of England. His proposal required two Coastals operating together and employing heavy calibre weapons. It was submitted to the Admiralty, which replied that this was the most sensible scheme submitted thus far but that it was not prepared to adopt it at that time, although it would retain it for future consideration. This was the first example of serious original thinking by Ralph on operational issues, and it certainly brought him to the notice of the Admiralty. Another idea was to attach a BE2 fighter to an airship and slip it to attack a Zeppelin when a commanding height had been achieved, something which the plane could not do on its own. This idea foundered at the test stage, although experiments were successfully carried out by rigid airships later in the war.

One alarming incident took place whilst Ralph was carrying out towing trials on an early Coastal model off Harwich in May 1916. The airship was successfully attached to the light cruiser HMS *Carysfort*, but when the cruiser gathered speed it began to yaw. The tow rope then parted, but another was dropped on to the quarterdeck, although the cruiser slipped it again after only a short time. The loose rope then fouled the forward propeller, badly damaging one blade, and also put a hole in the envelope, releasing gas. Ralph managed to pull some fabric over the hole, but the forward engine was running so roughly that it had to be stopped. This meant that not enough air was being generated for the ballonets, so Ralph had to clamber astride the nose of the car and saw off the opposite blade so that it was balanced with the damaged one, after which it worked sufficiently well to get the airship back to base.

At the end of July 1916 Ralph found himself back at Scapa, where a small two-Submarine Scout RNAS station had just been established to carry out anti-submarine patrols.[2] Although tucked away at the head of Scapa Bay, just south of Kirkwall, it proved to be exceptionally windy. On one occasion, returning from a patrol, the wind was so strong that, even with every available man on the ropes, it proved impossible to hold the ship, let alone walk it into the hangar. Ralph immediately vented some gas, but the handling party lost control and the ship collapsed. Although the envelope was undamaged and the only loss was in gas, Ralph found himself up before a Court of Enquiry. Whilst he avoided censure, he thought it ridiculous that nothing of the sort took place when the RNAS wrecked any of its much more expensive seaplanes; but it seems that an airship was classified by the Royal Navy as a ship, damaging which without good reason was a offence, and that an aeroplane was not.

There was another incident for which Ralph felt that he did deserve a reprimand, but avoided one. A Swedish ship had been sunk about 20 miles east of Scapa, and he was sent out to locate the submarine responsible. He passed the wreckage of the ship and spotted a conning tower about three miles away, sending a signal to alert a destroyer flotilla which was on its way. The submarine had dived before he reached the spot, so Ralph put the airship into a tight turn to circle the area. He then saw an oil slick, which he followed before it disappeared, so he executed another circle and again picked up an oil slick, which in due course disappeared too. This happened again and again, until he realized what was happening: the oil was coming from his own engine, only dripping down into the sea when he turned sharply. The submarine escaped!

By this time Ralph had established something of a reputation for himself as both an operational and a test pilot. His confidential report before leaving Kingsnorth for Scapa had described him as 'A most excellent young officer. Specially recommended for promotion', and he was indeed promoted to flight lieutenant on 30 June 1916. When he left Scapa his CO, Lieutenant Commander R. C. Hayes, wrote that he had conducted himself 'to my entire satisfaction, both as a flying officer and as executive officer of the Station. I consider Flight Lieutenant Cochrane to be an officer of exceptional ability.' His immediate future, however, was to lie in testing new airships rather than conducting operations.

Up to this point Ralph had had no experience of rigid airships. The rigid programme had come to an abrupt halt in September 1911, when His Majesty's Airship No. 1, also called *Mayfly*, had broken in two during testing. The evident success of the Zeppelins, however, caused a rethink at the Admiralty and, in April 1913, it was decided to reopen the rigid programme. By their very nature the rigids were much more complex than the non-rigids, and the design and construction of new airships was not undertaken by the RNAS. A contract was instead awarded to Vickers, already a significant builder of warships, and a design team was formed consisting of H. B. Pratt and a young draughtsman called Barnes Wallis. Construction work on what was designated HMA No.9r was carried out at Walney Island near Barrow-in-Furness, where a very large shed was erected. The contract was cancelled in March 1915, on the grounds that the war would be over before long, but reinstated three months later, when it became clear that this was not to be the case. The ship was rolled out on 16 November 1916, a week after Ralph had been posted to Barrow, and its first test flight took place eleven days later.

Ralph now became intimately involved with the flight testing programme of No.9r, at the same time making a good friend of Wallis. Much of the testing actually took place at RNAS Howden in Yorkshire and included the longest flight in an airship recorded in Ralph's log book at 12 hours and 45 minutes. Rather extraordinarily, he had to take time off in June 1917 to re-graduate as an airship pilot at the RNAS Training Establishment at Cranwell. This establishment had only been opened on 1 April 1916, primarily to train new pilots of both airships and fixed-wing aircraft, but it was decided that all those who had gone through the very much more informal process at Kingsnorth would have to qualify again, doubtless in the interest of applying common standards.

Ralph also became involved with the new 23 Class rigid airships, which were based on No.9r, but were longer and faster, with greater capacity in the envelope and a much improved lift. Contracts were placed with three firms, one of which was Vickers at Barrow. However, as Ralph had been designated as the trial pilot of No.24r, which was being built to Vickers design by Beardmores near Paisley, he had to spend a lot of time there supervising construction work.

Ralph was never to pilot No.24r, the deployment of the 23 Class being overtaken by events when a Zeppelin crashed in Essex more or less intact, an event which led to immediate changes in future rigid design. Instead, promoted to flight commander, he found himself posted back to Kingsnorth and to the continuing non-rigid programme, which now included a wider range of airships, including the very effective Submarine Scout Zero, the Coastal Star and the North Sea, the last the largest of them all with a 360,000cu.ft. envelope and a potential flying time of up to 48 hours. Ralph, who was in charge of the erection and testing of all new airships, once again earned the approval of his superiors, not just as a capable and skilful trial pilot, but as an officer who could produce new ideas, which included schemes for mooring and proposals for improving the reliability of the engines.

On 1 April 1918 the Royal Flying Corps and the Royal Naval Air Service were absorbed into the new Royal Air Force and Ralph exchanged his rank of flight commander for that of substantive captain and temporary major in the new service. In practice very little changed as, for the time being, the Admiralty retained operational control of the airships, almost all of which were employed in conjunction with the surface fleet.

In July 1918 Ralph was ordered by the newly formed Air Ministry to report to the Directorate of Airship Production, still part of the Admiralty, where he was told that he had been selected to travel on its behalf to Italy to carry out flight testing of a semi-rigid airship and, once he had completed the trials, to hand it over to the Directorate of Airship Operations, which would arrange for one of its officers to fly the airship to the UK. Ralph thought this arrangement ridiculous, a waste of manpower caused by the rivalry between the two directorates, but he lacked the authority to object.

There had been scant interest up to that time in the semi-rigid variety of airship design, but the Italians had had some success with it, and it was decided that one would be purchased for eventual testing in an operational environment. The SR.1 was one of the M Class of semi-rigid airships, designed by the remarkable Umberto Nobile.[3] It lacked a frame, but differed from non-rigids in that it had a keel which ran underneath the envelope along the length of the airship, conferring a higher degree of strength and rigidity. It was larger than any of the British non-rigids, but smaller than the rigids.

The party left the UK on 22 July and travelled by boat and train to Ciampino,[4] south-east of Rome. It consisted of Ralph, who was in overall charge and would carry out the trials, Captain F. M. Rope, who would be advising on engineering and the installation of machinery, Captain George Meager, who was to accept the airship on behalf of the Directorate of Airship Operations and pilot it back to the UK and who stopped off in France to inspect landing sites en route, and Captain T. D. Williams, who was to act as the second officer. In addition, the party was accompanied by Captain Parry Jones and Mr A. D. Ritchie, who were visiting Italy in connection with fabric work, and it also included the non-commissioned members of the crew, three coxswains, three engineers, two wireless ratings and four spare hands.

When the party arrived at Ciampino, SR.1 was by no means ready to fly. Although the British officers were able to keep a close eye on the remaining construction work and to fly in some of the operational semi-rigid airships to gain experience of their characteristics, they also had a lot of time on their hands, which enabled them to make a number of visits to Rome and the surrounding area. Their Italian hosts were charming and entertained them to guest nights and to other dinners away from the base.

Ralph himself spent some time at the British Embassy, where his brother Archie was staying. Archie had had a highly eventful war. A submarine commander, he had made his name in the summer of 1915, during the Gallipoli campaign, by carrying out a devastating series of attacks on Turkish shipping in the Sea of Marmora and even, on more than one occasion, blocking a railway line with his deck gun and destroying the train which was trapped behind it. He even succeeded in firing a torpedo into the Turkish Imperial Arsenal. Having escaped through the Dardanelles, his submarine E-7 came to grief on his second foray into the Sea of Marmora six weeks later, when it became entangled in an anti-submarine net in a minefield. Forced to surface and surrender, he was sent to a prisoner-of-war camp but escaped, only to be recaptured. He was then sent to another camp deep in Anatolia, escaped once again and this time he and his companions made it to the coast, stole a boat and sailed to Cyprus. For his exploits he earned himself a DSO and bar.[5]

SR.1 flew for the first time on 26 August, handled by an Italian crew but with Ralph, Meager and Rope aboard. A number of problems were identified which would take time to fix, so Ralph and Meager were able to visit other airship stations at Ferrara and at Campalto, near Venice, enabling them to visit that city. Speed trials on SR.1 were carried out during late September and into early October, but there was still a great deal of spare time, and Ralph, Meager and Williams kept fit by walking in the Alban Hills. Rope, however, succumbed to the Spanish Flu epidemic which was by now sweeping Europe and was very ill in hospital in Rome, although he recovered in due course.

The final acceptance trials took place in October, and in mid-month Ralph formally handed over the airship to Meager, with whom he had at times had a somewhat testy relationship, with differences of opinion as to how the airship should be handled and on the composition of the crew to fly it back to England. SR.1 eventually departed from Ciampino on 28 October and arrived at Kingsnorth three days later. Ralph returned to England by train and was back in London comfortably before the Armistice on 11 November.

On 29 November, Ralph was posted to RAF Pulham, a long established airship base in Norfolk. SR.1 was now based there and was to form part of the escort for the German U-boat fleet on its voyage to surrender at Harwich, although it was scrapped less than a year later; Ralph himself always believed that it conferred no real advantage over the more advanced non-rigids. At Pulham he served initially as Chief Experimental Officer, in which role he developed a much better relationship with Meager, who was now also based at Pulham, piloting initially SR.1 and later a Submarine Scout Twin, a class of airship which had only come into service just before the end of the Great War. The station was already in the throes of demobilization, which caused considerable disruption and, at one point, a mutiny. Captain Frederick Boothby RN, the station commander, announced that there would be a holiday, arranged for a section of Royal Marines to be available from the nearby depot and, at 4.00 in the morning, arrested all the ringleaders in their beds, after which there was no more trouble.

In the New Year Honours of 1919 Ralph was awarded the Air Force Cross. He had been mentioned in despatches in 1917, but this distinction was evidence of the continuing regard in which he was held by his superiors. The AFC was granted at that time 'for an act or acts of valour, courage or devotion to duty whilst flying though not on active operations against the enemy',[6] and, in Ralph's case, it clearly related to his career as a test pilot. In his congratulatory letter, the Director of Airships, Brigadier-General Edward Maitland, wrote that 'no one has merited the award more than you for all the good work you have done during the War.' A few days later, he received a letter relating to his work in respect of SR.1. from the Secretary to the Air Ministry, who wrote that the Lords Commissioners of the Admiralty 'would be glad if this officer could be informed that the various reports which he has compiled have been read by them with great interest and reflect very creditably on him; also that My Lords have noted with satisfaction the manner in which this officer has carried out the various duties entrusted to him.'

In May 1919, like most of the officers holding acting or temporary rank, Ralph had to relinquish his rank of major, but three months later his permanent commission as a flight lieutenant in the RAF was confirmed. After all the plaudits he had received, it was probably with some disappointment that in September Ralph found himself appointed as First Officer to Godfrey Thomas in the new R.33. Thomas had been one term junior to him at Osborne and Dartmouth and they had served together in the *Colossus*, so they knew each other well. As commander of R.29 Thomas had been awarded a Distinguished Flying Cross for the airship's part in sinking a German submarine, and Ralph himself held a high opinion of him, believing that he would have been in the running for Chief of the Air Staff many years later, had he not been killed in 1921 in the disastrous crash of the R.38. It was some consolation that Ralph's former station commander at Capel, Alexander Cunningham, now serving as deputy to Maitland, wrote to say that the appointment was being made to enable him to gain experience of the new class in order to be able to take command of a sister ship at an early date.

As events turned out, Ralph was never to command another airship. On the other hand, in contrast to his professional frustration, his private life was enhanced by the first taste of a sport which he was probably to enjoy more than any other – skiing. In January 1920 he accompanied his sister Dorothy[7] to Mürren in Switzerland. He loved the whole experience and looked forward to going again. Only weeks after his return, however, he learnt that he was to be posted abroad on special duty. By the middle of June he was in Egypt.

Chapter 4

Heavier than Air

Ralph was posted to Air HQ Middle East in Cairo, although he lodged with 216 Squadron at RAF Heliopolis,[1] just outside the city. He was there for two reasons. The first was to select the site for the Egyptian station of what was expected to become the great airship route from the UK to India and Australia. The second was to carry out tests in local conditions on a range of fabrics which might be used for the envelopes of the airships, which had hitherto only been employed in a cool climate. He was accompanied by Sergeant Green from the airship service, and one or other of them was taken up in a borrowed DH9a twice daily to 10,000ft to take temperature readings there and at lower levels, whilst also testing the fabrics. Although he had to write regular reports, the work was not arduous, and Ralph had plenty of opportunity to develop a social life, to play squash and tennis in Cairo and to visit Luxor, Thebes, Karnak and other sites of antiquity.

In March 1921, the Cairo Conference was held to agree on a number of issues concerning the Middle East in the aftermath of the Great War. Chaired by Winston Churchill, the Secretary of State for the Colonies, it was attended by a number of Arab leaders, with whom it was agreed that the British mandate in Mesopotamia would become the new Kingdom of Iraq under the Emir Feisal, son of the Sharif of Mecca, and that Transjordan would be ruled by Feisal's younger brother, Abdullah, although both would remain British Protectorates. Palestine would remain under a British mandate.

Among the delegates to the conference,[2] on the express invitation of Churchill, was Air Marshal Sir Hugh Trenchard. Rightly called the 'Father of the RAF', Trenchard had fought hard to establish the independence of the new service against the strong and persistent opposition of both the Royal Navy and the British Army, and he continued to battle to preserve it. He had, however, had one recent success. Towards the end of 1919, the activities of Mohammed Abdullah Hassan, nicknamed the 'Mad Mullah', threatened the colony of British Somaliland, and the Army's solution was to send two infantry divisions to put down the revolt. On being asked for his opinion, Trenchard replied that the situation could be contained by a squadron of DH9a bombers and the local colonial forces. A very brief bombing campaign forced the Mad Mullah to flee to Abyssinia, and peace was restored. Trenchard now proposed to do much the same in Iraq, where an uprising in the north of the country was being supported by Turkey. His offer to send six squadrons there was accepted by Churchill and the new King, not least on the grounds of cost, which was a small fraction of what would be required for a purely land-based campaign. A similar arrangement was concluded with Transjordan.

This was to have implications for Ralph before very long, but in the meantime Trenchard, carrying out an inspection of local RAF units, asked to meet him to find out what he was doing. In Ralph's words:

> I had my speech all ready, pointing to where the airship mast would be, and visualising the ships coming in from England and refuelling before setting out for India and Australia. But it didn't go a bit like that. Rocking back on his heels he looked down on me and said, 'Young man, you are wasting your time, go and learn to fly an aeroplane.' This at a time when scientific opinion still put the maximum all-up weight of an aeroplane at 30,000lbs with a range of perhaps 1,000 miles, leaving the airship as the only real contender for Empire and ocean routes. We had all been brought up on the 'square/cube law' and believed it implicitly, so my immediate reaction was that the old man had never heard of it – and he probably hadn't, but as in so much else his intuition proved right.[3]

On 18 March, just a few days after his meeting with Trenchard, Ralph began his flying training on a relatively informal basis with the Special Instruction Flight at Heliopolis, whilst at the same time continuing with his work on fabrics. He learnt on the Avro 504, the RAF's basic trainer from 1914 to 1933, and he had an excellent instructor, Flying Officer L. G. 'Splinter'

Wood.[4] He went solo for the first time two and a half weeks later, the flight being a very short one, largely due to Ralph's failure to set the correct fuel mixture, which caused the engine to splutter and reduce power so that he had to land on the open desert, fortunately on hard sand.

His more formal flying training began with his posting on 26 May to the recently opened 4 Flying Training School at Abu Sueir, near Ismailia on the Suez Canal, with a temporary attachment to and accommodation at 70 Squadron. He retained responsibility for the testing of fabrics, but delegated much of the work on this to Sergeant Green in his absence. At 4 FTS he moved on in due course to instruction on the Bristol Fighter, which he considered a joy to fly. Abu Sueir was a long way from the fleshpots of Cairo, but there were compensations, the most notable of which was the ability to sail on Lake Timsah, through which the canal runs south of Ismailia. On one weekend he and three fellow students sailed down to the Great Bitter Lakes to fish. However, the northerly wind which carried them there so effortlessly continued to blow, and they had to tow the boat back for about ten miles, getting very sunburnt in the process.

Ralph was due for a month's leave at the end of August, and he and three friends decided to charter a Greek caique and sail to Cyprus. Ralph was delegated to identify a craft and travelled up to Port Said to do so. He eventually struck a deal with the captain of the *St Nicholas*, the cost of the voyage being partially offset by buying a cargo of sugar, the profit on selling which would then be split 75 per cent to Ralph and his friends and 25 per cent to the captain. They sailed from Port Said on 2 September, but adverse winds meant that they took three and a half days to make the passage to Larnaca. There they discovered that another boat had arrived just before them with a cargo of sugar, which took the edge off the market, although they still made a small profit. After visiting Nicosia they sailed to Paphos and on from there to the island of Kastellorizo, occupied since the war by the Italians. On being told by an official that they would have to remain in quarantine for fourteen days, they asked him to convey an invitation to the Governor for drinks that evening. The Governor turned out to be a naval commander who had served with the Royal Navy during the war, and there was no more talk of quarantine! Leaving Kastellorizo they sailed for Rhodes, but sharply deteriorating weather meant that they were forced to seek shelter. By the time it had cleared, they were due to return to Egypt, so sailed directly to Alexandria.

Ralph passed out from 4 FTS on 12 October, but for the time being remained at Abu Sueir, pending a permanent posting. He was still involved with fabric testing for the airships, but this, too, came to an end when he completed his final report on 9 November. He knew by this time that his new posting would be to the newly re-formed 45 Squadron[5] and he was able to meet some of the first intake of officers, but none of its aircraft were yet ready for operations, so it was not until 7 January 1922 that he joined the squadron at Heliopolis.

Initially, 45 Squadron was equipped in part with the Vickers Vimy, but it soon standardized on the Vimy's derivative, the Vickers Vernon. Thus, from one of the smallest aircraft in the RAF, the Bristol Fighter, Ralph moved to one of the largest. The Vernon was a sizeable biplane, with a length of nearly 43ft and a wingspan of 68ft, and was powered by two Rolls-Royce Eagle engines, later replaced by the more efficient Napier Lions. It was designed as a transport aircraft, with a cruising speed of 75mph and a range of 320 miles. It had a crew of four, the pilot, co-pilot, wireless operator and a fitter, and its bulbous fuselage could carry up to six passengers, although that number could be significantly reduced by both the amount of fuel on board and the weight of cargo, and in practice there were more often only two or three. Ralph had his first lesson in a twin-engined aircraft on one of the squadron's Vimys a few days after arriving, graduating quickly to a Vernon and carrying out his first solo flight within a fortnight.

It was already known that the squadron would be based in Iraq and that its primary role, in conjunction with the identically-equipped 70 Squadron, would be to operate the mail and cargo route between there and Egypt. However, it needed to complete its build-up first, and this turned out to be very slow, although the first draft of ground crew, together with a significant volume of stores, departed by ship to Iraq on 21 February. New aircraft, when delivered, were almost invariably unable to operate to their full potential and required a great deal of work to make them fit for purpose. The officers also arrived piecemeal. The Commanding Officer, Squadron Leader E. M. Murray, of whom Ralph formed a high opinion, was already in the post when he joined the squadron, and on 4 March a new batch arrived, which included Flight Lieutenant Robert Saundby, who was to command A Flight, whilst Ralph commanded B Flight, both comprising six aircraft in theory, if not always in practice. In contrast to Ralph, Saundby was a very experienced aeroplane pilot, having been a flight commander in a fighter squadron on the Western Front and an instructor at 1 FTS in the UK. The two men formed a close relationship, and Ralph later wrote that Saundby was the greatest help in giving him the confidence he lacked.

The first two aircraft of 45 Squadron set out for Iraq on 2 April, taking with them Air Vice-Marshal Ellington,[6] the recently appointed AOC Middle East. Five more, all those that were serviceable, departed from Heliopolis twelve days later. Saundby led, with Flying Officer H. I. T. Beardsworth on his starboard beam, followed by Murray, Ralph and Flying Officer C. N. Ellen in line astern.

The 866-mile air route between Cairo and Baghdad had been established less than a year earlier. The first leg was relatively straightforward. It ran from Heliopolis to the shore of the Mediterranean east of Port Said, following the coast as far as Rafa before turning east towards Beersheba. It then crossed the Judean Hills and the Dead Sea before arriving at a makeshift airfield at Ziza, 12 miles south of Amman, the capital of Transjordan, and next to a station on the old Hejaz Railway. Thus far the route was relatively easy to navigate by sight, with plenty of natural features. After Ziza, however, it ran east by north-east across the Syrian Desert, which was uninhabited except for nomadic Bedouin tribes and featureless from the air, albeit not at all homogeneous on the ground. About 60 miles after leaving Ziza, for instance, it crossed a belt of basalt, itself 60 miles wide, which even the Bedouin avoided. This was covered in black boulders which would do considerable damage to any aircraft attempting to land on them. There were, however, a number of mud flats which made good landing grounds when they were dry, but the lack of any features meant that pilots found it difficult to judge their altitude, and hard landings were frequent. The next 150 or so miles ran across a featureless plain with sparse or no vegetation, until a line of low hills was reached, with wells at El Jid on the west side and Rutbah on the east. Thence the country sloped gradually downhill towards the Euphrates, which was crossed at Ramadi, after which there was a relatively easy run across more populated country to Baghdad, with the RAF station at Hinaidi situated close to the city's south-eastern suburbs.

Much of the country between Ziza and Ramadi lay at a height of between 2,000 and 3,000ft. This had implications for aircraft taking off into relatively rarefied air. Moreover, in a very hot climate the air becomes thinner as the temperature rises, so the best time to take off was at dawn. In the light of the unreliability of aircraft at that time, it was decided to create along the route twenty-four unmanned landing grounds, some of which contained reserves of fuel in underground tanks, at intervals of between 15 and 30 miles. Although not far apart, it was necessary that the route between them should be clearly visible from the air and this was achieved by dragging a plough along the track.

Ralph and his fellow pilots arrived at Ziza without incident, refuelled and took off early the next morning, hoping to make Hinaidi before the end of the day. On reaching Azrak, only two landing grounds along, Ellen was forced to land with a boiling radiator and was followed by the others. On taking off again, one of Murray's engines cut out and his aircraft slewed round, wrecking the undercarriage. Ralph landed once more to get details of the damage, before following the others. Seven landing grounds further along, Ellen was forced down yet again. Ralph landed to help him, whilst Saundby and the only other remaining aircraft carried on to Hinaidi. It was clear that there was something badly amiss with one of Ellen's engines, and a signal was sent to Amman, which resulted in the arrival of a DH9 with orders for Ralph to return with its pilot to Azrak, where he found Murray, still waiting for his aircraft to be repaired.

Ralph was by now feeling very ill, with a raging sore throat, and spent the next day in his makeshift bed. On the following day three desert tenders appeared with the necessary spare parts. Accompanying them, by sheer happenstance, was a doctor, who ordered Ralph to return with them to Amman. The next morning he awoke to find himself salmon pink all over! Scarlet fever was diagnosed and he was rushed in a Bristol Fighter to Ramleh, where he was admitted to the Palestine General Hospital.

The next few weeks proved extremely tedious. Ralph was only allowed out of bed on 2 May and it was the end of the month before he was released. He spent the next few days visiting the sights in and around Jerusalem. After a short stay at Abu Sueir he appeared before a medical board in Cairo on 9 June and was granted a month's sick leave. As it happened, his brother

Archie, who had resigned his commission in the Royal Navy, was in the Eastern Mediterranean at the time, having acquired a Buckie drifter and sailed it to Cyprus with a view to fishing for tuna and selling the catch in Egypt. Archie invited Ralph to join him and they sailed around the island for the next twelve days, but the tuna proved elusive. Ralph decided to return to Egypt early, requested and appeared before a medical board immediately and was passed fit for duty. He went up to Aboukir to pick up a new Vernon, but as usual there was a delay whilst the aircraft was made ready for service and it was 7 July before he was able to leave, taking as passengers two academics from McGill University, on their way to visit ancient sites in Iraq, and in company with a Vimy. They reached Ziza without incident and on the next day arrived at Hinaidi, the flight only interrupted by the need to land to fix a leak in the Vimy's water pump, effected by the application of chewing gum!

Hinaidi was a huge mud airfield lying east of the Tigris and just north of its junction with the River Diyala. It was protected from flooding by a high embankment or 'bund' and was home to four RAF squadrons, Nos. 1, 8, 45 and 70, an RAF armoured car company and a general hospital. Ralph thought it untidy and dusty, although the officers' quarters were good, their thick mud-brick walls and fans keeping the rooms relatively cool. There were some good places to swim and fish in the Diyala and opportunities for shooting: either doves and sand grouse close to Hinaidi, geese and duck in the marshes north-east of Baghdad or, best of all, black partridge in a liquorice patch near Hillah, 60 miles to the south, all of which made good eating. Ralph established contact with Air HQ in Baghdad, where he found that his former station commander at Capel, Alexander Cunningham, was on the staff.

Although the primary function of the two Vernon squadrons had been to operate the mail route between Baghdad and Cairo, most of their aircraft were diverted for the time being by a revolt in Kurdistan, where the dissident leader, Sheikh Mahmud Barzanji, had declared his independence from Iraq, supported by Turkey. The Kurds were proving difficult to suppress, in spite of the implementation of Trenchard's policy, with one of the Kurdish leaders, Karim Fattah Beg, proving so troublesome that he was widely referred to as 'the Director of Training of the RAF'. The RAF was, indeed, heavily involved, with the ground forces consisting of two British and four Indian Army battalions, plus locally enlisted Assyrian levies and armoured cars.

Ralph made his first round trip to Kirkuk on 4 August with supplies for the detached flights of 1 and 8 Squadrons and was to make many more. In early September a punitive column was forced to retreat, with a number of fatalities and injuries, the latter evacuated by the two transport squadrons, as were the European civilians in the area. In early October one of 45 Squadron's Vernons crashed en route to Kirkuk, killing a passenger and the fitter and gravely injuring the pilot, who died twelve days later. However, by the end of the month the impact of further bombing had produced the required result: the Turks in the area retreated behind the frontier and the Kurds largely surrendered.

At the same time Murray left the squadron. 'A thoroughly good CO', wrote Ralph in his diary, 'nothing makes him "spin", he never worried & consequently never worried other people.' His replacement was Squadron Leader Thomas Hazell DSO, MC, DFC & Bar, the fifth most successful British 'ace' of the Great War, with forty-three victories to his name. Less than three weeks later, the news came that he was to return to his former squadron, No 55, in Mosul, possibly because his knowledge of Northern Iraq was invaluable. He was to be relieved by Squadron Leader A. T. Harris, whose reputation preceded him, Ralph writing in his diary after the news had been received: 'General groans have been heard ever since.'

Arthur Harris joined the RAF in 1915 after serving with the Rhodesia Regiment during the successful campaign in German South-West Africa. His active service began on BE2s in the defence of the UK against the Zeppelins, and he was subsequently posted to the Western Front, where he flew Sopwith 1½ Strutters and Camels. He had been a flight commander in both 45 and 70 Squadrons and briefly commanded the former. After the war he attended a course on navigation and then became the first CO of 3 FTS, before being posted to India to command 31 Squadron, flying Bristol Fighters on the North-West Frontier. Harris became deeply unhappy about the RAF's relationship with the Army in India, the latter being unquestionably in charge of all operations, inclined to treat the RAF with some contempt and place it low on the priority list for spare parts, so that its aircraft were frequently unserviceable. Harris's loud complaints, along with those of others, reached the ears of Trenchard, who sent Air Vice-Marshal John Salmond[7] out to investigate. Salmond's report was highly critical of affairs in India and made a number of recommendations, although these took some time to be implemented.

Salmond was impressed by Harris and persuaded the younger man to join him in Iraq, where Salmond had been appointed not only AOC but also Commander British Forces, with authority over all operations in the country, both in the air and on land. Harris's reputation as a hard taskmaster was burnished by his few months spent on the staff at Air HQ in Baghdad and it was as such that his arrival at 45 Squadron was greeted with some trepidation.

The relationship between Ralph and Harris, which was to assume great significance later in Ralph's career, was established over the following months. It was as Ralph's co-pilot that Harris had his first flight in a Vernon, and the former quickly realized that his new CO was a man of some quality. The regard was mutual, Harris writing many years later:

> My Flight Commanders were R. H. M. S. Saundby and R. A. Cochrane, whom I then met for the first time. They were both outstanding men and later both of them held high posts under me in Bomber Command.[8]

The relationship was to develop some way beyond a professional one. Harris invariably addressed Ralph, except on formal business, as 'Cocky', the only person ever to be allowed do so to his face, although his subordinates in Bomber Command twenty and more years later often called him that behind his back, as an expression of regard bordering on affection rather than a description of his character.

Within days of arriving, Harris had come to one particular conclusion, that the Vernons would make excellent bombers, carrying on one aircraft as many bombs as a squadron of DH9s. He persuaded Salmond to let him cut a circular hole in the nose of a Vernon, for use by a bomb aimer lying on his stomach and using a course-setting bomb sight, with racks for the bombs and an improvised release mechanism fixed up by the squadron workshop. In tests carried out in the first two weeks of December, the average error was initially 100 yards, but this was speedily reduced to 40 yards. A challenge was issued to one of the DH9 squadrons, and 45 Squadron came out comfortably on top.

Harris made an immediate impression in other ways, tightening up discipline, instituting a daily parade and requiring all officers to carry out regular physical training. He also laid emphasis on continuous flying training and technical instruction. Morale, never in any case very low, improved yet further.

Despite all the work being carried out supplying the squadrons and ground forces in Kurdistan and converting the Vernons to bombers, it was not forgotten that one of the primary roles of 45 Squadron was to carry the mail from Baghdad to Cairo and vice versa. As it turned out, in just over a year spent in Iraq, Ralph only flew the return mail route once, and it was fortunate for him that the Baghdad to Cairo leg took place on 20 and 21 December 1922, which enabled him to spend Christmas and the New Year in the Egyptian capital. Iraq was an unaccompanied posting for the RAF and the Army, so there were few British women in the city, whereas Cairo was full of them. Ralph met up with John D'Albiac, a friend on leave from Transjordan, and the two men engaged in a lively social round. Among other excursions they took two young ladies to see the Pyramids on Christmas Day and then travelled down to the Valley of the Kings, where Tutankhamun's tomb had been discovered a month earlier but was not open to the public. They were back in Cairo for the lively festivities on New Year's Eve.

The return trip was not entirely straightforward. The flight to Ziza was uneventful, but on the next leg to Ramadi they had to leave late due to fog and then found that the track had been washed away by heavy rain, so the flight had to proceed by compass alone. A track was spotted running north to south and Ralph decided to land there for the night, during which they worked out their position, which turned out to be to the south of El Jid, by dead reckoning. In the morning they took off, found the correct track and reached Hinaidi before midday.

Three weeks later, 45 Squadron moved to Mosul to counter a new threat. This time it was the Turks, who were making bellicose noises about regaining part of the old Ottoman Empire, infiltrating men into the country and stirring up the local population. On 3 February there took place the first and only bombing attack in which Ralph participated during his period of service with the squadron, the target being the village of Khoram, 70 miles east of Mosul. In Ralph's words:

> The villagers have been indecently independent for a long time & have taken to harbouring Turkish irregulars, so punishment in the shape of some hundred heavy bombs was decided on.[9]

Three planes from each flight, accompanied by DH9s and Sopwith Snipes, attacked the village, whose inhabitants had left, having been warned by leaflets in advance. Khoram lay at the foot of a 6,500ft mountain, which made the approach very difficult and from whose slopes the villagers and Turks fired their rifles at the aircraft. About 80 per cent of the bombs fell in the village. Two days later, three Vernons, including those piloted by Harris and Saundby, attacked a second village. The operation appeared to have worked, so A Flight and Harris returned to Hinaidi, leaving B Flight under Ralph at Mosul.

Ralph remained at Mosul until 22 March. Accommodation was in a bare stone house, which was made habitable with purchases in the bazaar. By borrowing a pony he was able to visit the nearby site of Nineveh and on one occasion flew to Hadra, whose Parthian ruins marked the limit of the eastern expansion of the Roman Empire. Harris came up to visit from time to time, provoking a revealing entry in Ralph's diary:

> He is still full-out but looks worried & restless which results in his interfering in little matters. People who see only this side of him consider him impossible – but given time I think he will make the Squadron a real success, though possibly never a very happy home.[10]

Back at Hinaidi, the operational priority remained the support of the continuing campaign in Kurdistan which, whilst of low intensity, was to rumble on until 1932. There were frequent flights to Kirkuk, bringing up supplies and evacuating sick and wounded. Although not called upon for further aerial bombardment, 45 Squadron continued to practise and, in a competition with 30 Squadron's DH9s, scored an average error of 25 yards to its opponent's 64 yards.

Ralph continued to participate in a number of leisure pursuits, which now included polo, a game which he had never played before. The price of ponies was set at virtually nothing and Ralph acquired two in succession, first 'Haifa' and then 'Bronzo', who were small but nimble and easy to ride. His main handicap was that, although he wrote right-handed, almost certainly a legacy of the classroom in his childhood, he was naturally left-handed at tennis and other games, and hitting the ball with his stick in the right hand was never easy, although by dint of much practice he could make a reasonable showing in a match.

Longer excursions included a weekend expedition to Samarra, but for his two months' local leave, which came up at the beginning of August 1923, he was far more ambitious. He and Flight Lieutenant Percy Maitland, formerly a colleague in the airship service, decided that they would travel around Persia, Iraq's next door neighbour and a country of much interest. Obtaining permission to do so proved difficult, as relations between Great Britain and Persia were somewhat fractious at the time. The former was concerned by the activities of Shia clerics in Iraq, a country now ruled by a Sunni dynasty, and a number of them had been expelled; whilst the Persians believed that the British had too much influence on the south-west of their country, where there was a large Arab community. As a result, all leave there was stopped and Ralph and Maitland began to plan a trip to Syria and Lebanon instead. A week before they were due to leave the order was rescinded and they were free to go.

Armed with a number of introductions from the Baghdad agent of the Imperial Bank of Persia[11] and carrying a mail bag from the British Consul, which transformed them temporarily into *couriers diplomatiques*, Ralph and Maitland set off for the border in the former's Ford. Into this small vehicle was loaded a large spare petrol tank, two sets of kit for two months, food, water, oil and spare tyres, all of which was secured by the liberal use of rope and on top of which perched Ralph's 14-year old bearer, Mirza. They headed north-west, crossing the border at Khanikin and travelling thence over the Paitak Pass via Kermanshah, Hamadan and Kasvin to Teheran. Their letters of introduction proved most useful, as they were able to stay either with the local British consul or with the managers of the Imperial Bank of Persia or the Anglo Persian Oil Company. In Teheran they were the guests of the British Military Attaché, who advised them not to go into the city, where anti-British feeling was rife.

Ralph and Maitland spent the next three weeks in the Elburz Mountains, their objective being to stalk and shoot ibex, which had an excellent reputation as sporting game. As it turned out, the ibex were cleverer than the hunters and, although they spotted a number of them, they never got close enough even to fire a shot. There was a great deal of mist and fog and at times heavy rain, and the locally recruited guides proved to be useless. 'The Persian mountains' wrote Ralph in his diary 'are rather like the Persian state – soft and degenerate.'[12] They managed to shoot some small game, hares and partridges, and saw a leopard but were unable to follow it, so conceded defeat rather earlier than they had hoped.

After two days in Teheran, much of which was devoted to acquiring the necessary road pass, they set off for Isfahan. Ralph was not particularly taken by the city and decided to travel on to Persepolis and Shiraz in the company of two locally based British diplomats. He was most impressed by Persepolis, less so by Shiraz, whose famous cypress groves and gardens he thought too few and far between. Having rejoined Maitland, the two of them retraced their steps and arrived back at Hinaidi on 5 October, with the car still in one piece in spite of the terrible roads.

Seven days later, Ralph handed over B Flight to Flight Lieutenant Henry Scroggs, yet another former airship pilot, and took a troop train to Basra, where he boarded the SS *Glengorm Castle* for the voyage back to Southampton. His services in Iraq did not go unrecognized. On 10 June 1924, amongst a relatively small number of officers and men from the British and Indian Armies and the RAF, he was mentioned in Salmond's despatch 'for gallant and distinguished services in the field'.

Chapter 5

Moving Up

Ralph was entitled to yet more leave on the termination of his overseas service. After catching up with family and friends, he travelled to Switzerland with his brother Archie, who had returned to the UK after the failure of his fishing venture in the Mediterranean and was now contemplating entering politics. The two of them had decided to spend three weeks over Christmas and the New Year in Pontresina. The weather in the Engadine in the winter of 1923/24 was extremely cold, so much so that Ralph suffered from frostbite on one of his ears, and the snow was deep, with a great risk of avalanches. On one occasion he managed not only to injure himself, fortunately only slightly, but also to rescue some others who were at the point of exhaustion. In spite of this, his enthusiasm for skiing was rekindled and, following instruction from professional guides and some newly made friends, he managed to pass all parts of the second class test.

On 14 January 1924 Ralph assumed command of No. 3 Squadron of the Boys' Wing at RAF Cranwell. Cranwell had been set up as the RNAS Training Establishment in 1915, and Ralph knew it from his re-graduation there as an airship pilot in 1917. Subsequently it became an important part of Trenchard's strategy to carve out an independent identity for the RAF. Geographically it was divided into three areas, of which the East Camp housed the Boys' Wing and the West Camp the Cadet College, whose two-year course was the entry point for all those hoping to gain permanent commissions. The third area, known as 'Lighter than Air', consisted of a small airship hangar and some huts, but by this time was little used.

Trenchard's original intention had been for all those intending to serve in technical trades to undertake their training at RAF Halton, but when Halton opened in 1920 it was far from ready for occupation by Boy Mechanics, an important component of the CAS's plan. The first intake of these went instead to Cranwell and was succeeded by other intakes until 1926, when they at last moved to Halton, which had itself begun to accept Boy Mechanics in 1924. There were three squadrons at Cranwell, each consisting of 350 boys aged fifteen to eighteen, a third of whom entered each year on a three-year course. The CO of the Boys Wing was Wing Commander Robert Barton and the Adjutant was Flight Lieutenant Leslie Hollinghurst, with whom Ralph became particularly friendly but who left four months later to attend the RAF Staff College. Ralph got on well with Barton, although he believed that he was dominated by his mother, with whom he lived. Within 3 Squadron, Ralph was assisted by two junior officers and a flight sergeant.

The emphasis for the Boys in their first few weeks at Cranwell was on drill, and it was only when a satisfactory level of proficiency had been reached that they moved on to the classroom, to learn the theory of the various ground trades, and to the workshop, to gain practical experience. A DH9a, a Bristol Fighter, two Avro 504s and a Vickers Vimy were available to help them convert theory into practice. There were searching exams at the end of each year.

Discipline for the apprentices was particularly strict. Due to a lack of experienced NCOs, a problem throughout the service at this time, it had to be maintained to a considerable extent by Leading Boys, who tended to overdo the punishments and were greatly resented as a result. On the other hand, there were plenty of opportunities for sport, in which some participation was compulsory. There was no lack of choice, with soccer, rugby, cricket and hockey being the major sports, whilst squadron teams were also formed for athletics, fencing and tug-of-war. Matches were held frequently, both inter-squadron and inter-station.

Ralph developed his own sporting interests. He played squash, both at Cranwell and on some much better courts at Melton Mowbray, and participated in the rifle, revolver and pistol championships at Bisley, doing particularly well with the pistol. His main sporting activity during the season, however, was hunting. He acquired from his predecessor at 3 Squadron a horse called 'The Major', who turned out to be both a comfortable ride and a very good jumper, but not particularly fast, and thus an excellent mount for a beginner. The nearest hunt was the Blankney, but Ralph preferred the Belvoir, further away but in excellent country. He made a special visit to Crawford Priory to pick up his father's old hunting kit, which fitted very well, and in order to get to the hunts and to drive himself further afield, he bought the first car he had owned in the UK, a Cluley 10/20, for the princely sum of £250.

Towards the end of June Hollinghurst came on a visit to Cranwell and strongly advised Ralph to take the RAF Staff College entrance exams. Ralph applied and was sent the papers, which he duly completed and returned to the college by the end of September, having found them fairly straightforward. Not long afterwards he was informed that that he had been accepted for entry in May 1925. He was, however, undecided on whether or not to take up his place, due to his continuing interest in rejoining the airship service.

Ralph had kept broadly up to date with developments on airships whilst he was in Iraq. The airship programme had experienced mixed fortunes in the meantime. Since the Great War all the emphasis had been placed on rigid ships, which still seemed to hold great promise for long distance travel. However, only R.33 and R.36 remained in service, the former at Cardington, the latter at Pulham. R.34, which had made the first trans-Atlantic crossing in 1919, had come to grief two years later, happily without any casualties, whilst R.38 had suffered a catastrophic accident in August 1921, when it collapsed over the estuary of the Humber. Edward Maitland, whom Ralph had known well as Director of Airships, was among the twenty-eight fatalities, and there were only five survivors.

Not long after Ralph returned from Iraq, the British Government announced a new airship policy. The two remaining airships would be reconditioned and used for experimental work, whilst two new ships were to be built, R.100 by Vickers at Howden and R.101 by the Royal Airship Works at Cardington. Encouraged by this, Ralph expressed his continuing interest to the Director of Airship Development, Group Captain P. F. M. Fellowes, who told him informally that he would ask for him in the spring of 1925. Ralph took the opportunity to visit both Cardington and the Head Office of Vickers in London, where he met Dennis Burney, managing director of the subsidiary set up to build the R.100, and his old friend Barnes Wallis, head of the design team.

Ralph's enthusiasm was expressed most forcefully in an extraordinary entry in his diary:

I sit in front of the fire and I dream. And the dreams I dream are these.
In the Spring of 1925 I am posted to airship development & assist in the experiments on R33.

In the Summer I am sent to Egypt in charge of the experimental mooring mast & take, whilst there, every opportunity to assist Scott[1] in flying the ship.

In the late Autumn I proceed to India to supervise the erection of the Airship base there & to carry out certain fabric tests. In the Autumn of 1926 I go to America to watch the progress of the new American ship, & from there return to Cardington for the command of the 5 million ship in the Spring of 1927.

After initial experiments lasting 6 months I resign from the Air Force & join up as Chief Pilot to the Orient Line.

In 1932 I retire from active flying & am elected Supervisor with a seat on the Board.

Perhaps!!![2]

It was not to be. Most of the relatively few RAF appointments relating to airships had already been filled and, when Ralph discussed his career options with Alexander Cunningham, himself back from Iraq and now on the staff of the Directorate of Personnel Services at the Air Ministry, he was strongly advised to take up his Staff College place. On the same day he wrote to Group Captain Fellowes to withdraw his application. He was to maintain his contacts with the airship service for as long as it existed, but was never to rejoin it.

The Fourth Course at the Royal Air Force Staff College in Andover opened on 5 May 1925. Like Cranwell and Halton, this was the brainchild of Trenchard as part of his long campaign to establish the full independence of the RAF, in the face of attempts by both the Army and the Royal Navy to have it broken up and the parts returned to their control. The other two services had long-established staff colleges, whose purpose was broadly the same, to prepare the most promising officers of the rank of captain/major in the Army and lieutenant/lieutenant commander in the Navy for higher command and staff appointments. The emphasis of each was slightly different. The course at the Royal Naval Staff College at Greenwich was for a year and was focused on staff duties, but in terms of an officer's promotion, greater emphasis was placed on sea time and on specializations such as gunnery, whilst service on the staff was not so highly regarded. In the Army the opposite was true. The courses at the Army Staff Colleges in Camberley and Quetta lasted for two years and, some thought, were designed to create generals rather than staff officers. Few Army officers had any prospects of promotion beyond lieutenant colonel without a staff college qualification.

The RAF Staff College also selected its most promising officers, but as a very young service it could not afford the luxury of a two-year course, so limited it to eleven months, with the main emphasis being placed on staff work rather than on the higher direction of war, although there were many lectures on the latter. Unlike the imposing edifices of its sister colleges at Camberley and Greenwich, it was housed in a relatively modest building, although Ralph was pleased to be allocated two comfortable rooms.

The Commandant was Robert Brooke-Popham, who had been responsible for drawing up the plans for the college and then for implementing them; together with Trenchard and a few others, he could be regarded as one of the founding fathers of the RAF. The Directing Staff was a strong one. Christopher Courtney, the Deputy Commandant, Bertine 'Bertie' Sutton, Douglas Evill and Guy Garrod were all to serve on the Air Council during the Second World War, whilst Grahame Donald became Director General of Organization and AOC-in-C Maintenance Command. Amongst the RAF cadets, thirteen out of twenty reached air rank, of whom five – Ralph himself, Robert Foster, Hugh Lloyd, Trafford Leigh-Mallory and Charles Medhurst – became air chief marshals. There were also two students from the Royal Navy, two from the British Army, one from the Indian Army, two from the Royal Australian Air Force and two from the Royal Canadian Air Force, one of whom was William Barker, the most decorated serviceman in Canada's history, with a Victoria Cross, a Distinguished Service Order and bar and a Military Cross and two bars. Ralph was somewhat disparaging of Barker, writing of him, 'He has few brains and absolutely no fear. He is a moderate pilot but a crack shot and he owes most of his success in the War to this.'[3] Leigh-Mallory was another to receive criticism: 'He is his own worst enemy as he suffers from a cocksure manner which can only be the result of his never having been sufficiently well-kicked at school … he is also quite without tact.'[4]

Ralph thought that the members of the Directing Staff were good, but that the overall approach was rather amateur, based as it was on the experience of the Great War. However, he appreciated being taught to write accurate English and to understand the basics of staff work. He had a particularly high regard for Courtney, with whom he had a number of discussions about Technical Officers, of which there was at that time a great deficiency, as Ralph had found at Cranwell. As far as Brooke-Popham was concerned, he thought him 'a curious mixture – on one side the visionary, on the other the practical. A great brain, but I would say that he was apt to see too much of both sides of a question to allow him to take a very drastic course of action.' He went on to compare him with John Salmond, formerly the Commander British Forces in Iraq and now the AOC-in-C Air Defence of Great Britain ('ADGB'). Ralph held a very high opinion of Salmond as a decisive man of action: 'Salmond as the C-in-C with Brooke-Popham as his Chief of Staff would win a war.'[5]

Ralph's first piece of individual written work arrived back liberally covered in red ink, which he accepted was fully deserved. However, his writing improved so much so that, towards the end of the course, his essay on Morale was published for the benefit of others. This was the start of a successful career of writing on aviation, military and political issues, which would result in his winning a number of prizes and becoming, much later and particularly in retirement, a sought-after commentator.

In addition to lectures and classroom work, the course included a number of visits, including one to the Royal Navy in and around Portsmouth, which took in the gunnery school on Whale Island, the submarine base at Fort Blockhouse and the Fleet Air Arm station at Gosport, and others to the School of Chemical Warfare at Porton Down and the Royal Aircraft Establishment at Farnborough. There were also joint exercises with the other staff colleges at Camberley and Greenwich, with Ralph playing the part of fleet aviation officer to the Mediterranean Fleet at the latter, and he was attached to the 2nd Cavalry Brigade for three days of joint manoeuvres around Whitchurch.

As far as leisure pursuits were concerned, Ralph brought 'The Major' down from Cranwell and hunted with the South-West Wiltshire and Tidworth Forest Hunts, although he did not consider their country to be as good as that of the Belvoir or even of the Blankney. In January of both 1925 and 1926 he went skiing with Archie, since October 1924 the Unionist Member of Parliament for East Fife, and in 1926 they were accompanied by Archie's new wife, Dorothy, the daughter of Lord Cornwallis, whom Ralph thought 'really splendid'.[6]

For the one-month summer vacation of 1925, Ralph and a fellow student, Flight Lieutenant Walter Park,[7] who had also served in Iraq, embarked on an ambitious trip to Yugoslavia. They travelled by train via Paris to Ljubljana, Belgrade and then to Novi Sad to pay a courtesy call on the Royal Yugoslav Army Air Force. They were very well received and were each given a brief flight in a Breguet XIX, which turned out to be rather alarming in Ralph's case when the pilot, who had done very little flying on this type, attempted to carry out a loop, only for the aircraft to collapse sideways when just over the vertical. The seat belt was inadequate and Ralph had to tuck his feet under some bracing wires and hold on tight in order to avoid falling out. Moving on to Zagreb they had a similar welcome, this time enjoying a flight in a Breguet XIV. From there they travelled to Fiume, where they were entertained by the Royal Yugoslav Navy. The local Vickers representative arranged a passage for them in a tug down the Dalmatian Coast via Sibenik to Djenovici, where they enjoyed a flight in an Icarus flying boat, before travelling to Cattaro and then on the narrow gauge railway to Dubrovnik.

The return to Belgrade began with a train ride to Mostar, where Ralph and Park once again enjoyed the hospitality of the local air base and were taken up in a Brandenburg and then a Potez XV. They then spent three days in the resort town of Vranjska Banja, staying in a chalet run by a charming Swiss woman, before arriving back in Belgrade. From the Yugoslav capital they travelled by train to Vienna and then by plane in a terrifying flight amongst the mountains in thick cloud to Innsbruck, where they boarded the Balkan Express to Paris, flying from there to Croydon by Imperial Airways.

Ralph, who had been promoted to squadron leader on 1 July 1925, passed out of the Staff College on 25 March 1926 and began his new job as Training Officer at HQ Wessex Bombing Area, conveniently also in Andover, just over a fortnight later. The Wessex Bombing Area controlled all the regular bomber squadrons in the UK as one of the components of ADGB, the other being the Fighting Area, which performed the same function in respect of the UK-based fighter squadrons. The latter were positioned substantially in South-East England.

The Wessex Bombing Area was, however, a misnomer. Of the seven stations under its command, only three were within what might be considered the historic boundary of Wessex: Andover itself – 12 Squadron with the Fairey Fox and 13 Squadron, which was actually engaged in Army Co-operation, with the Bristol Fighter; Netheravon – 11 Squadron with the Hawker Horsley; and Worthy Down – 58 Squadron with the Vickers Virginia, the most recent derivative of the Vimy. Two stations were in Kent: Eastchurch, 207 Squadron with the DH9a, and Manston, 9 Squadron with the Virginia. Another two were much further north: Bircham Newton in Norfolk with 7 Squadron, which moved to Worthy Down in April 1927, with the Virginia, and 99 Squadron with the Handley Page Hyderabad; and Spitalgate in Lincolnshire, 39 Squadron with the DH9a and 100 Squadron with the Fairey Fawn, later replaced by the Horsley.

The wide geographical dispersion meant a great deal of travel for Ralph, largely undertaken by piloting himself in one of the Andover Communication Flight's Bristol Fighters. He had flown from time to time whilst at both Cranwell and the Staff College, the former usually to give Boy Mechanics their first experience in the air, the latter on occasion further afield, but both the frequency and the distance of his flights now increased substantially.

His new appointment combined the two specializations for which he would become best known in the RAF, bombing and flying training, and thus may well have had some influence on the course of his future career. The job involved carrying out regular inspections of all the squadrons under the area's command to ensure that the authorized training regimes were being applied and that the prescribed standards of flying training were being met. On occasion he was even required to carry out airmanship tests on pilots himself. In this he had the full support of the AOC, Air Vice-Marshal John Steele, who he described as 'a magnificent naval warhorse who Boom Trenchard had brought in to give some naval balance to the Air Force. He was not a pilot but had a good eye for efficiency and was much liked by us.'[8]

Steele's own inspections were exhaustive affairs and his methodology clearly rubbed off on Ralph, who was also an admirer of his AOC's habit of getting exactly what he wanted in his visits to the Air Ministry. On being asked by Ralph how he managed this, his answer was that he took care to know more about the subject under discussion than his interlocutor.

Ralph's diaries show that he was far from impressed by some of the squadrons, with adverse comments on certain commanding officers and criticisms related not only to training but also to more general failures, particularly of discipline and morale. As throughout the RAF, the key virtue was 'efficiency', a word which expressed a great deal more than the dictionary definition and was used to describe the highest standards of organization and control. One squadron which was beyond reproach on this score was No. 58 at Worthy Down, which since May 1925 had been commanded by Harris, with Saundby as one of his flight commanders. Ralph described Harris as 'struggling hard against adversity',[9] probably alluding to his efforts to bring the squadron up to his own very high standards, but he still gave a good account of himself on one of Steele's rigorous inspections. He was majoring in night flying, in the belief that day bombers would be highly vulnerable to attack by faster fighters; he was to write later in his memoirs that he believed that his squadron did more of this than all the world's air forces put together. Ralph accompanied him on a number of night flights and was quick to appreciate the difficulties, in an aircraft completely devoid of the sophisticated navigational aids which would emerge fifteen or more years later.

In April 1927 Worthy Down received a second squadron which transferred from Bircham Newton. This was No. 7, commanded by another officer who was to have a significant impact on Ralph's career, Wing Commander C. F. A. ('Peter') Portal. Portal was as capable a commanding officer as Harris, and there was considerable competition between them to prove whose was the better squadron, although they became good friends. Like Harris, Portal believed that the ability of bombers to fly at night would be essential. Ralph was immensely impressed when he took on a bet with a tank commander that he would stay in touch with his column on an exercise throughout the hours of darkness. Portal positioned his aircraft over the tanks at nightfall and was still there at daybreak, winning the bet comfortably.

There were two notable breaks from the routine of training. Ralph's sister Kitty[10] had married Edward Bruce, the Earl of Elgin, in 1921, and when Elgin was appointed Lord High Commissioner to the General Assembly of the Church of Scotland, the King's personal representative to that body for 1926, he asked for Ralph to be temporarily seconded to him as one of his three aides-de-camp. Having secured permission, Ralph spent the first ten days of July in Edinburgh, staying at Holyroodhouse and attending both the Assembly itself and a number of other functions, including lunches, dinners and garden parties, not only for the delegates, but for the Edinburgh and wider Scottish communities. Among many others, he met and was particularly impressed by Stanley Baldwin, the Prime Minister, who had come to address the Assembly.

By this time Ralph's enthusiasm for flying for the sake of flying had grown considerably, and he became interested in acquiring a light aircraft of his own for recreational purposes. One which caught his eye was a relatively new design by Westland Aircraft, the Widgeon III, a two-seater parasol monoplane. In August 1927 he flew down to the company's works at Yeovil and was taken for a test flight, finding the aircraft 'delightful'.[11] With a month's leave due shortly, he wrote to Westland, suggesting that they might like to lend it to him for a trip round Europe, on which he would write a report as an owner-pilot. Perhaps unsurprisingly, the company declined the offer, but agreed to hire it to him for a month for £50.

Ralph took delivery of G-EBRO and with his companion, Flight Lieutenant Hedley Drew, an old friend from the airship service who was also serving at Andover, took off on 1 September on a 3,860-mile tour around Europe. Their initial focus was on Germany, after a stop in Brussels on the first night. Over the next week they flew down the Rhine from Cologne to Frankfurt, across from there to Leipzig and Berlin, on to the Baltic Sea at Warnemünde and Lübeck, then back to Berlin via Hannover and Magdeburg. On the whole they were received with great friendliness, although they encountered bureaucracy in Leipzig, where a demand for certain papers which were no longer necessary caused a modest delay. The one incident of note took place on their way to Travemünde, just outside Lübeck, when they spotted what looked suspiciously like a fighter flying at the same height and about a mile away. As fighters were strictly forbidden to

Germany by the Treaty of Versailles, they decided to develop engine trouble and land on the airfield to which the mystery plane was descending. They learnt that the airfield was a preliminary training centre for Lufthansa airline pilots and, although the other aircraft was hidden by a rise in the ground, the incident gave some credence to early Air Ministry concerns, long before Adolf Hitler's rise to power, that the newly-formed Lufthansa was being used as cover to train a new air force.

Ralph was impressed by Germany, writing prophetically in his diary following the flight down the Rhine:

> I defy anyone after flying down the Rhine to deny that the Germans are a great people. To one's airy sense the idea of holding them down appears too ludicrous for words; it might be a good thing for a few French politicians to make the trip, it would at any rate give them a wider outlook.

With Drew at the controls for the first time on the tour, they set off from Berlin to Belgrade and thence to Venice, where they planned to stay for six days. Their objective was not so much to visit the sights of the great city – Ralph had been there in 1918 in any event – as to watch the Schneider Trophy races for seaplanes and flying boats, in which the British team was highly fancied. The Schneider Trophy had been first competed for prior to the Great War and was revived in 1920. Great Britain had won in 1922, but had lost in 1923, 1925 and 1926 (the race was not held in 1924). The winning country from the previous year hosted the race, and in 1927 this was Italy.

Ralph and Drew landed on the airstrip at the Lido, where they were initially told that they were not permitted to remain and would have to fly on to Padua. They managed to convince the authorities that permission had been arranged for them by the British team and were able to leave the Widgeon there and head off to the Excelsior, where rooms had been booked. The next few days were spent in visiting the seaplane base to look over the competing aircraft, watching the trials of the various competitors and, indeed, doing some sightseeing as well. The race itself was held on 25 and 26 September and it was very clear that the main contenders for the trophy would all be seaplanes, Mario Castoldi's Macchi M.39s and M.52s and Reginald Mitchell's Supermarine S.5s. When the time came, the Italian planes were all forced to withdraw with engine failure, and it was the two S.5s which triumphed, Flight Lieutenant S. N. Webster taking first place with an average speed of 281.65 mph, and Flight Lieutenant O. E. Worsley coming in second.

The celebrations in the British camp lasted into the early hours of the next morning and it was with heavy heads and much depleted pockets that Ralph and Drew took off from the Lido, reaching Nice that evening, Dijon on the following evening and Croydon on the next day. On 30 September Ralph delivered the Widgeon back to Westland and later wrote an account of the journey for *Flight* magazine, extolling the virtues of private flying and touring.

Ralph's posting to the Wessex Bombing Area came to an end in March 1928, but not before he was able to get in a fortnight's skiing in the Bernese Oberland, albeit without Archie, who had flu. His new destination was to be at the opposite end of the climate spectrum, back in the Middle East.

Chapter 6

Squadron Commander

The port of Aden was ceded to the British by the Sultan of Lahej in 1838, its initial purpose being to combat piracy against British ships in the Arabian Sea, and it subsequently served as a coaling station as steam first complemented and then superseded sail. Its value became even greater with the opening of the Suez Canal in 1869, which placed the port on the direct route to India and South-East Asia. It was administered initially by the East India Company and from 1858 by the Government of India and was garrisoned by British and Indian troops. In the course of time, treaties were concluded with the small states in the interior, including Lahej, offering them protection in return for their agreement not to commit hostile acts against Aden.

With the neighbouring state of Yemen forming part of the Ottoman Empire, the Turks made incursions over the border into the Protectorate during the Great War, causing the garrison of Aden to be significantly strengthened at that time. Following the defeat of Turkey, Yemen came under the control of the Zaydi Imams, who now threatened not only the Protectorate but the port itself. The peacetime garrison of one British and one Indian battalion, together with a flight of Bristol Fighters, was no longer considered sufficient to counter the threat, and the Army in India was requested to put forward new proposals for defence. The Army's solution was an Indian Division, supported by an RAF Squadron for army co-operation, but this was considered by the British Government to be prohibitively expensive. Once again, Trenchard argued that the territory could be secured by air control, which had worked so well in British Somaliland and Iraq. This was agreed, and 8 (Bomber) Squadron was deployed from Iraq to Aden in February 1927. The Indian battalion left in 1928, whilst the British battalion remained until early 1929 to allow time for the locally enlisted Aden Protectorate Levies to be raised, after which defence, as in Iraq, was placed entirely under the control of the RAF. The total force comprised 8 Squadron, an armoured car company, a few small Army units, notably engineers, and the Levies, the last commanded by an Indian Army officer, Colonel M. C. Lake, who spoke fluent Arabic and knew the local tribes.

At the end of the first week of March 1928 the advanced element of the staff of the new Aden Command met at Waterloo station to travel down to Southampton for the voyage to South Arabia. The Officer Commanding was Group Captain William Mitchell, known to all as 'Ginger Mitch'. In Ralph's words he was 'a splendid man, large, red-headed, extrovert with enormous hands much battered through playing wicket keeper'.[1] Making up the party in addition to Mitchell and Ralph himself, who was to be responsible for air staff duties and to act as Mitchell's deputy, were Wing Commander Edward Sayer, formerly of the Royal Army Service Corps in which he had won a Military Cross, who was to run the Stores branch, and Flight Lieutenant Ernest Borthwick-Clarke, the Personnel Officer. They were to be joined in Aden by Flight Lieutenants Aubrey Rickards and Charles Attwood, responsible respectively for Intelligence and Signals, and three officers in the Accountants and Medical branches. These nine officers formed the entire commissioned staff of the headquarters. Mitchell's predecessor as military commander, the CO of the now defunct Aden Brigade, embarked for India soon after the party's arrival, but not before predicting disaster under the new arrangements.

At the time of Ralph's arrival in Aden the situation was, indeed, far from satisfactory. The Yemeni forces, about 6,000-strong and still trained by Turkish officers and NCOs, had recently occupied the Emirate of Dhala, part of the Protectorate, in which they had built a substantial fort, and were now advancing from there towards Aden. The British strategy was to bomb the Yemeni towns and military bases on the other side of the border, thus threatening the enemy's lines of communication, at the same time raising a force from the tribes of the Protectorate to advance on to the plateau between Aden and Dhala. Flight Lieutenant Rickards, equipped with a radio and accompanied by a bodyguard provided by the Sultan of Lahej, was sent up to join the tribal force, which initially proved reluctant to move. Rickards decided to push on alone with his bodyguard, and gradually the tribesmen followed him. In the meantime, the fort at Dhala was subjected to intense bombing, as were the nearest Yemeni towns. Their inability to hit back meant that morale fell amongst the Yemenis, with a significant percentage of the population of Sana'a, the capital city which was never bombed, evacuating their homes. The Imam, under attack from the air and also potentially on the ground, gave the order to withdraw, and Rickards and his tiny force reoccupied Dhala. The total casualties on the British side amounted to one officer, killed flying into the ground in a sandstorm.

During the brief campaign Ralph had taken part in two reconnaissance flights in a DH9a, and now that hostilities were at an end, he was keen to get to know 8 Squadron better. The squadron was in the course of converting from the DH9a to the Fairey IIIF, a more advanced light bomber, in the prior knowledge of which he had flown one of the latter briefly before leaving England. His first flight in the type at Aden was to nearby Perim Island. Mitchell was also keen to fly and, as he had ordered that the squadron should be able to operate by night, was determined to set an example. Taking Ralph as a passenger, he carried out a few circuits before returning to the airfield at Khormaksar. The approach was over the sea and Ralph, who thought they were coming in somewhat low, looked over the side as they approached the landing strip and saw the reflection of the moon just beneath him. As he shouted a warning, the plane hit the sea and, when the fixed undercarriage engaged the water, turned over on its back. Mitchell's seat belt held and he hung upside down above shallow water, but Ralph was thrown clear into warm sticky mud, hitting the gun ring hard with his knee.

The two men were rescued immediately, but whilst Mitchell was undamaged, Ralph's knee was in very bad shape and he was removed to the military hospital, where he was to spend the next six weeks. The accident happened on 2 May and it was 18 August before he was passed fit for flying, with his knee still rather loose at the joint, but functioning well enough for most purposes.

On 1 February 1929 Ralph took over as Commanding Officer of 8 Squadron. Command of a squadron is one of the most important steps in the career of any officer in the General Duties branch of the RAF, and to Ralph, at the age of nearly thirty-four, it came relatively late; a number of his near contemporaries who had served in action in the Royal Flying Corps had commanded squadrons in their mid-to-late twenties. He was delighted with his new appointment and not just because it made a welcome change from staff work.

His new command had been first formed in the UK on New Year's Day 1915, crossing to France just over three months later. From then onwards 8 Squadron was constantly in action, operating the BE2 and later the Armstrong Whitworth FK8 in reconnaissance, artillery spotting and light bomber roles during most of the major battles on the British sector of the Western Front. Disbanded in January 1920, it was raised again in Egypt nine months later, transferring from there first to Basra in Iraq and then to Hinaidi and later Kirkuk during the Kurdish revolt, where Ralph had known it well. It had been sent to Aden in February 1927 in response to the deteriorating security situation and, apart from a period in 1945 and 1946 when it was disbanded and re-formed twice, was to remain there for an astonishing forty years.

The squadron consisted of twelve aircraft, divided into three flights. Ralph was by this time fully conversant with the Fairey IIIF and liked to lead the squadron in the air whenever possible. As it happened, on his very first day in command the squadron was engaged in a bombing raid and on this occasion he acted as observer to one of his flight commanders to gain experience, but he flew as a pilot more often than not thereafter. With the defeat of the Yemenis, all offensive actions were now directed at troublesome tribes, and in early 1929 these were the Subehis, who lived in the foothills about 50 miles north-east of Aden. They had no one leader, unlike most of the other tribes, and were particularly difficult to manage; some thought that, in this respect, they resembled the Pathans of the North-West Frontier. On this occasion they had not only conducted raids into Lahej, stealing livestock, including camels from a police post, but had also murdered a girl. On being ordered by the British Resident in Lahej to make full reparation, they refused to do so. Warnings were issued to the tribesmen that their villages would be bombed until they complied, and they drove their animals off into the mountains whilst this took place. Bombing began at the end of January and continued into early March, by which time the tribesmen had had enough, sending a deputation to ask what they should do to bring a halt to this calamity. By the end of the month the camels and other livestock had been returned and full compensation had been paid to the murdered girl's family. It was a very effective demonstration of air control.

Although practice bombing remained high on the squadron's agenda, with many days devoted to it each month, other priorities emerged. One was to mark out and build a number of landing strips in the tribal areas in the western part of the Protectorate[2] between Aden and the frontier with Yemen, as the lack of these had been a handicap in the past. For Ralph this meant many journeys in his Ford, with Rickards in a Morris six-wheeler truck, along the coast and into the interior, sometimes accompanied by Colonel Lake, who distributed cash to the local chiefs by way of keeping them happy.

The success of such visits encouraged Ralph and his colleagues to widen their horizons by visiting the eastern part of the Protectorate, a much bigger area than its western equivalent, bordered in the north by the Empty Quarter of Saudi Arabia, in the east by the Sultanate of Muscat and Oman and in the south by the Arabian Sea. It consisted substantially of the Hadhramaut, for the most part a desert plateau, but with two relatively well populated areas, the coastal strip and the Wadi Hadhramaut. The latter is a very large valley which lies parallel to the coast and through which runs a seasonal watercourse, making it unusually fertile. Of the two sultanates occupying the Hadhramaut, the more powerful was the Qu'aiti, covering much of the coastal strip, including the main port of Mukalla, as well as the greater part of the Wadi, including the town of Shibam, whilst the smaller Kathiri sultanate occupied much of the north-east of the territory including the towns of Sayun and Tarim in the Wadi. All the towns are noted for their substantial mud buildings, including palaces and 'skyscrapers'.

The Hadhramis were much more sophisticated than their fellow Arabs in the western part of the Protectorate, with a tradition of venturing far afield in their ships as traders to India and South-East Asia, returning with their fortunes made. Ralph and his colleagues made a detailed reconnaissance of the area, receiving a friendly welcome and giving the Qu'aiti Sultan his first ride in an aeroplane. They were astonished to find in the towns of the Wadi Hadhramaut cars which had been broken down into parts for transportation by camel and reassembled at their destination by their wealthy Hadhrami owners.

Back in Aden, Ralph enjoyed two forms of relaxation. The first was polo and, as in Hinaidi, ponies were inexpensive, so he acquired two, 'Tommy' and 'Curley'. The second was sailing. The squadron owned a miniature dhow, which provided employment for a very small Arab boy who kept it clean. Whilst its lateen sails had been much patched, it was an excellent sailer and ideal for the local conditions. Races were held regularly, mostly against the gigs and cutters of visiting Royal Navy ships. In one such race, the captain of the frigate concerned fancied the chances of his crew but was beaten by the dhow's ability to make good way in the lightest of airs and by the local knowledge of its crew, who knew that the wind would shift dramatically late in the afternoon, catching their opponents unawares. There was also a swimming club in a sheltered bay, protected from sharks by nets. Social life was otherwise somewhat limited, due in part to the lack of European women, but it was enlivened by a visit in December 1928 by the Prince of Wales, who was on his way back to the UK from a tour of Africa.

Once it could be spared, 8 Squadron detached a flight at a time to British Somaliland, on the other side of the Gulf of Aden, and Ralph went there on inspections both by air and by sea, in the case of the latter loading his car on the ship so that he could use it on his one month's local leave. Accompanied by Flying Officer Geoffrey Pilcher, one of the younger officers in the squadron, and by his bearer and an old shikari, his intention was to spend the time shooting all sorts of game, focusing on the west of the colony, where the mountains rose towards the Abyssinian border and the rainfall was higher. The party followed several lions, without getting close enough to take a shot, but managed to bag a Greater Kudu, whilst Lesser Kudu were shot for the pot. On the advice of the shikari they had brought a kid with them to attract bigger game, but although they stayed up all night, much plagued by insects, nothing emerged, so the kid made an excellent meal as they retraced their route to the coast.

Ralph's second overseas tour came to an end in the late autumn of 1929. Commanding a squadron, especially one which had been engaged in combat, had been a highly valuable experience. At the same time, his knowledge of a little understood part of the world led to his being asked to give a number of lectures, the first at the Royal United Services Institution, of which he became a keen member, and the second at the Royal Geographical Society, both of which brought him for the first time to the attention of a much wider audience than his own service.

Chapter 7

Staff Officer

Ralph's new appointment was for two years back at the RAF Staff College, this time as a member of the Directing Staff. The course dates had changed since his time as a student and now ran from January to December, with Ralph taking up his position in time for the 1930 course and staying until the end of 1931.

Brooke-Popham had moved on some years earlier, to be succeeded as Commandant by Air Vice-Marshal Edgar Ludlow-Hewitt. A non-drinking, non-smoking Christian Scientist with little in the way of a visible sense of humour, Ludlow-Hewitt nevertheless possessed one of the best brains in the RAF, for which he was much admired, by Ralph amongst others. He was succeeded in September 1930 by Air Commodore, later Air Vice-Marshal, Philip Joubert de la Ferté, whose charm provided a contrast to Ludlow-Hewitt's rather austere manner but who lacked his predecessor's great intellect, although he was by no means short of brains. He was to achieve distinction during the Second World War as C-in-C Coastal Command.

The Directing Staff were also men of future distinction. In addition to Ralph himself, Arthur Barratt, Norman Bottomley, Roderic Hill, Charles Medhurst and George Pirie were all to become air chief marshals, whilst Arthur Tedder became Chief of the Air Staff and a marshal of the RAF. Hill had succeeded Harris in command of 45 Squadron and, shortly before Ralph arrived back at the college, had published a book on the Baghdad Air Mail, so they had much in common and were to become good friends. Ralph had visited Tedder, then in command of 2 FTS, on a tour of the Wessex Bombing Area and had been much impressed by him at the time; when he got to know him better he was to consider him outstanding.

Ralph was to recall later that Tedder's lecture on the Seven Years' War was a masterpiece, but his own intellectual credentials had also been recently burnished by winning the Special Prize for the R. M. Groves Memorial

Essay in 1929.[1] The essay considered the influence of aircraft on the strategic problems in the Mediterranean confronting not only Great Britain, but also France and Italy. This was a subject which clearly intrigued him, as he was to win an RUSI Gold Medal in 1935 for an essay updating and expanding on the same subject and focusing particularly on British interests in the area.

The years 1930 and 1931 were not particularly vintage ones at the staff college as far as its students were concerned, although many years later, Conrad Collier would be Ralph's deputy in Transport Command and John Baker would succeed him as Vice-Chief of the Air Staff. Moreover, one of the two Canadian students in 1930 was Clifford McEwen, later to be one of his fellow group commanders in Bomber Command.

With the prospect of two years in Andover, allowing him more free time than he might expect in a staff or command appointment, Ralph decided that he would buy his own aircraft. In early 1930 he agreed with Westland to purchase G-EBRO, the Widgeon in which he had flown around Europe in 1927, for £350. He took delivery of the aircraft on 15 April, during the college's Easter break, and two days later began another tour. This time he was part of a considerable company of amateur flyers, all of whom were members of the flying club at the Heston Air Park formed by Nigel Norman, whom Ralph described as 'a very remarkable man having gifts of far sightedness, engineering competence, financial wisdom and with great personal charm'.[2] Norman was an entrepreneur, the co-founder of Airwork Services, which was to carry out a number of activities on behalf of both the RAF and other organizations, including maintenance and flying training, and which owned Heston Aerodrome. Moreover, he was also a flight commander in 601 (County of London) Squadron, Auxiliary Air Force, and would become its CO in the following year.[3]

Twenty or so light aircraft left Heston on the morning of 17 April, following a large breakfast. Most were De Havilland Gipsy Moths, but there were a few other types, including the Widgeon. They flew initially to Douai, where they were welcomed by Louis Breguet, the leading French aircraft designer and manufacturer, and the Secretary-General of the French Air Ministry, together with a number of French private pilots from the Aero Club de France. Speeches of welcome were followed by a champagne reception and a large lunch, at which Ralph found himself sitting next to

Adrienne Vinchon-Bolland, a notable French aviatrix. She told him that she had accumulated nearly 3,000 flying hours, mostly travelling around South America, following which he was very careful with his remarks![4]

The British aircraft flew on to Brussels after lunch. The majority of them were carrying passengers, so Ralph went out to dinner with another solo flyer, John Shand, with whom he struck up a friendship. After a day grounded in the Belgian capital by thick fog, compensated for by a visit to an excellent variety show that evening, the fliers set off for Cologne and then Frankfurt, from where Ralph accompanied Norman to Darmstadt to have a look at a new German light aeroplane, the Darmstadt D-18. This was a cantilever biplane, designed specifically as a sports aircraft, with a top speed of 140mph. It took off in about 40 yards and shot up like a rocket, impressing the visitors enormously.

On the following day the party flew to Stuttgart and then on to Friedrichshafen, where they were taken to see the Zeppelin works and given a meal on board the *Graf Zeppelin*. Ralph was disappointed that it was by then too dark to be able to see the girder construction, but he was delighted to talk shop afterwards with some of the ship's officers, notably Hans von Schiller, who had taken part in several raids on the UK during the Great War.

On the next morning the party was taken across Lake Constance to the Dornier works to see the giant DO X flying boat being built, Ralph taking the view that it would certainly be seaworthy because of its strong hull, but might, in spite of its six engines, prove to be underpowered. In the event, notwithstanding their luxurious interiors, the three that were built were never a commercial success.[5]

It was now 20 April, and the party moved on to Vienna and Prague that afternoon, all except for Ralph and Shand, who decided to get in some late season skiing in the Arlberg. They took a train up to St Anton and kitted themselves out, but due to the thaw only managed to get in a single run before having to call it a day. There ensued a very tedious train and boat journey back to Friedrichshafen, where they picked up their aircraft and flew to Berlin via Nuremberg and Leipzig, catching up with the rest of the party. The highlight of the stay in the German capital was a dinner given by the Berlin Aero Club at which one of the hosts was Bruno Loerzer, a famous fighter pilot of the Great War.[6]

Ralph subsequently spent a day in bed with what he thought was flu, but he was well enough by the following day to fly in company with Shand to Antwerp via Brunswick and Düsseldorf, arriving back at Heston on 30 April.

There was a coda to this trip a few days later, when Ralph and Shand flew up in their two planes to Gloucestershire to meet Norman and several others, who included Geoffrey de Havilland in the new Moth III. Coming in to land near Cirencester in a small field with no wind, Ralph found that his speed was too high, overshot the landing point and crashed into a ditch at the other end, damaging the propeller, one side of the undercarriage and the underneath of the fuselage. Handing over the remains to Norman, who promised to get it back to Heston for repair, he was given a lift back to Andover by Shand. He was nervous about his insurance claim, but Captain A. G. Lamplugh of British Aviation Insurance decided that the presence of a number of other planes made the site an authorized landing ground and agreed to pay. Seven weeks later, Ralph was able to pick up the Widgeon from Heston.

The year 1930 closed with a momentous event in Ralph's life, when he married Hilda Wiggin in the Church of St Simon Zelotes in Milner Street, Chelsea on 22 December. Ralph's bachelor existence had hitherto suited his career, as appointments in Iraq and Aden at this time were specifically 'unaccompanied'. His diaries through the 1920s provide no evidence of other close friendships with women, although he led an active social life and was clearly comfortable in mixed company. His relationship with Hilda, however, whilst conducted for the most part at a distance, was a longstanding one, going back for very nearly ten years to Cairo, which she had visited with her Aunt Eva. She and Ralph had enjoyed each other's company there, in particular whilst visiting the archaeological sites of Upper Egypt and sailing on the Nile at Aswan.

After Hilda's return to England they struck up a correspondence, which had lasted ever since. Whilst on postings in the UK, Ralph had visited her from time to time and had been particularly impressed by her driving ability. Then, seemingly out of the blue, he fell in love with her, proposed marriage and was, after some hesitation, accepted. She met his parents in London and then, rather bravely, went to stay at Crawford Priory by herself. Happily, Lord and Lady Cochrane strongly approved.

Hilda Frances Holme Wiggin was born on 26 July 1901, the sixth of seven children and the third of four daughters of Francis Holme Wiggin and his wife Margaret, née Carey. Her father was a tea planter in Ceylon and her mother had been born there, although educated in England. When Hilda was just four years old, her father died at the age of just forty-six. The children's guardian, a Mr Michie, travelled out to bring her mother and siblings back to England, where they lived with her father's unmarried sister, Eva Wiggin, at Langton Lodge in Charlton King's, just outside Cheltenham. Shortly afterwards, her mother committed suicide. Hilda and her younger sister Frances continued to live with their aunt for many years and were educated at Cheltenham Ladies' College.

The family tragedies were by no means over, since two of Hilda's brothers were to die during the Great War, Noel, the eldest, in 1917 at Kut-el-Amara during the campaign in Mesopotamia, and Douglas, the third son, in France in 1914. Her surviving brother, Arthur,[7] who gave Hilda away at the wedding, served in the Rifle Brigade in the Great War and then joined the Diplomatic Service, whilst her three sisters, Eva, Mary and Frances, all married in due course.

Hilda's sister Frances later told her own children that Hilda had had a relationship with a British Army officer in Egypt, although this cannot be confirmed. She was certainly a frequent visitor to the country, travelling there in every year but three between 1921, when she met Ralph before his posting to Iraq, and 1930. She had also ventured further afield in the Middle East and visited Europe on a number of occasions.

Ralph and Hilda had contrasting personalities. He was decisive, down-to earth and, on occasion, somewhat brusque. She was gentle, kind and sensitive, with a highly developed artistic temperament, which she put to good use as a sculptress. She was also very much a character in her own right, with a lower profile than Ralph but not overshadowed by him. They were to have a very happy marriage, although it did not start particularly auspiciously, as Hilda went down with jaundice on the day of the wedding and did not feel at all well. Instead of going straight to St Moritz, as had been their intention, they spent the first three days in Paris for her to recover, at least partially. On their arrival in St Moritz they were given a very poor room in the annexe of the hotel, and when Ralph decided after three days that they would move instead to Klosters, the manager demanded payment for a full week. The owner of the hotel in Klosters, a good friend of Ralph's, was the chairman of the Swiss hoteliers' association and he persuaded his colleague in St Moritz to see reason. The rest of the honeymoon, although Hilda took some time to recover fully, was more satisfactory.

Ralph and Hilda had a second honeymoon during the Staff College's Easter holiday in 1931, when he flew her round Europe in the Widgeon. She had experienced some short flights hitherto, but this was to be a three-week marathon. They were delayed for a day at Lympne by thick fog over the English Channel, but then flew from there all the way to Essen, landing at Antwerp to refuel en route. Their route took them directly over the Ruhr Valley, and Ralph's diary entry on what he saw was prophetic:

> Some people talk rather glibly of destroying industrial areas by bombing them, but one only needs to look down on the triangle of country which includes DUISBURG, ESSEN, MUHLHEIM to realize what such a policy would mean. One goods yard alone must have extended over 200 acres while the industrial plants themselves are not only scattered, but also the buildings within the plants. It is true that certain buildings contain key machinery, but even if these are known it would be no easy matter to hit them. So one is really driven back to the question of moral affect, & there as the opponents of bombardment point out one is on very uncertain ground. This of course applies to any country in a future war in which aircraft play a predominant part but the sight of these great industrial areas makes me wonder what their fate will be.[8]

Just over a decade later, Ralph would be totally immersed in tackling the conundrum which he foresaw.

The three core cities which Ralph and Hilda visited were Berlin, Leipzig and Vienna, the last being Ralph's own favourite, and in each their focus, reflecting Hilda's interests rather more than Ralph's, was on visiting the museums and palaces. Flying over the border between Germany and Czechoslovakia, Ralph noted the military preparations on the Czech side of the border, a contrast with the evident lack of such activity on the German side. After a brief stay in Budapest they arrived in Salzburg, Ralph's intention, as in the previous year, being to get in some late skiing. They made their way by train to Zell am See, where there was some satisfactory snow on their first two days, after which it turned to rain. They retraced their steps to Salzburg and thence back to England. Hilda, however, never really shared Ralph's great enthusiasm for skiing, and on future visits to the Alps he would usually go by himself or in company with other members of the family or with friends.

In 1931 Hilda started a business of her own, the Wednesday-Thursday Gallery in London's Brompton Road. As the name might suggest, it was initially open on only two days a week, selling woodcuts and greeting cards. In 1933 she was joined as a partner in the venture by Ala Story, and the name was changed to the Storran Gallery. It quickly became highly fashionable, exhibiting some of the well known artists of the period, including Gertrude Hermes, Duncan Grant and André Derain, and it brought Hilda into contact with a number of even more famous personalities, including Jacob Epstein and Henry Moore, who were said to have asked why they had not been invited to exhibit there.

Following two enjoyable years at the Staff College, Ralph's next posting was to the Directorate of Operations and Intelligence at the Air Ministry, with Ludlow-Hewitt as Director. In fact, his job had nothing to do with either operations or intelligence. Instead he found himself in a very small team dealing with Plans under Portal. The two of them and Squadron Leader Gerald Gibbs[9] shared a tiny office in Adastral House on Kingsway. When the window was open the noise was intolerable and when it was closed the air was unbreathable. This was at a time before German rearmament had come to be seen as a serious threat; indeed, it was the French who were perceived as the greater danger, and it was only after Hitler became head of state in the second half of 1934 that the priorities changed. The work of the Plans team thus focused much more on inter-service issues, of which two were particularly prominent, Singapore and the North-West Frontier of India.

On Singapore the arguments were with both the Royal Navy and the Army over the proposed installation of a number of 15-inch guns to counter the threat of landings from the sea. The possibility of an attack from the landward side was completely discounted as the Malayan jungle was believed to be impenetrable. The other two services wanted to have aircraft to spot the fall of shells from these guns, and it was evident that the spotters would themselves need fighter protection. The RAF argued that, if this was the case, it would be better to do without the guns altogether and instead to employ torpedo-carrying aircraft to sink enemy ships.

The opposition to the RAF case was mounted not only by the other services, but also by the immensely powerful Secretary to both the Cabinet and the Committee of Imperial Defence, Sir Maurice Hankey, who was considered by the government of the day to be an expert on defence matters. As a young man Hankey had been commissioned into the Royal Marine Artillery, serving in a battleship and on land, and Ralph believed him to be a dyed-in-the-wool coast gunner. Hankey argued that, once installed, the guns would always be there, whilst aeroplanes could never be guaranteed to be anywhere. His weight proved to be decisive, and work began on the guns.

As far as the North-West Frontier was concerned, the RAF's opponent was the Army in India, especially its Indian Army component, which saw that part of the world as very much its own responsibility, indeed virtually as the reason for its existence. The RAF, since the days of Harris and Salmond, and even before then, had been very much the junior partner in the policing of the Frontier and, notwithstanding the successes which had been achieved in British Somaliland, Iraq and Aden, the Army was implacably opposed to handing over the full responsibility.

Ralph himself felt that the North-West Frontier issue, whilst symptomatic of the Army's innate conservatism, was less important than another controversy which arose with the Royal Navy. The Senior Service had made available the old battleship HMS *Centurion* as a radio-controlled training target for RAF dive-bombers. These managed to score a significant number of hits, only for the Navy to assert that the bombers would have been shot down by anti-aircraft fire. No amount of analysis or argument could force a change of mind, and it was not until the Norway campaign and the Dunkirk evacuation in 1940 that the Navy was forced to accept the vulnerability of its vessels to air attack.

Ralph was immensely impressed by the lucidity of Portal's mind on these and other issues. On arrival in the office, Portal would sit at his desk and write in long-hand for an hour or so, before ringing for a copy typist from the pool, who would take his paper away and bring back six copies an hour later. These would then be circulated to the Chief of the Air Staff – at that time Sir John Salmond, succeeded in 1933 by Sir Edward Ellington – and to the appropriate service and civilian members of the Air Council for their comments. Such comments would usually come back during the afternoon, in time for the agreed paper to be submitted to the Committee of Imperial Defence before the end of the day. It is difficult to imagine such a fast turnaround in later years, even in the digital age.

If lucidity of expression was one of Portal's great qualities, then tenacity of purpose was another. This was demonstrated when Ralph played golf with him. Ralph was a capable golfer himself, if anything somewhat better than Portal. However, time and again Ralph would find himself in the lead on a round, only to be overhauled, shot by shot, by Portal's sheer determination.

Ralph's formerly unmarried status had entitled him to live in accommodation provided by the RAF, but at the beginning of their married life he and Hilda started on what was to be a very long succession of rented properties. The first of these, a small cottage in Abbotts Ann, not far from Andover, was one of the best, with a lovely garden. It was followed over the next few years by three houses in London, respectively in Knightsbridge, Gerald Road and South Place, all conveniently sited for both Ralph's work and Hilda's gallery. Their first child, Ann Grizel Cochrane, always known by her second name, was born on 26 June 1932, her arrival necessitating an increase in the domestic staff, with a nurse and a nursemaid in addition to a cook and a 'tweenie'. In spite of Ralph's relatively modest salary, increased when he was promoted to wing commander on 1 July 1933, they were able to afford this establishment, but it left little to spare for entertaining.

Shortly before the end of 1933, Ralph took a series of trains from London to Brindisi and, on New Year's Day 1934, boarded an Imperial Airways flying boat to take him from there to Alexandria, where he landed two days later after overnight stops at Corfu and Crete. He was on a temporary attachment as a staff officer to the AOC Middle East, Air Vice-Marshal Cyril Newall who, with an Army general, was to undertake a review of the defence of East Africa. Ralph's role was to represent the Air Staff view and to act as the Joint Secretary with an Army officer.

Much of this odyssey was undertaken in two Vickers Victorias, a larger development of the Vernon, although on some legs Ralph flew in a Fairey Gordon, a derivative of the Fairey IIIF which he knew so well. The party's route ran from Cairo to Khartoum, on to Entebbe and Nairobi and then down to Livingstone and Salisbury, thereby taking in the Sudan, Uganda, Kenya, Tanganyika, Nyasaland, Northern and Southern Rhodesia. One of the Victorias was flown by Flight Lieutenant Bill Markham, who was a magnificent pilot but regarded in the service as quite mad. This was demonstrated on one occasion at a sloping airfield on which it was considered highly advisable to take off downhill, even when the wind was blowing in the same direction, which it was on this occasion. The first Victoria did just this and took off satisfactorily. The second, piloted by Markham with Ralph as one of the passengers, took off uphill against the wind and was about 50ft off the ground by the end of the strip. Thereafter the ground rose at exactly the same rate of climb as the aircraft, whose wheels were brushing the tops of the trees. It was only after some nerve-wracking minutes that the Victoria succeeded in out-climbing the hill!

After some three weeks the party had seen and heard enough to come to a conclusion, which was that the method of air control used in Iraq and Aden would not be appropriate in the territories that it had visited and that British-led locally enlisted troops, together with a small number of aircraft to provide mobility and fire power, could keep the peace without difficulty. The report and recommendations were put together in Nairobi, Ralph taking advantage of a free weekend to spend it with a friend, Sir Pyers Mostyn, at his farm on the slopes of Mount Kenya.

Whilst still in Kenya and on a trip to the north of the country close to the Abyssinian border, Ralph received some terrible news. His brother Tom and Tom's wife, Nellie,[10] of whom Ralph was very fond, had themselves been on a visit to Egypt at this time, during which Nellie had been killed in a car accident. He was desperately sorry for Tom, but his first thought was for the eldest of his and Nellie's children, Anthony, who was physically disabled.

On the journey back to Cairo the party had reached Juba in the Sudan when Ralph went down with malaria and was rushed into the local hospital. The doctor pronounced that he would have to stay there for ten days, but Newall told him that he would 'fetch the body'[11] at 6.00 on the following morning, which he duly did. Still feeling very poorly from the effects of malaria and devastated by the family tragedy, Ralph spent a miserable few days in Cairo before retracing his steps back to England via Brindisi.

Whilst Ralph had been away, Portal had left the Air Ministry on his posting as Officer Commanding British Forces in Aden. His successor as Deputy Director of Plans was Harris, bringing Ralph once more into close contact with another officer he knew well and admired greatly. Not long after his arrival back in London, however, he learnt that he had been selected for the next course at the Imperial Defence College, which he duly joined nine months later, in January 1935. The IDC was still a young institution, having opened its doors as recently as 1927. It was the brainchild of Winston Churchill, who had chaired the cabinet committee recommending its establishment. Its objective was to prepare officers in the three British armed services, the Indian Army, the armed services of the Dominions and the civil service, for high responsibility in their respective organizations. Selection for the course was therefore itself an accolade, an early indication that the career prospects of the student held some promise. A number of officers who Ralph held in particularly high esteem, notably Portal and Tedder, were graduates of the college.

The IDC was housed in 9 Buckingham Gate, a relatively modest building opposite the side of Buckingham Palace and convenient for Ralph, who could walk to work from home, which was now in Cliveden Place. It comprised a lecture room, a library, half a dozen classrooms for syndicate work and offices for the Commandant and Directing Staff. For the most part uniforms were not worn, and a Monday-to-Friday working week was followed by weekends off, so in some respects it was an opportunity to recharge the mental batteries.

The Commandant of the IDC in 1929 was Major General Robert Haining, who at that time was very highly regarded in Army circles, but who never quite reached the top of his profession. There were only three members of the Directing Staff, one from each of the British armed services, two of whom were to achieve five-star rank, Arthur Power from the Royal Navy and Sholto Douglas from the RAF. In his memoirs Ralph wrote that these were all able men, albeit not very receptive to new ideas, but he was somewhat dismissive of his fellow students, the outstanding one in his opinion being a civilian, Robert Harvey of the General Post Office, who was to become an Under-Secretary at the Treasury and, in due course, Director of Inland Telecommunications. Ralph was also later to describe another student, Lieutenant Colonel Giffard Martel, as a brilliant tank officer, which indeed he was.[12] There were, moreover, others who made names for themselves subsequently, one of the most distinguished being Lieutenant Colonel (later General) Richard O'Connor, who was to defeat the Italians decisively in Egypt and Cyrenaica in 1940, only to be taken prisoner when Rommel entered the scene; he was later to escape and to command a corps in North-West Europe in 1944/5.

Another fellow student was Lieutenant Colonel Arthur Percival, the ill-fated defender of Singapore in 1942. As it happened, the threat from Japan was one of the two main issues placed before the IDC students in 1935, and here Ralph was on strong ground, having considered the defence not only of Singapore, but also of Hong Kong and the Indian ports, whilst at the Air Ministry. Singapore was the subject of a major exercise for the students in which O'Connor acted as the Japanese commander and successfully took the island, whilst Percival was amongst the defenders. Ralph was to say subsequently[13] that Percival was an able staff officer but should never have been sent as a commander to Singapore.

The IDC was run in a relatively relaxed fashion, but its purpose was deadly serious: to consider the defence problems of the British Empire from every angle and to produce solutions for them. The Directing Staff were given access to highly confidential information, including intelligence, by the service and other ministries, and it highlighted growing concerns about international developments. Japan was now seen as a potential threat, hence the focus on Singapore, but much closer to home, the rearmament of Germany was now well under way: in March 1935 Hitler announced that the new Luftwaffe, which had been officially established only a month earlier, was as strong as the RAF. Moreover, Italy invaded Abyssinia in October 1935 and was adopting an increasingly bellicose stance in its own imperial expansion. These and other events led to the war-gaming at the IDC of a number of scenarios for a European war. As a key component of the course, talks were given by senior officers, cabinet ministers, ambassadors, industrialists, bankers and trades unionists, who delivered alternative views on the issues in question.

There were two breaks for Ralph from the IDC routine, one planned, the other not. The first was a trip to the battlefields of northern France. The party stayed in Soissons, where Martel took Ralph to see the site of the bridge he had constructed in 1914 to replace the one blown up by the Germans in their retreat from the Marne.[14] The second was a stay of ten days in the RAF hospital at Uxbridge when Ralph's knee blew up, a recurrence of the injury which he had suffered in the crash in Aden.

Ralph enjoyed the course and particularly the opportunities to stand up and express his opinion. He came away with a better understanding of the momentous changes taking place in international affairs and their implications for Britain: these now included the rapid expansion of the RAF, blocked hitherto by the Ten Year Rule, which had presumed that there would be no major European war for the next ten years and was only abandoned in 1932. His next appointment, to the staff of Inland Area, would be at the heart of the transformation now taking place.

Inland Area had been formed in 1920, initially to take command of all those groups engaged in training and subsequently to control all the RAF units in Great Britain with the exception of those included in ADGB and Coastal Area, together with Cranwell and Halton, which ranked as separate commands. This was still the case when Ralph arrived a few days before Christmas 1935, but there was a major reorganization in the spring and early summer of 1936, when Bomber Command and Fighter Command were created out of ADGB, Coastal Area became Coastal Command and Inland Area became Training Command. Training Command comprised 23 (Training) Group, 24 (Training) Group, the Armament Group and Cranwell. The RAF Flying Training Schools, the Central Flying School, the School of Air Navigation and the Air Observers' School were controlled by 23 Group, while 24 Group controlled all technical training, including Halton. The Armament Group consisted of the Air Armament School and the Armament Training Camps. Training Command also had direct responsibility for overseeing the Civil Flying Training Schools, under which a number of aircraft manufacturers had been contracted to train pilots for the Reserve of Air Force Officers ('RAFO') on their own airfields.

Inland Area's and initially Training Command's HQ was located at Bentley Priory, Stanmore, so Ralph and Hilda, with Grizel and the couple's second child, John Alexander Cochrane, born on 6 January 1935, moved to a flat in a more conveniently located building. The AOC-in-C was Air Marshal Sir Charles Burnett, with Air Commodore Lionel McKean as the Senior Air Staff Officer.

Ralph's immediate subordinate in his first few months was Squadron Leader G. S. Oddie, who was well qualified for the position, having attended the Flying Instructors' Course at the Central Flying School (CFS), served as a pilot in the experimental section of the Royal Aircraft Establishment and then been chief instructor at 3 FTS. He was at the time engaged in a heated debate with the CFS, which Ralph described as 'the acknowledged fountain head of flying orthodoxy'.[15] The subject was instrument flying, on which Oddie was an expert, having been on a recent tour of the USA which had included opportunities to see how the USAAF handled this particular task. The question was eventually resolved in Oddie's favour, but not without some resistance on the part of the CFS, which disliked this sort of oversight.

In July 1936 HQ Training Command relocated to Buntingsdale Hall, a beautiful eighteenth century country house near Market Drayton in Shropshire. The expansion of flying training had been particularly rapid, with Nos. 6, 7, 8, 9, 10 and 11 Flying Training Schools forming between April 1935 and March 1936, along with a number of armament training camps. The FTSs now became focused on advanced training, so more civilian-run schools were opened, not only for RAFO training, but also for the primary training of RAF and RAuxAF pilots. The training facilities which Ralph had to visit were thus spread all over the country, from Montrose and Leuchars in the north to Netheravon and Manston in the south As a result, he flew himself more often than he had done since Aden, mostly in a Tiger Moth, which by this time was starting to replace the Avro Tutor as the RAF's basic trainer, but occasionally in a Hawker Hart light bomber or its Audax variant, which were much faster aircraft. The Widgeon had been sold some years earlier, possibly because it had proved difficult to justify keeping it during his four years of postings in London.

In between the hectic activity caused by expansion there was some scope for leisure, especially after the move to Market Drayton, and it was whilst Ralph was enjoying a round of golf at a local course that he received an urgent message to ring Harris, who was still Deputy Director of Plans at the Air Ministry. He called back immediately, only to be asked a question: would Ralph be interested in going on a short term assignment to New Zealand?

Chapter 8

New Zealand

On further enquiry, Harris explained that the Government of New Zealand had asked for an RAF officer to be sent out to write a report on the country's air defence. This was by no means the first time that this had happened; indeed, there had been two previous occasions on which advice had been sought, the first in 1919, when Colonel Arthur Bettington was despatched to New Zealand with a small team. Bettington proposed an air force establishment of seven squadrons, formed initially on a cadre basis, with 70 regular officers and 299 airmen, supported by 174 territorial officers and 1,060 airmen. His report was rejected by a government whose country had suffered such severe casualties, proportionate to its size, in the Great War. Instead, a much smaller Permanent Air Force (PAF) was set up under the control of the General Officer Commanding New Zealand Forces and equipped with thirty-five aircraft, which over the next decade saw little use and gradually became obsolete.

The second report was produced in 1928, when John Salmond was sent out to advise both the Australian and the New Zealand Governments on air defence. By this time the strength of the PAF had been reduced to a mere five officers and fourteen airmen. Salmond recommended the formation of a nine-squadron force, whose Director of Air Services, whilst still subordinate to the GOC, would have direct access to the Minister of Defence. His report met much the same fate as its predecessor, although RAF ranks were adopted for the first time and two Fairey IIIFs were acquired for maritime reconnaissance, together with a few other aircraft, including four Hawker Tomtit trainers and a flying boat. In 1934 the name of the PAF was changed to the Royal New Zealand Air Force, but it remained subordinate to the GOC New Zealand Forces. In the following year the RNZAF took delivery of twelve Vickers Vildebeest general purpose biplanes, but without any bombs, and four Avro 625 trainers. By March 1936 it numbered 20 officers and 107 airmen, whilst an additional 74 officers held a Territorial commission.

At the end of November 1935 a general election was held in New Zealand and the Labour Party came to power for the first time, winning 46 per cent of the popular vote and 66 per cent of the seats in Parliament. The electoral platform of the incoming government had been focused on social security and similar issues, with defence a very low priority. However, the belligerent noises now beginning to emerge from Germany, Italy and, most worryingly of all for a Pacific nation, from Japan, together with the effective demise of the League of Nations, resulted in a change of heart, and the British Government was requested to send out a new advisor. The recommendations of a very senior RAF officer having been largely spurned in 1928, the Air Ministry considered that a middle-ranking officer was all that could be spared, and Ralph, whose intellectual talents were by this time widely recognized, fitted the bill. He accepted the posting with alacrity and embarked for New Zealand in the RMS *Mataroa* on 2 October 1936.

It was not until 8 November that Ralph disembarked in Auckland. The voyage across two oceans via the Panama Canal, in a vessel with a theoretical cruising speed of 13.5 knots, which was rarely achieved, gave him plenty of time to consider the issues, as well as to read the recently published blockbuster novel, *Gone with the Wind*. Armed with some good maps and briefed by the Air Ministry on the likely scale of such threats as might be encountered, he had a complete draft of his report written before his arrival.

In his private memoirs, in an interview he gave to the Air Historical Board in 1975 and in a speech which he prepared for an award ceremony at the Museum of Transport and Technology in Auckland in 1977, which he was unable to attend due to ill-health, Ralph wrote of borrowing a private plane to see as much of the country as possible before submitting his report. His New Zealand flying log book, which brings forward the correct total of flying hours from his RAF log book, shows no flights before 4 January 1937 as a passenger and 26 March as a pilot, whilst his short-lived New Zealand diary does not begin until 20 November 1936 and makes no reference to this journey. It is thus impossible to determine where he went, whether in both the North and the South Islands or just in the former, and exactly whom he met, but he wrote in his memoirs that he used the airfields of flying clubs, which by that time were thriving concerns established near many cities and large towns.

In addition to developing a better understanding of the country through this journey, it was clearly necessary for Ralph to consult a number of people in New Zealand before he could complete and submit his report. Inevitably these included the relevant members of the Labour Government, to which he would be answering. The Prime Minister, Michael Savage, took an interest, but with much else on his plate at the time was happy to delegate most of the discussions to others. The responsible cabinet member was Fred Jones, the Minister of Defence who, whilst not opposed to the expansion of the country's air force, was most concerned about cost, a sentiment shared by Walter Nash, the Minister of Finance. Jones found it difficult to grasp some of the issues. 'He is obviously entirely in the dark and has no one to turn to who can give him advice',[1] wrote Ralph at the time. A much more important ally turned out to be Peter Fraser, who was later to succeed Savage as Prime Minister and to lead his country through the Second World War. Fraser was enthusiastic from the outset and, despite the fact that his ministerial portfolios were Health and Education, was to prove highly effective in his support. It was helpful that he and Ralph had something in common as fellow Scots, and they got on particularly well at a personal level. Ralph believed, probably correctly, that Fraser was already the power behind the throne within the Government.

Whilst it was the Government which would decide the outcome in due course, it was the leading officers of the RNZAF who Ralph also needed to be fully supportive. The most senior of these was the Director of Air Services, Wing Commander Tom Wilkes, and it was due to him that Ralph was there at all. Wilkes had been asked to produce the plan for expansion himself, but declined on the grounds that the scheme would prove to be very expensive and was likely to be rejected if proposed by an insider; in his opinion it needed to be put forward by someone entirely independent to have any chance of success. Wilkes, who had spent two years in London as the New Zealand liaison officer at the Air Ministry, had done more than any other person to keep the PAF, and later the RNZAF, alive against the indifference of successive governments. He now became a strong supporter of Ralph's proposals, as did the two next most senior officers, Squadron Leaders Leonard Isitt, who had spent two years with the RAF in the late 1920s to gain experience of new developments and had subsequently been responsible for flying training in the RNZAF, and Arthur Nevill,[2] who had succeeded Wilkes at the Air Ministry in London.

Ralph also established a good relationship with the New Zealand Division of the Royal Navy.[3] The division's commander, Rear Admiral the Hon. Edmund Drummond, gave Ralph the impression that he would back the air arm in any dispute with the Army. The next most senior officer in the division turned out to be Captain Robert Oliver, who had been in Ralph's term at Osborne and Dartmouth. Ralph showed him the full report and asked for his comments, which were few.

Ralph was also obliged to consult the General Officer Commanding, New Zealand Military Forces, Major General Sir William Sinclair-Burgess, under whose command the RNZAF still sat. In Ralph's view the Army was in a parlous state, with an establishment too large for the funds available to maintain it, and it had lost much credibility as a result. Moreover, the arguments in favour of keeping the RNZAF under overall Army command had by this time already been lost, so the meetings were little more than a formality.

Finally there was the Governor General, Viscount Galway, who made him very welcome at Government House. Galway was encouraging, but publicly he was bound to remain strictly neutral on what was a political matter.

Following all these meetings, Ralph found that he only needed to make modest changes to his draft, and the final report went to the printers on 26 November, less than three weeks after his arrival in the country. When it appeared in print the *Report on the Air Aspect of the Defence Problems of New Zealand* ran to a modest ten pages, plus some maps and a short appendix on operation and training. It began with an analysis of defence problems, which Ralph divided into three – the defence of New Zealand itself, the defence of the country's communications, especially those with the United Kingdom, and the security of the United Kingdom. As far as the first was concerned, he discounted the threat of invasion, although he considered that the country might be subjected to raids by ships or by aircraft carried on ships. The defence of communications was vital, especially if it proved desirable to concentrate the RAF in the United Kingdom, in which case it might be necessary for New Zealand to help to reinforce Singapore. The defence of shipping in New Zealand waters was clearly a prime responsibility of that country. The security of the United Kingdom might well require assistance from New Zealand and other countries in the Empire, whether by way of complete units or of trained personnel.

Ralph proposed that the duties of the air force should address these issues and went on to consider the types of aircraft which would be required. As far as offensive aircraft were concerned, they would need to be able to fly the longest leg on the route to and from the UK, between Darwin and Singapore, carry a bomb load sufficient to destroy or cripple any raider and have a sufficient reserve of engine power in the event of damage. This pointed to a long-range multi-engine aircraft capable of carrying two tons of bombs for 1,000 miles at 200mph, a requirement which could be met by one of the new types of medium bomber now under development in the UK. Ralph had in mind the aircraft currently being developed to an Air Ministry specification by Vickers and designed by his old friend Barnes Wallis,[4] with whom he was conducting a correspondence about its capabilities. He recommended that two squadrons should be formed, each of twelve such aircraft,[5] located at the same base in order to economize on equipment and control. Ralph ruled out the need for fighters, as the likelihood of air attack on New Zealand was small and no adequate early warning system was available in any case. There should, however, also be a squadron of lighter aircraft, capable of operating from small landing grounds, for army co-operation duties.

As far as organization was concerned, Ralph proposed that the two bomber squadrons should be established on a permanent basis, without which efficiency and readiness for action would be compromised. He also proposed that there should be an air force reserve, sufficient to provide the flying personnel required to keep two medium bomber squadrons and one army co-operation squadron flying in time of war. He suggested an overall build-up to 250 pilots, 125 wireless operators and 125 air gunners, for whom a sizeable training establishment would be required. He proposed that preliminary flying training should be carried out by New Zealand's aero clubs, with advanced training centred on Wigram Aerodrome, outside Christchurch on the South Island.

On higher organization, Ralph recommended that the Royal New Zealand Air Force should be constituted as an independent armed service, controlled by an Air Board under the direction of the Minister of Defence. Other recommendations were that civil air transport should be encouraged in order to provide an effective transport system, that the aero club movement should receive some financial support for training and that the UK Government should be invited to co-operate in developing facilities for aircraft operations in the Pacific Islands.

Whilst the report was being printed, Ralph visited the South Island, travelling there by ship in rough weather. He stayed in Christchurch with Air Marshal Sir Robert Clark-Hall, who was, like Ralph, a former officer in the RNAS, so they had much in common.[6] Whilst there, he was able to visit Wigram, where he was disappointed by the size of the buildings, including the hangars, a direct result of government parsimony. During his stay in Christchurch he met two former shipmates from HMS *Colossus*, one running an engineering business and the other the secretary of the Christchurch Club. To his astonishment, shortly after his return to Wellington on 3 December, he met two more, both serving on HMS *Dunedin*, one of the cruisers in the New Zealand Division.

The cabinet met to consider the report on 8 December, immediately prior to which Ralph held a meeting with Jones and another Labour politician, John A. Lee, who had been expected to join the cabinet after the election but was disliked by Savage, who made him an under-secretary. Lee was highly influential with the left wing of the party and was even more supportive than Jones, who was still concerned about cost implications. Ralph was in due course called in to the cabinet meeting to answer a few inconsequential questions and to be asked what should happen next. He replied that he would like to form a committee to deal with practical aspects, and the report was accepted without modification.

After the cabinet meeting both Jones and Lee asked Ralph if he would consider staying on to put his recommendations into effect. This had already been suggested by a number of others, including Wilkes, who Ralph thought would have been perfectly suitable for the role but who unfortunately carried little credibility with the politicians. In the knowledge that Wilkes himself agreed with the Government's proposal, Ralph replied that he would be honoured to be asked, but that the decision would have to be made by the Air Ministry. On 17 December a formal offer was made and Ralph sent a telegram to London recommending that he should allowed to stay on.

Whilst awaiting developments, Ralph took a holiday over Christmas and the New Year, largely spent fishing with some success around Taupo and Rotorua and enjoying the hospitality of many new friends. One of those to whom he was introduced was Jean Batten, the now famous aviatrix who had recently made the first solo flight from England to New Zealand. On 4 January 1937 he was flown to Auckland in a Moth piloted by Flight Lieutenant M. W. Buckley[7] and on the next day took a train to Wellington in order to resume his discussions with the Government; these included the terms of his secondment, in connection with which he cabled the Air Ministry to ask if he could be given the acting rank of group captain, which was readily agreed to with effect from 1 February. He also sent a telegram to Hilda at Crawford Priory, followed up by a telephone call, asking her to book a passage to New Zealand for herself and the children on the first available ship.

Ralph's immediate task was to produce two Acts of Parliament, one to create the Royal New Zealand Air Force as a separate service within the country's armed forces, the other to establish an Air Board. The drafting was delegated to Nevill, who made an outstandingly good job of it. Ralph was insistent that the Air Board should include a civilian secretary, responsible among other things for finance. One of those recommended to him was Tom Barrow, a civil servant in the Public Works Department. Ralph interviewed Barrow and found that he was eminently suitable, only to be told by the Public Works Commissioner that he was too junior for the job. Ralph appealed to Fraser, who had Barrow transferred into what would be a sixteen-year career on the Air Board, providing a welcome degree of continuity up to, through and beyond the Second World War.

The man who had recommended Barrow in the first place was Esmond Gibson, who combined a job as a civil engineer in the Public Works Department with a reserve commission as a flight lieutenant. Gibson was responsible for airfield construction and was now placed at Ralph's disposal to build two new RNZAF stations, rather than the one suggested in Ralph's report. Of the two already in existence, Hobsonville, near Auckland, was to be converted to accommodate the training of ground crew and to be the central depot for stores and repairs, whilst Wigram was to be used almost exclusively for advanced flying training, initially on the Vickers Vildebeests, Avro 626s and Hawker Tomtits already in the country. Five Airspeed Oxfords were also ordered, four to provide training on multi-engined aircraft, one to be used on aerial surveys.

It had been decided that the two new airfields would both be situated on the North Island, and Ralph requested and received plans of typical RAF stations on which they could be modelled. The area in the immediate vicinity of Wellington was not suitable for an airfield operating large bomber aircraft, so a site was sought well to the north of the capital. It needed to be out of range of cruiser fire from the sea, yet far enough away from the mountains for them not to be a hazard, and to enjoy good weather conditions. The area with the most promise was around Palmerston North, which was notably free from fog and low cloud. Ralph and Gibson had visited the place before Christmas 1936, following which surveys had been carried out. After a number of other visits, the site chosen was sixteen miles north-west of Palmerston North and was to become RNZAF Ohakea.

With Hobsonville now allocated for other purposes, another site was sought near Auckland. The ground conditions in much of the area, either former peat swamp or with a sub-stratum composed of viscous clay, were not generally suitable for the construction of the large buildings required, particularly the hangars. There was a good area of flat land which consisted of more suitable volcanic clay, but Gibson was dubious about this and insisted on driving a pile down to test the conditions. At the first blow the pile disappeared through the clay into the swamp below. After some months of searching and surveying, an area only three miles north of Hobsonville and some ten miles north-west of Auckland proved to be suitable and was developed into RNZAF Whenuapei.

On both the two new airfields work began as soon as the sites had been selected. The hangars, in particular, posed a problem, as they would have to accommodate much larger aircraft than those already in the country. Charles Turner, the chief design engineer of the Public Works Department, devised a novel concrete structure which had no internal support, being held together instead by an underground steel girder. Despite concerns among other architects about the hangars' safety, they proved to be immensely strong and are still in use today at both Ohakea and Whenuapei. The other buildings were of similarly high quality, also constructed out of concrete, unlike those made of wood on other military bases; complaints about expense from the

Ministry of Finance were defused by demonstrating that the higher capital cost would reduce the need for maintenance.

On the family front, Hilda sailed for New Zealand in the *Mataroa* on 22 January with Grizel, John, a nanny, a nursemaid and a car, and arrived at the end of the following month.[8] They were able to move into Overton House, the home of Mrs A. D. Crawford, who was spending six months in England. Blessed with a large and attractive garden, it was situated in Miramar, a suburb of Wellington conveniently close to the civil airfield at Rongotai. Rongotai was considered unsuitable for general military use, due the high winds to which it was frequently subjected, but it was to prove essential to Ralph for his many light aircraft flights around the country, more often than not piloting himself in either a Percival Gull or a Miles Whitney Straight.

On 1 April 1937 the Air Force Act and the Air Department Act took effect, and Ralph became the RNZAF's first Chief of the Air Staff. The Air Board, concerned with military aviation, consisted of Fred Jones as Chairman, Ralph as CAS, Isitt as Air Member for Personnel, Nevill as Air Member for Supply and Barrow as Air Secretary. The new Air Department had a separate branch for civil aviation, with Wilkes as the Controller; he also sat on the Air Board as an extra member when issues were discussed involving both military and civil matters.

Ralph was to spend nearly two more years in New Zealand and they were action-packed. The emphasis was not only on the building of two large airfields. The most pressing immediate need was for pilots, and although there was no lack of volunteers, the means to train them were as yet limited. Ralph had numerous meetings with representatives of the twelve aero clubs, and a scheme was devised whereby young men who committed to join the RNZAF Reserve would get free initial flying training at the clubs. Whilst many young New Zealanders were happy to be trained as pilots within their own country and to serve in the RNZAF, others were keen to join the RAF. This had been the case from the early days of military flying, and large numbers of them had volunteered for the RFC during the Great War, some of whom went on to have most distinguished flying careers.[9] All of these had travelled to the UK at their own expense, with no certainty that they would pass the selection board on their arrival. It was now decided to establish a selection board in New Zealand and to pay the passages of those selected. In addition, in order to share both knowledge and experience, a number of RAF officers were seconded to the RNZAF, whilst RNZAF officers went on exchange in the other direction.

Advanced flying training was now concentrated at Wigram, where pilots were trained not only for the RNZAF and its reserve but also directly for the RAF, which provided a subsidy. The lack of sufficient aircraft for training and other purposes was solved by the British Government agreeing to sell twenty-nine surplus Blackburn Baffins to the RNZAF, together with full sets of spare parts, all at a knock-down price. These had recently been replaced as torpedo bombers in the Fleet Air Arm by the Fairey Swordfish, but were in generally very good condition. They were now used to equip three territorial squadrons, one each for Auckland, Wellington and Christchurch, allowing many of the remaining older aircraft to be released for training. A further territorial squadron was planned for Dunedin.

An unusual problem at Wigram, at least as far as Ralph was concerned, was a longstanding ban on alcoholic consumption on military premises, brought about by the lobbying of New Zealand's very strong temperance movement. This proved to be especially unpopular amongst those in married quarters, often located close to civilian homes where no such restriction existed, and was considered to be manifestly unfair. Ralph pressed very hard and succeeded in having the ban lifted.

Another issue which needed to be addressed very quickly was a major shortage of ground engineers and mechanics with specialist skills. Ralph discovered, however, that there was a very efficient apprentice engineer training scheme run by the New Zealand Railways Department. The course lasted for five years, and Ralph obtained agreement that the last year should be focused on aeronautical engineering. In due course this produced some high quality riggers, fitters and other members of the ground crew.

In his report to the New Zealand Government Ralph had raised the issue of the Pacific Islands, which in the event of a war needed to be secured against occupation by the enemy. Some of the groups of islands to the north, notably Fiji and Tonga, were under British governance, whilst New Zealand was itself responsible for Western Samoa and the Cook Islands. In the event of an attack from that direction, these would all be of great strategic importance. Although bellicose noises were emerging from Japan, it was not that country which was now causing concern, but the actions of a supposedly friendly nation, the United States. The British Government had laid claim to Canton Island, in the Phoenix Group, in the middle of the nineteenth century and had reasserted this claim in August 1936. The US Government, however, also had a claim on the island, which was formally placed under its control by President Roosevelt in March 1938. After some tense moments, which at one point included British and American warships exchanging shots across each other's bows, it was agreed about a year later to hold the island under joint control, but in the meantime it was identified as a base for the expansion of the long-distance services of Pan American Airways. Ralph had met and become friendly with Harold Gatty, who had made his name as the navigator on a record-breaking aerial circumnavigation of the world in 1931 and was now Pan American's South Pacific manager.

The New Zealand Government, with British agreement, decided that steps should be taken to identify sites in the islands for airfields or flying boat stations, to be built when the need arose, but in the meantime to limit the further expansion of Pan American as a surrogate for the United States. HMS *Leander*, now serving in the New Zealand Division, was ordered to sail north on a cruise round the islands during the last three months of 1938, with Ralph and Gibson, together with a representative of Imperial Airways, on board to survey the likely islands for possible sites. The ship sailed via Fiji as far north as Christmas Island, just over the Equator, where an aerodrome was marked out and notices erected, announcing the intention to build there, in the hope that this might deter Pan American. It then retraced its course to Fiji, where two good sites were marked out, and sailed on to Tonga, where Ralph and some others from the ship dined with Queen Salote and marked out yet more sites. In general they were optimistic that the coral could be easily flattened to allow strips to be built. On several occasions reconnaissance was made much easier by the use of *Leander*'s Supermarine Walrus flying boat.[10]

Although the demands of his appointment were enormous, Ralph still found time for the family and for recreation. He played both golf and tennis regularly, and there were opportunities during his periods of leave for travel in both Islands, skiing in the winter and fishing in the summer. In the autumn of 1936 the return of Mrs Crawford required the family to move out of Overton House, and after much searching, another suitable house was found to rent for a year It was, however, some fifteen miles away at Maoribank in the Hutt Valley, not nearly as convenient as Overton House for travelling to the centre of Wellington or the airfield at Rongotai. It was whilst they were living there that a local surgeon carried out a skin graft to repair the effects of Bell's palsy on John's face, a deformity which British doctors had said could not be alleviated. This was successful, although John then fell and badly bruised the spot, which turned septic. Happily, the infection was cured and the graft held.

Hilda continued to indulge her keen interest in the arts by meeting and promoting the careers of New Zealand artists, particularly those who were up and coming. She hung their works prominently in whichever house the family was living, where they would be seen by influential visitors who were being entertained there. One of those whom she particularly supported was Mountford 'Toss' Wollaston, who many years later was to become the first New Zealander knighted for services to art.

In February 1938 Ralph's parents came to stay for a month. Lord Cochrane was particularly interested in dairy farming, in which he had been a pioneer of both artificial insemination and mobile milking parlours. He was keen to discover if there were any new ideas which he could use in his own herd at Crawford Priory, where he was experimenting with feeding the cattle during the winter with alternatives to hay, so Ralph arranged for him to meet a number of local farmers. Later in the year, there was a new addition to the family with the birth of Malcolm Ralph Cochrane on 8 August 1938.

At the end of their year in Maoribank the Cochranes moved again, this time to a modern house in Murphy Street in the centre of Wellington, only a few hundred yards from Ralph's HQ and close to a school for Grizel. Whilst there they engaged a cook called Doris, a woman of great character who became a good friend of the family and was to send them food parcels during the coming war!

Ralph's term of appointment expired in the spring of 1939. His successor was Group Captain Hugh Saunders, who arrived in New Zealand on 26 February, fresh from a year at the IDC. A South African by birth, Saunders had been on the staff of the Directorate of Training whilst Ralph was at

Training Command. Ralph had briefed him extensively by letter in advance and, on the day of his disembarkation, they set off on a series of flights in Ralph's Whitney Straight from Hobsonville to Invercargill at the far end of the South Island, stopping at all the key locations, and then back to Wellington, where they arrived on 4 March. Saunders succeeded Ralph as CAS five days later.

There was an extensive round of farewell engagements for Ralph and Hilda, his former staff presenting him with an album filled with photographs of the mountains, lakes, rivers and forests of New Zealand. The family sailed for England on 25 March. Ralph and Hilda had considered leaving the ship at Panama and travelling up through the United States, but the worsening political situation in Europe persuaded them that they should sail on.

Ralph's achievements in New Zealand had been appreciated on both sides of the world. He had been appointed a Commander of the Order of the British Empire in the New Year's Honours of 1939, whilst Lord Galway wrote to the Secretary of State for Dominion Affairs to say that 'His Majesty's Government in New Zealand wish to express their sincere appreciation of the excellent service rendered by this officer and of the conscientious and able manner in which he assisted and supervised the re-organization and expansion of the Royal New Zealand Air Force.'[11] Sir Harry Batterbee, the British High Commissioner in Wellington, sent the Secretary of State an account of the New Zealand Government's farewell function in Ralph's honour, emphasising the sincerity of the speeches made by Fred Jones and Peter Fraser and saying that there was no doubt that Ralph had won their confidence to a remarkable degree.

Chapter 9

Training

On 30 May 1939, following a short period of leave, Ralph reported to the Air Ministry as Deputy Director of Intelligence (2). His immediate superior was Group Captain, shortly to become Air Commodore, K. C. Buss, the Director of Intelligence. Buss was eight years older than Ralph and had served most of his career in the Middle East, including in Iraq. In Ralph's opinion, 'He was a confirmed Arabist with his methods based on what he had learnt there.'[1] He was almost certainly an unsuitable superior for a sub-directorate whose purpose was to establish the strength and disposition of the Luftwaffe.

As a result of the deteriorating international situation, there had been a very significant increase in the establishment of every part of the Air Staff, and with the RAF commands also crying out for experienced men, the numbers had been boosted by retired officers, all of whom in the case of DDI(2) had served their time in the British Army rather than the RAF. On the other hand, there were two highly capable wing commanders as Ralph's deputies, Frank Inglis, who went on to have a distinguished career in Intelligence during the war and was, moreover, the brother-in-law of a close friend of Ralph's from the airship days, Victor Goddard,[2] and Claude Pelly, who was himself to become an air chief marshal many years later.

The task of DDI(2) was made much easier than it might have been by the poor signal security of the Luftwaffe, which was to persist throughout the forthcoming war, much to the benefit of the Allies. The Luftwaffe used wireless when testing new aircraft on factory airfields, and from this source it was possible to identify each one as it left to join its unit. The Germans themselves tended to rely on information published in the aeronautical press, which, as Ralph suggested to the Air Attaché at the German Embassy, made their task very much easier. The attaché denied this, telling Ralph that he had two assistants who spent their lives poring over the press without gaining much useful information.

There were other sources of information for DDI(2), and it is tempting to think that these included Ultra, the product of the German wireless messages sent on Enigma machines and decoded at the Government Code and Cypher School at Bletchley Park. However, in spite of Ralph referring to 'secret sources' in his memoirs, it would be another year before Ultra yielded much of real value. Nevertheless, when hostilities began on 3 September and the German diplomats departed for their own country, they left behind, whether by design or by mistake, a draft of their latest handbook on the RAF, which suggested that the RAF knew more about the Luftwaffe's organization and order of battle than vice versa.

Towards the end of 1939 it was apparent that Ralph and Buss were never going to be able to work in harmony, and the latter asked that the former be posted elsewhere. Ralph spoke to Portal, at that time the Air Member for Personnel, who offered him the command of the RAF station at Abingdon, which he was delighted to accept. In early December he and Hilda moved into married quarters there, whilst the children were sent to stay with their maternal grandmother's formidable sister, Blanche Carey, at her house in Oddington in Gloucestershire.

RAF Abingdon, situated five miles south of Oxford, had opened in 1932 as a station in the Wessex Bombing Area. It had housed a number of light bomber squadrons as well as the Oxford University Air Squadron, and there had always been a strong emphasis on training. In addition to the squadrons, it was the site of the headquarters of Central Area from late 1933 until the formation of Bomber Command in 1936, when it became the HQ of 1 (Bomber) Group. In September 1939 1 Group was re-designated the Advanced Air Striking Force and moved to France with the British Expeditionary Force, to be succeeded at Abingdon by the HQ of 6 (Operational Training) Group.

In early 1939 it had been decided to relieve the majority of the squadrons of Bomber, Fighter and Coastal Command of their training duties by designating a small number of them for that specific purpose, and 97 and 166 Squadrons, together forming 4 Group Pool, arrived at Abingdon in September. They were each equipped with twelve Armstrong Whitworth Whitleys, one of three relatively new types of monoplane medium bomber, the others being the Handley Page Hampden and the Vickers Wellington, and four Avro Anson twin-engined training aircraft. In April 1940 the squadrons themselves were disbanded and 4 Group Pool was re-designated as 10 Operational Training Unit (OTU).

The purpose of the OTUs, which formed part of Bomber rather than Training Command, or later Flying Training Command, was to provide the final stage of training for aircrews, using the type of aircraft which they would fly operationally. In the case of pilots, they had previously attended Elementary and then Service Flying Training Schools, whilst the bomb-aimers, navigators, wireless operators and air gunners had been through the equivalent specialist schools. The OTU course lasted six weeks, during which crews were formed, effectively through self-selection by the men themselves. On completion of the course at the OTU they were posted to operational squadrons, by which time the average crew should have had some 60 hours of flying time on the relevant aircraft.

The Whitley, which had entered squadron service as recently as March 1937, was by this time seen as a stopgap, pending the introduction of four-engined heavy bombers. In its design and capability it was years ahead of the Vickers Vernon and that aircraft's descendants, but such had been the pace of aircraft development that it was already effectively obsolete. Nevertheless, along with the lighter but faster Hampden, the inadequate Bristol Blenheim and the outstanding and thus much longer-serving Wellington, it was to carry the weight of the bombing campaign against Germany until well into 1941, and it remained in front line service until early in 1942. The Whitley could carry a heavier bomb load than the Wellington, but the largest bomb it could accommodate in its narrow bomb bay was only 1,000lbs. As a training aircraft it was a significant step up from the twin-engined types found at the Service Flying Training Schools, such as the Airspeed Oxford, and it had the virtue of providing relevant experience for every member of its crew, which would stand them in good stead if they survived long enough to move on to a heavy bomber. Among other aspects of training, blindfold cockpit drill, whereby the pilot had to carry out all his tasks whilst unable to see, was introduced at Abingdon and later became accepted practice at other OTUs.

Ralph enjoyed his relatively brief posting as a station commander. The winter of 1939/40 was particularly cold, characterized by freezing fog and ice, which were serious hazards to training, although, on a lighter note, the family was able to cross the Thames at Abingdon on foot. One amusing visitor was the artist Paul Nash, who was attached full-time to the RAF and commissioned to produce, among other things, a series of paintings of its aircraft. He was, however, an unreliable time-keeper. Invited to lunch at his house in Oxford, Ralph and Hilda arrived promptly at 1.00 as instructed, only to sit down more than two hours later.

The Air Officer Commanding 6 (Operational Training) Group was Air Commodore W. F. MacNeece Foster, yet another officer who had served in Iraq at the same time as Ralph. In 1934 Foster had been placed on the half-pay list at his own request, only to be recalled in 1939. Ralph found him a strange character, erudite and capable of holding his own at the high table of any Oxford college, but with some odd views on training. Having been away from the service for five years, he was out of date on current practices. Moreover, he insisted on flying with crews under training, including at night, which Ralph felt imposed a great strain on both him and them. Foster was clearly impressed by what he saw of Ralph, as in February 1940 he had him transferred to the group HQ as his Senior Air Staff Officer. Ralph clearly did not enjoy the experience, although it at least meant that he did not have to move from Abingdon.

The already high and still increasing demand for operational training now required the establishment of more OTUs, and it was probably with both anticipation and relief that Ralph was appointed to form 7 (Operational Training) Group as Air Officer Commanding, with promotion to air commodore. The group opened at Brampton Grange, near Huntingdon, on 15 July and took over four existing OTUs: 13 OTU carried out training on Blenheims at Bicester, 14 OTU on Hampdens and a Hampden variant, the Hereford,[3] at Cottesmore, 16 OTU on Hampdens and Herefords at Upper Heyford and 17 OTU on Blenheims at Upwood. All the OTUs also had a small complement of Ansons.

The throughput of the OTUs was substantial, with a planned intake of twenty crews every fourteen days, filling the seats of those posted to operational squadrons. In August 1940, the first full month after the formation of 7 Group, it was not yet hitting this target, the deficiency being most marked in the Blenheim OTUs, although over fifty crews each for Blenheims and Hampdens had by then been posted to operational squadrons. Training involved conversion on to the aircraft, followed by exercises on the practice-bombing and air-firing ranges, in the Fens for 14 and 17 OTUs and on the West Berkshire Downs for 13 and 16 OTUs, with all the OTUs also using ranges further away in the South Cambrian Mountains. Photographic training, formerly carried out at Service Flying Training Schools, was now also moved to the OTUs.

One imaginative scheme, involving the purchase of a model railway for range estimation, was designed by 14 OTU and approved by Bomber Command. A small model aircraft, representing an enemy fighter, was mounted on a bicycle spoke and pulled along the track by an electric engine to simulate the effect of an attack being made from astern. With a reflector sight at one end and a 'sky background' at the other, this proved to be a useful form of practice for air gunners.

Towards the end of their course, the aircrews flew further afield, including over enemy-occupied territory, where they engaged in 'nickelling', the dropping of leaflets. These sorties were carried out at night, and such was the ineffectiveness of the German air defence at this time – the Luftwaffe's night fighters, mostly Messerschmitt 110s, lacked airborne interception radar and were dependent on moonlight or on picking up targets in searchlight beams to have any chance of success – that there were very few casualties.

Ralph's period of command coincided almost exactly with the Battle of Britain. Bomber Command played only a supporting role in the battle and the two operational training groups were not directly involved, but they were potentially affected by the threat of a German invasion, which gave rise to a plan under the name of Operation BANQUET. In BANQUET, 7 Group's role would be to provide every available aircraft of an operational type for anti-invasion sorties, together with Ansons modified for the purpose. Moreover, under a secondary operation, BANQUET TRAINING, the stations in 7 Group were to be reinforced by aircraft from Flying Training Command if the need arose.

The Operational Instruction for BANQUET was issued on 7 August; 7 Group was to be directed in the first instance against the invasion ports on the Continent and later against the surface craft conveying the invasion force, whilst escorting warships were to be ignored. In the event that landings were effected, attacks were to be mounted in co-operation with Army formations or units. The bombs to be used for each type of attack were set out in the instruction. In order to avoid congestion at the group's airfields, relief airfields were designated, where arrangements were made for refuelling and re-arming. Each station was also affiliated to the nearest army command or formation.

Although the risk of invasion diminished during the winter of 1940/41 and effectively evaporated after the German invasion of Russia in June 1941, BANQUET was not finally cancelled until as late as October 1943, long after any real threat had disappeared.

Ralph was by now developing a reputation for original thought amongst both his subordinates and his superiors. Among the former was Squadron Leader Sam Elworthy, the Chief Instructor at 13 OTU. Elworthy only served briefly under Ralph at this time, as he was posted to an operational squadron in August 1940, but he was later to say of their first meeting at Bicester that 'I realized immediately that I'd come across a man of enormous ability.'[4]

The family had moved temporarily to Crawford Priory, whilst Ralph looked for somewhere to rent. In late October, after many weeks of searching, he found The Field House, a delightful Georgian village house in Buckden, less than ten minutes drive from his HQ. He had just moved in, and Hilda and the children were due to arrive on the next day, when Portal arrived on a visit to 7 Group. Portal had been AOC of Bomber Command, and thus Ralph's immediate superior, for the previous six months and had without doubt played a significant part in choosing him to be 7 Group's AOC. He had recently been selected as the new Chief of the Air Staff, an appointment which he was due to take up a few days later. In Ralph's words:

> Peter Portal came to have a look round and having served with him I knew him well and I opened my mouth rather wide on the failings of the Flying Training Command to train pilots who were coming to us and to train them on the lines that were wanted, now there was a war on. When Portal left us in the afternoon we shook hands and I thought he would do something. But, six o'clock in the morning, my telephone rang. 'This is the Air Ministry. You are to report forthwith as Director of Flying Training.'[5]

This was an immense accolade. It was also a great inconvenience, as the family arrived later that day to be told the news. Ralph decided to continue with the tenancy and, for nearly two years, circumstances at the Air Ministry permitting, which they frequently did not, he became a weekly commuter, catching an early train from Huntingdon to London on a Monday morning and getting home late on the following Saturday afternoon. For the rest of the week he stayed at the RAF Club on Piccadilly. This was convenient for travel by London Underground into his office at Adastral House, but it exposed him to the Blitz, which by this time was at its height. There was one near miss, when a bomb left a big crater just outside the front door of the club. Ralph was woken by a slab of concrete landing on the roof above his bedroom and he reached the ground floor just in time to see an Austin Seven approaching from the direction of Hyde Park Corner and vanishing into the hole. A rescue party pulled out two drunken young men! In the meantime, Hilda made a real family home out of The Field House, improving its garden and making for the three children their own small plots. In 1941 her Aunt Eva, who had provided Hilda with a home after the loss of her parents, came to live at The Field House until her death in the following year.

At much the same time as Ralph was appointed Director of Flying Training he came to the end of another, more unusual, position. On 1 September 1939 he had been appointed one of two Air Aides-de-Camp to the King, succeeding John Slessor. This was not in any way a full-time role, indeed it impinged very little on his day-to-day duties, but there were occasions on which he was required to accompany the King when His Majesty was visiting RAF establishments. The two men had Osborne and Dartmouth in common and got on well together.

The demands of the air war against Germany and Italy had been and would continue to be enormous, on both equipment and personnel. As far as the latter was concerned, the single most inhibiting factor was the amount of time required to turn new recruits from complete novices into fully trained aircrew and ground crew; in the case of bomber pilots, this could take eighteen months or even longer. In order to address this and other issues, significant changes in the whole apparatus of training took place in the summer of 1940. At the Air Ministry this was effected at the top by the creation of a new seat on the Air Council for an Air Member for Training, who now joined the CAS, the VCAS, the DCAS and the Air Members for Personnel and for Supply and Organization as one of the service representatives. The position of Director-General of Training was abolished and three new directorates were set up, for Flying Training, Operational Training and Technical Training. This was reflected in the splitting of Training Command into Flying Training Command and Technical Training Command, whilst Bomber, Fighter and Coastal Commands continued to be responsible for operational training through the OTUs. Army Co-operation Command, controlling two more groups, one of which focused on training and development, was formed in December 1940.

The division of responsibility between the Air Ministry and the various Commands was, in essence, a simple one. The Air Council, operating through its members and their various directorates, was charged with formulating policy and strategy, which it conveyed to the Commands by directives. The Commands were responsible for devising the appropriate tactics and for undertaking operations in line with the directives. In reality there was some blurring of the lines between strategy and tactics, which on occasion led to tension. However, the basic structure withstood the test of time.

Ralph's immediate superior as Air Member for Training was Air Marshal Guy Garrod, whom he had known as a member of the Directing Staff at the staff college in 1925/6. Ralph was later to describe him as an able man who let his subordinates get on with their jobs. There was a large staff in the Directorate of Flying Training, with no fewer than four Deputy Directors. This was just as well, as the demands were immense. Bomber Command, hitherto largely restricted to operations against ports and ships and to leafleting, was now gearing up for a sustained bombing campaign against German cities, spurred on by the London Blitz and the bombing of Coventry, the latter event taking place less than a month after Ralph took up his appointment. The casualties incurred in the Battle of Britain and the continuing threat of invasion imposed equally pressing demands on Fighter Command, and the success of the U-boat campaign had a similar impact on Coastal Command, whilst hostilities against the Italians in the Western Desert and East Africa required a constant flow of trained aircrew in that direction.

There were three stages of flying training to be undertaken before aircrew could be handed over to the OTUs in the various commands. The first consisted of the Initial Training Wings (ITWs), sometimes called the Initial Training Schools, in which potential pilots and observers/navigators were given classroom instruction on the principles of flying and basic navigation, accompanied by the inevitable drill to establish discipline and by physical training to build up fitness. In due course, as Bomber and Coastal Commands began to receive aircraft with much larger crews, their prospective wireless operators, air gunners, bomb aimers and flight engineers also attended ITWs. Those deemed suitable, following written exams and psychological tests, were then passed on, in the case of pilots to Elementary Flying Training Schools, where they learnt to fly on light aircraft such as the Tiger Moth. After graduating from these they moved to Service Flying Training Schools, in which those intended for Bomber and Coastal Command converted to multi-engined aircraft, whilst those destined for Fighter Command graduated to more sophisticated and higher performance single-engined aircraft. If they passed out satisfactorily they were sent to OTUs. There were similar streams for the specialist training of other members of the aircrew.

The requirement to accommodate rapidly increasing numbers of operational squadrons in all the commands meant that a number of airfields, hitherto used for training, would have to be taken over by the operational home commands pending the building of new ones. This, together with satisfying a goal of carrying out pre-OTU training free, as far as possible, from enemy attack, had led in December 1939 to a conference in Ottawa attended by representatives of the British, Canadian, Australian and New Zealand Governments, whose purpose was to discuss arrangements for much of the training of aircrew to take place outside the UK. The result was the signing by the four nations of the Air Training Agreement, the blueprint for the most ambitious programme of air training ever conceived, the British Commonwealth Joint Air Training Plan, sometimes known as the Empire Air Training Scheme.

The Agreement provided for training schools to be established in all the countries concerned; the list was later extended to include South Africa and Southern Rhodesia. For the most part the Commonwealth countries trained their own personnel, but the relatively short distance to Canada meant that very large numbers of RAF aircrew were trained there in both Elementary and Service Flying Training Schools and in other specialist schools for non-pilots. The Canadian scheme, by far the largest of them all, came under the overall supervision of Air Vice-Marshal Lionel McKean, who took up his position in March 1940. The RAF set up its own schools there which by September 1941 numbered eight Elementary and fourteen Service Flying Training Schools, with six specialist schools and three OTUs. These were, however, heavily outnumbered by the RCAF schools, which trained both RCAF and RAF personnel.

Schools were also formed in due course in India, whilst 4 FTS, at which Ralph himself had learnt to fly, relocated from Abu Sueir to Habbaniya in Iraq at the beginning of the war, where it became a SFTS; in May 1941 its motley collection of training aircraft successfully defended the airfield against a new Iraqi Government which had ousted the pro-British king and was backed by Germany.[6] Much more significantly, with the entry of the United States into the war at the end of 1941, British aircrew were also trained in large numbers there, whilst American instructors had been employed in Canada from the early days of the scheme.

The US schools were of two types. One consisted of civilian schools, which obtained first-class results. However, places were also offered at USAAF service schools, whose administration was based on the strict discipline traditional at West Point. The British response to such a regime came to light when an American general on an inspection found a British trainee sleeping on the floor of his quarters. Asked why he was doing this, the trainee explained that he had just succeeded in getting the turn-down of his bed correct to the nearest eighth of an inch, as demanded, and the corner to within two degrees of what was required, and that there was no way in which he was going to disturb it! With a certain amount of tact, such cultural differences were overcome.

There was some concern that the failure rate for would-be pilots at the Canadian Elementary FTSs was very high at 50 per cent. It had been possible to give preliminary flying training to some of the students at schools in the UK which were due to close, and, after being passed for the next stage, these now had to go to Canada to finish off their course. To the surprise of Ralph and his colleagues, half of them were failed, and it turned out that the Canadian instructors, used to failing 50 per cent, were continuing to do just that. The failures were sent down to schools in the USA, where most passed without difficulty The Canadians were persuaded to adopt more sophisticated measurements of ability; failures continued, but those concerned were usually re-mustered in alternative aircrew functions, often as bomb aimers or air gunners, who required less technical training than pilots or navigators.

Although the day-to-day control of training schools in the Commonwealth had to be exercised locally, their syllabus and methods of training were largely determined by the Directorate of Flying Training to meet the very specific requirements of the home and overseas commands. In Ralph's words, 'As the users of the product we clearly had the right to have a say.'[7] There were inevitable disagreements and tensions, although overall the scheme turned out to be highly successful. A high degree of uniformity at all levels of flying training was achieved by the production of official manuals, which were written in as simple and unambiguous a way as possible. One of those recruited by Ralph into the navigation branch for this purpose was Francis Chichester, whom he had known in New Zealand and who was later to achieve fame as the first solo round-the-word sailor.

On a more informal basis, a magazine called *Tee Emm* (short for Training Memoranda) was produced monthly, each section of the Flying Training Directorate sending to the editor, Anthony Armstrong,[8] a summary of an issue which it wanted to get across to instructors and trainees. Armstrong would then recast it in a particularly humorous way, often through the words of the fictitious Pilot Officer Prune, who urged readers to 'Take *Tee Emm*. Prevents that Thinking feeling!'[9] Prune, who was depicted in the cartoons of Bill Hooper, was 'the embodiment of a pupil's difficulties and failings, the kind of fellow who does some of the right things at some of the wrong times and all the wrong things at some of the right times, but never all the right things at all the right times'.[10] Ralph's patronage of the magazine was confirmation that he did not lack a sense of humour!

Planning output to meet the requirements of the various commands was always difficult, especially for Bomber Command, where the rate of casualties grew significantly with the expansion of the bombing campaign. Initial forecasts of the availability of trained crews were quickly proved to be too high – it was taking eighteen months or more to train a bomber pilot before he was qualified to join an operational squadron – and the problem was only solved by a decision that the heavy bombers would require a single pilot instead of the two originally planned, some of the second pilot's tasks being assumed by the flight engineer. This new policy was clearly instrumental in permitting full crews to be formed at a greater rate, but it had its critics. Foremost amongst these was Donald Bennett, who in 1942 commanded 10 Squadron, equipped with one of the new heavy bombers, the Handley Page Halifax, and who was, in the autumn of that year, to form 8 (Pathfinder) Group. His criticism was founded on the understandable concern that new pilots on operational squadrons would not have had any previous experience as second pilots. They might have gone on a few operations as a 'second dickey', sitting alongside an experienced pilot, but they would lack the deeper experience of a much longer-serving second pilot. In Bennett's words:

> A change of policy in the training of aircrews had been brought into effect, which not only affected the efficiency of the Pathfinder Force itself but in my view seriously impaired the whole strength of Bomber Command ... This policy was forced on the Air Staff by the Training Staff at the Air Ministry, headed by Guy Garrod who, I believe, was principally influenced by Ralph Cochran [sic], who at the time the decision was taken was Director of Flying Training.[11]

This attribution of blame, for a policy which arguably contributed to the higher than average losses of aircraft undertaking operations with novice pilots but which was equally essential for the manning of the number of aircraft required for Bomber Command's campaign, was misdirected. In an interview with the Air Historical Board in 1975, Ralph explained the decision as the result of planning which had gone wrong: 'The planning was based on two pilots per aircraft. With the stroke of a pen the Commander in Chief said that in future he only wanted one pilot per heavy bomber.'[12] The C-in-C concerned was unnamed, but must have been Harris, AOC-in-C of Bomber Command since February 1942. Harris himself attributed the decision partly to the requirement to include a specialized bomb-aimer in every heavy bomber crew:

> It was impossible to give the two pilots an equal amount of training unless the whole crew went through double the number of flights, circuits and landings they needed, and the result was that neither pilot was trained to the standard that was rapidly becoming necessary, the standard required for the heavy bombers. So the second pilot was left out of the crew, and the air bomber put in his place.[13]

An earlier problem had arisen when it became clear that the Bomber Command OTUs, whose largest aircraft had hitherto been the Wellington, were not training crews sufficiently well to be able to take over any of the new types of heavy bomber which began to enter squadron service in late 1940 and to undertake operations in the spring of 1941. It was eventually decided to set up a Heavy Conversion Unit for each bomber group, the first of which were formed in 3 and 4 Groups in early January 1942, with the objective of training crews respectively on the Short Stirling and the Handley Page Halifax. Shortly afterwards, another HCU was formed to provide training on the Consolidated Liberator to crews destined for the Middle East. As the groups expanded, so additional HCUs were formed, with the first Avro Lancaster HCU being set up in 5 Group in May 1942. The first HCU for Coastal Command was not formed until October 1943.

Ralph's appointment as Director of Flying Training at a critical period in the expansion of the RAF had been both challenging and stimulating, but after nearly two years he was ready for a change. He was thus delighted when it came in September 1942, in the shape of a posting to Bomber Command as Air Officer Commanding 3 Group.

Chapter 10

3 Group

Ralph took over 3 Group from Air Vice-Marshal J. E. Baldwin on 12 September 1942. Jackie Baldwin had been a popular and highly respected commander of the group since shortly before the beginning of the war, at which time it was the most powerful of all the bomber groups, having been fully equipped with the Wellington, the best medium bomber of the day. In addition to Baldwin's duties as AOC, he had been appointed Acting AOC-in-C of Bomber Command for just over a month in early 1942, following the posting of Air Marshal Sir Richard Peirse as AOC-in-C of the Air Forces in India. Peirse had lost the confidence of both Portal and the Secretary of State for Air, Sir Archibald Sinclair, following disappointing results from the bombing campaign. It had been Baldwin's misfortune that his brief tenure as Acting AOC-in-C coincided with the 'Channel Dash', the escape of the German battleships *Scharnhorst* and *Gneisenau* and the cruiser *Prinz Eugen* from Brest to Kiel, in which Bomber Command had not distinguished itself, or so it seemed at the time. Late in the day, it was decided to cease the fruitless attempts to sink the ships by bombing and instead to lay mines along their likely course; subsequent intelligence showed that both of them had indeed been damaged by mines, although these had probably been laid on an earlier occasion. In any event, the incident did not harm Baldwin's personal reputation and he was now to follow Peirse to India to serve as his deputy.

The decision to appoint Ralph as Baldwin's successor was made ultimately by Portal, but there can be no doubt that he was asked for by Harris, who had assumed the leadership of Bomber Command from Baldwin seven months earlier. Harris arrived back in England from Washington, where he had been the Head of the British Air Staff at an important time, during which the United States entered the war and the USAAF hugely accelerated its own programme of expansion. His impact on Bomber Command was immediate, exemplified by his mounting of the first 'Thousand Bomber Raid' on Cologne at the end of May. Ruthlessly focused on a campaign against German cities, he needed men whom he could trust implicitly as the leaders of his bomber groups, and Ralph matched his specifications perfectly. With 'Sandy' Saundby as his Senior Air Staff Officer at Bomber Command's HQ near High Wycombe, Harris now had both his two former flight commanders in 45 Squadron as immediate subordinates.

Ralph's new headquarters were in Exning House, in the village of the same name, half way between Cambridge and Bury St Edmunds. It was conveniently close to the RAF station at Newmarket, where the 3 Group Communications Flight was based, and it was from there, on his very first day in command, that Ralph began a tour of his stations and squadrons, flying the Airspeed Oxford allocated to him for his personal use. The stations were located over a wide area of Eastern England, from Lincolnshire to Essex and from Bedfordshire to Norfolk. Of the mainstream bomber units, XV Squadron[1] was at Bourn, 75 Squadron at Feltwell and then Newmarket, 90 Squadron at Bottesford and then Ridgewell, 115 Squadron at Marham, Mildenhall and then East Wretham, 149 Squadron at Lakenheath, 214 Squadron at Stradishall and then Chedburgh and 218 Squadron at Downham Market; 101 Squadron, which had been in 3 Group since July 1941, left on transfer to 1 Group two weeks after Ralph arrived.

In addition, there were two Special Duties squadrons, Nos. 138 and 161, both of which were located at Tempsford, whilst the latter maintained a detached flight at Tangmere in Sussex, flying Westland Lysanders on missions to the French Resistance. These squadrons were not under Ralph's or, indeed, Bomber Command's operational control. Ralph was responsible for their administration, but for operational purposes they were at the disposal of the Special Operations Executive, undertaking missions to Occupied Europe. Unlike any of the other squadrons in the group, their most numerous aircraft was the Handley Page Halifax, although in late 1942 they were still employing the Whitley and, in the case of 161 Squadron, the Douglas Boston, an American medium bomber. Their airfield at Tempsford was a curious choice for two such secretive units, flanked as it was by the London and North-Eastern Railway's main line to Scotland on one side and by the A1 Great North Road on the other.

Throughout his term as AOC, Ralph would visit one or two squadrons by air every week, flying himself more frequently than he had done since leaving New Zealand, and go to see others by car. The group was approaching the end of a long conversion to heavy bombers, and it was its misfortune that the aircraft chosen to replace the robust and reliable Wellington was the Short Stirling. By the time that Ralph arrived, all the squadrons were equipped with the Stirling except for No. 75, which would fly its last Wellington sortie at the end of October 1942, No. 90, which was to reform on Stirlings in November after having been disbanded as a Blenheim squadron in the previous February,[2] and No. 115, which in March 1943 would become the only squadron in the group to convert directly from the Wellington onto the Avro Lancaster.

The Stirling was the first of the British four-engined heavy bombers to come into service with the RAF, initially in late 1940 with 7 Squadron, which at the time was part of 3 Group. Considering that it had been ordered to meet a specification issued as recently as in 1936, this was a remarkable achievement on the part of the manufacturer, which had been largely realized on the back of using the same wing design as the already successful Sunderland flying boat. However, the Air Ministry insisted that the wing span be reduced from 112ft and 9½ inches to 99ft and 1 inch in order to meet its requirement that the aircraft could be housed in a standard hangar. This was a fatal flaw, since the Stirling was unable as a result to achieve its planned operational altitude of 20,000ft; indeed, with a full bomb load its ceiling was no more than 12,000ft. On the introduction of the two other heavy bombers, the Halifax and the Lancaster, this meant not only that the Stirlings were far more vulnerable than the others to fighter attack and flak, but also that, whilst flying over the target, they were at risk from bombs raining down from above.

Having said that, the Stirling was popular with its pilots for its manoeuvrability in the air, which allowed them to throw it around the sky and often escape from attacking fighters as a result. Its very long undercarriage, however, created serious challenges on take-off and landing. Moreover, not long after Ralph arrived, another concern emerged. As he wrote later:

> Reports started to come in of rogue aircraft which when fully laden and at a height of above 10,000 feet would put one wing down and

require the combined strength of two pilots to raise it. There seemed no obvious cause and repeated defect reports only brought the answer that each aircraft had been thoroughly tested before delivery and had nothing wrong.

This was true when flying lightly loaded and at low height. To break the deadlock I did the only thing likely to create a stir and grounded the Group. Within 24 hours we had senior members of the Ministry of Aircraft Production, the chief designer of the firm making the Stirling, the chief test pilot et al. The fault was found by one of the Group's engineers who noticed that a small piece of fairing on the leading edge of the elevator was slightly higher one side than on the other. With a hammer he tapped it down and the trouble was cured. It was a good example of the small causes which can lead to serious aerodynamic changes.[3]

Ralph was also unhappy with the general serviceability of the aircraft, which he described to Harris as shocking. He believed that this was due to over-driving the engines when climbing and overheating them when on the ground. He had his senior engineering officer replaced and also arranged for a competent electrical engineer to be posted in, which helped to resolve the problem.

The squadron in the middle of conversion to Stirlings when Ralph arrived was No. 75, for the formation of which he had himself been indirectly responsible. His report in 1936 to the Government of New Zealand on the air aspects of the country's defence had recommended the purchase of twenty-four long-range medium bombers, and in subsequent discussions he had persuaded his political masters that the most suitable aircraft would be Barnes Wallis's Wellington. As a result of this, the New Zealand Flight had been established at RAF Marham in June 1939, initially as a RNZAF unit. Training on the new aircraft began with a view to flying them down to New Zealand, but the declaration of war by Great Britain and the Dominions three months later put paid to the plan. The New Zealand Government very generously donated the aircraft to the RAF, and it was decided to go ahead with forming a new squadron, with New Zealanders under training in the UK as its aircrew. The New Zealand Flight relocated to RAF Harwell, where it stayed until January 1940, when it moved first to Stradishall and then to Feltwell, where in April 1940 it became 75 (New Zealand) Squadron.

Ralph took a particular interest in the squadron, which shortly after his arrival moved to Newmarket, close to his HQ. A number of its officers were men whom he remembered from New Zealand. The squadron was to go on to earn an outstanding record, converting on to the Lancaster in early 1944. Its 8,017 wartime sorties were the highest achieved by any squadron in Bomber Command; on a sadder note, however, it also suffered the second highest number of aircraft losses.

A month before Ralph's appointment to 3 Group, a new formation had made its appearance within Bomber Command. At the time it was called the Pathfinder Force, but in January 1943 it became 8 (Pathfinder) Group. The genesis of this formation was in a report commissioned in mid-1941 by the Prime Minister's Scientific Adviser, Lord Cherwell. With doubts being raised in a number of quarters about the accuracy of bombing raids, Cherwell instructed his private secretary, David Butt, to conduct an analysis of the photographs taken over the targets by the bombers during their raids. The Butt Report was issued in August 1941 and its overall conclusion was both sensational and deeply disturbing: of those aircraft which had claimed to attack the target, only one in three had come within five miles of it. The figure dropped to one in five as a proportion of total sorties and to one in ten over the heavily defended Ruhr, whilst in the new-moon period it dropped overall to one in fifteen. Churchill was outraged and ordered Portal to produce proposals as quickly as possible to remedy the situation.

There were two strands to the development of more accurate bombing. One was the adoption of a number of aids to navigation, the first of which, Gee, appeared in early 1942. The use of radio beams for navigation was not new, indeed the Luftwaffe had employed three of them – *Knickebein*, *X-Gerät* and *Y-Gerät* – with some success in their raids on British cities following the Battle of Britain, although their impact was subsequently diminished and then negated by the invention of effective counter-measures. Gee was rather different in that there were no beams, but a series of pulses, sent by a master and two slave stations. The navigator on a bomber would measure the differences in their time of arrival, which would identify two co-ordinates from which the aircraft's position could be determined very accurately using a lattice framework overlaid on a map. The system had two problems. The first was that, due to the curvature of the earth, its effective range was only 350 miles, which reached as far as the Ruhr Valley but no further. The second was that the Germans learnt how to jam the signal, although as it was a passive system, the aircraft's location could not be detected. Gee remained in use and was particularly valued by aircrews for its ability to guide them home.

The second system was Oboe, which came into general use in December 1942. This was also governed by ground stations, two in this case, which sent out pulses and received them back, enabling the controllers and the navigator to determine not only the position of the aircraft but also the point at which bombs should be released. It was inhibited by the inability of the stations to control more than one aircraft at a time. For the same reason as Gee, its range was limited, but it proved to be much more difficult for the Germans to jam. Together with Gee, Oboe took the science of navigation well past the system of dead reckoning, impacted by wind direction and speed, on which navigators had relied in the past.

Finally, at least during Ralph's term of appointment at 3 Group, there was H2S, introduced in January 1943. This was a self-contained radar mounted in the aircraft and looking down on the ground over which it flew, displaying an impression on a screen in the navigator's compartment. It proved to be most useful when there was a feature which stood out, such as a coastline or a river. It had one serious drawback, that its transmission could be picked up by the Naxos radar warning receivers in German night fighters, enabling them to home in on their targets.

These aids, alone and in combination, made a significant difference to accurate navigation to and from the target. They did not, however, solve the problem of target marking once the bombers had arrived there. Within the Air Ministry the officer most concerned with finding a solution for this was Wing Commander, later Group Captain, S. O. Bufton, the Deputy Director of Bombing Operations. In January 1942 Bufton put up a paper to his Director, Air Commodore John Baker, proposing the allocation of squadrons specifically to target-marking along the lines of Kampfgruppe 100, a Luftwaffe formation which had carried out this activity with much success during the bombing campaign over the United Kingdom in

1940/41. The arrival of Harris at Bomber Command in the following month put paid, at least temporarily, to his proposal. Harris believed that marking could be carried out by specially trained crews in his existing squadrons and was totally opposed to the creation of an elite force, as were his group commanders, including Baldwin, although canvassing by Bufton of station and squadron commanders elicited greater enthusiasm.

With no progress by early June, and in the absence of Portal overseas, Bufton enlisted the support of Air Chief Marshal Sir Wilfrid Freeman, the Vice-Chief of the Air Staff. Freeman agreed to argue the case with Portal, by whom he was much respected, and on Portal's return persuaded him of the need for a discrete target-finding force. Harris was summoned and, not for the last time, was compelled to agree to a proposal to which he was opposed. To give him credit, once the order had been received, he carried it out to the best of his ability. He reserved for himself two important decisions, the name of the formation and the choice of its commander. For the first he rejected the name proposed by the Directorate of Bomber Operations, the 'Target Finding Force', in favour of the 'Pathfinder Force'. For the second, he declined the suggestion of Basil Embry, a forceful and occasionally unorthodox leader who would have filled the position well and who had, moreover, been one of Ralph's fellow members of 45 Squadron under Harris. Instead, Harris chose another protégé, Donald Bennett, an Australian who had served under him in the early 1930s and whom he admired for his skills as a navigator at Imperial Airways, which Bennett had joined after leaving the RAF in 1935.

Bennett rejoined the RAF in 1941 after helping to set up the Atlantic Ferry Organization, which delivered aircraft built in the USA and Canada to the UK. By the summer of 1942 he had had an eventful war, which had included being shot down over Norway whilst flying a Halifax in command of 10 Squadron and escaping though the snow to Sweden, whence he made his way back to the UK. On his appointment to command the Pathfinder Force on 15 August 1942, a month short of his thirty-second birthday, he was promoted from wing commander to group captain and was made up to acting air commodore before the end of the year.

Harris had reluctantly agreed that every bomber group should provide a squadron of aircraft to be trained as Pathfinders. These were 7 Squadron with Stirlings from 3 Group, 35 Squadron with Halifaxes from 4 Group, 83 Squadron with Lancasters from 5 Group and 156 Squadron with Wellingtons from 1 Group. In addition, 109 Squadron, whose Mosquitoes were carrying out trials of the various electronic warfare aids, including Oboe, was transferred to provide the benefit of its experience.[4] The transfers were not well received by the group commanders, with the exception of Air Vice-Marshal Roderick Carr at 4 Group, under whom both Bennett and Bufton had served as squadron commanders, as well as Bennett as a staff officer and Bufton as a station commander. The AOCs' unhappiness was compounded by the fact that the Pathfinder crews would wear a distinguishing badge and would be promoted one rank above that which they would otherwise have held, although the latter was compensation for having to undertake a tour of forty-five operations instead of the usual thirty.

All of this was a fait accompli when Ralph arrived at 3 Group a month after the Pathfinder Force had been formed. He had not been involved in any way whilst Director of Flying Training and had not previously met Bennett. However, Wyton, where 83 and 109 Squadrons were located and where Bennett initially established his Group HQ, had been a 3 Group station, and the group was still providing administrative services to the Pathfinders and also acting initially as the day-to-day link with Bomber Command, pending the formation of a fully functional HQ. As Ralph wrote later in his memoirs, 'I thus saw a good deal of him and admired his drive and ways – if somewhat unorthodox – of getting things done.'[5] His first impressions of Bennett were given a slightly different slant in a letter to Harris:

> I will do all I can to help Bennett. I foresee no difficulties providing that he does not make them. I think you are aware that he has certain defects as well as tremendous qualities. One of his defects is his ability to antagonise all those people who are most ready and willing to help him. So far there has been no trouble, but he is apt to be temperamental.[6]

There is no evidence that the relationship was hostile at this time, but it was certainly to deteriorate significantly a year and more hence, as the bombing campaign developed. For reasons which will become apparent, Bennett, whilst continuing to profess friendship with Ralph, actually developed considerable animus towards him, which was reflected at some length in his wartime memoirs. As far as Ralph's arrival at 3 Group was concerned, Bennett wrote:

> When he first came to the command, he was given No. 3 Group in place of Baldwin. Having no experience of bomber operations in the current war, he immediately complimented his predecessor by grounding practically all his squadrons for intensive training, thus weakening the Group's operational strength very considerably for a period. Whether the quality was better after the training period or not, is something which was hard to discern.

The last fortnight of September 1942 was, in fact, a relatively quiet period for Bomber Command. The largest raid was on Essen on the night of 16/17 September, which, whilst successful, incurred considerable losses, particularly of aircraft from the OTUs; 3 Group provided aircraft, as it did for smaller raids on Saarbrücken and Munich three nights later. Otherwise operations were small scale and largely devoted to 'gardening', the dropping of mines in sea areas from the Oslo Fjord in the north to the mouth of the Gironde in the south. Ralph did, of course, ground his Stirlings very briefly for technical reasons during this period, but there is no evidence for Bennett's claim. In any event, it is difficult to imagine Harris permitting the withdrawal of large numbers of aircraft for training purposes if the campaign demanded their contribution.

The first half of October saw the tempo of raids on German cities increased, with operations against Lübeck, Krefeld, Aachen, Osnabrück, Kiel and Cologne. With Wellingtons still equipping many squadrons in 1, 3 and 4 Groups and the Pathfinders, it was the most numerous of the aircraft involved, but was now comfortably outnumbered overall by the four-engined bombers. There was a change of emphasis towards the end of the month, when Bomber Command was ordered to provide support for Operation TORCH, the Allied landings in French North Africa in early November, by bombing ports and industrial centres in Italy. Over the next seven weeks, Genoa was attacked twice, Milan once and Turin on no fewer than five occasions. These were interspersed with raids on German cities, Hamburg, Stuttgart, Frankfurt, Mannheim and Duisburg.

All the raids during the last three months of 1942 were led by Pathfinders. They produced indifferent results, although those on Italian cities were markedly more successful. At the same time losses, particularly over Germany, were high, and morale plummeted. Ralph was particularly concerned by the incidence of 'early returns', aircraft which had failed to reach their target before flying home. In the event that there was no obvious reason, he made a point of interviewing the captain concerned:

> I remember one sergeant who had turned back near Hamburg on the grounds that they had strayed away from the main stream. When I asked what made him decide to do this he replied that they discussed it on the intercom and the majority decided that they should turn back. When I asked him why he as captain hadn't taken the decision he replied that they were all members of the sergeants' mess and it was their lives as well as his so obviously he had to consult them. That small incident led to a number of changes which could not be fully brought in until later in 5 Group.

Ralph's concern was that many of the pilots coming to the group were NCOs – flight sergeants and sergeants – and they lacked a sufficient level of authority over their crews, particularly if some of the others were commissioned officers, as was sometimes the case. He felt strongly that the captain of the aircraft should be given every assistance to exert his authority and that this would probably mean commissioning him if he was a NCO. This was a far from universal view in Bomber Command, let alone the Air Ministry, but in the meantime Ralph proposed to sort out crews arriving at the Heavy Conversion Unit so that there was either a commissioned officer or an NCO with officer potential in each, with a view to promoting the latter as quickly as possible. In terms of on-board discipline, he also ordered crews to address each other by their functions, for instance 'pilot to navigator', rather than by first names or nicknames, although this was commonly ignored.

When Ralph arrived at 3 Group, his experience of bombing was very out-of-date. There was little resemblance between the operations of 1942/43 and the activities of the Wessex Bombing Area in the late 1920s, let alone those of 45 Squadron in Iraq and 8 Squadron in Aden. His focus at 7 Group had been on training on two types of aircraft which were now obsolete, at a time before the bombing campaign against German cities had begun in earnest. Ken Batchelor, the Wing Commander Operations at 3 Group, was later to say that he arrived with preconceived ideas, some of which proved to be quite inappropriate, and that his Senior Air Staff Officer, Group Captain John Gray, sometimes found it difficult to persuade him otherwise. There were a number of occasions on which, having gone to Ralph with the plans for that night's operations, Batchelor had to retire discreetly whilst Ralph and Gray resolved their differences.[7]

Ralph was by no means deaf to argument born of experience, but neither did he accept conventional wisdom before he had put it to the test. His fertile brain was all the time looking for ways to conduct operations more successfully, and it was at this time, for instance, that he conceived what was to become known as time-and-distance bombing, whereby the bombs would be dropped when the aircraft had travelled for a precise period of time from a given point. He first raised the idea with Harris in a letter of 12 January 1943, asking for permission to try it out. In his reply, Harris thought that such a bombing method would be valuable in circumstances in which the aiming point could not be identified. However, he insisted that aircraft should always bomb on markers dropped by the Pathfinders whenever they could see them.

Next to Gray, the member of the HQ Staff closest to Ralph was Section Officer Carol Durrant of the Women's Auxiliary Air Force, who became his personal assistant, staying on with him for several years through multiple appointments and becoming a longstanding friend of the family, to whom she was known as 'PA'. She was highly effective at ensuring that Ralph's time was never wasted, and was, he wrote later, 'a most loyal and helpful assistant, with a sense of the ridiculous that sometimes got out of hand'.[8] Ralph was occasionally accused, by Batchelor amongst others, of lacking a sense of humour, but his tolerance of S/O Durrant, added to his support for *Tee Emm* whilst Director of Flying Training and the recollections of a number of those who knew him well, provides evidence that one was lurking beneath the surface, even if it was not often apparent. War for Ralph was a serious business and not to be conducted with undue levity.

The year 1943 began quietly, with no major raids for the group until the middle of the month. When they restarted, the target was a very different one, the U-boat pens at Lorient. The Battle of the Atlantic was to reach its climax in the first half of the year, and the Admiralty was desperate to reduce the attacks on the North Atlantic convoys. Harris, who was keen to resume the bombing of German cities, was deeply frustrated by a direct order to attack the bases at Lorient, St Nazaire, Brest and La Pallice, but had no alternative other than to comply. Whilst some raids were mounted on Berlin during this period, the Stirlings were exempted from them. As it happened, the new Stirling III was now beginning to replace the earlier models in 3 Group, with improved engines and a more aerodynamic design to the mid-upper turret. However, although the engines proved to be easier to maintain and more reliable on operations than their predecessors, they only delivered more height at the expense of reducing the bomb load, and there were no other discernible advantages.

Between mid-January and late February 3 Group participated in no fewer than six raids on Lorient, doing a great deal of damage to the town but very little to the U-boat pens, which by this time were fully protected by enormous reinforced concrete roofs, impervious to any of the bombs of that period. However, these raids provided some opportunities for experiments with timed runs. The results were far from compelling, and Harris, at least for the time being, insisted that the aircraft should always bomb in the centre of any pattern of flares or marker bombs laid by the Pathfinders, regardless of how they had arrived in the target area.

Participation in raids on Germany recommenced with Cologne on the night of 2/3 February. A modestly successful raid on Hamburg on the following night, at least in terms of the damage done, was overshadowed by the loss of eight aircraft. Cologne was revisited twice in the second half of the month, along with Wilhelmshaven and Nuremberg.

By the second half of February, after more than five months in the job, Ralph had settled down to prosecute a campaign whose end was far from being in sight. He had gained considerable knowledge of up-to-date bombing techniques and was beginning to formulate a number of ideas of his own as to how these might be improved. To his surprise, however, he was not to be able to test them out at 3 Group. Instead, on 27 February, he received an order to take up a new appointment on the following day, as Air Officer Commanding 5 Group.

Chapter 11

5 Group

Shortly after Ralph's arrival at 3 Group, he had written to Harris with his first impressions, saying that it had always been a first-class group but that 'all in it now realise that the leadership [of Bomber Command] has passed to 5 Group.'[1] This clearly had much to do with the recent conversion of the whole of 5 Group to the Avro Lancaster, the outstanding British heavy bomber of the war, but there was more to it than that. Writing many years later in the foreword to W. J. Lawrence's history of the group, Ralph expressed it thus:

> Those of us who served in No. 5 Group will be allowed our own belief that it had a special zest and spirit of its own. Mature reflection may convince us that we were in fact like other groups and differed only in our good fortune to be given chances that were denied to them; yet it may be that those very chances and the opportunity which they gave of saying 'those were our results' bound all ranks together and made it easier to bear the many disappointments.
>
> Similarly, we may each think that the period in which we served in the Group represented its Golden Age, and in that we may be right, for the development of the Group was a continuous process in which each advance was made possible by the efforts of those who went before.[2]

From the very start of the war, 5 Group considered itself a cut above the rest. This may, of course, have also been true of the other groups at the time, but as the war evolved, both good fortune and good leadership would contribute to the creation of an identity which was not necessarily superior in all respects but was certainly unique, and good fortune came first and foremost in the shape of its leadership.

With the exception of its first AOC, Air Commodore W. B. Callaway, who had raised the group in September 1937 but was to be posted elsewhere eleven days after the declaration of war on Germany, 5 Group was to be commanded by a succession of highly distinguished officers, all of whom went on to become air chief marshals, with two rising still further to become marshals of the RAF. No other group was able to come close to this record. It was also highly significant that the first of them was Harris himself, who was to retain a particularly deep interest in and regard for the group.

Although Harris had enjoyed a typically varied career, he was a bomber man to his core. His command of 45 Squadron at Hinaidi and 58 Squadron at Worthy Down had been followed, albeit after a gap of ten years, with an appointment as AOC of 4 Group in 1937, at a time when it was in the course of converting from the descendants of the biplane Vickers Vernon to the first of the new medium bombers, the Whitley. This brought him fully up to date with recent developments in aircraft design and operating capability, but his long-held philosophy, that bombers were going to have to operate at night to mitigate the impact of fighter defence, remained the same, and he trained his squadrons to that end.

By the time of Harris's appointment to 5 Group two years later, it was equipped not with the Whitley but with the Hampden. This aircraft was faster and more manoeuvrable than either the Whitley or the Wellington and could still carry 4,000lbs of bombs, but in many ways it was unsuitable for the purpose for which it had been intended. Constructed to a 'pod and boom' design, with a very narrow fuselage, it was cramped and uncomfortable for its crews. It also had a woefully inadequate defensive armament, although Harris improved this by privately arranging for a local engineering company to design and manufacture a new gun mounting which effectively doubled the aircraft's firepower, arguing about the question of cost with the Air Ministry only once it was a fait accompli.

This happened too late to save five aircraft out of eleven from being shot down in a daylight operation over the Heligoland Bight on 29 September 1939. All Harris's fears about daytime bombing were realized by this event and, although Bomber Command initially blamed the disaster on poor formation flying, by the end of the year the group was refocused on night operations. At this early stage of the war there was a general prohibition on carrying out any operations in which civilians might be killed, and the targets were mostly German naval bases and ships. The invasion of Norway prompted a move to mine-laying, which Harris himself felt was a much more appropriate task for the Hampden. The opening of the German offensive in France and Belgium, however, prompted yet another set of priorities, with the group's aircraft targeting German communications and, after Dunkirk, the potential invasion ports.

On the night of 12 August 1940, the first Victoria Cross to be awarded in Bomber Command was won in 5 Group by Flight Lieutenant R. A. B. Learoyd of 49 Squadron, in a low-level attack on the Dortmund–Ems Canal, a target which would continue to attract the group's attention right up to the end of the war. This was followed a month later by the award of a second VC in the group, to a wireless operator, Sergeant John Hannah, who had fought a fire in his aircraft rather than bale out, sustaining serious injuries but enabling the pilot to bring it safely home.

For much of the summer and early autumn of 1940 Harris had been in close contact with Ralph who, as AOC of 7 Group, was responsible for training the aircrews destined for 5 Group at 14 and 16 OTUs. The two men moved to the Air Ministry at much the same time, Ralph as Director of Flying Training in October and Harris as Deputy Chief of the Air Staff in November. The latter was succeeded at 5 Group by Norman Bottomley, who had been one of Ralph's fellow instructors at the Staff College in 1930/31. Bottomley lacked the long history of Harris in bombers, but he had been the Senior Air Staff Officer at Bomber Command since February 1938, so was well suited to his new appointment. He held it for a mere six months, however, during a difficult period in which Bomber Command, with Peirse having succeeded Portal as AOC-in-C, began its long campaign against German cities, prosecuted initially without much success. The focus switched to oil installations early in the New Year of 1941, but the ability of the bombers to hit such small targets was minimal. The emphasis then moved again, this time to support the campaign against the U-boats by bombing the yards in which they were built and the ports where they were based. Once again, the results were modest.

Bottomley moved on in May 1941 to relieve Harris at the Air Ministry, where he would remain for the rest of the war, becoming in the process something of a thorn in Harris's side. His successor at 5 Group was Jack Slessor, just over two years younger than Ralph and already recognized as one of the stars of his generation. Two months after Slessor arrived, the focus switched back from the war at sea to a renewed assault against Germany itself, but neither the aircraft nor the techniques employed by their crews were equal to the challenge of making a major dent in the enemy's economy, and the results were substantially outweighed by the casualties; the latter were caused to a great extent by the increasing sophistication of the German defences, which included a new early warning radar system, a deep belt of searchlights and anti-aircraft guns and the beginnings of effective night-fighter operations. However, for 5 Group in particular there was some light at the end of the tunnel, although most would not have realized it at the time. It came in the shape of a new and highly effective aircraft.

In November 1940, the first Avro Manchester had been delivered to 207 Squadron at Waddington, and the maiden operational sortie, by six Manchesters flying alongside Hampdens, was carried out against Brest on the night of 24/25 February 1941. Avro had submitted the design for the Manchester in response to Air Ministry specification P.13/36, which also elicited a successful bid by Handley Page with the Halifax. Unlike the Halifax, however, the Manchester was designed with two instead of four engines, and these were to be the new Rolls-Royce Vulture. It was these engines which resulted in the Manchester proving a serious disappointment, as they were both underpowered and unreliable; but due to the lack of alternatives, these major defects did not prevent the equipping of seven squadrons of 5 Group with the Manchester between November 1940 and April 1942.

However, even before the Manchester had flown its first operational sortie, Roy Chadwick, Avro's chief designer, had completed the prototype of its successor, the Lancaster. The major improvement was a new wing centre section, which allowed for the installation of four Rolls-Royce Merlin engines. The Lancaster proved from the start to be an outstanding aircraft, with a service ceiling of 24,000ft and a normal carrying capacity of 14,000lbs of bombs. It began to replace 44 Squadron's Hampdens at the end of December 1941 and progressively re-equipped all those squadrons employing Manchesters by the end of July 1942; 5 Group now had the weapon it needed.

Before this process took place, and just over three months before the end of Slessor's term as AOC, the *Scharnhorst* and *Gneisenau* made their dash up the Channel. Slessor put as many aircraft into the air as possible on 'that foul February day',[3] but their attempts to bomb the ships proved fruitless, and it was only at dusk that he sent out twenty Hampdens to mine the estuary of the Elbe. Nine out of the fifteen aircraft lost to Bomber Command came from 5 Group. Thereafter, naval targets began to be replaced by German cities, with the exception of one particularly successful raid on the Renault factory at Boulogne-Billancourt, to which 5 Group contributed 48 Hampdens and 26 Manchesters out of a total force of 235 aircraft, the greatest number in the war to that date.

Slessor left to become an Assistant Chief of the Air Staff on 6 April 1942, and it was not until 25 April that his successor, Alec Coryton, arrived to command 5 Group. In the interregnum, one of the most remarkable bombing operations took place, which among other things announced the arrival of the Lancaster to both the British public and the Germans. This was an initiative undertaken by Harris, who had only arrived at Bomber Command less than two months earlier and was desperate to score a resounding success. The target was the MAN factory at Augsburg, which manufactured U-boat engines. The raid was carried out on 17 April by six aircraft each from 44 and 97 Squadrons, under the overall leadership of Squadron Leader John Nettleton of the former, and took place in daylight, with the aircraft flying at a very low level to avoid enemy radar. Whilst the factory was damaged, seven planes were lost. Nettleton was awarded a VC, but it was very clear that daylight raids over Germany without any fighter escort were likely to be highly costly, even for an aircraft as versatile as the Lancaster.

Coryton was a longstanding protégé of Harris, having served under him as a flight commander in 31 Squadron on the North-West Frontier of India in 1921/22 and in the Directorate of Operations and Intelligence, where he also became a friend to Ralph, in the mid-1930s. He turned out to be a forceful and energetic commander during a period in which the first navigational aids, notably Gee, came into use, the Pathfinders were formed, with 83 Squadron transferred from 5 Group, and Lancasters replaced the last of the Hampdens and all the Manchesters. The upgrading to new aircraft was seriously disruptive for a time, but the introduction of first one and then two more HCUs within the group eased the process. In spite of all this, and by dint of using aircraft from the HCUs, 5 Group was able to put seventy-three Lancasters, forty-six Manchesters and thirty-four Hampdens into the air for Harris's first 'Thousand Bomber Raid' on Cologne on the night of 30/31 May, of which only one Lancaster and four Manchesters were lost. One of the latter was piloted by Flying Officer L. T. Manser, who ordered his crew to bale out of the fatally damaged aircraft whilst he held it steady, thereby saving all their lives but losing his own, for which action he was posthumously awarded 5 Group's third Victoria Cross.

Whilst the Augsburg Raid had proved very costly and Harris was in general opposed to daylight operations, he made one more exception, in which ninety-four Lancasters, from all nine squadrons in 5 Group, attacked the Schneider factory at Le Creusot on 17 October. Once again the bombers flew at a very low altitude, making a long detour out over the Bay of Biscay before turning at a right angle towards their target, thereby avoiding most of the defences. With the exception of one which turned back with engine problems, all the aircraft reached their target and bombed from heights of 2,500 to 7,500ft. The only casualty was a Lancaster which crashed after hitting a building. The results of the raid were disappointing, however, with most bombs falling well wide of the factory. Harris recognized that the techniques for target recognition and marking were still quite inadequate, and low-level daylight operations were abandoned until they could be made more effective.

For the first two months of 1943, 5 Group formed part of the Main Force of Bomber Command, participating in raids on Lorient and the other U-boat bases and on German and Italian cities, with mixed success. It was during this time that Harris lost confidence in Coryton. Whilst he was complimentary about the planning and execution of group's operations, he was highly critical of the differences of opinion which arose frequently between Coryton on the one hand and the staff at Bomber Command on the other. He wrote to Coryton on 23 February:

> I have repeatedly reminded you that it is for me to say what shall be done and when, and broadly how; and for you to accomplish it. The responsibility for the outcome is mine and mine alone, subject only to a subordinate commander's observance of instructions and of customary procedures. While, therefore, I am always open to representations – even

amounting to protests – I am not prepared to bear further the perpetual and persistent disputes which have characterised your relationship with my operational Staff, still less with the attitude you evinced, for example, apropos the proposal to continue, with a few Lancasters on a clear night, politically necessary attacks on Berlin which the Mosquitos found it practicable to carry out in daylight with cloud cover …

I fully recognize that throughout you have been actuated solely by the highest motives of duty and, especially, devotion to your crews. Nevertheless, as I have so often tried to explain to you, the responsibility and the moral onus of all decisions within the Command are mine alone. Where you fail therefore is through your inability to divest yourself of a moral responsibility which is not yours.[4]

The Mosquito attacks on Berlin had taken place on 30 January with the specific aim, achieved to some extent, of disrupting rallies addressed by Hermann Goering and Joseph Goebbels on that day. Donald Bennett, in his memoirs, alleges that both Coryton and Ralph had been ordered to detail twelve Lancasters for the night-time attack and that 'Cochran [sic], being new to the Command and being Cochran, immediately replied, "Yes". Coryton, on the other hand, declared the great risk for the crews concerned was unjustifiable, and said that he would not order aircraft on such a raid.'[5] 3 Group had not begun to re-equip with Lancasters at this time, but there is no record of any raid by Stirlings in small numbers on Berlin in the first two months of 1943, so it must be assumed that, even if Bennett was correct, the proposed 3 Group element of such an operation was not sent out on its own.

Harris consulted Portal in the hope that there would be another job available for Coryton, who he assured would not be the subject of an adverse report. It would, however, be nearly six months before he was appointed Assistant Chief of the Air Staff (Operations) and, in the meantime, he was employed on other duties at the Air Ministry and in the Middle East.[6] He was still at 5 Group's HQ at St Vincent's Hall, a large Gothic Revival mansion on the outskirts of Grantham, when Ralph arrived on 27 February, ready to assume command on the following day. Ralph and Hilda were looking for a suitable prep school for John and Malcolm at the time, and it was whilst they were staying with the Corytons at the AOC's large house, Norman Leys, that they learnt from them about Spyway School in Langton Matravers in Dorset, run by an eccentric pair of bachelor brothers, Geoffrey and Eric Warner; the boys were sent there in due course. Grizel, in the meantime, who had been boarding initially at the preparatory Barn School at Much Hadham in Hertfordshire, moved on to Tudor Hall, which was initially located at Burnt Norton,[7] near Chipping Camden in Gloucestershire, before moving in 1943 to Wykham Park, near Banbury.

Ralph found that he had inherited a good team at Grantham. The Senior Air Staff Officer was Group Captain, later Air Commodore, Harry Satterly, who had begun his RAF career as an apprentice at Halton before retraining and qualifying as a pilot. He had commanded 83 Squadron in 1941, at a time when it was operating Hampdens, and had been awarded a DFC. He then became Station Commander at RAF Swinderby, which housed 455 Squadron, an Australian unit, and 50 Squadron, both of which were also equipped with Hampdens. In the spring of 1942 the airfield was closed for concrete runways to be laid, and Satterly moved on shortly afterwards to be SASO to Coryton.

Of the other members of the staff, those in the General Duties branch and particularly on Operations were very often officers taking a breather between operational tours, but even those with more administrative or technical functions tended to be on relatively short postings. There were some civilian members, notably a meteorologist, R. H. Matthews, nicknamed by some 'The Gremlin', whom Ralph held in particularly high regard for his willingness to give an opinion on the weather which did not always follow the line adopted by his colleagues at Bomber Command HQ. Last but far from least, he was able to engineer the transfer of Carol Durrant from 3 Group.

As had been his practice at 3 Group, Ralph was from the start a frequent visitor to his stations, either by car or by flying in the Percival Procter reserved for his personal use in the 5 Group Communications Flight at RAF Grantham, which Ralph had known as Spitalgate[8] in the Wessex Bombing Area in the late 1920s. Satterley's old station, Swinderby, remained in 5 Group for the time being as the home of 1654 HCU and then 1660 HCU. Most of the stations housing operational squadrons were, like Swinderby, in Lincolnshire. From north to south they were Scampton (57 Squadron),

Fiskerton (49), Skellingthorpe (50), Waddington (9 and 44) and Woodhall Spa (97). In addition, there were Syerston (61 and 106) and Langar (207) in Nottinghamshire and Bottesford (467) straddling the Leicestershire/Lincolnshire border.

Ralph had been familiarizing himself with 5 Group for just over two weeks when he was summoned at short notice to a meeting with Harris at Bomber Command HQ at High Wycombe to be briefed on a special operation, for whose successful execution he was to take full responsibility.

Chapter 12

UPKEEP

Ralph's meeting with Harris on 15 March marked the beginning of his involvement in what was to be, by some way, the most famous Bomber Command raid of the war. Harris told him that he was to take personal control of the planning of this operation, which would have to be carried out within the next two months, to form a new squadron specifically for the purpose and to supervise the squadron's training, whilst at the same time carrying out his normal duties as AOC of 5 Group. In order to deploy a new type of weapon, the squadron was to fly specially converted Lancasters, which would become available over the following weeks. In the meantime, training on aircraft currently available would involve all the crews becoming expert in very low flying, by night as well as by day. Within 5 Group, only Ralph himself, Satterly, one of the station commanders and the yet to be appointed CO of the new squadron would be aware of what was being planned, and the highest level of secrecy would need to be maintained until the last moment.

Whilst the coming to fruition of this operation was to be brief, its gestation had by then already been a long one, going back some three years. The prime mover was Ralph's old friend Barnes Wallis, who had been toying with a number of alternative ways of destroying the dams which supplied the Ruhr Valley with electricity and water and were thus vital to the effective functioning of Germany's greatest industrial area. He had particularly focused on the potential of using shock waves to achieve this goal and initially proposed using an enormous bomb, which would have to be carried by a very large aircraft which he called the 'Victory' bomber. In late 1940 experiments were carried out at the Road Research Laboratory at Harmondsworth to simulate the impact of such a weapon on 1/50 scale models of the Möhne Dam, the most significant of those supplying the River Ruhr itself, and the Eder Dam, which controlled the water to the River Weser and the Mittelland Canal. These were modestly encouraging, but far from conclusive.

With official support at best lukewarm, Wallis then produced a paper entitled 'A Note on a Method of Attacking the Axis Powers', which identified dams as particularly suitable targets, although many others were considered, including dock gates and canals. The paper met initially with a cool reception. However, Wallis had gained the support in particular of Wing Commander (later Group Captain) F. W. Winterbotham, whose relatively modest rank belied his importance as a key figure in the dissemination of Ultra, the product of the decryption of the German Enigma cypher machines. Winterbotham's work brought him into close contact with the service chiefs, including Portal, politicians, not least Churchill himself, and scientists. The last category included Sir Henry Tizard, the Scientific Adviser to the Ministry of Aircraft Production, to whom Winterbotham sent a copy of Wallis's paper, and it was with Tizard's backing that Dr David Pye, the Director of Armament Development at the Ministry, set up the Aerial Attack on Dams Advisory Committee (AAD Committee) in March 1941 to consider the potential of Wallis's proposals.

Whilst Wallis had his supporters, there were some big guns lined up against him, the most powerful of whom was Frederick Lindeman, Lord Cherwell, Churchill's scientific adviser. Cherwell did not know Wallis personally, but he was an enemy of Tizard and others who were generally supportive of Wallis. In addition, the Air Staff rejected the 'Victory' bomber on the grounds that it would be a hugely expensive project with a limited use. Unsurprisingly, the AAD Committee in due course rejected both the big bomb and its carrier.

Wallis was not deterred and began to think of other ways to deliver the explosive force needed to destroy the dams, using a type of aircraft currently or shortly to be in service. By the use of models he discovered that a smaller charge would be effective if detonated in direct contact with the dam wall. At the beginning of 1942 he began to put together some ideas for a device launched from an aeroplane which would skip across water to the top of the dam, sinking then to the required depth, at which it would be detonated. Where the skipping idea emerged from is not entirely clear, as it was only subsequently that he learnt that the Royal Navy in the late eighteenth and early nineteenth centuries had discovered that the range of a solid canon ball could be extended if it ricocheted off water on its way to the target.

He began to experiment with a catapult, his children's marbles and a tub of water, from which he could calculate the range of a spherical device dropped from an aircraft at a particular speed. This time, in the knowledge that the Air Staff had been sceptical about his ideas, he sent a paper on the subject to Professor P. M. S. Blackett, Director of Operational Research at the Admiralty. Blackett was enthusiastic and passed the paper to Tizard. Far from being upset at apparently being bypassed, Tizard authorized the use of the ship model tank at the National Physical Laboratory at Teddington for further experiments.

The experiments proved that the theory was sound, although practical implementation would require a great deal of trial and error. In terms of explosive power, Wallis was able to demonstrate what would be necessary by carrying out tests at the small and disused Nant-y-Gro Dam, against the wall of which a charge was lowered. The second such test, in July 1942, was spectacularly successful, and Wallis was given permission to convert a Wellington bomber to carry and test out prototype bombs. On 4 December 1942 a Wellington piloted by 'Mutt' Summers, the chief test pilot of Vickers, with his deputy Robert Handasyde as flight test observer and Wallis as bomb-aimer, dropped the first dummy spherical bombs off Chesil Beach. The bombs all burst on impact with the water, but Wallis was undeterred, strengthening the casing so that, at the next attempt eleven days later, the bombs were damaged but did not shatter.

By this time there were two potential bombs in contemplation. The smaller, codenamed HIGHBALL, was designed to be carried by Mosquitoes and deployed by the Royal Navy against surface ships. The other, UPKEEP, was much larger and could only be carried satisfactorily by a Lancaster, which would have to be extensively modified to accommodate it. Test runs at Chesil Beach took place throughout January 1943, and shortly before the end of the month, Wallis was able to show films of them to audiences of senior officers in the Royal Navy and RAF and civil servants in the Admiralty and the Ministry of Aircraft Production.

February 1943 turned out to be the critical month for the decision to go ahead with the production and, in due course, the deployment of Wallis's unorthodox weapons. In the belief that he would have to overcome Cherwell's opposition, Wallis had sent him a copy of a new paper, 'Air Attack on the

Dams', which set out the results of his experiments, described the weapons being developed and considered the targets and the impact on the German economy of their destruction. Cherwell was not sufficiently impressed to withdraw his opposition, but support was growing elsewhere at such a rate that his stance was no longer a barrier.

On 13 February a key meeting was held at the Air Ministry, chaired by Air Marshal Ralph Sorley, the ACAS (Technical Requirements). Amongst the other officers from the Air Staff were Bottomley, the ACAS (Operations), and Bufton, the Deputy Director of Bombing. The Ministry of Aircraft Production team was led by Air Commodore G. A. H. Pidcock, the Director of Armament Development, and included Ben Lockspeiser, the Director of Scientific Research. There were two representatives from the Admiralty and, significantly, two from Bomber Command, one of whom was Group Captain Sam Elworthy, the Group Captain Operations. Wallis was not invited.

The meeting began with an introduction by Sorley, after which Lockspeiser explained the principle of HIGHBALL and UPKEEP, saying that, from the results obtained with models, there was every chance of the weapon being a success, at least on calm water. However, it would not be possible to produce UPKEEP before April, and the earliest possible date for an attack was six months hence. As far as HIGHBALL was concerned, Lockspeiser favoured it over UPKEEP, but Sorley felt that the use of the former against ships would give away the whole idea to the Germans.

Elworthy undertook to brief Harris on the position. In fact he briefed Saundby and, on the following day, Saundby sent the AOC-in-C a summary of the meeting and its conclusions. As far as UPKEEP was concerned, he explained that it would be carried by a specially modified Lancaster and dropped at a speed of 220mph from a height of between 80 and 120ft. He set out a number of issues which would need to be resolved, including, as far as Bomber Command was concerned, how many aircraft would need to be modified, what length of training would be required and whether it would possible for the attack to be made in bright moonlight rather than in daylight. Saundby gave his own opinion, which was that sufficient aircraft should be modified to equip one squadron, that three weeks should suffice for training as the tactics were not too difficult and that it was perfectly possible for the operation to be carried out by moonlight.

Harris's handwritten response was withering:

This is tripe of the wildest description. There are so many ifs & ands that there is not the slightest chance of it working. To begin with the bomb would have to be perfectly balanced round its axis otherwise vibration at 500 RPM would wreck the aircraft or tear the bomb loose. I don't believe a word of its supposed ballistics on the surface.

It would be much easier to design a 'scow' bomb[1] to run on the surface, bust its nose in on contact, sink and explode. This bomb would of course be heavier than water and exactly fit existing bomb bays.

At all costs stop them putting aside Lancs and reducing our bombing effort on this wild goose chase. Let them prove the practicability of the weapon first. Another Toraplane[2] – only madder. The war will be over before it works – & it never will.[3]

By now, however, the momentum was unstoppable. Another meeting, chaired this time by John Baker, the Director of Bombing Operations, was held on 15 February, at which it was decided to manufacture one UPKEEP bomb and modify a single Lancaster in order to test it. Moreover, on 19 February Wallis was able to show his films of the trials to some interested audiences, which included Portal, Admiral of the Fleet Sir Dudley Pound, the First Sea Lord, and Sir Charles Craven, the Chairman of Vickers. Portal, who had received a letter from Harris following the 15 February meeting objecting, among other things, to the diversion of his precious Lancasters to a wild goose chase, had by that time arranged for Elworthy to spend time with Wallis at Teddington and to fly in a Wellington carrying out a test drop off Chesil Beach. Elworthy was not entirely convinced as to the feasibility of the new weapon and was mindful of Harris's warning that he should treat 'mad scientists' with great circumspection, but he had nevertheless been impressed by his experience and urged Harris to meet Wallis. It seems likely that Ralph, too, although not privy to the circumstances at this time, was asked to use such influence as he had with Harris to encourage him to listen to his old friend. Even more importantly, the fact that Portal, a man whom Harris respected above all others, was taking the project seriously and had written to Harris to tell him to do the same, persuaded him that

Wallis should be given a hearing. He accordingly invited him to come to High Wycombe on 22 February.

Wallis took Mutt Summers with him to answer questions on flying the aircraft. They were given a somewhat hostile reception, with Harris telling Wallis that his aircrews' lives were too precious to be wasted on crazy schemes. Wallis responded by giving the AOC-in-C a measured explanation in layman's language of exactly what was being proposed and then suggested showing the films. Harris had the projection room staff removed and a somewhat hamfisted Saundby was ordered to act as projectionist. Harris's reaction during the film show was a series of grunts, and he declined to commit himself in any way before Wallis and Summers left, but he did reveal that Portal had now authorized the conversion of three Lancasters.

If the news about the Lancasters had given Wallis some hope that his project was to go forward, this was almost immediately dashed. On the day after his meeting with Harris he was summoned to see Craven at the head office of Vickers. Standing like a naughty schoolboy in front of the headmaster, he was told that he had been making a complete nuisance of himself with the project and, in particular, that the Controller of Research and Development at the Ministry of Aircraft Production, Air Marshal Francis Linnell, had asked that he should cease work on it immediately. Wallis immediately tendered his resignation, which was refused by a furious Craven. It took a lunch with Winterbotham to calm him down.

Two days later, Wallis was asked to attend a meeting at the MAP on the following day. When he arrived he found Linnell in the chair and Craven present, as well as Lockspeiser and Roy Chadwick, Avro's chief designer. To his astonishment, the position had changed completely. Instead of reverting to other work, notably on a new bomber – later to be called the Vickers Windsor – the immediate focus was to be on completing the work on both the UPKEEP bomb and the converted Lancasters and on forming the squadron to deliver them, with a view to attacking the dams by 26 May at the latest, after which the water levels were expected to fall too far to make the operation viable. Avro would focus on producing the required number of modified Lancasters, whilst Vickers would take responsibility for the bombs and for the attachment holding them.

It was clear that Portal had now thrown his weight behind the operation, supported enthusiastically, it would seem, by his former Vice-Chief and now Chief Executive of the MAP, Wilfrid Freeman. Once again, as with the Pathfinders, Harris had come reluctantly to the party, but once again he was now to give it his full backing and to ensure that all the resources it required were made available.

Delighted though Wallis was at the decision to go ahead, the timescale within which he would have to operate was daunting. He had an absolute maximum of thirteen weeks to turn his prototype into a fully functioning and tested weapon of war. In order to do this he would not only have to produce a device which did exactly what was expected of it, but also calculate how it was to be delivered, at what speed and at what height. UPKEEP has been known as 'the bouncing bomb' ever since it first engaged the popular imagination, immediately after its operational deployment, but it was not, in reality, a bomb at all. It would be better described as a mine or, indeed, a depth charge, as it did not explode on impact but through the triggering of three hydrostatic pistols, setting off the explosion of 6,000lbs of Torpex at a depth of 30ft. If the pistols failed, then a self-destruct fuse, triggered when the device was released, would detonate after 90 seconds.

When Wallis left the meeting of 25 February, his thoughts were still focused on a spherical shape, although he had decided long beforehand that the spinning technique would only work if the bomb was launched with backspin, which would itself require a motor to be installed on the attachment to the bomber carrying it. There was an immediate setback when the Ministry of Supply announced that it could not provide enough steel for the dies for spherical bombs. This required a complete redesign, and Wallis opted initially for a cylindrical core with wood casings in a spherical shape. This, too, shattered on impact with the water and, over the course of the next few weeks, it became apparent that the best option would be a cylindrical shape without any extra casing; but it was not until the end of April that this was successfully tested.

Much else had taken place before then.

Chapter 13

617 Squadron

Written confirmation of the verbal order to Ralph from Harris to form a new squadron specifically for the raid arrived two days after their meeting. This document was extraordinarily complacent on the risks involved, with an assertion that 'The operation against this dam will not, it is thought, prove particularly dangerous'[1] and a recommendation that 'Some training will no doubt be necessary.'[2] It emphasised the urgency of the operation due to falling water levels, but made no reference to the identity of the new commander of what was initially called Squadron X. Harris, however, had already nominated his choice at the meeting.

Wing Commander Guy Gibson DSO and Bar, DFC and Bar, had been well known to Harris during the latter's own period of command at 5 Group. Aged only twenty-four, he already had an outstanding record of service. He had joined the RAF on a short service commission in November 1936 and his first operational posting had been to 83 Squadron, then flying Hawker Hinds. Conversion to the Hampden took place during 1938, by which time the squadron was in 5 Group at Scampton. After a slow start to the war, with the squadron mostly involved in attacking maritime targets, the focus switched to operations over enemy territory following the German invasion of Belgium and France. Gibson completed thirty-seven operations by the end of his first tour in September 1940, earning himself a DFC, promotion to flight lieutenant and the admiration of Harris, his AOC for all except the first few days of the war.

After the normal rest from operations, spent as an instructor at 14 OTU and then 16 OTU, he switched to Fighter Command. The reason for this was an urgent appeal by Air Vice-Marshal Trafford Leigh-Mallory, the AOC 12 Group, for pilots with experience of night-time operations to fly night fighters during the German bombing campaign of 1940/41. Gibson was personally recommended by Harris and was posted to 29 Squadron, flying Bristol Blenheims out of Digby and its satellite airfield at Wellingore. After he had completed only six operations, the squadron was converted on to the much more effective Bristol Beaufighter. It was then transferred to West Malling in April 1941, where Gibson completed his tour in December 1941, having achieved four confirmed kills, a bar to his DFC and promotion to acting squadron leader.

Gibson was frustrated by his inevitable appointment to another OTU, this time No. 51 at Cranfield, as Chief Flying Instructor. When Harris was appointed AOC-in-C of Bomber Command in February 1942, Gibson appealed directly to him to be returned to operations as soon as possible and was called in for an interview. As a result, Harris wrote to Slessor, then AOC 5 Group, recommending him for promotion to wing commander and command of a Lancaster squadron. Slessor appointed him to 106 Squadron at Coningsby, which was still flying Manchesters but due to begin its conversion to Lancasters within the next two months, although it would be July before Gibson went on his first operation on the type. He quickly gained a reputation as an intrepid commander, but this did not mean that he was universally admired; he gave some of his aircrews a very hard time and was generally unpopular with the ground crews for what was sometimes perceived as high-handed behaviour. During a period in which 5 Group was very much part of the Main Force of Bomber Command, he flew as often as possible, including on the daylight raid on the Schneider factory at Le Creusot and the attacks on Italian cities in the autumn of 1942. The squadron moved to Syerston in October 1942, and it was from there that Gibson completed his tour on the night of 11/12 March 1943 with a raid on Stuttgart, on most of which he flew at a low level as a result of the failure of one of his aircraft's engines. By this time he had certainly deserved the award of a bar to the DSO which he had been awarded in November 1942.[3]

Gibson was expecting to spend some time on leave with his wife, Eve, in Cornwall and was dismayed to be posted instead to HQ 5 Group, apparently to write a book on his experiences. After two days toying with ideas for such a book, he was summoned to see Ralph on 18 March. It has been assumed by some historians that Ralph had not met Gibson before, but it is certainly possible, even likely, that he had. Gibson had been serving at 14 and then 16 OTU at a time when Ralph was commanding the group to which they belonged. Moreover, Ralph's flying log shows that he visited Syerston on both 11 March, the day on which Gibson set off on his last operation from there, and 14 March, whilst he was still there. Even if this was the case, however, he certainly did not know him well and, new to the group himself, was only too happy to accept Harris's decision. Gibson later described their meeting at St Vincent's:

> In one breath he congratulated me on my bar to the DSO, in the next he suddenly said, 'How would you like to do one more trip?'
> I gulped. More flak, more fighters; but said aloud, 'What kind of trip, sir?'
> 'A pretty important one, perhaps one of the most devastating of all time. I can't tell you more now. Do you want to do it?'
> I said I thought I did, trying to remember where I had left my flying kit.[4]

Ralph was not in a position to divulge any more information at the time, but Gibson was summoned back the next day to find a third man in the room, Group Captain J. H. N. Whitworth, always known as Charles. Whitworth was the station commander at Scampton, and it was there that the new squadron, which Gibson was now ordered to form and train, would be based. Apart from Ralph and Whitworth, Satterly was the only other person in 5 Group to know what was afoot, but in the meantime the staff had been ordered to provide Gibson with anything he needed, without questioning why.

On the face of it, there could not have been two more dissimilar characters than Ralph and Gibson. The former was a model of controlled restraint, a man of considerable intellect and of ideas as well as action, who was considered by many who did not know him well to be somewhat austere and even to lack a sense of humour. Gibson was much more of an extrovert, a leader by example rather than by the force of argument, capable of high jinks in the officers' mess but not by any means liked by all. Ralph was in a stable marriage with a strongly supportive wife, Gibson's relationship with Eve was falling apart. Both, however, demanded high standards of their subordinates; moreover, they shared a strong sense of duty and an absolute determination to succeed. In the event, they got on well together, Gibson respecting Ralph as 'a man with a lot of brain and organizing ability',[5] whilst Ralph later wrote that 'Gibson was an obvious choice and an undoubted leader, could be head prefect at any school and a good organizer.'[6] This last characteristic must have held considerable appeal for Ralph, whose watchword was 'efficiency'.

Gibson's orders from Ralph were to make an immediate start on forming his squadron. He was told that specially modified Lancasters would be arriving over the course of the following weeks, but that in the meantime, standard models of the aircraft would be made available for training on low flying, expertise in which would be absolutely essential to the success of the operation. Scampton, some six miles north of Lincoln, was well known to Gibson from his time at 83 Squadron. A large airfield opened in 1936 during the RAF's Expansion Period, its grass surface had suffered from the introduction of heavy bombers and it had been already designated for closure during 1943 to allow concrete runways to be laid. As a result of this, one of its occupants, 49 Squadron, had already moved elsewhere and, although 57 Squadron remained, there was plenty of room for Squadron X, although some of its more immediate mundane requirements had to be scrounged or even, on occasion, stolen from its neighbour.

The original intention was for the new squadron's aircrews to be selected from those in 5 Group who had either recently or nearly completed a tour of operations. Moreover, according to Gibson himself, Ralph told him that he could pick his own crews. Neither of these criteria proved capable of being completely satisfied, but they were true of those pilots who had served under Gibson at 106 Squadron. Flight Lieutenant John 'Hoppy' Hopgood DFC and bar had been one of his inner circle in the squadron and instrumental in his squadron commander's conversion on to Lancasters. Hopgood's tour had finished in October 1942 and had been followed by some short postings on test flying and training duties, so he was readily available. Flight Lieutenant David Shannon DFC, an Australian, had also been close to Gibson at 106 Squadron. When Gibson approached him he had completed his first tour there and had recently been posted to 83 Squadron in 8 (Pathfinder) Group, but he jumped at the chance to join his old CO again. Pilot Officer Lewis Burpee DFM, an RCAF officer, had finished his first tour on the day after Gibson himself and was thus immediately available; unlike Hopgood and Shannon, he came with a complete crew.

The whole of C Flight of 57 Squadron, Squadron X's neighbour at Scampton, was posted across the airfield. The flight commander, Squadron Leader Henry Young DFC and bar, had acquired the nickname 'Dinghy' following two ditchings, one in the Atlantic flying a Whitley of 102 Squadron on loan to Coastal Command, the other in the North Sea in the same type of aircraft returning from a raid on Turin. He had had a varied wartime career, which had included flying in a Wellington squadron out of Malta and then in Egypt. On his return from the Mediterranean he had been posted to 57 Squadron but had not undertaken any operations with it before transferring to the new squadron. He was highly experienced and was to become one of Gibson's two flight commanders and his effective deputy. Flight Lieutenant Bill Astell DFC had also served in Malta and Egypt, where he had been involved in two serious crashes, from the second of which he had to walk back to the British lines. On his return to the UK he had been posted to 57 Squadron, carrying out his first operation in January 1943, so was in the middle of a tour when he moved. The third pilot from 57 Squadron, Pilot Officer Geoff Rice, was a novice on his first tour, with barely a month on operations behind him. Flight Sergeant Ray Lovell was equally inexperienced and, in his case, it showed to such an extent that he was posted back to 57 Squadron shortly afterwards, to be replaced by Flight Sergeant Bill Divall, another rookie pilot but one who was expected to make the grade. Flight Sergeant George Lancaster was the fifth pilot from 57 Squadron and, like Rice and Divall, was yet to complete his first tour; subsequently, his navigator was unable to reach the standard demanded by Gibson, and Lancaster insisted that the whole crew should leave with him.

The other pilots all came from squadrons in 5 Group. Three of them arrived from 50 Squadron, the most senior of whom was Squadron Leader Henry Maudslay DFC, an Old Etonian who had been an outstanding athlete at school. After training he had joined 44 Squadron at a time when it was still flying Hampdens. Following his first tour he had returned to the squadron as an instructor on the conversion flight as it moved on to Lancasters, in which role he had participated in all three of Harris's Thousand Bomber Raids of May and June 1942. He returned to operational flying with 50 Squadron, but had only completed thirteen more operations when he was posted to join Gibson, becoming his second flight commander. Flight Lieutenant Harold 'Mick' Martin DFC was an Australian who had served with 455 Squadron

RAAF before transferring to 50 Squadron. His crew was all Australian apart from the flight engineer and included two men who would play a leading part in the forthcoming operation, Flight Lieutenants Jack Leggo DFC and Bob Hay DFC, who were appointed respectively the Squadron Navigation Leader and the Squadron Bombing Leader. Gibson had met Martin at an investiture at Buckingham Palace, where the latter expounded on the virtues of low flying, and he asked for him as soon as he heard that this was to be a feature of the special operation. The third pilot from 50 Squadron was another Australian, Pilot Officer Les Knight, who, unlike most of the others, brought with him a complete crew.

Three pilots were supplied by 97 Squadron. They included one of the only two RNZAF officers in the new squadron, Flight Lieutenant Les Munro, who had flown on his first operation over Germany in a Wellington whilst still at an OTU. He had subsequently completed the best part of a tour on Lancasters before his posting to Scampton. The second of the three was unique in the squadron, a US citizen who had volunteered to join the RCAF in 1941, Flight Lieutenant Joe McCarthy DFC. McCarthy was one of those who had just completed his first tour. The final pilot of the trio was Flight Lieutenant David Maltby DFC, who had completed one tour and had just returned for a second when his posting came through.

Two other squadrons supplied more than one pilot to the new squadron. Two came from 49 Squadron, both of them NCOs. Flight Sergeant Bill Townsend had almost reached the end of his first tour, but Flight Sergeant Cyril Anderson had only completed seven operations. Flight Sergeant Ken Brown, an RCAF pilot in 44 Squadron, had the same number of operations to his name, but he was amongst the last to join, by which time Gibson was desperate to make up the numbers. His fellow member of 44 Squadron, Flight Lieutenant Harold Wilson, was much more experienced but still did not have a complete tour under his belt. Three squadrons supplied one pilot each. Flight Lieutenant Robert 'Norm' Barlow DFC of 61 Squadron was two operations away from the end of his first tour, whilst Pilot Officer Warner Ottley DFC, a Canadian in 207 Squadron, had just finished his and had applied to join the Pathfinders; after learning that he had been unsuccessful he heard that Gibson was seeking crews, approached him directly and was accepted. Pilot Officer Vernon Byers, another Canadian, but this time from the otherwise Australian 467 Squadron, was the least experienced of all the pilots, with a mere four operations to his name.

At the same time as the aircrews were being recruited, both ground crew and administrative staff were transferred from other units. Across the airfield from 57 Squadron came Flight Sergeant George Powell, known to all as 'Chiefy', who was to take charge of the practical aspects of administration, including the selection of the ground crews and the furnishing of the accommodation. An adjutant was appointed to oversee the administration, but he proved to be unacceptable to Gibson and was replaced by Harry Humphries, his deputy adjutant at 106 Squadron, who was promoted to flight lieutenant.

On 24 March, before most of its pilots and other aircrew had arrived, Squadron X was officially designated as 617 Squadron. Training in low-level flying began three days later on ten borrowed standard Lancasters, and it was not until 8 April that the first Type 464 Provisioning Lancasters became available, their name derived from the official designation by Vickers of their payload as a Type 464 bomb. Their most obvious special features were the removal of the bomb bay doors, the insertion of a number of attachments to hold, spin and then release the bomb, and the removal of the mid-upper turret. The mid-upper gunner became the front gunner, a role usually adopted by the bomb aimer except during the run towards a target. In the forthcoming operation the bomb aimers would have the task not only of dropping the bomb, but also of assisting with visual navigation and watching out for low-level obstacles such as electricity pylons and lines. The front gunner, in the meantime, would engage any anti-aircraft defences, his legs lifted above the bomb aimer's face by specially fitted stirrups.

At this time Gibson had no idea about the identity of the targets, but he was advised by Satterly that the squadron should practise carrying out their attacks over water, flying at 100ft and 240mph. In addition to this, the crews would have to learn to navigate by moonlight, picking up the features of their route as they flew over them. Satterly suggested nine stretches of inland water, including Bala and Vyrnwy Lakes in North Wales and a number of reservoirs in the Midlands and North of England.

In the meantime, Gibson had met Wallis for the first time, travelling down to Weybridge by train on 24 March, from where he was driven by

Summers to Wallis's office. Wallis was taken aback to find out that Gibson knew nothing of the identity or even the nature of the targets, but he told him as much as he could in spite of this handicap, showing him the films of the bombing trials with the half-size version of UPKEEP and explaining the requirement for absolute accuracy, to be achieved by speed, height and precise distance from the target.

Gibson was not to be kept in the dark for long. Five days later, having in the meantime carried out his own first low-level run over water at the Derwent Reservoir near Sheffield, which he found exceptionally difficult, he met Ralph at St Vincent's and was shown scale models of both the Möhne and Sorpe Dams. Gibson's immediate reaction was to be grateful that the target was not the German battleship *Tirpitz*, as he had feared since his first meeting with Ralph. He was told to fly down to see Wallis again for a more comprehensive briefing on the nature of the targets, with Summers once more present to elaborate on the flying issues. At this meeting Wallis queried whether a daylight attack might not be appropriate, but this was comprehensively ruled out by Gibson.

Wallis's main concern was the progress of the trials, which had now moved from Chesil Beach to the Thames Estuary, off the North Kent coast at Reculver. The results had been more encouraging for him than for many of the other observers, who witnessed the bombs breaking up more often than not. Wallis was still using wooden outer casings at this time, and it was not until late April, a month or less before the deadline for the raid, that it was decided to use the cylinders without them. Gibson watched the trials for the first time on 13 April, accompanied by Bob Hay, his Bombing Leader, and saw the casing shatter on the first run, although the cylinder broke free and ran on. The same thing happened on the second run, but Wallis was not perturbed. Whilst waiting for the third run, due to take place early in the evening, Gibson decided to borrow a Miles Magister from the airfield at Manston, so that he and Hay could see for themselves what it was like over the bombing range at Reculver. The engine cut out at 300ft and the aircraft did not have enough height or speed to avoid a crash landing; both men were uninjured, but the Magister was a write-off. They drove back to Scampton without waiting for the third drop.

Further trials took place, but Gibson was unable to attend any more until 29 April, when bare cylinders were dropped and bounced satisfactorily, but tended to veer off a straight line to the target. From his calculations, Wallis was now asking the aircraft to drop their loads at precisely 60ft. Gibson and Hay were deeply concerned about how this could be achieved, as no altimeter could perform at that height with any degree of accuracy. A solution was sought and it came in the form of a proposal from Ben Lockspeiser at the MAP. He suggested attaching two spotlights to the aircraft which would be fixed in such a way that they came together at exactly 60ft. When told of this, Harris doubted that it would work; he had tried it on the flying boats of 210 Squadron in the early 1930s and the beams broke up on entering the water. Lockspeiser believed that this was because the sea was too rough and that it would work on the calm waters of an inland lake. So it proved, and the problem was solved.[7]

Another major problem was exactly when to drop the bomb. Conventional bomb sights, however sophisticated, were of no use whatsoever. The solution was proposed by Wing Commander C. L. Dann of the Aeroplane and Armament Experimental Establishment at Boscombe Down, who produced an even lower-technology device than the spotlights. This took the form of a small wooden equilateral triangle, with a peephole at the apex, a nail at each end of the base and a handle. The bomb aimer would look through the peephole and, in the case of the main target, the Möhne Dam, would release the bomb when the nails were in line with the towers on the dam wall. By no means all the bomb aimers were happy with this, and a number came up with their own solutions, including making marks on the clear-vision panel, to which string was attached to create the triangle. This proved to be somewhat more stable than the Dann sight, which was difficult to hold steady in a low-flying aircraft.

In spite of having to continue his normal duties in respect of the rest of 5 Group, Ralph was keeping his finger firmly on the pulse of what was happening with 617 Squadron and the operation as a whole and, with Satterly and Whitworth, had embarked on its detailed planning. In early May an alarming breach of security was brought to his and Satterly's attention by Gibson, who had sent his Armament Officer, Pilot Officer Watson, down to Manston on a three-week attachment to learn about UPKEEP. Watson told him that, within three days of his arriving there, he had been shown a file which included sectional diagrams of 'certain objectives', a map of the Ruhr showing these objectives and various other secret details in connection with UPKEEP. Watson also revealed that the same information had been shown to Flying Officer Rose of 618 Squadron, whose Mosquitoes were training to deliver HIGHBALL. The file was shown to both of them by Wing Commander Garner of the Directorate of Research and Development. Gibson, who had meticulously ensured that only he and Whitworth knew the full details of the forthcoming operation – even Hay had no idea of the nature of the targets, although he had seen the prototype bombs in action – was absolutely furious. He passed on his concerns to Ralph, who wrote immediately to Saundby, suggesting that the file should be withdrawn from Garner and steps taken to ensure that there were no further breaches of security. Saundby in turn referred the matter to Bottomley, who spoke both to Ralph and to Garner's superior, the Deputy Controller of Research and Development, Air Commodore B. F. McEntegart, as well as to the Director of Intelligence (Security), who was instructed to take the appropriate steps.

On 5 May Ralph attended an important meeting at the Air Ministry, chaired by Bottomley, with Saundby, McEntegart, Bufton, Wallis and Dr W. H. Glanville from the Department of Scientific Research as the other participants. The object of the meeting was to discuss operational and security issues, the state of technical readiness and the date for which the operation should be planned, bearing in mind the optimum water levels in the dams. The third of these was debated first, with input from Glanville, who had worked with Wallis to agree the optimum depth for detonation of the charge. This was now set as 30ft, to permit which the water level would need to be no more than 5ft below its maximum. The latest reconnaissance on the night of 4/5 April had shown the level to be 2ft below the maximum. The May moon period was agreed to offer suitable conditions for attack, but the risks of waiting until the June moon period were considerable. It was agreed that further reconnaissance flights should be laid on immediately.

As far as UPKEEP was concerned, Wallis reported that, with the cylinder alone, and at air speeds of 210 to 220mph, a range of 450 to 500 yards could be obtained. Confirmatory trials on the rate of revolution induced by the spinning mechanism were about to be carried out.

Ralph now reported on the training programme, saying that it was well advanced and that he was anxious that all crews should have the opportunity to drop two or three cylinders against a representative target, in response to which McEntegart said that aiming marks representing the towers on the Möhne Dam were being erected on the sea wall at Manston. Ralph went on to inform the meeting that twenty converted Lancasters were now available to 617 Squadron and the pilots were ready to undertake training at 60ft with the spotlights. He pressed for the operation to take place on or as soon as possible after 14/15 May, after which he believed that any delay would be detrimental to the crews' enthusiasm.

He went on to outline the plan which he had in mind. He proposed establishing VHF/RT control of the aircraft in the target area so that, if success was achieved against the primary target X (the Möhne) in the earlier phases of the attack, subsequent aircraft could be diverted to a secondary target Y (the Eder). He planned to detail four crews who had not reached the highest standards of accuracy in training to attack target Z (the Sorpe), where the method of attack was simpler but where Wallis believed that it would offer good prospects of causing the dam's destruction, although this might not be immediately apparent to the crews, because it would be caused by seepage through the walls.

Further test bombing flights took place at Reculver over the following days and continued, with a brief interruption for bad weather, right up to 13 May. Gibson himself went down to Manston for the last time on 7 May. Back at 617 Squadron, activity remained at a high pitch as bombing runs were made over the sea at Wainfleet on the Lincolnshire shore of the Wash, where white cricket screens were erected to represent the towers on the dams, whilst low flying training continued over the Eyebrook and Abberton reservoirs to simulate the Möhne and Eder Dams and the Howden and Derwent reservoirs to represent the Sorpe. The usual radio sets were stripped out of the aircraft and replaced by the VHF sets used in Fighter Command, to allow the type of control over the target area which had been proposed by Ralph. As the UPKEEP bombs arrived, the attachment mechanism was balanced to be able to spin them to the rate of revolutions required without shaking the aircraft to pieces. All leave for the squadron was stopped from noon on 7 May.

There had been two important visitors to Scampton on the previous two days. The first and less surprising one was Lord Trenchard. The RAF's founder and first CAS had taken it on himself to visit as many units as he could, not only in the UK but also in the Middle East, and, with his avuncular style that appealed to all ranks, was always warmly welcomed for the boost to morale that his interest engendered. It was probably no coincidence that he had chosen this day to visit 617 Squadron, although he was unlikely to have known any details of the operation. The second was Harris himself on 6 May, and this was certainly out of the ordinary. Harris normally spent all of his time at High Wycombe, except when he was attending meetings at the Air Ministry or on special occasions such as visiting Churchill at Chequers. He spoke nearly every day to his group commanders by phone, and often on a conference call, and summoned them on occasion down to High Wycombe, but he very rarely visited them, let alone the stations under their command. Ralph was later to say that Harris made only three visits to him in the two and a half years of his command of 3 and 5 Groups, one of which was shortly to take place. This was thus a special distinction and an indication of the support he was now giving to an operation which he had initially decried in unambiguous terms.

On 10 May Satterly, following discussion with Ralph, sent the draft operation order to Whitworth, asking him to consider it immediately with Gibson and then either to rewrite it as appropriate or to attach any suggested amendments. He requested that it should be returned by no later than 1600 hours on 12 May. In fact, after further iterations, the final order was not released until the day of the operation, when two copies were sent to Whitworth at Scampton and three to Bomber Command, but another working draft was considered in the meantime by Ralph, Satterly, Whitworth and Gibson. After an introduction which justified the raid in the expectation of the damage it would inflict on German industry and the general disruption it would cause to the Ruhr Valley, the order set out the targets. In addition to Targets X, Y and Z, three additional dams were included as 'Last Resort Targets', D (the Lister), E (the Ennepe) and F (the Diemel). Of the twenty Lancasters available, the First Wave was to consist of nine aircraft to attack Target X and, only when it was breached, to move on to Y; should both be destroyed, the remaining aircraft would attack Z.

The Second Wave would comprise five aircraft, flying on a more northerly route but crossing the Dutch coast at the same time as the First Wave; these would attack Z. The Third Wave would consist of the remaining aircraft as an airborne reserve under the control of 5 Group HQ and would take off at such a time that they could be recalled before crossing the Dutch coast if the First and Second Waves had breached all the targets.

Detailed instructions were included as to the spacing of the waves and sections, the heights at which they should fly, the use of radio in the attacks, the assumption of leadership and deputy leadership if those originally nominated fell out, the direction of attacks and the decision to attack secondary and last resort targets. Routes were set out in an appendix. The signals procedure, including codenames for the results of the bombing, was set out in another appendix. Further elaboration was also provided on diversions, armament, fuel, navigation and intercommunication.

All that remained was to set a date, and this was nearly jeopardized at the last moment by the intervention of service politics. The original intention had been for UPKEEP and HIGHBALL to be deployed in action at the same time, and the latter device was by no means ready for use. The Royal Navy was nevertheless reluctant for an UPKEEP operation to go ahead on its own, for fear of compromising the secrecy of its weapon. The British Chiefs of Staff, who would have to make the final decision, were all at the Trident Conference in Washington. The Vice-Chief of the Naval Staff was under orders from the First Sea Lord not to concede in his absence, so Air Marshal Sir Douglas Evill, who had succeeded Freeman as VCAS, sent a signal to Portal strongly recommending that the two operations be disassociated. On the afternoon of 14 May a signal was received confirming that the operation could go ahead. Nothing now stood in its way.

Chapter 14

Operation CHASTISE

T he formal order from the Air Ministry to carry out what had now been designated as Operation CHASTISE was sent by Bottomley to Bomber Command at 0900 on 15 May. Ralph drove over to Scampton later that morning to tell Whitworth and Gibson that the operation would take place little more than twenty-four hours later. He took Gibson back to Grantham with him in the afternoon to go over the final details with Satterly and 5 Group's Chief Signals Officer, Wing Commander W. E. Dunn. Just as they left Scampton, Wallis arrived there in a Wellington piloted by Summers. When Gibson returned, he held a meeting at Whitworth's house with his two flight commanders, Young and Maudslay, together with Hay and Hopgood, the latter designated as his deputy for the attack on the Möhne, so that he and Wallis could brief them. Hopgood was able to point out that the outbound route took the bombers over a concentration of flak which had been recently identified, and it was modified accordingly. As Gibson left the meeting he was taken aside by Whitworth, who broke the news that his dog Nigger had been killed by a car when crossing the road outside the station gate. This was a severe personal blow to Gibson, who had owned the dog since he was a puppy, but he refused to let his distress show.

On the following day a number of further briefings took place, by Gibson and Wallis for the pilots and navigators and by Dunn for the wireless operators, and later they were joined by the bomb aimers and gunners to study the models and photos of the targets which Gibson had first seen in Ralph's office. The weather was fine and clear and, with the full moon only three days away, no other Bomber Command operations would be taking place that night, other than a few Mosquito sorties and some 'gardening' in the Bay of Biscay and amongst the Friesian Islands. Due to serviceability problems, only nineteen Type 464 Lancasters were available that morning, but illness in the crews of Wilson and Divall meant that there were also only nineteen crews. In the afternoon, however, another aircraft was flown up from Boscombe Down; it turned out to have an engine problem, but this was fixed by the ground engineers, providentially as it would turn out.

At 1800 all the crews assembled to hear the final briefings, delivered by Gibson and Wallis. When they had finished, Ralph gave a short speech, concluding with the words, 'I know that this operation will succeed.' Following this, the crews went off for the traditional pre-operation meal, distinguished by the presence of two eggs with their bacon. Ralph drove over to the dispersals to talk to the ground crews, telling them that he understood the last weeks had been particularly difficult, but that he hoped that they would realize over the coming hours how worthwhile their work had been.

As it was taking a longer route, the Second Wave took off shortly before the First. It had been Ralph's original intention for this wave to be composed of some of the less experienced pilots. However, relatively late in the planning of the operation, he and Gibson had decided that Byers and Rice, both of whom had only a modest number of operations under their belt, should be joined by the experienced Barlow, Munro and McCarthy, the last of whom was designated the leader. Four of the aircraft lifted off between 2128 and 2131, but McCarthy, to his fury, found that his aircraft had sprung a glycol leak in one of its engines. The crew disembarked and switched to the aircraft which had arrived that afternoon from Boscombe Down. An increasingly irritated McCarthy then discovered that there was no compass deviation card, something essential to accurate navigation. Locating a new one took yet more time and it was not until 2201, half an hour late, that his aircraft lifted into the air.

In the meantime, the First Wave had taken off in three sections. Gibson led the first at 2139, alongside Hopgood and Martin, the squadron's low flying expert. The second section, comprising Young, Maltby and Shannon, followed eight minutes later and the third – Maudslay, Astell and Knight – twelve minutes after that. With a long time to go before the Third Wave was due to leave, Ralph, who had stayed at Scampton to see most of the squadron off, returned with Wallis to Grantham, where they found Harris and Satterly in the Operations Room and Dunn sitting by the phone to monitor the incoming messages. It was unprecedented for Harris to be present at a group headquarters during an operation and a clear indication of the importance which he now attached to CHASTISE.

The Second Wave proved to be deeply unlucky. Passing over the island of Texel, Byers' aircraft was hit by light flak and crashed into the sea with no survivors. At much the same time and slightly further south, Munro's aircraft was also hit, putting his transmitter, intercom and master compass out of action and forcing him to abort. Rice was flying so low that his UPKEEP hit the sea and was ripped off, whilst a great deal of water was scooped into the plane. With no weapon, he too was forced to return. This left only McCarthy, trying to catch up after his delayed departure, and Barlow, but the latter crashed less than an hour later and the whole crew was lost, almost certainly after colliding with high tension cables. The UPKEEP being carried in his aircraft failed to detonate and was captured intact by the Germans.

Leading the First Wave, Gibson encountered serious flak at Dorsten and then again at Dülmen, and radioed back to the following aircraft to take avoiding action. Hopgood's aircraft was hit by anti-aircraft fire and several members of the crew were slightly injured, including Hopgood himself, but he flew on nonetheless. Astell was less fortunate; his aircraft suffered the same fate as Barlow's and, once again, it was flying too low for any of the crew to survive.

At shortly after midnight the leading section of the First Wave reached the Möhne, followed by the second section, which was also intact, and then Maudslay and Knight of the third section. After an initial recce, Gibson made the first attack on the dam at 0028 and released his bomb, but it fell short and to the left of its intended target. Although it exploded, it failed to do any serious damage. Hopgood attacked next, but by this time the defenders were well and truly alerted and he attracted heavy anti-aircraft fire, which hit the aircraft. The bomb was released late and bounced straight over the dam wall, detonating on the far side, where it destroyed the power station. With the aircraft on fire and clearly doomed, Hopgood ordered the crew to get out. Flight Sergeant Fraser, the bomb aimer, managed to escape via the nose hatch, whilst Pilot Officer Burcher, the rear gunner, pushed out Sergeant Minchin, the wireless operator, who was badly wounded. Burcher was blown out himself, parachute deployed and in his arms, when the aircraft exploded. He woke up on the ground, and he and Fraser, who had also landed safely, were taken prisoner. Hopgood and the other members of his crew were lost.

The next attack was delivered by Martin, with Gibson flying on his starboard side and slightly ahead to create a diversion. However, although the bomb was released, it veered off to the left even further than Gibson's before it exploded. Martin was followed by Young, whose bomb was dropped exactly as Wallis had intended and sank right in the middle of the dam wall. There was a tremendous explosion and a vast fountain of water, but the wall seemed to be intact. This left Maltby, Shannon, Maudslay and Knight from the First Wave, and it was the first of these who made the next bombing run, with both Gibson and Martin creating diversions for the German gunners. As Maltby approached he could see that the top of the dam was beginning to crumble, but as he was about to call off his attack, his bomb aimer released the UPKEEP. Once again the drop was accurately delivered, creating a huge explosion and tower of water. Several seconds elapsed before the circling aircraft saw that the top of the wall was indeed crumbling fast, creating a huge gap through which the pent-up waters of the lake began to pour. Within seconds what looked like a tidal wave began to pour down the valley.

Back at Grantham, Wallis was beginning to despair. 'Goner', the code word for a drop without a breach of the dam, had been received four times, from each of Gibson, Young, Martin and Maltby. Shortly after the last of these, at 0056 on the morning of 17 May, a new signal was received, this time from Gibson. Having sought and obtained confirmation, Dunn called out, 'Nigger', the code name for success. The tension broke immediately. Wallis pumped his arms up and down and was warmly congratulated by Ralph, whilst Harris shook his hand and told him that he hadn't believed a word he had said when they first met, but that now he could sell him a pink elephant!

CHASTISE, however, was far from over. Gibson immediately ordered Martin and Maltby to head for home, whilst he, with Young as his deputy and Shannon, Maudslay and Knight with their bombs still aboard, set off for the Eder. Unlike the Möhne, the Eder had no anti-aircraft defences, but it was far more difficult to attack. High hills surrounded the lake, requiring a sharp descent, whilst a very tight turn to port had to be made not long before the bombs were released, by which time the aircraft needed to be at

60ft. Shannon lost his way and had to be summoned by Gibson firing Very lights. He made the first run, which turned out to be unsatisfactory, followed by others. Maudslay also tried twice without success. Shannon was then sent in again and, after two more dummy runs, released his bomb, which blew up against the dam wall, albeit to the right of centre. No breach was detected, so Maudslay made a third attack. He eventually dropped his bomb, but it struck the top of the dam and exploded, doing no great harm to the structure, but almost certainly causing some damage to Maudslay's aircraft, which now lost radio contact. It was learnt later that Maudslay and his crew survived their experience at the Eder only to be shot down just short of the Dutch border near Emmerich.

This left Knight as the last as yet uncommitted member of the First Wave. Only minutes after Maudslay had disappeared from view, he began his first run. This proved to be unsatisfactory but, advised over the radio by Shannon, he tried again and this time he achieved a perfect approach and dropped his bomb, which bounced towards its target and settled by the dam wall. The resulting explosion blew a huge hole, through which the water rushed. The Eder had been breached, and 'Dinghy', the codeword for this event, was sent to Grantham, where it was jubilantly received. Harris rang Portal in Washington, who congratulated all those involved and promised to inform Churchill.

At much the same time as Maltby was carrying out his successful attack on the Möhne, McCarthy, flying the only remaining aircraft of the Second Wave, delivered his attack on the Sorpe. This required an entirely different approach from the other dams, due to the Sorpe's construction, consisting as it did of earthern banks on either side of a concrete core. Wallis believed that flying along the top of the dam rather that at right angles to it and dropping an UPKEEP right on its crest from a low height in such a way that it rolled down the reservoir side and exploded at the right depth, without using the revolving mechanism, would do the trick. After no fewer than nine dummy runs, McCarthy executed this perfectly and the bomb exploded, but apart from some crumbling along the top, there was no apparent damage. His mission complete, McCarthy turned for home.

Only a matter of minutes before Gibson delivered the first attack on the Möhne Dam, the Third Wave took off from Scampton, with Ottley in the lead, followed by Burpee, Brown, Townsend and Anderson. At the time they approached the Dutch coast, the Eder was still intact, so there was no question of recalling them. Burpee's aircraft was the first casualty; he lost his way close to the German night-fighter airfield at Gilze-Rijen, where the flak gunners were fully alert. Shot down at a very low level, there was no hope for the crew. The same fate befell Ottley and his crew, shot down by the formidable German anti-aircraft fire over the railway centre at Hamm, except that in this case one man miraculously survived. Sergeant Tees, the rear gunner, managed to escape from his turret and wandered off into the nearby woods, where he was taken prisoner by two members of the Hitler Youth.

This left Brown, Anderson and Townsend. The first two were directed by Group HQ to the Sorpe, which Brown found and attacked at 0315. Using the same approach as McCarthy and after the same number of dummy runs, he dropped his bomb on the crest of the dam, whose surface crumbled yet further, but with no sign of a clear breach. Anderson, however, whose compass was unreliable, failed to find the target and got completely lost. With his rear turret out of operation, he decided to abort and return to Scampton. Townsend was allocated Target E, the Ennepe Dam. Quite why he had been directed there is not known; it might have made more sense for him to drop yet another bomb on the Sorpe, where the damage inflicted by McCarthy and Brown might as a result have been enlarged sufficiently to create a breach. In any event, he encountered serious difficulty in locating the Ennepe and almost certainly attacked the Bever Dam, which was not even one of the other 'Last Resort Targets'. He had great difficulty in making his approach and only succeeded in dropping his bomb on the fourth attempt. It sank well short of the dam wall and no damage was incurred. This, the last attack of Operation CHASTISE, was made at 0337, after which Townsend headed for home, a long way behind his comrades.

The operation at an end, Harris, Wallis and Ralph left the Operations Room at Grantham and drove to Scampton. By the time that they arrived there, the surviving aircraft of the First and Second Waves were all back, Gibson himself only a short time earlier, so Harris and Ralph were able to attend his crew's debriefing. There had been one further casualty on the return journey in addition to Maudslay. 'Dinghy' Young's aircraft was brought down in the sea shortly after crossing the Dutch coast and it was third time unlucky for him; none of his crew survived. Harris and Ralph were out on the airfield to greet the three remaining crews, those of Anderson, Brown and Townsend, on their return, much to the surprise of some of the crew members.

The atmosphere at Scampton after the raid was one of exhilaration for most, with Whitworth inviting the pilots and some others to an impromptu party in his house, whilst the rest celebrated in the officers' mess with the help of a number of WAAFs roused from their beds. There was one exception, Wallis, who was in tears. He had been thrilled by the success achieved at the Möhne and Eder Dams, but his mood had changed considerably as he learnt of the loss of life. Eight aircraft out of nineteen had been brought down, 42 per cent of the total, an appalling statistic even by the standards of Bomber Command. Fifty-three young men had died.[1] Wallis seemed to be inconsolable and went to bed well ahead of the others.

The news of the operation was broken to the world later that day and made the headlines in the British press on 18 May. Congratulations to those involved poured in and, on the following day, Churchill referred to the raid in an address to a joint session of Congress in Washington. Ralph had returned to Grantham on the morning of 17 May, one of his first actions being to send written congratulations to Gibson:

> All ranks in 5 Group join me in congratulating you and all in 617 Squadron on a brilliantly conducted operation. The disaster which you have inflicted on the German war machine was a result of hard work, discipline and courage. The determination not to be beaten in the task and getting the bombs exactly on the aiming point in spite of opposition has set an example others will be proud to follow.

He also wrote a personal letter to Wallis, expressing admiration for his perseverance and determination and telling him that he had discussed his proposal for a big bomb with Harris, who was now keen to move ahead with trials. Following his 'pink elephant' comment, Harris had become a strong supporter of the inventor, which was to pay dividends later in the war. The AOC-in-C had also said that he would work towards getting him

Thomas Cochrane, 10th Earl of Dundonald, Ralph's great-grandfather and his most famous ancestor.

Ralph as a young boy, clearly already destined for the Royal Navy.

Crawford Priory, Ralph's birthplace in Fife and the seat of his father, the 1st Lord Cochrane of Cults.

Non-rigid Submarine Scout airships undertaking mooring trials.

The first trial of Rigid No. 9r at Barrow.

Semi-rigid SR.1 during trials in Italy.

The crew of SR.1 at Ciampino. Seated from left: Captain F. M. Rope, Captain George Meager, Ralph, Captain T. D. Williams.

Ralph with his future wife, Hilda Wiggin, on the River Nile at Aswan in late 1920 or early 1921.

The *St Nicholas*, chartered by Ralph and colleagues for a voyage from Egypt to Cyprus and back.

Vickers Vernons on the landing ground at Ziza in Transjordan.

Ralph at RAF Hinaidi near Baghdad.

Ralph's Ford, heavily loaded for his trip to Persia with Percy Maitland.

The Directing Staff and students at the RAF Staff College, Andover in the spring of 1926. Seated from left: Ralph (2), Robert Brook-Popham (4), Lord Trenchard (5), Christopher Courtney (6), Bertine Sutton (7). Second row from left: Robert Foster (8), Trafford Leigh-Mallory (9), Graham Donald (10), Douglas Evill (13), Guy Garrod (14), Walter Park (16)

Ralph (second left) as CO of 8 Squadron in Aden.

A Fairey IIIF at Mukalla.

Constructing a landing ground in the Aden Protectorate.

The Directing Staff and students at the Imperial Defence College in 1935. Seated from left: Richard O'Connor (2), Sholto Douglas (4), Robert Haining (5), Arthur Power (6). Second row from left: Robert Harvey (10). Back row from left: Arthur Percival (2), Ralph (3), Giffard Martel (6)

Ralph escorting Lord Galway, Governor-General of New Zealand, at an air display at Rongotai. (*Air Force Museum of New Zealand*)

Ralph in New Zealand with Wing Commander Leonard Isitt and other RNZAF officers. (*Air Force Museum of New Zealand*)

Air Chief Marshal Sir Arthur Harris, AOC-in-C of Bomber Command 1942–45.

The Royal visit to RAF Scampton on 27 May 1943, following the Dams Raid. Front row from left: Ralph (2), King George VI (3), Queen Elizabeth (4), Charles Whitworth (4), Guy Gibson (5). Barnes Wallis is in the second row, partially obscured by the King. Mick Martin stands behind and between the Queen and Whitworth, with David Maltby behind Whitworth and Richard Trevor-Roper of Gibson's crew behind Gibson.

Ralph escorts the Queen at Scampton with Wallis on the far right.

Gibson describes the Dams Raid to the King with the help of the models, with Ralph on the left and Whitworth on the right.

Senior USAAF officers in the UK visiting RAF Woodhall Spa on 31 March 1944. From left: Ralph, Unknown, Lieutenant General Carl Spaatz, Lieutenant General Jimmy Doolittle, Leonard Cheshire, Brigadier General Curtis LeMay.

Ralph with Harry Satterly, his Senior Air Staff Officer 1943–44.

Sir Archibald Sinclair with Willie Tait at Woodhall Spa on 15 November 1944, following the sinking of the *Tirpitz*.

Ralph, as AOC-in-C Transport Command, meeting Churchill on the Prime Minister's return from the Potsdam Conference, 25 July 1945.

Hilda presenting a prize at the WAAF Athletics Championships at RAF Uxbridge in the late 1940s.

One of Ralph's favourite pastimes – skiing in the Alps in 1951.

The 1st Lord Cochrane of Cults and his immediate family in 1950 – relationships to Ralph in brackets. Seated from left: Kitty Bruce, Countess of Elgin (sister), Michael Wemyss (great-nephew – son of Jean Wemyss), Lord Cochrane of Cults (father). Standing from left: Andrew, Lord Bruce (nephew – son of Kitty), Lady Jean Wemyss (niece – daughter of Kitty), Mary Cochrane (sister-in-law – Tom's second wife), Archie Cochrane (brother), Hilda, Dorothy Cochrane (sister-in-law – Archie's wife), Edward Bruce, Earl of Elgin (brother-in-law), Julian Cochrane (nephew – son of Tom), Tom Cochrane (brother), Lady Martha Bruce (niece – daughter of Kitty), Ralph, David Wemyss (husband of Jean Wemyss).

Ralph at a passing-out parade at RAF Halton, October 1949.

Ralph at Exercise Ariel with (left) Hugh Saunders, Air Member for Personnel, and (right) Arthur Tedder, CAS.

Ralph with Jack Slessor, CAS, and Wilf Curtis, CAS RCAF.

Ralph and Hilda at Grizel's wedding to Bobby Stewart, May 1953.

Ralph being welcomed by Air Vice-Marshal Cyril Kay, CAS RNZAF, on his arrival in New Zealand for the 21st Anniversary of the independent RNZAF in 1958.

Ralph representing Rolls-Royce at the Military Industrial Conference, Chicago in 1958, with Colonel Walker of the Industrial College of the Armed Forces, Brigadier General Vogel, Retired Chairman of the Tennessee Valley Authority, and Major Alexander De Seversky, Aeronautical Designer & Inventor.

Ralph, flanked by Leonard Cheshire and Willie Tait, is welcomed to Canada for the 617 Squadron Reunion, 1972.

Ralph shaking Molly Wallis by the hand at the dinner given by the 617 Squadron Association to celebrate Barnes Wallis's ninetieth birthday in September 1977. Wallis himself is receiving the congratulations of 'Bomber' Harris, whilst Leonard Cheshire stands behind Lady Wallis.

Sam Elworthy, Ralph's Senior Air Staff Officer in 1944–45 and in due course Chief of the Defence Staff, unveils the portrait of Ralph at the Museum of Transport and Technology in Wellington, New Zealand, October 1977.

Ralph and Hilda in 1975, with their immediate family (all Cochrane unless otherwise stated). Standing left to right: David Stewart, Catriona, Countess of Romney (Grizel's daughter), Julian, Earl of Romney (Grizel's son-in-law), Grizel Stewart, Malcolm with William, Mary, Bobby Stewart, John Stewart. Seated from left: John with Phoebe and Thomas, Ralph, Hilda, Margaret with Alexandra.

a knighthood, which he and many others thought he richly deserved. He did just that but, shamefully and due largely to the machinations of Wallis's enemies in high places and to jealous colleagues who had not yet been so honoured, this was not to be granted for another twenty-five years. Instead, he was awarded a CBE.

Ralph flew himself up to Scampton twenty-four hours later to express his thanks both to the aircrews, who were about to go on seven days leave, and to the ground crews, who were also given leave, but limited to three days. Gibson remained for the time being at Scampton, among other things, and with the help of Humphries, writing letters to the next of kin of those who had died.

In the meantime, Ralph and Whitworth were working on the decorations to be awarded. Thirty-four recommendations were made and accepted. The five commissioned pilots who had attacked one of the dams and survived to tell the tale, other than Gibson himself, were awarded the DSO, whilst the two non-commissioned pilots, Brown and Townsend, received the Conspicuous Gallantry Medal, which was much more rarely awarded and thus particularly highly prized.[2] Ten officers received the DFC, whilst four who had already received it, including Hay and Leggo, were awarded a bar. Eleven non-commissioned officers were awarded the Distinguished Flying Medal and one a bar. Every single member of Gibson's own crew was included in the awards, as were all the surviving navigators and bomb aimers of those aircraft which had bombed the dams. For some reason, no fewer than five members of Townsend's crew were decorated.

Gibson received the Victoria Cross for outstanding bravery. It was fully deserved. Gibson had led the squadron on an exceptionally dangerous and technically difficult mission with great skill and had shown cool-headed gallantry over the dams themselves, staying on the scene directing operations until both the Möhne and Eder had been destroyed and drawing the anti-aircraft fire from the Germans over the former to allow his pilots to have as clear a run at the target as possible. Harris had thought that he deserved the VC at the time of the award of a bar to his DSO and had now proved to be fully justified in his selection of Gibson to command 617 Squadron.

Ralph was keen that those on the ground should not be forgotten, and Commendations for Meritorious Service were awarded to Satterly,

Whitworth, Dunn, the Engineering and Armaments Officers at both 5 Group HQ and Scampton and five members of the ground crew at the latter. As the architect of both the unusual training regime and the successful operational plan, it might be thought that he should have received an award himself, but he would not have expected one. In any event, he had been made a Companion of the Order of the Bath in the relatively recent New Year's Honours, and further recognition was unlikely for the time being.

The investiture for most of those who were decorated took place at Buckingham Palace on 22 June and was followed by a riotous dinner at the Hungaria restaurant, also attended by Wallis, Whitworth, Summers, Chadwick and many others who had been involved. There was an even more significant expression of royal approval on 27 May, when the King and Queen visited Scampton.[3] Accompanied by Ralph, Whitworth and Gibson, they were introduced to all the crews, as well as to a number of other personnel, and shown both the models used for the pre-operation briefing and some reconnaissance photos of the damage which had been done to both the dams themselves and the areas downstream affected by the floods. The King was also asked to approve a squadron badge. Out of the two options placed before him he chose the one showing a broken dam with lightning bolts above and water pouring out below and the motto 'Après moi le déluge'. Wallis was also invited and attended.

Was Operation CHASTISE worthwhile? There have been many views expressed on this, some of which have concluded that it was not. The overall consensus has been that it did cause considerable, albeit temporary, disruption to the German war economy in a number of ways. The destruction of the Möhne Dam was a major short-term blow to industrial activity in the Ruhr. The power stations at the dams themselves were destroyed and a number downstream were flooded and put out of operation. Production of steel and coal were both adversely affected. Water supplies were significantly reduced over many months, necessitating rationing and again having an impact on industrial production. Flooding also had a significant impact on transport, with both road and rail bridges destroyed and railway lines left under water. Upwards of 1,300 people were killed, the vast majority by the breach of the Möhne, of whom by far the largest component were prisoners of war and forced labourers from Eastern Europe, many of them women.

Had the Sorpe Dam, of a completely different type of construction, also been breached, the damage would have been significantly increased, as it was second only to the Möhne in terms of the volume of water contained in its reservoir. UPKEEP, however, was not specifically designed to destroy it, and a different method of bombing was required. Although McCarthy and Brown dropped their bombs as instructed, they seem to have made little impact.

The effect of the destruction of the Eder Dam was less marked. The valley below it leading to the Weser was much less densely populated, and below Kassel there was a relatively modest impact on the river and the Mittelland Canal. Nevertheless, there was a similar interruption of water and electricity supplies, albeit to an area which in no way matched the Ruhr in its importance to German industry. Had the secondary target been one or more of the other Ruhr Valley gravity dams of much the same construction as the Möhne, including the Lister and Ennepe, this would have added to the damage there, although the capacity of their reservoirs was very much smaller than that of the Möhne.

One of the major adverse consequences for the Germans was an indirect one, the diversion of some 7,000 construction workers, mostly belonging to the Todt Organization, from their work on the Atlantic Wall to repairing the dams. The highly capable Albert Speer, Reich Minister of Armament and War Production, was deeply depressed by his initial visit to the area affected, but rapidly took control. The Möhne Dam was back in operation in September 1943, just in time to store water over the winter. The Eder Dam was ready at much the same time.

The raid had a positive effect on Great Britain's wartime reputation; indeed, it was widely admired not only in the United States, but also in the usually highly sceptical Soviet Union. The composition of the aircrews, with strong representation in particular from Australia and Canada, was much appreciated in the Commonwealth. At home morale was significantly boosted, as was the reputation of Bomber Command.

The conclusion must be that the raid was tactically worthwhile; indeed, it is difficult to imagine comparable damage being done at this stage of the war for the loss of eight aircraft and fifty-three men. However, it was certainly not a decisive stroke in the bombing campaign, let alone the war-winning operation conceived by Wallis, due entirely to the modest resources devoted to it. It was also incapable of being repeated.

Ralph's own contribution had been immense. He was the prime architect of the plan, whose conception and preparation was limited to only four individuals. This is all the more remarkable for having taken place during a period when Ralph himself and Satterly were also fully involved with other operations – the Battle of the Ruhr was at its height between 15 March and 17 May, with the rest of 5 Group fully committed to it – whilst Whitworth had a second active squadron to look after at Scampton and Gibson was diverted by visits to Weybridge, Reculver and London and also had to fit in low-flying training. Ralph himself provided the main link to Bomber Command and, alongside Wallis and Gibson, shared the heavy responsibility for the operation's success.

There was one significant bonus as a result. Ralph now had a force trained in precision bombing operations at low level and, with Harris's support, he was determined to make the most of it. However, No. 617 was only one of eleven squadrons in 5 Group, and huge demands were also being made on all the others.

Chapter 15

Time and Distance

Ralph's appointment as AOC 5 Group at the end of February 1943 came at a promising time for Bomber Command. During the previous month the British and American political and military leaders had met in Casablanca for one of the key conferences of the war. Out of this emerged the directive for the Combined Bomber Offensive, whereby Bomber Command and the US Eighth Air Force would mount a sustained campaign against Germany, the British by night and the Americans by day, the objective being 'the progressive destruction and dislocation of the German military, industrial, and economic system, and the undermining of the morale of the German people to a point where their capacity for armed resistance is fatally weakened'.[1]

The Combined Bomber Offensive was further formalized in the subsequent order for Operation POINTBLANK, which among other things, set out the target priorities. These were to be refined later, but were initially: (a) German submarine construction yards (b) the German aircraft industry (c) transportation (d) oil plants and (e) other targets in the enemy war industry. Whilst the Americans under Major General Ira Eaker, with whom Harris had established an excellent relationship, took this literally, Harris did not. His interpretation was that it gave him the authority to attack any German city with significant industrial activity, in the belief that doing so would not only destroy industrial facilities but also undermine the enemy's morale to the extent that they would no longer be able to continue the conflict. Although he was to use 617 Squadron to deliver precision attacks on certain small but highly important targets, this was not the case for the Main Force, which would continue with what was still effectively area bombing. Harris frequently expressed a strong antipathy to attacks on what he called 'panacea' targets such as synthetic oil installations or ball-bearing factories.

Harris's attention now became focused on the Ruhr, by some way the largest industrial area in Germany and known ironically in the RAF as 'Happy Valley'. As well as providing an abundance of targets, it was within the operational radius of Oboe, which was now carried in a number of Mosquitoes in 8 (Pathfinder) Group. These were employed in primary target marking as 'blind markers', dropping flares of a certain colour when Oboe indicated that they were over the target, and were followed by Lancasters acting as 'backers-up', dropping target indicators of a different colour aimed visually at the primary markers. In order to cater for the increasing demand for marker aircraft, Bennett received two further squadrons of Lancasters, one of which was No. 97 from 5 Group on 18 April. Three crews were left behind as the first element of 619 Squadron, which began forming at Woodhall Spa on the same day.

The Battle of the Ruhr, of which Operation CHASTISE may be seen as a part, began on the night of 5/6 March with a raid on Essen by 442 aircraft, including 140 from 5 Group. With considerable damage caused and a loss rate of 3.2 per cent, which was regarded as acceptable for this well-defended target, it was judged to have marked a successful start to what would be five months of intensive action. Essen was to remain a primary target throughout the battle, due to the numerous factories there operated by Krupp, Germany's largest armament company, with raids on the nights of 12/13 March and 3/4 April putting most of its facilities out of action. However, many other Ruhr towns were attacked, including Bochum, Dortmund, Duisburg, Düsseldorf, Gelsenkirchen, Krefeld and Wuppertal, as well as nearby Cologne, although raids on these were interspersed with other targets far from the Ruhr, including Munich, Nuremberg, Stuttgart and even Berlin.

In spite of his close involvement with Operation CHASTISE, Ralph had his finger firmly on the pulse of what was going on in the rest of the group. He was keen to try out alternative tactics whenever possible. In a raid on Dortmund on the night of 4/5 May, the largest in the war to date other than the three Thousand Bomber Raids in mid-1942, he specifically banned evasive action being taken in the run up to the target, with everything subordinated to accurate bombing, no matter what the apparent risk might be. Harris seized on this, pointing out to the other group commanders subsequently that 5 Group's losses had nevertheless been very modest. He cited the opinion of the Operational Research Section at Bomber Command HQ that evasive action was just as likely to attract flak as to avoid it and urged the AOCs to experiment with such an approach themselves, pointing out that vastly improved accuracy should result.

Ralph raised a number of questions about the accuracy of the Pathfinders' marking, one of which concerned an unsuccessful raid on the Škoda factory at Pilsen, well beyond Oboe range, on the night of 16/17 April. The factory itself was not hit, indeed only a tiny minority of aircraft bombed within three miles of it. Ralph's own interpretation of the photos was that many of the target indicators went down on a village seven miles south-west of the city. In a letter to Harris on 17 April he made two suggestions. One was that a Pathfinder squadron should be trained to specialize in low-level marking. He cited the example of the two Special Duties squadrons for which he had been responsible at 3 Group, which had managed to arrive at pinpoint targets in Poland without flying above 2,000ft, whilst 617 Squadron was currently being trained in low-level flying, with good results being achieved in terms of their navigation. Not only at this time, however, but throughout the war, Bennett remained strongly opposed to low-level marking, which he believed to be too dangerous, and nothing came of this suggestion, leaving Ralph in due course to develop it himself within 5 Group.

His other suggestion, made in the same letter, was that 'time-and-distance' bombing, which 3 Group had tried out with little success at Lorient earlier in the year, should be attempted again. This did not find favour immediately, but Ralph continued to advocate the tactic and Harris eventually sanctioned it for a raid on the Zeppelin factory at Friedrichshafen, memorably visited by Ralph back in 1930, on the night of 20/21 June. For this raid 5 Group provided fifty-six aircraft, drawn from all the squadrons in the group other than No. 617 and joined by four Pathfinder aircraft from 97 Squadron. A number of crews were detailed to bomb on the Pathfinders' target indicators, whilst the remainder would use the time-and-distance method. It was decided that the bombers should not return to their airfields in England, but instead fly on over the Alps and Italy to North Africa, now wholly occupied by the Allies.

There was another major innovation in this raid, the employment of a Master Bomber. Gibson had effectively invented the role over the Möhne and Eder Dams, but that was at the time seen as a one-off requirement. Now a single officer, Group Captain L. C. Slee, the station commander at Dunholme Lodge but previously the CO of 49 Squadron in the low-level attack on Le Creusot, was given the overall leadership of the raid, with Wing Commander C. L. Gomm, the CO of 467 Squadron, as his deputy. The aircraft were equipped with VHF sets as used by 617 Squadron for the Dams Raid.

The Lancasters of Operation BELLICOSE flew out over the English Channel and then crossed France, thereby avoiding the heavy flak and night-fighter concentrations to be found over the Netherlands and Germany, before turning east near Orleans to cross the Rhine and the Black Forest to Lake Constance. There was, however, some anti-aircraft fire encountered crossing the French coast, and it may have been this which caused a problem to one of the engines of the 49 Squadron Lancaster in which Slee was travelling in the flight engineer's seat. He was accordingly forced to hand over the Master Bomber role to Gomm.

On arrival over the lake, the 97 Squadron 'Illuminators' released their flares over the Zeppelin shed. The defences were heavy, so Gomm ordered the force to climb another 5,000ft, which required them to begin circling the target and thus delay their attack. When Gomm established which of the target indicators were closest to the factory he called in the first wave to attack, following which the Pathfinders re-illuminated the target. Gomm then gave the order to the time-and-distance bombers to begin their run, starting from an easily identified landmark, also illuminated by the Pathfinders, on the shore of the lake. At a precise number of seconds after this, the bombs were released and, although not all crews were able to achieve a good result, due to lack of practice, most dropped their bombs on target. Photo reconnaissance on the next day showed considerable damage to the Zeppelin factory and two others close by. Although nobody on the Allied side knew it at the time, part of the complex was manufacturing major components for the V-2 rocket, production of which was compelled to move elsewhere.

Disappointing any German night fighters lying in wait for their return, the Lancasters then turned south to cross over Switzerland, Italy and the Western Mediterranean and land at airfields at Blida and Maison Blanche near Algiers, where it was found that there had been no losses at all. The facilities for repairs and maintenance, especially at Maison Blanche, a USAAF airfield, were far from ideal, but after some improvisation and some welcome relaxation for the crews, most of the aircraft were fit to fly back to England on the night of 23/24 June, bombing La Spezia on the way.

Following the completion of Operation CHASTISE in mid-May, Ralph had more time to consider a number of other issues. He was not a great admirer of conventional wisdom on any subject, and there were many aspects of running a group which he thought could do with improvement. He was open to new ideas from anyone and even provoked them himself. Sam Elworthy, who had become the station commander at Waddington, was called to see him at St Vincent's one day, to find to his horror that Ralph wanted him to write an appreciation of the USAAF raid on Ploesti in Romania. Elworthy protested that he was quite untrained in staff work, only to be ordered to get on with it. He later realized that Ralph was just testing him to see if he had any ideas of his own.

Ralph brought a number of concerns with him from 3 Group, where he had not had the time to address them. One of the most important of these related to the status of the pilot of the aircraft. By convention this crew member was considered to be the captain and was often called 'Skipper' by his crew, but he was sometimes of a lower rank than one or more of the others. This problem became particularly acute when the pilot was a flight sergeant or sergeant and another crew member was a commissioned officer, not least because, in their time off operations, they were members of different messes. Ralph insisted on the maintenance of the captain's authority at all times and, later in the war, used specially equipped aircraft to monitor intercom exchanges over the target, something which was not popular with the crews for understandable reasons.

A related issue which Ralph had encountered at 3 Group was an unhealthy regard for democracy, particularly when all the crew members were NCOs, with the captain allowing votes to be taken on aborting an operation if mechanical or other difficulties were encountered en route to a target. Like all his fellow AOCs and the station commanders, Ralph wanted to keep 'early returns' as low as possible and came down hard on those considered unnecessary, with some pilots even being sent for court martial and a small number dismissed the service.

Ralph believed that the decision from on high on whether or not a pilot should be commissioned was based not so much on his ability to fly on operations as on what were known as 'officer-like qualities', very often a matter of education or even of accent, particularly when it came to the British. The problem was often compounded by poor morale, always a big problem when losses were high and when every crew knew that their chances of completing thirty operations were low. In order to enhance the captain's authority, which Ralph also believed would improve morale, he introduced two new measures. The first was that all captains in 5 Group, if not commissioned already, should be so on joining their squadrons. The second was that the captain should be responsible for the operational briefing of his crew. As he wrote later:

> The standard briefing procedure in the command was for all crews to be brought into a large room where they were told the target and given any special instructions by the squadron commander and his specialist officers. This was changed to two sessions. In the first the Squadron Commanders briefed the Captains, whilst the navigation, bombing and gunnery specialists briefed the members of the crews. In the second session each crew had a table in the main briefing hall at which the captain sat at the head and discussed the raid with his crew. I believe this system helped those captains, who were often a bit younger than their crew members, to gain confidence in their ability to command.[2]

These changes took some time to implement, but Ralph continued to hammer home the concept of leadership in talks he gave to the captains whenever he visited their stations.

Ralph was also very concerned about training at the HCUs, particularly when he was ordered to release twelve Lancasters from them to boost the numbers in operational squadrons. He reminded Harris that the AOC-in-C had asked him to look very specifically at training when he took over the group. The conclusion he had reached was that crews had been leaving the HCUs quite unpractised in any tactics other than violent evasive action, and he had subsequently ensured that proper tactics were first conceived and then taught in the syllabus. Notwithstanding that the bare minimum of time was available for such instruction, there had subsequently been a significant drop in the percentage of aircrew lost on their first five sorties.

Ralph made the point that if such training was halted in the HCUs due to the lack of aircraft, the crews would have to rely on such time as was available for it in their operational squadrons and on experience, which he thought was unsatisfactory. Withdrawing Lancasters from the HCUs was more likely, in his opinion, to lead to a reduction in operational efficiency than to an increase. He asked for six months to demonstrate better results, which he was granted. The Lancasters remained in the HCUs.

Ralph was equally concerned about lax flying standards in operational squadrons. He selected Flight Lieutenant P. D. Bird, a former flying instructor, to undertake a review. Bird was given as much petrol as he required and ordered to visit every squadron in the group, accompanied by a flight engineer, and to select crews who had completed ten and twenty operations. He would fly with them, in daylight and not on an operation, to see how they reacted to certain problems, such as the sudden loss of an engine shortly after take-off. He would then write a report for Ralph. This was understandably unpopular with squadron commanders and crews, but it resulted in much improved flying standards. As a reward, Bird was promoted to squadron leader and made a flight commander in the squadron of his choice.

In the meantime, the Battle of the Ruhr ran its course, effectively coming to an end in late July. It was judged a success at the time and was later found to have caused a significant drop in steel production and, even more pertinently, in aircraft manufacture, which stalled between July 1943 and March 1944 and was to have a significant impact on both the campaign in Russia and those by the Western Allies in Italy and, in due course, in North-West Europe. Locomotive production, vital for Germany's supply chain, ceased completely for some time at Krupp.

Four raids now took place on Hamburg, Germany's second city after Berlin. It was just beyond Oboe range, but natural features, not least the River Elbe, made it ideal for H2S. The first of these raids, on the night of 24/25 July, also saw the first use of Window, aluminium-backed paper cut into strips and dumped from aircraft, confusing the German radar used for anti-aircraft guns and searchlights, and for night-fighter ground control and airborne interception. This so baffled the defence that only 1.5 per cent of the force was lost, although the results of bombing were relatively modest. The second raid, three nights later, was devastating. The ground temperature was high and there had been no rain for a long time, so the buildings were tinder-dry. The target marking was accurate, as was the bombing, and incendiaries started a firestorm, which caused huge damage and by far the largest number of casualties on the ground in the war to that date. Elworthy, flying in a Lancaster of 9 Squadron, could smell the smoke at a height of 20,000ft. Two more raids over the next few days completed the effective destruction of the city.

Harris now turned to other German cities, but one special raid on the night of 17/18 August allowed 5 Group to employ time-and-distance bombing once again. In the aftermath of the Friedrichshafen raid, the group had been practising at Wainfleet, using well chosen landmarks as the starting points for their runs, and had succeeded in reducing the bombing error to no more than 300 yards. The new target was the German manufacturing and testing facility at Peenemünde on the Baltic coast, which intelligence had revealed was engaged in bringing to fruition Hitler's secret weapons, the V-1 flying bomb and the V-2 long-range ballistic missile. The buildings were widely dispersed, with large empty spaces between them, making it a much more difficult target than Friedrichshafen, but this time all the groups of Bomber Command were involved, providing ten times the number of aircraft, whilst a Master Bomber, Group Captain J. H. Searby of 8 Group, was to control the raid for the first time in a Main Force operation.

The attackers initially followed the route taken frequently for attacks on Berlin, which helped to deceive the defenders, at least initially, as night fighters were deployed to protect the capital. Moreover, eight Mosquitoes were despatched to Berlin to drop markers on the city and thereby bolster the deception. The Pathfinders at Peenemünde laid the initial markers for the first wave of bombers from 3 and 4 Groups, with a view to placing them on the housing estate where the scientists and other key personnel were living. However, most fell on another part of the complex, which housed largely Polish forced-labour workers, among whom there were considerable casualties.

The second wave consisted of 1 Group aircraft attacking the main V-2 works. A number of the markers were misplaced, but Searby was able to correct the attack, which succeeded in destroying a rocket store. The third wave, consisting of 61 aircraft from 6 (Canadian) Group bombing on pre-agreed markers and 117 from 5 Group employing the time-and-distance technique, arrived over the target area between 30 and 60 minutes after the first wave; 5 Group used the island of Rügen as its landmark from which to start the timed run, with instructions to bomb green target indicators close by when the time had elapsed or, if there were none, to release their bombs at that point. The Master Bomber circled over the area throughout, correcting aircraft when necessary. A subsequent analysis of the results showed that those bombers which had dropped blind at the end of the timed run, because the markers were obscured by smoke, were, in fact, far more accurate than those who had bombed the nearest visible marker. Further study showed that the markers had overshot the aiming point by 300 yards initially and by as much as 3,000 yards in the final stages of the raid.

The raid was considered to have been a success. It was later believed that the V-2 programme had been delayed by anything from four to eight weeks, with production having to be moved to the Harz Mountains and testing to Poland, whilst a small number of key scientists had been killed. Since Poland was out of range of the bombers and the new factory was deep underground, this made them effectively immune to attack in the future, and it would be only when the weapons were deployed at their launch sites in the following year that Bomber Command, and particularly 5 Group, would have another chance to deal with them.

For 5 Group this turned out to be an expensive night. Whereas the first wave had been the beneficiary of the deception scheme and got off very lightly, by the time that 5 Group's aircraft turned for home, the night fighters were fully alerted and the group lost 17 aircraft out of the 117 despatched, 14.5 per cent, against 6.7 per cent for the total force. It was no comfort that the losses in 6 Group had been proportionately even higher. On the other hand, it confirmed to Ralph that time-and-distance was now the most accurate method of bombing available, although he accepted that it could only be used on the relatively rare occasions when there was a distinctive feature from which to start, and that the crews who would use it required considerable training.

Chapter 16

Cheshire

On 17 April 1943, just under a month after Gibson first met Ralph regarding Chastise and exactly a month before the breaching of the Möhne and Eder Dams, a memo arrived at St Vincent's from the Senior Air Staff Officer at Bomber Command HQ. It was headed 'The Policy regarding the operational role of No. 617 Squadron' and read as follows:

1. The above Squadron was formed in order to perform a special operation which entailed using new equipment of a most secret nature. When this commitment has been completed this squadron will not revert to normal bombing operations but will retain its identity as a Special Duty Squadron under the operational control of A.O.C. 5 Group.
2. The duties of this Squadron will be laid down from time to time by this Headquarters. These duties will consist of performing operations that entail special training and/or the use of specialist equipment. It is not thought likely that this Squadron will ever be called upon to take part in sustained operations.
3. The aircrew personnel for this Squadron should, as far as possible, be recruited from within the Group. As the work is not expected to be arduous full use should be made of crews who have completed two operational tours and who apply to take part in further operations. It is not intended that the crews at present in this Squadron should be moved, but the future policy should ensure that a high percentage of the aircrew personnel are time expired experienced crews that need a rest from normal operations but are capable of performing special tasks that may be allotted to this Squadron.[1]

Having been initially highly sceptical about the Dams Raid, Harris was, as usual, not only making the best of things, but looking to the future. If a squadron had been highly trained in low flying, night-time cross-country navigation and a method of bombing which was, to say the least, unusual, he was not going to squander it by returning it to normal duties. He was sure that he would have a number of uses in the future for such an unusual unit, and he was subsequently proved to be correct.

Ralph was concerned, he was delighted to be given the opportunity to break the mould where bombing was concerned and he relished the independence that this would give him, at least as far as a small part of his group was concerned. As he wrote later, 'Whereas main force attacks were laid on from command H.Q., I had complete freedom regarding the tactics of 617 Squadron and their subsequent adoption to the Group as a whole.'[2]

All the pilots who had returned from Operation CHASTISE, with one exception, remained in the squadron, together with Divall and Wilson, who had been left behind due to illness. The exception was Cyril Anderson, whom Gibson, dissatisfied with his reasons for returning from the raid without attacking one of the dams, had posted back to 49 Squadron.[3] In the other direction came Flight Lieutenant Ralf Allsebrook DSO, DFC, who had completed the best part of two tours with 49 Squadron, the first on Hampdens. With the loss of the two flight commanders, he effectively became one of them, with Maltby, promoted to squadron leader, as the other. Allsebrook was followed into the squadron by two other experienced pilots, Flight Lieutenant W. H. Kellaway DSO and Pilot Officer 'Bunny' Clayton DSO, CGM, at the beginning of July.

Ralph was nevertheless experiencing great difficulty replacing all the losses. He wrote to Harris on 2 June to say that he envisaged the squadron remaining at its existing strength for some time, with there being little possibility as a result to undertake any training in high-altitude precision bombing, and suggesting that he might take another existing squadron in the group and train them accordingly. Harris remained sanguine, writing to the AOCs of all groups on the following day:

> I feel confident that the importance and interest attached to work of this type will make a greater appeal to any experienced aircrews than any of the alternative forms of employment open to those who have completed their second tour, and have no doubt that if the proposition is put to them, there will be no shortage of applicants.[4]

Gibson remained in the squadron for six weeks after CHASTISE and later joined the Prime Minister on his visit to Canada for the Quadrant Conference with the Americans. His relief was Wing Commander George Holden DSO, DFC and Bar, who, notwithstanding Bomber Command's edict that aircrew should come whenever possible from within 5 Group, came instead from 4 Group. It turned out subsequently that he was establishing a precedent, the next three COs also being posted in after serving in 4 Group.

Holden had begun his operational career in September 1940 flying Whitleys in 78 Squadron. After twenty operations, one of which involved the dropping of a paratroop unit in Operation COLOSSUS, the demolition of the Tragino Aqueduct in Italy,[5] he transferred early in the following year to 35 Squadron, which was just converting onto Halifaxes. Having completed his first tour he went through a typical period of training pilots at a HCU, before commanding the conversion flights of first 405 and then 158 Squadron. In October 1943 he took over as CO of 102 Squadron, but stood down in the following April until his posting to 617 Squadron on 2 July 1943, where he inherited most of Gibson's crew.[6]

The first post-CHASTISE operation for 617 Squadron took place on 15 July, two weeks after Holden's arrival. Two separate flights under Holden and Maltby attacked the electrical transformer and switching stations at Aquata Scrivia and San Polo d'Enza in North-West Italy at between 800 and 1,600ft. The attacks were modestly successful, and the aircraft, emulating those on the Friedrichshafen raid, flew on to Blida in Algeria. A second visit to Italy, at the time deemed ripe for capitulation in the aftermath of the invasion of Sicily, followed on 29 July, with three crews dropping leaflets on Milan and two each on Bologna, Turn and Genoa, once more returning after a brief stay at Blida.

These operations provided some much needed action for 617 Squadron, but they were otherwise hardly worthy of such a specialized unit. Other minds, however, were at work on alternatives. Much of the focus was on the further employment of UPKEEP, to which end Ralph attended a meeting on 8 June at the Air Ministry. It was chaired by Bottomley, whilst Wallis was among the attendees. Among other matters it was reported that trials of the weapon had taken place on land and had been perfectly satisfactory. The major targets under consideration for either this type of attack, or the one over water which had proved so successful in CHASTISE, were all inland waterways, respectively the Rothensee Ship Lift, the Dortmund–Ems Canal and the Mittelland Canal. As far as the first of these was concerned, Wallis thought that it was more suitable for HIGHBALL, but it was agreed that 4,000lb bombs should also be considered. Ralph also requested that the possibilities of the new 'deep penetration' bomb being designed by Wallis should be investigated, and Wallis agreed to produce details of its likely effect. In the meantime, Ralph suggested that the 12,000lb High Capacity bomb already available might be used instead of UPKEEP, although trials would be necessary to ensure that it could be used at a low altitude on a canal. In a letter to Harris on the next day he gave his opinion that such an operation should be both feasible and successful.

Over the next two months a number of trials were carried out, the result of which was that 617 Squadron was detailed to attack the Dortmund–Ems Canal on the night of 14/15 September. The canal was a key artery for German industry, carrying war materiel in barges for 167 miles from the heart of the Ruhr to the port of Emden. It had already attracted the attention of 5 Group on the night of 20/21 August 1940, when Squadron Leader Learoyd had won Bomber Command's first VC.

As suggested by Ralph, the weapon to be used was not UPKEEP, but the 12,000lb HC bomb, the largest employed by the RAF at the time. It had considerable destructive power which, when the bomb was dropped into the canal where it ran along an embankment and across the River Glane on two aqueducts, was expected to breach it in such a way that the water would drain out, stranding the barges which used it. The bomb, however, had poor aerodynamic qualities, which meant that it would have to be dropped at low level to ensure accuracy.

Eight crews were detailed for the operation, flying in two sections, the first led by Holden with Knight, Maltby and Wilson, the second by Allsebrook, with Divall, Rice and Shannon. Each of the aircraft carried three gunners rather than the usual two, with the front turret permanently manned. They flew out from the squadron's new station, Coningsby, whither they had moved on 30 August as Scampton had been closed to have hard runways laid. Whilst still over the North Sea the aircraft were recalled, following a report from a weather Mosquito that conditions over the target were poor.

Turning his Lancaster round at low level, Maltby crashed into the sea, but although Shannon remained over the site of the accident to direct the air-sea rescue operation, the entire crew was lost.

The operation was rescheduled for the following night, with Martin replacing Maltby in the first section. It turned out to be a major disaster. Having crossed the Dutch border into German airspace, Holden increased height to avoid a church steeple, only to attract light anti-aircraft fire which hit one of his fuel tanks, causing a fatal explosion and the death of all aboard, including Holden himself and four former members of Gibson's crew. Martin took over as the leader of Holden's section, whilst Allsebrook assumed overall command of the operation. The weather now deteriorated, with mist obscuring the ground for the rest of the way to the target. Beacons and flares were dropped, but disappeared from view under the blanket. The next aircraft to crash was Wilson's, once again hit by flak. Knight flew so low that his two port engines ingested large amounts of foliage and had to be shut down. He received permission to jettison his bomb and turned for home, but there was little chance of his crossing the North Sea, so he ordered his crew to bale out, whilst holding the aircraft as steady as he could. All of them parachuted to safety, but he lost control and died when the aircraft hit the ground. Two of the crew were taken prisoner, but the rest managed to evade the Germans and get back to England via the Resistance network.

Allsebrook was the next to succumb to flak, followed by Divall. Shannon managed to drop his bomb over the canal due to a break in the mist, but it exploded on the towpath and failed to cause any breach in the embankment. Rice, who was quite unable to locate the target, was given permission by Martin to head for home, dropping his bomb in the sea on the way. Martin himself stayed on the scene for another forty minutes, in due course getting a better run at the canal, but the bomb dropped in the water without creating any damage. He arrived back to find Ralph at Coningsby, where he pleaded to be allowed to try again the following night. He was refused, but made flight commander on the spot. Shortly afterwards he was promoted to acting squadron leader and given temporary command of 617 Squadron.

This was unquestionably No. 617's darkest hour. To many it looked like a suicide squadron and, as Ralph was later to write, 'It would be hardly true to say that volunteers were queuing up for admission.'[7] On the basis that if one falls off a horse the best remedy is to get on again immediately, the six crews which had not been involved in the Dortmund–Ems Canal raid were sent to bomb the Antheor Viaduct in the South of France on the following night. The viaduct itself was undamaged, but subsequent reconnaissance showed that there were a number of near misses, which provided some encouragement. Ralph wrote to Harris on the next day regarding the future of the squadron. He was now thinking in a new direction, bearing in mind both the capability of the aircrews and the *esprit de corps* which he strongly believed still existed:

> I therefore strongly recommend that No. 617 should continue its existence as a special precision bombing squadron concentrating mainly on extremely accurate high level attacks using the Mark IIA S.A.B.S. Now that we are over-stocked with crews [he was referring here to the group, not the squadron], I suggest that I might draw some of its new material from crews who are completing their normal tour. If the few remaining members of the original Squadron can communicate their spirit to the newcomers, the unit will pay a high dividend in terms of results achieved even though the weight of its bombs may be somewhat below that of its fellow Squadrons.[8]

Harris did not reply until 1 October, but when he did it was to accept Ralph's proposals:

> I am anxious to keep in being a unit for which special training and equipment are required. This is the purpose for which No. 617 Squadron was formed, and I want to keep it going ...
> I think that a very good form of training on which you can safely concentrate is the achievement of a very high standard of accuracy with the S.A.B.S Mark IIA sight.[9]

Although it was unsaid, it was likely that both men had in mind Wallis's new 'big bomb', the employment of which Harris had effectively agreed to in the aftermath of CHASTISE, but which had yet to be produced. It was known, however, that this would be a deep penetration bomb, which would achieve its purpose not by explosion when it hit the ground but through shock waves when it detonated deep beneath the surface after being dropped from a great height. This would require a much greater degree of accuracy than achieved hitherto, and the choice of bomb sight was thus critical to Ralph's plan.

Since the Great War the RAF had used various versions of the Course Setting Bomb Sight and entered the Second World War with the Mark IX. This was a vector sight, which required data to be fed into it on the aircraft's speed and altitude, the flight characteristics of the bomb carried and, most importantly, the wind. By mid-1942 the most recent model, the Mark XIV, had been introduced, initially with the Pathfinder squadrons and later with the rest of Bomber Command. It had a higher degree of automation and was simpler to use. It also allowed evasive action to be taken right up to the point of release of the bombs and was very acceptable for area bombing, remaining in service until well beyond the end of the war

The Mark II Stabilised Automatic Bomb Sight, on the other hand, was a tachometric sight, which was superbly accurate but required a straight and level approach to the target. It still demanded the input of key information and required considerable practice by bomb aimers, but it was capable of an average error of 80 yards from a height of 20,000ft, and many crews regularly achieved half that or less. It was to be the critical tool in high-level precision bombing, restricted in its use to 617 Squadron. Ralph was keen to try out the sight for himself:

> On one occasion getting Martin to take me up on my first use of the sight I scored 38 yards average of 8 bombs from different directions. This shook the Squadron but they did not know how much bombing practice I had in 45 and 8 Squadrons.[10]

Training on SABS became the priority throughout October 1943 and continued thereafter. More new crews were posted in and, on 11 November, Martin was able to assemble eleven of them for a new attack on the Antheor Viaduct, although Shannon encountered an engine problem on take-off and was forced to abort. The raid was as unsuccessful as its predecessor, with many of the aircraft bombing the wrong bay, whilst those that dropped their bombs in the right place were unable to get close enough to do significant damage. The crews flew on to Blida, but on the flight back one of them was lost over the Bay of Biscay.

They returned to a new commanding officer. Leonard Cheshire DSO and Bar, DFC had learnt to fly in the Oxford University Air Squadron and was commissioned into the RAFVR in November 1937. He obtained a permanent commission in the RAF in October 1940 and underwent training before joining 102 Squadron in 4 Group in June 1940, initially as the second pilot in a Whitley and then, after ten operations, as the captain. He won his first DSO for an attack on marshalling yards near Cologne. His plane was very badly damaged on his first run and caught fire, but he recovered control, the fire was put out by members of the crew and he delivered his bomb load accurately before getting the damaged aircraft back to England.

When his first tour was completed in January 1941, Cheshire volunteered to continue operations and was posted to 35 Squadron, where Holden was one of his fellow pilots. The squadron was in the process of converting to Halifaxes, but Cheshire was unable to complete a tour before the aircraft were withdrawn from service for urgent modifications. Whilst waiting to return to operations he obtained a temporary posting to the Atlantic Ferry Organization, which was responsible for flying new American-built aircraft to the UK. During his stay in the USA he met Constance Binney, an American actress, whom he married three weeks later. In due course he flew a new Lockheed Hudson back to the UK, thereafter rejoining 35 Squadron and completing his tour. Cheshire was then posted to 1652 Heavy Conversion Unit at RAF Marston Moor, but still managed to fly on two of the three Thousand Bomber Raids as well as on a number of other operations, on one of which his younger brother, Christopher, was also flying and was shot down, becoming a PoW for the rest of the war. Whilst at the HCU Cheshire found time to write a book on his experiences, which was published as *Bomber Pilot* in early 1943.

In August 1942 Cheshire was promoted to acting wing commander and appointed CO of 76 Squadron at RAF Linton-on-Ouse, once again in 4 Group and once again flying Halifaxes. The squadron was in the process of re-forming after heavy losses, which had led to poor morale. Cheshire addressed this both through personal example, flying on operations himself at every opportunity, and through force of character, helped by learning the names of every man in his squadron, including the ground crew, whose importance he frequently emphasised to them. He discovered that the morale problem was largely down to the Halifax's inability to fly as high as the Lancasters of other groups, so he had their weight reduced by ordering the shedding of what he considered to be unnecessary bits of equipment or aircraft fabric, improving both ceiling and speed. Losses fell and morale rose.

Cheshire's tour at 76 Squadron came to an end in April 1943, recognized by a bar to his DSO. He was promoted to acting group captain, at the age of twenty-five the youngest in the RAF's history, and appointed station commander at Marston Moor, where the only unit was 1652 HCU, which he knew all too well. He had, by this time, persuaded the authorities to allow his wife to join him, and the two of them lived there in a converted railway carriage, the station commander's house being excessively damp. Cheshire immediately lobbied for a return to active operations, but without initial success. He then met Bennett and requested a transfer to 8 Group, where the rank of group captain was held by all squadron commanders, but was refused. He next approached Charles Whitworth, who had been one of his instructors at the University Air Squadron, about the possibility of relieving Gibson at 617 Squadron, but was told that Holden had already been appointed as Gibson's successor. After Holden's death, however, when Ralph consulted his fellow AOCs about a replacement, Roderick Carr at 4 Group suggested Cheshire, who was invited to an interview and offered the job, albeit with a reduction in rank back to wing commander. He accepted with alacrity, only to be told that he would now have to attend a course at the Lancaster Finishing School. With three tours on operations and one as an instructor behind him, he raised an objection to this, but was told by Ralph to get on with it. He later realized that it probably saved his life.

Cheshire did not find immediate favour at 617 Squadron, especially amongst the CHASTISE veterans. He was quite different in character to Gibson, who radiated energy and enthusiasm, whereas Cheshire, whilst friendly to all and notably to the ground crews, was more thoughtful and quietly spoken. It did not help that the aircrews were getting fed up with endless bombing practice and with little immediate opportunity to put their new found skills to the test.

There was, indeed, a pause in operations after the second Antheor raid, broken only, to Cheshire's displeasure, by the attachment of four of his aircraft and their crews to 138 Squadron at Tempsford to carry out drops to the French Resistance. Two were lost to flak on 9/10 December and, although they were replaced for a second attempt twelve days later, neither operation was successful. Just over a month after Cheshire's arrival, however, he led three operations over six days which were a more suitable use of his crews, directed as they were onto a new type of strategic target which was causing a great deal of concern in the corridors of power.

The Peenemünde raid had put back the design and production of Hitler's 'secret weapons', but only for a relatively short time, during which the Germans had relocated the production and testing facilities. Now, for the first time, intelligence had identified a number of sites in North-West France which were to serve as launch pads for the V-1 flying bomb. Cheshire led the first raid of a long campaign, known as Operation CROSSBOW, on a site at Flixecourt, near Abbeville, on the night of 16/17 December. The nine Lancasters were preceded by a single Oboe Mosquito, but it dropped its markers 350 yards from the target. The 12,000lb bombs were well grouped around the markers, indeed none was more than 100 yards away, but the target itself was untouched. In a raid by twenty-six Stirlings on the same day on a second CROSSBOW target, the same thing happened.

Four nights later, Cheshire led another raid, this time on an armaments factory near Liège, but the markers could not be seen through cloud and all the aircraft except two returned with their loads. One of the Lancasters jettisoned its bombs over the rough position of the target, whilst another, piloted by Geoff Rice, who was by that time one of a dwindling number of CHASTISE survivors,[11] was shot down. Rice himself was the only man to parachute to safety, going on the run for five months before being picked up and then incarcerated by the Germans. Cheshire led another CROSSBOW raid to Abbeville on the night of 20/21 December, but once again the markers were invisible. The last operation of 1943, a return to Flixecourt on 29/30 December, this time led by Squadron Leader W. R. Suggitt DFC, an RCAF officer from 6 Group who had arrived at the end of October to join Martin as the second flight commander, was no more successful than the last one, due once again to inaccurate marking by the three Oboe Mosquitoes from 8 Group.

The year 1944 began for 617 Squadron with a move from Coningsby to Woodhall Spa, only a few miles away, where it would remain for the rest of the war. The officers' mess was located in the comfortable Petwood Hotel, which boasted extensive grounds and became a home from home and, on occasion, the venue for some uproarious parties.

It was clear to both Ralph and Cheshire that much more accurate marking was to be required in the New Year if 617 Squadron was to achieve the potential promised by its bomb sights. It was to discuss the best way of achieving this, in the specific context of an attack on the Rothensee Ship Lift, that Ralph, Cheshire and Bennett attended a meeting at High Wycombe on 18 January. Saundby was in the chair and the other participants from Bomber Command HQ were Air Vice-Marshal R. D. Oxland, the SASO, and Group Captain N. W. D. Marwood-Elton, the Group Captain Plans. The bomb to be used was Wallis's new TALLBOY, whose genesis went back to 'A Note on a Method of Attacking the Axis Powers' in 1941, which had led ultimately to UPKEEP and the Dams Raid.

TALLBOY was produced in three sizes, Large, Medium and Small, but the last of these was a development weapon not intended for operational use, and it was the employment of the medium-sized bomb of 12,000lbs which was considered at the meeting. Two target-marking alternatives were discussed. The first was the 'Newhaven' method, whereby Pathfinder Mosquitoes would use Oboe for ground marking or H2S for sky marking, and a Master Bomber flying at 6,000 to 8,000ft would identify the target visually, drop a line of markers across the target and direct the bombing force in by VHF. The alternative was to illuminate the target by flares dropped by the marker aircraft, each individual bomb aimer then being responsible for visual identification of the target. After discussion, it was agreed that the 'Newhaven' method would be used. Marwood-Elton raised the possibility of using rocket projectiles, but no decision was made on these. It was also agreed that Ralph would decide the date of the operation, and he asked that it should come under cover of a Main Force attack. Bennett agreed to commit eight to twelve marker aircraft, whilst Marwood-Elton said that Mosquitoes would be laid on to provide protection for the Lancasters.

What the minutes did not record was an argument between Ralph and Bennett, the former pointing to 8 Group's inadequacy in marking thus far, whilst the latter queried 617 Squadron's capabilities. Cheshire also waded into the discussion by advocating low-level marking, which Bennett dismissed as both impractical and too dangerous. The relationship between Ralph and Bennett, which had been at least civil whilst Ralph was at 3 Group and during his early days at 5 Group, was now deteriorating fast, with Bennett quick to point out Ralph's lack of recent operational experience, something the latter shared with every group commander except Bennett himself and a few younger men appointed by Harris towards the end of the war.

The first use of TALLBOY was, in the event, not to take place for nearly five months, but in the meantime, 617 Squadron was well employed, carrying out three attacks on CROSSBOW sites during January 1944, the second of which was moderately successful. Cheshire and Ralph, however, were both now highly sceptical of the value of 8 Group's Mosquitoes to their operations and were keen to try out a new low-level marking technique, which Cheshire and Martin had been practising in a Lancaster. The opportunity emerged on the night of 8/9 February. Cheshire later recalled Ralph's orders:

> You've got one chance. Just one and you stand or fall by it. The target is the Gnome-Rhône aero-engine factory at Limoges. But it is in a built-up area, and there are 500 girls on night shift. You are to destroy the factory, but not take a single life inside it or outside. That's a direct instruction from the War Cabinet. If you fail, you'll never get another chance; but if you succeed ... well, wait and see.[12]

After making three low passes over the factory to warn the night shift to take cover, Cheshire dropped his markers from under 100ft, followed by Martin with incendiaries and spot fires and then the other Lancasters at a high level with 12,000lb bombs. The damage was immense and there were no French casualties.

During March no fewer than eight further attacks were mounted by 617 Squadron on French targets, all of which were led by Cheshire himself, marking at low level, and most of which were highly successful. The squadron's record in the first three months of 1944 was only blemished by yet another unsuccessful attack on the Antheor Viaduct on the night of 12/13 February, in which Bob Hay, still the squadron's Bombing Leader, lost his life when flak struck Martin's aircraft.

Cheshire had made an immense mark on 617 Squadron in less than five months and was now fully accepted by all for his leadership and personal bravery. It had not been long since the station commanders at both Coningsby and Woodhall Spa, Group Captains A. C. Evans-Evans and P. W. Johnson, had written of the frustration expressed by the members of the squadron, due largely to its lack of regular employment. Now those same aircrews understood the squadron's purpose and potential, as a result of which morale had risen dramatically.

The squadron's activities had also created a great deal of interest outside 5 Group and not only in the RAF. On the last day of March 1944 Ralph brought three important visitors to Woodhall Spa. They were Lieutenant General Carl Spaatz, the Commanding General of the US Strategic Air Forces in Europe, Lieutenant General Jimmy Doolittle, now Harris's opposite number as the commander of the US Eighth Air Force, and Brigadier General Curtis Le May, commander of the 3rd Air Division, who had come to see and hear for themselves what was happening. The Dams Raid, whilst much admired by all, had seemed to many people subsequently to have been a flash in the pan. Cheshire had now comprehensively demonstrated that 617 Squadron had much more yet to give.

Chapter 17

The Big City

In its four raids on Hamburg in July and August 1943, Harris had demonstrated the level of devastation which Bomber Command was capable of inflicting. The second largest city in the German Reich now lay in ruins, and he was determined to repeat the treatment on the largest city and the centre of government, Berlin. Despite all the evidence to the contrary from the London Blitz and other raids on the UK, he genuinely believed that widespread destruction in the capital city would deal a mortal blow to the enemy's morale and bring about a capitulation. He was to be proved very wrong; only the physical occupation of the city by the Russians and of most of the rest of the country by Allied forces would bring this about.

At the end of August and in early September 1943 there was a false start to Harris's campaign to destroy Berlin. The three raids at that time were failures, an early indication of the difficulty of the task which he had set himself. Hamburg was an old Hanseatic city with narrow streets and many buildings constructed substantially of wood, an ideal target for incendiaries. Berlin, always known to British bomber aircrews as 'The Big City', was quite different, a much more modern metropolis, dispersed over a very large area, with wide boulevards and concrete buildings in its centre. Although there was a river, and a number of lakes, it proved to be difficult to mark with H2S, whilst it was well beyond Oboe range. It was also all too frequently covered by cloud.

Harris resumed his attacks on Berlin with a raid on 18/19 November, which was followed by fifteen others up to the end of March 1944, accompanied by the same number of raids on other major German cities, notably Leipzig, Frankfurt and Stuttgart, all of which suffered multiple attacks. Early in the battle it became very clear to Harris that the Stirlings were no longer fit for purpose. Flying at a lower level than the Lancasters, they became the prime targets for German night fighters and flak, and their losses were crippling. From the end of November they were withdrawn from operations over Germany and diverted instead to 'gardening' and raids on flying-bomb sites. In the meantime, 3 Group continued its slow conversion to Lancasters which was only completed in the summer of 1944.

The same was to happen with the Halifax Marks II and V, which were not a great deal better than the Stirling in terms of their maximum altitude, although enterprising commanding officers like Cheshire had found ways of mitigating this to some extent. It was only when the Mark III and later the Mark VI, both powered by the Bristol Hercules radial engine and with an extended wing span, began to enter service in early 1944 that they were able to match the Lancaster in some degree, although this did not extend to the latter's increasingly heavier bomb load. The departure of some of the Halifax squadrons to other duties left Bomber Command with far fewer aircraft than Harris really needed and increased the pressure on the rest, with HQ Bomber Command almost invariably calling for 'maximum effort', for which every serviceable aircraft had to be committed.

The Lancasters remained the bedrock of Bomber Command and were to equip three and a half out of the five mainstream bomber groups by late 1944 and to provide the heavy bomber element of the Pathfinders. They were not, however, free of problems. Ralph believed that this was at least partly due to the RAF suffering from what he called 'over inspection', the conventional wisdom being that a graph of 'petty unserviceability' would show a steadily rising occurrence of problems until inspection, after which it would drop back to a low level. Ralph was able to obtain actual graphs which showed the exact opposite of the theoretical curve. 'Petty unserviceability' turned out to be at its maximum just after an inspection and dropped to its lowest just before the next inspection was due. A new policy was instituted in 5 Group which cut inspections drastically, thereby keeping more of the group's aircraft available for operations at any one time.

Whilst Ralph devoted more time to No. 617 than to any other single squadron, the majority of his energy was focused on the rest of 5 Group, which was fully committed to the Main Force throughout the Battle of Berlin. Since his arrival it had grown by the addition of three squadrons, No. 619 in April 1943, No. 463, an Australian unit formed initially from C Flight of 467 Squadron, in November 1943, and No. 630, also in November 1943. Scampton had been closed for hard runways to be built, whilst Bottesford and Langar had been transferred to the USAAF. Syerston was now the home of 5 Lancaster Finishing School, which provided the last stage of training for aircrews between leaving the HCUs and posting to an operational squadron, whilst 1654 HCU at Wigsley and 1661 HCU at Winthorpe also came under 5 Group control. The RAF stations at Bardney, Dunholme Lodge, East Kirkby, Metheringham, and Spilsby had been added to the group to accommodate operational squadrons.

With fifteen stations, thirteen squadrons and three training units in the group, Ralph might have found command and control difficult, had it not been for a change of structure in Bomber Command. In between the group and the station was now interposed the base, which itself controlled two or more stations. The first of these, 51 Base, comprising Swinderby, Syerston, Wigsley and Winthorpe and thus wholly devoted to training, was set up in March 1943. It was followed by 52 Base (Dunholme Lodge and Fiskerton, with Scampton added once it was reopened) in May, 53 Base (Bardney, Skellingthorpe and Waddington) in November, 54 Base (Coningsby, Metheringham and Woodhall Spa) in January 1944 and 55 Base (East Kirkby, Spilsby and a new station at Strubby) in April 1944. The last base to be formed in 5 Group was No. 56 in November 1944, consisting of Syerston, restored to an operational role, Balderton and Fulbeck. At much the same time, 52 Base was transferred to 1 Group and 51 Base to 7 Group, which took over all the HCUs, although 5 Lancaster Finishing School remained at Syerston.

Each base had a commander, who in recognition of his greater responsibility was accorded the rank of air commodore. It was he who now reported directly to Ralph, with the station commanders reporting to the base commander. In order that Satterly and the other Group SASOs should be able to deal with base commanders on equal terms they, too, now became air commodores. Not all the station commanders were happy with the change, as they had lost their direct reporting line to the AOC. Sam Elworthy, station commander at Waddington, thought that it was unnecessary and that some of those in the position were older officers who were not always of high calibre or destined for senior staff appointments. For Ralph, however, it did simplify things, although he remained a very frequent visitor to all his stations, whether or not they also housed a base headquarters.

On 14 November, as the Battle of Berlin was about to begin, 5 Group HQ relocated northwards from St Vincent's to Morton Hall, Swinderby, an otherwise undistinguished country house surrounded by Nissen huts and other temporary accommodation. With the transfer out of the group of Bottesford and Langar, its centre of gravity had moved north, and this was a far more convenient location, albeit that most of its stations stretched away to the east, with Strubby located not far from the Lincolnshire coast. The 5 Group Communications Flight, including Ralph's Proctor, was located close by at RAF Swinderby. He and Hilda, however, lived at Waddington, some five miles away.

Hilda was by no means idle during this time. Not only did she work raising money on behalf of the RAF Benevolent Fund, but she also had a very much more depressing duty. She was the one who was all too often deputed to convey the news of loss to the wives or families of those killed in action. A highly sensitive person herself, this was a great burden to her, but she took it on willingly as the least that she could do.

In the light of the group's geographical distribution, Ralph kept his finger on the pulse of activity not only by frequent visits to his stations by both car and plane, but also by one important innovation of his own, a conference call system. This allowed him to talk to all his stations at once, so that he could convene telephone meetings with base commanders and include, whenever necessary, station commanders as well. In setting this up he was taking a leaf out of Harris's book, as the C-in-C, always reluctant to leave High Wycombe for any length of time, used the same or a similar system to communicate with his AOCs.

Ralph knew the value of communication, not only with his base, station and squadron commanders and the group HQ staff, but also to the whole group. This was achieved by the distribution to the bases, who disseminated it further, of the monthly *5 Group News*. This publication, typewritten, but with a new cover each month designed by someone of artistic bent, had been started by one of his predecessors, but Ralph embraced it enthusiastically. The first page or two was always reserved for the AOC's Foreword and, whilst the focus was almost invariably on recent operations, it enabled him to seize on the most important issues of the moment, whether this was an analysis of a notable raid, the progress of the bombing campaign as a whole or the need for a specific type of training. It was followed by a description of the last month's operations and 'gardening' sorties, and then by sections written by the responsible group HQ officer on signals, navigation, bombing, which included the results of the squadron bombing competition, gunnery, engineering, tactics, training, flying control, accidents and education, together with a list of the decorations or other honours awarded during the previous month. It provided a vivid impression of the enormous amount of activity taking place in a bomber group, only a part of which, albeit the most important part, related to operations. *5 Group News* was also sent to Bomber Command HQ, all the Bomber and Coastal Command groups (except, perhaps unsurprisingly, 8 Group), the Air Ministry, the USAAF and numerous other recipients.

By the end of November 1943 Berlin had been visited four times in two weeks, with mixed results. The raid on 22/23 November did the most damage, among other things hitting the Kaiser-Wilhelm-Gedächtniskirche (Memorial Church), whose broken tower remains the most visible and moving monument of the battle to this day. The second raid of December, on the night of the 16th/17th, subsequently called 'Black Thursday', was notable for considerable losses other than through night fighters or flak. The returning bombers found the East of England covered by very low cloud and fog, and no fewer than twenty-nine Lancasters crashed, flying into the ground or abandoned by their crews when they ran out of fuel.

Probably because the weather conditions over its stations were not as bad as elsewhere, 5 Group was the least affected. However, Ralph had already given considerable thought to the question of his aircraft landing on their return from raids. As far as fog and very low cloud were concerned, there were only two areas in the country which were generally clear, but one was Cornwall and the other Lossiemouth in Scotland, both as far away from the group's own stations as they could possibly be. The problem of fog was to some extent mitigated by the installation of FIDO – Fog Investigation and Dispersal Operation – at a number of airfields, including Metheringham, Fiskerton, Sturgate and Ludford Magna, the last two of which, and Fiskerton from October 1944, were fairly close by but in the neighbouring 1 Group.

FIDO consisted of pipes laid on either side of the main runway through which oil was run and ejected into the air in jets, which were then ignited. Two rows of flame were thus created, which warmed the air, dispersed the fog and were clearly visible to the returning aircraft.[1]

For more normal weather conditions Ralph and his staff devised a new landing system, which was designed to get aircraft down on to the runway at a rate of one a minute:[2]

> We did this by cutting out a lot of control tower banter and making the aircraft position themselves. On crossing the coast on the return each squadron followed a 'Gee lattice line' which would take each aircraft over its aerodrome. This was an easy task for the navigator who only had to guide the pilot down the line showing on the scope. When the pilot saw the airfield lights ahead he would call up control and would be given a landing number, say 4. He would then turn into the circuit and listen for number 3 who would call out at every 90 degrees around the circuit including 'finals' as he turned into the runway tunnel. All number 4 had to do was to call out his positions 'upwind', 'crosswind, 'downwind, 'finals' keeping 90 degrees behind number 3. Number 5 would similarly keep 90 degrees behind number 4. This simple system not only speeded up landings but greatly reduced the risk of collision.[3]

This was a good example of Ralph thinking laterally and encouraging his subordinates to do the same. On operations this extended to a 5 Group instruction to fly straight and level on approach to the target, whereas other groups, including the Pathfinders, allowed their aircraft to weave about the sky. Supported by Operational Research, Ralph maintained that the risk of being struck by flak was no greater with a level approach, whilst the accuracy of bombing would be much improved.

He also introduced the '5 Group corkscrew' to escape a fighter attack from astern. The usual corkscrew involved the bomber going into a diving turn to port before climbing into a reverse turn, followed by other previously rehearsed manoeuvres, the intention being not just to escape the attacker, but to put it firmly in the rear gunner's sights. Ralph proposed the same initial manoeuvre but followed by a climb in the same direction, which he believed would allow the gunner to take the initiative that much more quickly. It was also adopted by 1 Group, but the others questioned whether the tactic was sufficient to escape from an attacking fighter. Whether in a corkscrew or not, Ralph placed considerable emphasis on aggressive gunnery, in which enemy aircraft would be engaged whenever possible. Instructions on these and other manoeuvres were set out in *No. 5 Group Tactical Notes*, a 61-page booklet issued to all aircrew, albeit strictly banned from aircraft engaged in operations.

The year 1944 began as 1943 had ended, with a raid on Berlin on the night of New Year's Day and five more on the same target before the end of January. On the night of 15/16 February the largest raid since the three Thousand Bomber operations of mid-1942 was mounted against the city, with 891 aircraft taking part. Considerable damage was caused, but it was clear by this time that Harris's expectations of landing a decisive blow on the enemy were not going to be met by a strategy of focusing on his capital city. It was just too big and too well defended for the returns to justify the investment, which had been extremely costly in terms of losses. These were 5.9 per cent overall, above the rate of 5 per cent which was judged to be the highest sustainable, and highly damaging to morale. That 492 aircraft had been lost against a forecast of 500 by Harris before the battle started was no comfort in the light of the results. Moreover, the Germans had been stimulated into tit-for-tat raids, engaging in the 'Baby Blitz' on London in the first three months of 1944, although the Luftwaffe's losses were proportionately even higher than the RAF's.

The Battle of Berlin came to its conclusion with a raid on 24/25 March which was notable for the high winds encountered by the attackers, causing many aircraft to go astray, a good number over the well-defended Ruhr on the return run, and serious difficulties with marking. It was the very last occasion on which the Big City would be targeted by the Main Force, although the Mosquitoes of 8 Group's Light Night Striking Force, each carrying a 4,000lb 'Cookie', would continue to give Berliners sleepless nights for the remainder of the war.

One more raid of consequence was mounted before Harris was compelled to turn his attention away from German cities, and it proved to be a complete disaster. On the night of 30/31 March 795 aircraft set out to bomb

Nuremberg. The German night-fighter controller ignored the diversions which had been mounted and cleverly positioned his aircraft along the very route which the bombers were following; eighty-two aircraft were lost on the outbound flight and another thirteen on the return journey, the biggest loss of the war for Bomber Command, whilst aircrew casualties on this single night were greater than those suffered by Fighter Command during the whole of the Battle of Britain. With twenty-one losses out of 201 aircraft despatched, 5 Group was only slightly less severely hit than the average. Due to extensive cloud cover and strong winds, the raid itself was a failure.

The raids on Berlin and other major German cities mounted during the last two months of 1943 and the first three of 1944 had failed to come anywhere close to Harris's objectives and must be regarded as a major defeat for Bomber Command. Harris's critics, notably Bufton as Director of Bombing Operations at the Air Ministry, were not slow to point out the deficiencies of his strategy and tactics, although Portal remained supportive. This was, however, although few may have realized it at the time, the darkest hour just before the dawn. Harris was shortly to be granted a respite, albeit initially against his will, which allowed his command to recover in terms of men and material and thus to form additional squadrons. Moreover, new Lancasters were leaving the factories at an increasing rate, and the improved models of the Halifax were also arriving in the squadrons.

Perhaps most significantly of all in the longer term, 100 (Bomber Support) Group had been formed in November 1943 and would play an increasingly important role in future campaigns. It had two purposes. The first was to deploy a range of electronic counter-measures, carried in specially equipped aircraft flying in or outside the bomber stream, either to jam or confuse the German ground and airborne radar. The second was to equip Mosquito night fighters with Serrate, an airborne homing system, enabling them to operate as intruders independently of the bomber streams and pick off German night fighters. These measures were to prove highly effective after Bomber Command returned to Germany in August 1944.

Throughout the Battle of Berlin, and indeed the Battle of the Ruhr before it, Ralph had been deeply concerned about the efficacy of target marking by 8 Group. Whilst bombing accuracy had improved very significantly over the previous eighteen months, it was still, in his opinion, far from completely satisfactory. There was, in particular, a tendency for the bombs to fall further and further from the target as the raid progressed, a fault attributed by Bennett to a lack of guts on the part of the crews concerned, who he believed wanted to get away as soon as they possibly could. Ralph was sure, from the reports of his own crews, that the bombs were falling on the right markers and thus that it was the markers which were not on the target. In order to prove this he managed to obtain some colour film from the Americans which showed quite clearly that this was the case.

Ralph believed that the problem lay with the Pathfinders' methodology. This involved them arriving over the target ahead of the Main Force and dropping first a large number of flares to light up the ground, followed by coloured markers on the target as seen by the light of the flares. The Main Force was ordered to drop its bombs on the latter, but as the attack progressed, the smoke from the bombs, drifting in the direction of the wind, obscured more and more of the markers and changed the pattern. When the Pathfinder 'backers-up' arrived with the Main Force to drop further markers they aimed at what they could see, which by this time was no longer what had originally been laid down. The effect would then be what was called 'creep-back', which could amount to as much as three to six miles.

All this was inherently unsatisfactory, and Ralph was not willing to defer to Bennett, who made it clear that 8 Group's way of marking was the only way. Cheshire's low-level marking at Limoges and subsequently other targets had, Ralph believed, disproved this and was fully capable of being extended beyond just 617 Squadron.

Chapter 18

The Independent Air Force

In April 1944, Bomber Command and the US Eighth Air Force were issued with a new directive. The campaign over Germany itself was now to be subordinated to the requirements of the Supreme Allied Commander, General Eisenhower, in preparation for and as support to the forthcoming invasion of North-West Europe. Neither Harris, who would have preferred to go on with his bombing campaign against German cities, nor Spaatz and Doolittle, who wanted to continue with Operation POINTBLANK, were happy about this, although Harris, as had happened with both the formation of the Pathfinders and Operation CHASTISE, gave it his loyal support once it had become a fait accompli. The two strategic bomber forces were placed under the command of Air Chief Marshal Sir Arthur Tedder, Eisenhower's deputy, not least because Harris had a poor relationship with Air Chief Marshal Sir Trafford Leigh-Mallory, once one of Ralph's fellow students at the staff college and now AOC-in-C of the Allied Expeditionary Air Force.

There had been much debate at the highest level on the priorities for the new campaign. Spaatz, in particular, had advocated concentrating on oil installations, but the weight of opinion was that this would take too long to have a significant impact. The alternative was a focus on German lines of communication, particularly the railways, and this became the blueprint for what was named the Transportation Plan. Although railway targets were by no means the only ones, they became the chief focus of attention for both the RAF and the USAAF. However, 617 Squadron's first operation in April, on the night of the 5th/6th, was mounted on a different type of target in conjunction with the rest of the group, which put 127 Lancasters into the air to add to seventeen from the squadron itself. The objective was a complex of factories around Toulouse and the operation was to be highly significant in both the squadron's and the group's history. For the first time No. 617 was marking for others in the group, in this case for the 54 Base aircraft from

Coningsby, Woodhall Spa and Metheringham, whose target was an aircraft repair plant.

Each base used a different marking methodology and, in the case of 54 Base, there was a significant innovation. With Ralph's backing and Harris's approval, Cheshire had managed to borrow two Mark XVI Mosquitoes, believing that this type of aircraft was much more suitable than the Lancaster for low-level marking, as indeed now proved to be the case. Flying one of these, he managed to place his spot-fires so accurately from 800–1,000ft that Munro and McCarthy, waiting in their Lancasters to back up with more markers from a medium level, found that these were no longer needed, but released their bombs with the rest of the squadron and the other 54 Base aircraft. The operation was completely successful, for the loss of a single bomber in the group.

Harris's reaction was immediate. When Ralph went to see him, asking for two more Mosquitoes to allow him to increase the number of operations marked at low level, he was given the most astonishing news. Not only would 617 Squadron be provided with an additional three Mosquitoes, but no fewer than three squadrons would be lent to 5 Group by 8 Group, No. 627 with Mosquitoes and Nos. 83 and 97 with Lancasters. In future, 5 Group would operate substantially on its own and only occasionally as part of the Main Force of Bomber Command. Ralph was later to say that he did not know who was the more surprised, he or Bennett, but the comment in his memoirs – 'Bennett was not amused' – was a major understatement of the latter's reaction:

> This was, in itself, a tremendous slap in the face to a Force which had turned Bert Harris' Bomber Command from a wasteful and ineffective force into a mighty and successful one. It meant in the eyes of the rest of the Command that in the opinion of their C-in-C the Pathfinders had apparently failed.[1]

This was nonsense and, writing it as he did fourteen years later, Bennett should have recognized it. The Pathfinders had by no means failed, indeed they continued to provide the marking for the Main Force of Bomber Command up to the end of the war. The result of this decision, however, despite Bennett's subsequent protestations to the contrary, was that the relationship between him and Ralph, which up to early 1944 had been at least civil, now turned positively rancorous, and Bennett was blind to any suggestions that what Harris had done was to a good purpose.

In fact, Harris had done something which had been in his mind even before the formation of the Pathfinders, establishing a marking capability within one of his groups. He had been overruled by Portal in his attempt to have this structure implemented throughout Bomber Command, but he had now succeeded in part and was going to make the most of it. Bennett appealed to Saundby to see if he could change the AOC-in-C's mind, but was advised to drop the matter, and 8 Group began to refer to 5 Group as 'The Independent Air Force', a name which spread through the other groups in due course, and also, rather less flatteringly, as 'the Lincolnshire Poachers'!

It was a great pity that the transfer of the Lancaster squadrons on 18 April was not better handled at 5 Group. When the aircrews of 83 and 97 Squadrons arrived at Coningsby, which had been vacated by 61 and 619 Squadrons, they were met by the commander of 54 Base, Air Commodore Bobby Sharp,[2] who had them taken to the station cinema, where they were subjected to a lecture by him on how they should now give up their 8 Group ways and adopt those of 5 Group. Although they were to retain their special badge and their rank, this was deeply resented by the crews, all highly experienced and proud of their Pathfinder achievements. Both squadrons had been 5 Group units in the past, but few if any of the personnel remained from those days, and it was to take a long time before sufficient crews had been lost or come to the end of their tours to enable the 5 Group spirit to predominate once again. In the case of 97 Squadron, Ralph decided after two months to replace the CO with Wing Commander Anthony Heward from 50 Squadron, a somewhat humourless man ironically nicknamed 'Smiler', but also a brilliant pilot and strong leader, whom he could trust to run the squadron in the way he felt was necessary.

Ralph was not at Coningsby on the day of the two Lancaster squadrons' arrival, but he had been at Woodhall Spa three days earlier to meet the arriving Mosquito crews of 627 Squadron. In the words of one pilot, Flight Lieutenant J. R. 'Benny' Goodman:

Within a few minutes I found myself looking into the cold eyes of a tall, rather ascetic man, who abruptly welcomed me to 5 Group and moved along the line. Why had he taken the trouble to meet us? Such a thing was unheard of in bomber circles. We all felt somewhat uneasy. Obviously something was 'up' and it promised to be bloody dangerous.[3]

Ralph went to Coningsby subsequently to explain to the combined crews of all three newly arrived squadrons what their role was going to be. He was accompanied by Cheshire, who described the new marking technique, whereby the 87 and 93 Squadron Lancasters would drop flares to illuminate the area below and would be followed by Mosquitoes, which would mark the precise aiming point with spot fires. The Marker Leader would then inform the Master Bomber in one of the Lancasters, who would direct the rest of the group's aircraft on to the target.

The first test of the new organization was a raid on the marshalling yards at La Chapelle, north of Paris, on the night of 20/21 April, with the force split into two parts, one arriving an hour after the other. Although 627 Squadron was involved, it was not yet fully trained in low-level marking and was used to drop Window well short of the target. There was a considerable amount of confusion initially, but Cheshire marked the aiming point accurately for the first wave, backed up by Flight Lieutenant Gerry Fawke in a second Mosquito. Shannon and Flight Lieutenant Terry Kearns did the same for the second wave. The operation was a complete success, with the marshalling yards devastated.

The next raid, over Brunswick on 22/23 April, was more challenging, as the target was a defended city, and 238 Lancasters and 17 Mosquitoes of 5 Group were accompanied by 10 Lancasters of 1 Group, which provided a radio counter-measures screen. The initial marking by Cheshire and three other Mosquito pilots from 617 Squadron was accurate, but the target was obscured by a layer of cloud and there was some confusion on the part of the Master Bomber and his deputies due to radio communication problems. A number of bombs were dropped accurately, but many were a long way off target.

Two nights later, a force of much the same size and composition, with 627 Squadron employed to drop Window as in the previous two raids, attacked Munich, one of the most heavily defended cities of Germany. Cheshire dived low over the city to drop his spot fires from 700ft directly on to the selected aiming point, backed up subsequently by two of the three other Mosquitoes and a Lancaster. Although some markers fell well off target, these were identified by the controller of the flare force, who organized a back-up of the original markers. The raid was by a long way the most successful on Munich during the war to that date.[4]

Two nights after the Munich raid, 627 Squadron provided the low-level marking for the first time at Schweinfurt. They were far from accurate, since their training was still in its early stages, but from this point onwards they and the two other former 8 Group squadrons, Nos. 83 and 97, would provide the marking for raids mounted by the group, whilst 617 Squadron reverted substantially to operations on its own. The exception was a raid on a large German military camp at Mailly-le-Camp by 346 Lancasters of 1 and 5 Groups on the night of 3/4 May, for which Cheshire and three other Mosquitoes carried out the low-level marking. The spot fires were dropped and backed up accurately, but when the Master Bomber tried to call in the bombers, his transmission was blocked by a programme on the American Forces Network. Whilst he was trying to correct the situation, German fighters were scrambled to intercept the raiders. His deputy eventually established radio control, and considerable damage was done to the camp, but the losses were substantial at forty-two Lancasters, 11.6 per cent of the force. Twenty-eight of these came from the 173 aircraft of 1 Group, which formed the second wave. This was a disaster, due not only to the jammed communications but also to the several briefings which had taken place and produced some contradictory instructions. Ralph insisted that in future all 5 Group aircraft should be equipped with VHF sets, as used in 617 Squadron since the Dams Raid, to improve communications on operations.

After Mailly-le-Camp the activities of 617 Squadron and the remainder of 5 Group diverged, with the former focusing on the employment of Wallis's new big bomb on CROSSBOW targets and U-boat and E-boat pens, and the latter carrying out more conventional raids, often directed at railways in support of the Transportation Plan, sometimes alone and sometimes in conjunction with one or more other groups, but what linked both was that the targets were substantially in France. There were two visits by 5 Group to

German cities, both with other elements of the Main Force, one to Duisburg, the other a return to Brunswick. The latter was a failure due to heavy cloud cover, but at least there were no losses.

It was in May 1944 that 5 Group began to adopt an entirely new system of marking, although it took some time to perfect. For Ralph the major obstacle to successful marking was the tendency for the markers to be obscured by smoke, driven over the pattern by the wind. The new method required the area to be illuminated by flares as before, but the marker, only one of which was usually necessary, was now laid, usually from low level, not on the target itself, but upwind of it and 1,000 or more yards away. The target itself was thus free from smoke. The Master Bomber's navigator then calculated the distance and bearing of the marker from the target and received from several aircraft in the flare force the strength and precise direction of the wind. He would then transmit a false wind to the bomb-aimers, to which was added the true measurement of the wind, the wind direction and the distance of the marker from the target, all of which data was fed into the Mark XIV bomb sight. If the bomb aimer then fixed his sight on the marker, it would be automatically corrected for the bombs to fall on the target. As Ralph wrote later, 'If all went well a devastatingly accurate attack resulted.'[5] This became known as 'offset marking' and was first used in two highly successful attacks, on a seaplane base near Brest on the night of 8/9 May and on marshalling yards at Lille two nights later.

By the middle of the month Ralph was able to write to Harris with a progress report on marking which concluded that the new method had led to a remarkable improvement in bombing accuracy, attributing this success to a well trained flare force in 83 and 97 Squadrons and the gallantry of the pilots of 627 Squadron. In his reply of 25 May Harris accepted this, but he went on to write:

> I would like to take this opportunity of saying that an equal share in the success is due to those who, under your direction, have not been content with things as they are but have given a great deal of time and trouble to thinking out new ideas and new tactics.[6]

As the invasion date approached, the tempo rose. One of the elements of the overall deception plan, Operation FORTITUDE, which was designed to persuade the Germans that the landings would be made in the Pas de Calais and which was very substantially successful, was achieved in part by Bomber Command spreading its operations over a wide geographical area of Northern France, so that the real objective, Normandy, would not be identified. There were more attacks on coastal batteries in the north, for instance, than in the Bay of the Seine.

A more complex ruse was executed by 617 Squadron in Operation TAXABLE and by the Stirlings of 3 Group's 218 Squadron in Operation GLIMMER. Its purpose was to make the Germans believe that invasion forces were actually approaching Cap d'Antifer, between Le Havre and Dieppe, and the Pas de Calais on the night of 5/6 June, just as the real force was heading for the beaches in the Bay of the Seine. For this reason, apart from the involvement of the Mosquitoes at Mailly-le-Camp, 617 Squadron undertook no operations between the raid on Munich and the night of the invasion itself, as TAXABLE required a considerable amount of training.

Sixteen of No. 617's Lancasters were involved, flying in two groups of eight. Each group was to fly towards Cap d'Antifer in line abreast at exactly 180mph, with two miles separating each aircraft from its neighbour. The aircraft then flew a precise seven-minute leg, before turning to port on a reciprocal course for six minutes and then turning back on to the original course for seven minutes, and so on. Every five seconds a bundle of Window would be thrown out of the aircraft, whose crew was significantly increased to handle the load. Below them a number of small boats deployed radar reflector balloons and simulated radio traffic. The effect, conceived by some brilliant scientists, was to create the illusion to the German radar operators of a fleet of ships heading for the French coast at a steady seven knots. The second group of aircraft, carrying out an identical manoeuvre, flew eight miles behind the first, whilst the Stirlings headed towards the Pas de Calais.

Operation TAXABLE required a great deal of practice over the English countryside and out at sea off the Lincolnshire coast and was, when it took place, conducted in complete darkness. It was only after four hours of meticulous navigation and precise flying and as dawn was breaking that the aircraft turned for home, but not before laying mines. There was only a modest response from the German side, with some searchlight activity, but the other elements of FORTITUDE worked well and the landings in

Normandy took the Germans completely by surprise. The rest of 5 Group was fully and successfully employed in bombing German positions.

Two nights later, 617 Squadron was back in action in earnest. This was the first occasion on which it deployed Wallis's 12,000lb TALLBOY bomb, formerly known as TALLBOY Medium. Unlike the 12,000lb HC bomb used on the Dortmund–Ems raid, the TALLBOY was aerodynamically highly efficient. Released at 18,000ft it achieved a speed of 750mph in its 37-second descent to the ground. With fins designed to generate a longitudinal spin and a specially hardened nose, it could penetrate the ground to a depth of about 25ft or concrete to 18ft. Its detonators could be set to a number of delays between impact and 30 minutes later, upon which its 5,200lbs of Torpex exploded. The effect was to create shock waves to destroy its target, as well as a gigantic crater.

TALLBOY was first used on the night of 8/9 June in an operation to destroy the Saumur Tunnel, through which ran a vital railway connection between South-West France and Normandy, which was about to be used by 17 SS Panzergrenadier Division hastening towards the front. The marking was carried out by only two Mosquitoes, as Shannon's developed engine problems. Cheshire marked the entrance to the tunnel from the south and Fawke the one from the north. The bombing was very accurate, with one TALLBOY falling directly on to the tunnel roof, bringing the hill above down on the track. Notwithstanding that the track was returned to service by the Germans in due course, the progress of the division was seriously delayed.

The next operation for 617 Squadron was as one component of a daylight raid on 14 June by aircraft from 1, 3, 5 and 8 Groups against E-boats in Le Havre, in order to reduce the threat to Allied ships crossing the Channel and anchored off the Normandy beaches. The squadron's specific task was to destroy the concrete E-boat pens with TALLBOYS. Cheshire marked the target so well that neither Shannon nor Fawke were necessary, and there were a number of direct hits, whilst the bombs of the other aircraft destroyed the jetties and those craft out in the open. The Le Havre raid was followed by a similar one on Boulogne on the next day, with a similar result. As a result, the E-boat threat was effectively eliminated.

For the remainder of June and into July, 617 Squadron concentrated on Operation CROSSBOW targets, mostly V-1 launch sites and storage facilities. In a raid on a site at Siracourt on 25 June, Cheshire marked the target flying a North American P-51 Mustang[7] for the first time. This was an even faster and more manoeuvrable aircraft than the Mosquito, although its single seat required Cheshire to do his own navigation. He did so again at St Leu-d'Esserent on 4 July, joined by the rest of 5 Group, 617 Squadron dropping TALLBOYS on underground caves, whilst the others focused on storage facilities. The main force lost 13 out of its 231 Lancasters, but the raid was judged to have been a success.

The Mustang was used again two days later in a raid on a site at Mimoyecques which housed a V-3 supergun designed to shell London. The gun, whose enormously long multiple barrels were substantially underground, was effectively put out of commission by this raid and one by 5 Group on the following night and could not be restored before the site was overrun by Canadian troops in early September.

On the morning after the Mimoyecques raid, Ralph told Cheshire that his time at 617 Squadron had come to an end. He had done more than enough over an eight-month period to justify a rest. Moreover, the last three pilots who had flown in Operation CHASTISE, McCarthy, Munro and Shannon, would be going too. There was a grand farewell dinner at the Petwood Hotel, attended by, among others, Satterly and Sharp and also by Mick Martin, who had left the squadron after the raid on the Antheor Viaduct in which Bob Hay had been killed and was now flying Serrate Mosquitoes in 100 Group. Harris was invited but was unable to attend, although he sent a message, read out by Ralph, thanking 'the old lags' for their magnificent contribution.

Cheshire had transformed the squadron from the one which had reached a very low point after the Dortmund–Ems disaster. He had not only restored its self-confidence but forged it into a unique weapon of war, the rapier to Bomber Command's bludgeon. By his courage and enterprise he had also fully realized Ralph's belief that there were ways of marking targets which could deliver a better return than those practised by the Pathfinders.

Although Harris was unable to attend the farewell dinner, Cheshire was to meet him nearly two months later, after attending a senior commanders' course at Cranwell. In the meantime, a recommendation for a third bar to his DSO had made its way up from Group Captain M. G. 'Monty' Philpott, the Station Commander at Woodhall Spa, via Sharp and Ralph to Harris.

Harris, however, now told Cheshire that he had been awarded a Victoria Cross, not for any specific action, but instead, and uniquely in the history of the decoration, for sustained courage over a long period, given in the citation as 1940 to 1944. It seems most likely that the recommendation came from Harris himself, whose views on the subject at the time of the award of a bar to Gibson's DSO had been clear. However, it is possible that it came with the endorsement of Ralph, whose admiration for Cheshire was considerable. It was mutual, as Cheshire wrote later about his departure:

> And there's something else I have to do. I must go to the A.O.C. and tell him that it was that rotten conversion course of his which pulled me through it all. It rankled at the time, but that's over now. Deep down inside me I know that it pays to be taught by those who know.[8]

Cheshire's successor was Wing Commander James 'Willie' Tait. Like Cheshire and Holden, Tait's operational career had been substantially pursued in 4 Group. He was a Cranwell graduate who had been commissioned in 1938, thereafter joining 51 Squadron and flying Whitleys out of Linton-on-Ouse and earning the DFC. He had led the air force contingent in Operation COLOSSUS, the dropping of paratroops to destroy the Tragino Aqueduct, in which Holden had also participated and for which Tait was awarded the DSO. After flying Halifaxes in 35 Squadron and earning a bar to his DSO, he was appointed to command 78 Squadron, also in 4 Group. In March 1944 Tait was posted to Waddington as 53 Base Operations Officer. In theory this was an office job, but in practice he went frequently on operations. Two months later, he was officially returned to flying duties as a Master Bomber[9] in 5 Group, for which he earned a second bar to his DSO.

Tait was quite different in character to either Gibson or Cheshire, quiet and seemingly rather shy, but also very stubborn. In Ralph's words, 'I got to know that when he put on what I called his "Mule face" there was no point in continuing the argument.'[10]

For 617 Squadron, operations continued against V-1 sites until the end of July, but August was to see a change of target. Following an unsuccessful attack on a bridge at Etaples at the beginning of the month, the focus turned to the U-boat pens at Brest, Lorient and La Pallice. Ten raids were mounted on these, interrupted only by an attack on the E-boat pens at Ijmuiden. In the early part of the month Tait carried out the marking himself, but he then decided to revert to flying a Lancaster, leaving the marking to Fawke. The squadron used a combination of TALLBOYS and 2,000lb armour-piercing bombs on their new targets with very satisfactory results. On 13 August it was joined for the first time by Lancasters from 9 Squadron, flying out of Bardney. No. 9 had by then become the second squadron to be trained in the use of the TALLBOY and would join the Dambusters on a number of future raids. It was still using, and continued to use, the Mark XIV bomb sight, but it achieved a high degree of accuracy with this.

Between May and August of 1944 the other 5 Group squadrons, including those theoretically on loan from 8 Group, operated substantially in line either with the Transportation Plan or with Operation CROSSBOW, or in direct support of the Allied ground forces, which until the end of August were all under the command of General Montgomery's 21st Army Group. The last of these included the largest operation of the period, with 942 aircraft bombing German positions on 18 July to clear the way for British armoured divisions breaking out to the south-east of Caen in Operation GOODWOOD.

There were, however, a number of exceptions. One of these came on the night of 21/22 June, when 5 Group was split into two to attack synthetic oil plants in the Ruhr, one at Wesseling and the other at Scholven. The former was a complete disaster. Because of 10/10ths cloud cover, low-level marking could not be used and it was decided to bomb on H2S instead. The damage to the plant was slight and no fewer than 37 Lancasters were lost out of 133, at a huge 27.8 per cent the highest loss rate of the war for the group. The losses at Scholven, where the marking was carried out by Oboe, were much lower at 8 aircraft out of 123, but the result was the same. This was the low point of the campaign, after which the Group's fortunes gradually improved, although a number of setbacks were experienced.

It would be mid-September before Harris was formally released from his responsibilities to Eisenhower, but other German targets began to creep into the bombing programme again during July and August. Towards the end of July there were three raids by 5 Group on Stuttgart. Considerable damage was done to the city, especially in the second of these on the night of 25/26 July. They came at a cost, however, with losses of 7.9 per cent on the last raid three nights later. Towards the end of August, 5 Group mounted an operation against Darmstadt, which had not been visited before. However, it was a failure as the Master Bomber had to return early and his deputies were both shot down. The illuminating flares were dropped well wide of the city and the Mosquito markers were unable to identify the target. Little damage was caused and seven Lancasters were lost. Darmstadt remained on the target list for the future.

A much more successful raid was mounted against Königsberg, on the Baltic coast of East Prussia, on the night of 29/30 August. This city was little short of 900 miles from Lincolnshire, at the extreme end of the Lancaster's range with a full bomb load. It had been visited three nights earlier, but photo reconnaissance revealed only modest damage, so it was decided to return. This time the attack was one of the most successful undertaken by the group, with considerable damage caused. Subsequent reconnaissance showed that some 20 per cent of the industrial targets had been destroyed and 40 per cent of the residential area. Losses amounted to 7.9 per cent, but this was considered acceptable in the light of the excellent results.

During this period Bennett had lobbied Harris more than once to have his squadrons returned to him and had tried to persuade Ralph that 8 Group could serve his needs. Ralph was still experimenting with refinements to 5 Group's marking techniques and asked Harris for a decision. Harris delivered his edict on 21 July, in a signal to both Ralph and Bennett:

> The position is that these detachments are to be regarded within Bomber Command as 'permanent detachments', and that administrative arrangements are to be based on the assumption that the squadrons concerned will not return to No. 8 (PFF) airfields within any predictable period of time.[11]

This could hardly have been clearer and was to remain the position until the end of the war. Bennett was furious.

Unbeknownst to Ralph, his own future had also been debated during this period. On 23 June Portal wrote to Harris, telling him that a series of moves of senior officers had left him without an ACAS (Policy), to whom he would look for help in the battles which would doubtless have to be fought with ministers and the other service chiefs, on the subject of the post-war Air Force:

> Looking down the list of Air Vice-Marshals I can see no-one who approaches Cochrane in suitability for this job and I am wondering whether you would be prepared to release him during the next two or three months. I know how very valuable he has been to you as a Group Commander but you may think that for his own sake and that of the Service at large he has been long enough in his present position.[12]

Harris's reply was forthright:

> Cochrane is in my view the best operational commander we have today and I personally think it would be entirely wrong at this stage of the War to send him back to Staff duties of which he has done such an enormous amount already. There is not the least doubt in my mind that it would have the most adverse effect on the efficiency of his group, no matter who replaced him, and also on the war effort generally ...
>
> I should have thought and hoped that Cochrane would have had a very high Command in the Japanese war if not in this one before it is finished. I had personally envisaged him as the obvious relief for me. I hope therefore that you will reconsider the proposition, particularly because I am quite certain that it would have a very adverse effect on the conduct of the War at the present juncture.[13]

Portal dropped the matter immediately. It would only be once Harris was confident that victory in the European War was undoubted that he would let Ralph go.

Chapter 19

Germany and the Tirpitz

Before the summer of 1944 was over, there was one significant change to Ralph's staff at Morton Hall. Harry Satterley, who had served very effectively as 5 Group SASO for over two years, was relieved by Sam Elworthy on 22 August.[1]

Elworthy although a New Zealander by birth, was educated in England and called to the bar after graduating from Cambridge. He decided not to practise law and, whilst working in the City of London, learnt to fly and was commissioned into the Reserve of Air Force Officers in 1933. He then joined the Royal Auxiliary Air Force as a pilot in 600 (City of London) Squadron, flying Hawker Harts, before gaining one of the few permanent commissions awarded to university graduates, following a period of probation in XV (Bomber) Squadron. After serving as personal assistant to Edgar Ludlow-Hewitt, AOC-in-C of Bomber Command in the immediate pre-war period, he was posted to 108 Squadron, flying Blenheims. The squadron later became part of 13 OTU, where Elworthy was awarded an AFC for his work on night-flying training. From the summer of 1940 to the spring of 1941 he served as a flight commander in 82 Squadron and later as its CO, carrying out operations in Blenheims against both naval and ground targets, for which he was awarded first a DFC and then a DSO. He then became an operations officer in 2 Group and, in due course, Group Captain Operations at Bomber Command HQ, where he was highly regarded by Harris and was one of those who persuaded the AOC-in-C to meet Wallis.

In April 1943 Elworthy was posted to Waddington as station commander, where he got to know Ralph well, before being summoned back to High Wycombe to serve as Harris's liaison officer to Eisenhower and Tedder in the run-up to and the first months of the invasion of North-West Europe. In mid-August he was promoted to air commodore and offered by Harris the choice of three jobs: to remain with Eisenhower, to become a Deputy SASO at High Wycombe or to be SASO at 5 Group. In his words:

There was no doubt in my mind about the choice, primarily because Ralph Cochrane was AOC, and I thought the job would be by far the most exacting and the most challenging and interesting one. I certainly never had any reason to regret my choice.[2]

Ralph was later to say that Elworthy relieved him of much of the day-to-day running of the group, allowing him to give more thought to the operational side. There was certainly no slackening of operations, indeed quite the contrary. Although Bomber Command was released from Eisenhower's control on 14 September, it was still required to support 21st Army Group from time to time in its advance from Normandy to the north, with raids in September on the defences of Le Havre, Boulogne and Calais, as well as Brest, where the German garrison was stubbornly holding out against the Americans. However, the month also saw the return in earnest to Germany and, in the case of 5 Group, to Darmstadt on the night of the 11th/12th. Whereas its earlier raid had been a failure, this one was devastating, destroying much of the city, causing over 10,000 deaths and making nearly 50,000 of its inhabitants homeless. A medium-sized city with relatively little industry, it is ranked with Dresden by the critics of area bombing.

The destruction caused at Darmstadt was at least partly the result of a variation of 5 Group's offset bombing technique, which was known as 'line bombing'. In this the force was divided into sections, each of which approached the aiming point from a different direction. The intention was to distribute the bombs more widely and also more evenly. For Darmstadt there were two sections attacking along two aiming lines, but there could be more, depending on the area to be covered. As Ralph wrote in *5 Group News* at the end of the month, 'I want to impress on crews that area bombing calls for every bit as much accuracy as attacks on the smallest factory or railway target.'[3]

A particularly successful raid on a more obviously military target was mounted on the night of 18/19 September against Bremerhaven, which up to then had only suffered light raids by Blenheims and Mosquitoes. The damage to the port and city centre was such that no further attacks were deemed necessary. On the following night the targets were the twin towns of Mönchengladbach and Rheydt, and for this operation the Master Bomber was Gibson, flying a Mosquito. He was serving as an operations officer at 54 Base at the time and not as one of the designated Master Bombers, but appears to have authorized himself to undertake the role, taking with him as navigator Squadron Leader Jim Warwick, the Coningsby Navigation Officer. The raid was successful, but Gibson and Warwick failed to return, for the former a sad and unnecessary end to a spectacular career.

On the same night as the Darmstadt raid, 9 and 617 Squadrons set out on the first stage of a particularly complex operation. For two and a half years the Prime Minister and the Admiralty had been obsessed with the threat posed to Arctic convoys by the *Tirpitz*, which by 1944 was Germany's only remaining seaworthy battleship. It had been deployed to Norway in early 1942, taking advantage of that country's deep fjords and high mountains for its protection. A number of attempts had been made to sink it, notably by X-craft midget submarines and by carrier-borne aircraft. Both had caused damage, the former of a serious nature, but the ship had been repaired after each attack and remained in commission. By the summer of 1944 it was fit for action once again.

The *Tirpitz* was moored in the Kaa Fjord in the far north of Norway and was thus out of range for bombers flying from the UK. It was therefore decided, with the agreement of the Russians, that twenty Lancasters from 617 Squadron, led by Tait, and eighteen from 9 Squadron, led by Wing Commander J. M. Bazin, together with a 463 Squadron Lancaster carrying a film crew, a Weather/Photo Reconnaissance Mosquito and two Liberators carrying stores, spare parts and ground crew, should operate from a grass airfield at Yagodnik, on an island in the River Dvina 20 miles south of Archangel. The whole force employed in Operation PARAVANE came under the command of Group Captain Colin McMullen, the station commander at Bardney, the home of 9 Squadron.

The flight out to Yagodnik was bedevilled by very poor weather in its closing stages. Many aircraft found the airfield difficult to locate and, whilst some found alternatives, two from 617 Squadron and four from 9 Squadron were compelled to make forced landings and written off. Due to the weather, the raid itself was delayed until 15 September, when all those aircraft serviceable, twenty Lancasters carrying TALLBOYS and six carrying 'Johnny Walker' mines,[4] set out for Kaa Fjord. The TALLBOYS were being carried at the insistence of Ralph, the experts at the Admiralty and the Air Ministry having argued that the only type of bomb able to do the job would be the 2,000lb armour-piercing variety. Ralph had approached Wallis to confirm that his bomb could penetrate layers of armour plate and was assured that this was the case, encouraging him to override the experts.

The weather for the attack was fine and the bombers located the *Tirpitz* satisfactorily. However, the ship was protected by a smoke screen, and this began to cover it as they approached. Two aircraft were completely unable to see the target and returned with their TALLBOYS, and two others found that their bombs hung up and had to release them later. The others all bombed, but the results were obscured by the smoke, although one big flash was spotted. This, it was discovered subsequently, was from a direct hit on the foredeck of the battleship, which caused serious damage and flooded the forward compartments. The *Tirpitz*, assisted by tugs, could still sail at a very reduced speed, however, and the Germans decided to move it to Tromsø, where it could be employed as a floating battery to defend the town against a possible Allied landing. The RAF aircraft returned to the UK, although one Lancaster of 617 Squadron crashed in Norway with the loss of its crew.

On the night of 23/24 September, just over a week after the *Tirpitz* attack, 617 Squadron revisited its old nemesis, the Dortmund–Ems Canal, but this time it was using TALLBOYS and being backed up by a much larger force from 5 Group armed with conventional bombs. The TALLBOYS proved to be highly effective on exactly the same stretch of the canal where Holden and so many others had lost their lives just over a year earlier. The canal was breached in a number of places and the water drained out for about six miles, although losses of 10 per cent, including one from 617 Squadron, were high. There were to be six other attacks by 5 Group on the Dortmund–Ems Canal and five on the adjoining Mittelland Canal before the end of the war, most of which were successful, leaving the canals drained and barges stranded.

No. 617's next operation, on 3 October and once again carried out in conjunction with the rest of 5 Group, was an attack on the defences of the island of Walcheren. Walcheren, which lies on the north side of the estuary of the River Scheldt, was occupied by the Germans, preventing access by sea to Antwerp, the largest port between Cherbourg and Rotterdam and absolutely vital to the supply of the Allied armies in their advance towards

Germany. The island is very low-lying and protected by large sea walls and embankments from encroachment by the sea. The objective of the operation was to breach the walls, flooding the interior of the island in order to facilitate a seaborne landing. In this case the bombing by the other squadrons was so successful that No. 617 was able to bring its valuable TALLBOYS home. However, it was to take a number of further operations before the island was taken, the last one by 5 Group on 30 October, the day before successful landings by commandos and other troops.

Four days after the first raid on Walcheren, and whilst the rest of the group carried out another attack on the island, 617 Squadron undertook an exceptionally difficult operation, the destruction of the Kembs Barrage. This dam-like structure, built to hold back the water of the Rhine on the Franco-German border just north of Basel, where the river divides into two streams running parallel, represented a potential problem to the US Seventh and French First Armies, which were planning to cross the river there and further north. The fear was that the Germans would release a huge volume of water, making such a crossing impossible.

For this operation the squadron, escorted by long-range Mustangs from Manston, was divided into two sections, the first of which, led by Fawke, was to drop its TALLBOYS, fused to detonate on impact, from between 6,000 and 8,500ft, in so doing drawing off the flak. The second, led by Tait, was to come in at 600ft, with its bombs fused to explode 30 minutes later. One of the high-level section managed to hit the dam, but the remainder missed it. The low-level section then attacked, with Tait placing his bomb exactly where he wanted it. The other aircraft missed the target, but Tait's bomb exploded in due course and breached the dam very satisfactorily; the water level upstream fell by over 11ft, stranding many barges. However, two aircraft of the low-level section were shot down, all the crew of one being killed immediately, whilst the other, piloted by Squadron Leader D. R. C. Wyness, ditched in the Rhine and the crew escaped unhurt. Four of them were captured and later shot by the Germans, and whilst the fate of the other three is unknown, as their bodies were never recovered, it is likely to have been the same.

During October 1944 two more squadrons were added to 5 Group, both initially at Bardney. No. 227 was formed from A Flight of 9 Squadron and B

Flight of 619 Squadron and moved two weeks later to Balderton, which had been used for the first nine months of 1944 by the USAAF for troop carrying. No. 189 was created from scratch and moved in early November to Fulbeck, which had also been used by the USAAF, where it joined 49 Squadron from Fiskerton, which airfield was now transferred to 1 Group along with Dunholme Lodge and Scampton. With eighteen squadrons, including the three in theory on loan from the Pathfinders, the 'Independent Air Force' was now, and remained until the end of the war, the largest group in Bomber Command.

October 1944 saw another innovation in the command, this time in 3 Group, which had been equipped with a new navigation and blind bombing system, Gee-H, which combined elements of both Gee and Oboe[5] to achieve very accurate results and which, unlike the latter, could be used by up to a hundred aircraft at the same time. It enabled the group to bomb blind through cloud, which was particularly attractive to Harris, as the uncertain weather of winter lay ahead. With a third of the group's aircraft fitted with Gee-H, it was now able to assume an independent role similar to that of 5 Group for the rest of the war, and Main Force of Bomber Command was reduced to 1, 4, 6, and 8 Groups. Harris now had his eggs in three baskets!

During the autumn of 1944 the Main Force turned back increasingly to the Ruhr. In addition to Walcheren and the canals, 5 Group was given a variety of targets in Germany, although it also bombed the U-boat pens in Bergen and Trondheim. Other than Munich and Nuremberg, the cities attacked were of a more modest size, such as Harburg, Homberg, Giessen and Heilbronn. The group also returned to Brunswick on the night of 14/15 October. Yet another variant of offset marking was used for this raid known as 'sector bombing', the purpose of which was to deliver the bombs over an area rather than tightly around an aiming point or along a line. This required every single aircraft to be given a separate heading, a fiendishly difficult exercise which required great precision, and 5 Group had failed over Brunswick before; this time it was to be completely successful, with the town centre, the railway station and a number of factories completely destroyed. This was the last big raid on the city, as no more were considered necessary.

A raid on Munich on 26/27 November was notable for being the first time that 5 Group as a whole used Loran, a new American hyperbolic navigation system, which was similar to Gee but had a much longer range of up to 1,500 miles. Installation was limited to the aircraft of 5, 8 and 100 Groups.

In the meantime, the *Tirpitz* had not been forgotten. Moreover, the battleship's move to Tromsø had brought it to just within range of aircraft flying directly from Lossiemouth in Scotland, once extra fuel tanks had been fitted and as much surplus weight as possible removed. In a letter to Harris of 19 October, Ralph set out how a successful attack could be made, and the first attempt took place on 29 October, when eighteen aircraft from each of 9 and 617 Squadrons, accompanied as before by the film unit, mounted Operation OBVIATE. Although a reconnaissance Mosquito reported the target area free of cloud, a bank drifted over the ship just as the bombers approached. Many of the aircraft nevertheless released their TALLBOYS, but neither they nor a subsequent reconnaissance were able to confirm a positive result, although it emerged long afterwards that additional damage had been inflicted. Not realizing this, and with daylight hours drawing in rapidly, it was decided that they would have to go again.

In the meantime, protection for the *Tirpitz* by the Luftwaffe had arrived in the shape of the fighters of Staffel 9 of Jagdgeschwader 5 at the airfield at Bardufoss, 68km to the south, not much more than ten minutes flying time for the Messerschmitt 109s with which the unit was equipped or the Focke-Wulf 190s to which it was in the process of converting. As Ralph wrote later,

> There came the question of whether or not to attempt a third attack. We knew that fighters had been sent to Bardufoss to protect *Tirpitz* and it was therefore extremely risky to hope that the squadron would not be intercepted. However we also knew from reconnaissance that there was a gap in the radar cover and by approaching through this there was a chance that the attack might be completed before the fighters could intercept. I decided that it was an acceptable risk although it was the worst decision I had to take during the whole period at 5 Group.[6]

On 12 November eighteen Lancasters from 617 Squadron, but only thirteen from 9 Squadron, as it had not been possible to de-ice the others in time, accompanied as before by the film unit, took off again for Norway in Operation CATECHISM. The aircraft arranged to rendezvous over Torneträsk Lake in neutral Sweden before setting course for Tromsø. The weather was clear, and Tait dropped the first TALLBOY at 0841. His own bomb hit the *Tirpitz* amidships on the port side, penetrating the armour just as Wallis had predicted, with another one landing just aft of it. Others fell closely around the vessel. It was enough to achieve complete success, and the film crew in the 463 Squadron Lancaster was able to confirm that the battleship had capsized.

As luck would have it, the fighter cover failed to materialize. Although it had been urgently requested by the *Tirpitz* immediately it was realized that an attack was imminent, a mixture of extreme confusion and gross inefficiency meant that, by the time the fighters had taken to the air and reached the site, the bombers were long gone. They all arrived back in Scotland intact, apart from a Lancaster of 9 Squadron, which was damaged by flak and landed in Sweden, where its crew were interned and then repatriated. Congratulations poured in, to the group and the squadrons, from King George VI and Crown Prince Olaf of Norway among many others, and on 15 November the Secretary of State for Air, Sir Archibald Sinclair, visited Woodhall Spa in person to express his appreciation.

Elworthy later attributed 90 per cent of the credit for the destruction of the *Tirpitz* to Ralph, which seems over-generous in the light of the exceptional planning by the staff and, even more so, the courage, skill and professionalism of the crews of the two squadrons. Nevertheless, it was Ralph's two major decisions, one to use the TALLBOY instead of the 2,000lb bomb, the other to proceed with the final attack in spite of the fighter danger, which were the most critical to success. If the raid had not taken place when it did, it would have been three months before there were enough daylight hours to mount another.

For the rest of 1944 the two TALLBOY squadrons joined forces with the rest of 5 Group to mount attacks on the Urft Dam in the Eifel mountains which were unsuccessful, and on a synthetic oil refinery at Pölitz which was seriously damaged. Shortly after Christmas, Tait's tour of operations came to an end. Recommended by Ralph and endorsed by Harris, he was to receive a third bar to his DSO, one of only eight to be awarded in the Second World War, during which the only other RAF recipient was Basil Embry.

Tait was succeeded by Johnny Fauquier, a Canadian serving at the time as SASO of 6 (RCAF) Group. Fauquier had begun his flying career as a bush pilot in Canada before joining the RCAF. He was much older than those of his rank at the time, but rapidly proved himself, initially in 405 Squadron in 4 Group, of which he in due course became the CO. He returned to the squadron in 1943 when it became part of 8 Group in which he acted as a Master Bomber; indeed, he had been Deputy Master Bomber at Peenemünde. By the time he was appointed SASO at 6 Group he had earned a DSO and bar and a DFC. He came warmly recommended by the AOC of the group, Air Vice-Marshal 'Black Mike' McEwen, but Ralph could only accept him if he agreed to a demotion from air commodore, although Ralph succeeded in having the job of CO at 617 Squadron upgraded to the rank of group captain. Fauquier's first operation with the squadron was an unsuccessful raid on Oslo Fjord on the last day of 1944 to attack German warships there, but he was to prove subsequently to be a thrusting commander, although perhaps not as popular as Gibson, Cheshire and Tait because of his more aggressive personal style.

The year 1945 began with a major surprise, if not for Ralph on the day itself, as he would have known some time beforehand, then for many others. In the New Year's Honours he was appointed a Knight Commander of the Most Excellent Order of the British Empire. Although by no means unprecedented, this was an unusual honour for an air vice-marshal, and even more so for a serving RAF bomber group commander. It has been frequently and erroneously written of Donald Bennett that he was the only bomber group commander not to be knighted. In fact, of the thirty-five officers who commanded bomber groups during the Second World War, twenty were never knighted. They included two Canadians, who were not permitted by their Government to accept knighthoods, and many who commanded only training groups, which might be supposed to have been less demanding than the operational groups, but also a number of men who may not have been as famous as Bennett but were in their own way just as distinguished. Examples were Edward Addison, who created in 100 (Bomber Support) Group an outstandingly effective response to the German night-fighter and anti-aircraft defences, which had been very substantially neutralized by the closing stages of the war, Richard Harrison, who led 3 Group from 1943 to 1946 and was the man behind its success in bombing with Gee-H, and Robert Oxland, who led 1 Group for over two years and then served for two more as SASO at Bomber Command, with particular responsibility for its operations in support of 21st Army Group.

Of those who were knighted, almost all were recognized by virtue of their subsequent appointments and their promotion to air marshal or beyond. This certainly applied to Ralph's four predecessors: Harris was knighted nearly three years after leaving 5 Group, Bottomley over three years later, Slessor just over a year later and Coryton over two years later and, in his case, after Ralph himself. The only other man to receive a knighthood whilst still in command of a bomber group was Edward Rice, on 1 January 1946, shortly before his retirement and after two years at 1 Group and one more at 7 (Operational Training) Group.

This, then, was recognition of exceptional achievement. The recommendation would have passed up from Harris to Portal and then to Sinclair, and would certainly have had the approval of the Prime Minister himself. Ralph had proved to be the most creative and imaginative of his peer group, never content with doing anything as it had always been done before, always looking instead for a better way. If he did not always earn the affection of those under his command, he had their undoubted respect and even admiration. Although 5 Group was not his creation, he was one of a series of AOCs who made it into the pre-eminent British bomber formation of the war, with a spirit uniquely its own; it cannot be entirely a coincidence that nine out of Bomber Command's nineteen VCs were earned by men serving in the group.

Ralph had had very little in the way of leave since joining 5 Group, but on 5 January 1945 he wrote to Harris requesting nine days from the 22nd of the month. He had staying with him at the time Hugh Lloyd, who he suggested should stand in for him temporarily. Lloyd had been previously the AOC Mediterranean Allied Coastal Force but was now designated the commander-to-be of the Very Long Range Bomber Force, also known as 'Tiger Force', which was intended to become the RAF's contribution to the bombing of Japan after Germany had been defeated.[7] Much of this formation was to consist of 5 Group squadrons, and Lloyd was there to become more familiar with them and with heavy bombers generally. He had been in Bomber Command early in the war, but his subsequent appointments had taken him in other directions.

Ralph was to get his leave, but he was also about to leave Bomber Command. On 16 January he handed 5 Group over to Air Vice-Marshal Hugh Constantine, one of a small number of talented younger officers who Harris wanted to get experience of command of a bomber group before the war was over. Just under a month later, on 15 February, he became AOC-in-C of Transport Command, with promotion to acting air marshal.

Ralph's service in Bomber Command was the most important period of his career, notwithstanding his subsequent promotions and more senior appointments. In retirement, the history of the command during that period was to be a subject on which he was frequently approached for comment. His personal reflections were encapsulated in his memoirs, written towards the end of his life:

Bomber Command was Harris, a man of great determination and a belief in running the show his way. He suffered throughout the war in having a command based in the U.K. Had it been based abroad he would have been given a broad task and forces considered necessary to achieve it and then left to get on with it in his own way, subject only to proddings from Winston. But based in this country it was entirely different, and led to anyone wanting squadrons, or trained pilots, getting them from Bomber Command. Again able staff officers at the Air Ministry could hardly help taking a closer and more personal interest in the day to day operations than would have been possible if the command had been abroad. This inevitably led to friction.

Harris believed that given an adequate force Bomber Command could bring Germany to the point of surrender, and that military occupation would follow without having to fight a major campaign. He was, therefore, constantly fighting for the resources he believed necessary, and this led to his entertaining any visitors and showing them what could be done. If this was often in somewhat optimistic vein it was only so in point of time for the results of the last six months of the Anglo American bomber offensive equalled anything that he had ever forecast.[8]

Ralph was right about the final months of the campaign, but it was probably his longstanding friendship with and loyalty to Harris, to whom he owed an immense amount, which led him to downplay his chief's huge over-optimism about the bomber offensive. The war against Germany could not, other than on a very much longer timescale, have been won by bombing alone; it also required both boots on the ground and command of the sea. However, he was right to make this point:

> Even as early as the autumn of 1942 the weak bomber offensive was tying up roughly one third of the enemy fighter force in local protection of their industries. This enabled the Desert Air Force to gain that air superiority which was such a vital ingredient in the campaign of Alamein.[9]

It is certainly true that the requirements for the defence of the Reich against Allied bombing diminished the Luftwaffe significantly in other campaigns, as the lack of air cover for the German defenders of Normandy was to demonstrate so visibly in June 1944.

Ralph had been unhappy about the large-scale bombing of civilian populations but had accepted that he had to obey orders. He was, however, always quick to point out both that the bombing campaign had been the only way to hit back at Germany in the early years of the war and that the civilian casualties were a small fraction of those suffered by the Soviet Union between 1941 and 1945 and by the inmates of the concentration camps, and were at least on a par with those incurred as a result of the Allied naval blockade of Germany in the Great War.

Along with the overwhelming majority of those who served in Bomber Command, Ralph was deeply upset by the treatment of Harris after the war had ended, by a government which seemed to want to distance itself from the controversy associated with area bombing. As far as he was concerned, Harris had carried out his orders to the very best of his ability, but in his own remarkable way:

> The individual crews knew him as a name only – but a name which had the power to make them go through with an operational tour of 30 sorties and a casualty rate of 4%. It was an interesting example of the many different ways in which leadership can be exercised.[10]

Chapter 20

Transport Command

During the inter-war years, transport operations were not a high priority for the RAF. Within the United Kingdom the railway network was capable of satisfying almost every requirement for the movement of goods and people, with road transport perfectly adequate for the last few miles if necessary. For transport between the United Kingdom and the outposts of Empire, everything went by sea; indeed, it would not be until after the Second World War that large-scale trooping began to be undertaken by air.

Transport aircraft did exist in the RAF, as Ralph himself experienced during his posting to 45 Squadron which, with its sister 70 Squadron, was primarily tasked with operating the mail service between Cairo and Baghdad. The two squadrons also carried a very modest number of passengers and some urgently needed cargo. Moreover, during the operations against the rebellious tribes in Kurdistan, they provided an early indicator of what was possible in wartime by transporting vital supplies from Hinaidi to Kirkuk and evacuating casualties.

Little further development of transport services, however, took place before 1939. The Vickers Valentia, a direct descendant of the Vickers Vernon which had equipped 45 Squadron, was still in service as the RAF's primary transport aircraft, although in the month that war was declared it had been joined in the role by its designated replacement, the Bristol Bombay. The Bombay could carry twenty-four troops, a similar amount to the Valentia, but at a higher speed over a slightly greater range.

As it turned out, the greatest initial spur to the future development of military air transport was not the need to carry men and material, but the urgent requirement for aircraft themselves in locations which were far from those in which they had been manufactured. From the entry of the Italians into the war in the summer of 1940 it became necessary to reinforce the RAF in Egypt on a continuous basis. Blenheims and Hurricanes, followed later by other types of fighter and light bomber, were despatched in crates by ship to Takoradi on the Gold Coast, assembled there and then flown in convoy along the West African Reinforcement Route to Lagos and Kano in Nigeria, across French Equatorial Africa and the Sudan to Khartoum and thence up the Nile to Cairo. The journey of some 3,700 miles took four days, with nights spent at permanently manned staging posts along the way. Larger aircraft with a longer range flew by an even more dangerous route, from Portreath in Cornwall to Gibraltar and then on to Malta and Cairo. Some even had the ability to fly directly from Gibraltar to Cairo across French North Africa and Axis-held Libya.

Even more important in the longer run was the Atlantic Reinforcement Route. The British aircraft industry did not have the capacity to satisfy all the RAF's needs, and a number of types of American aircraft were required, at first mostly Lockheed Hudsons for Coastal Command. The Atlantic Ferry Organization (ATFERO), which came under the control of the Ministry of Aircraft Production rather than the Air Ministry, was set up with pilots either from the British Overseas Airways Corporation (BOAC) or recruited directly in the USA and Canada. The departure point was Dorval, outside Montreal, and the first delivery of Hudsons was led across the North Atlantic by Donald Bennett in November 1940. These were followed in due course by the many other types of US aircraft used by the RAF and by Canadian-built Lancasters and Mosquitoes, flying on well-established routes to Prestwick via Gander or via Goose Bay and Reykjavik. Within the UK, inbound aircraft from North America and outbound aircraft to Gibraltar were handled by the Overseas Air Movements Control Unit (OAMCU), based in Gloucester.

In the second half of 1941 there was a change in organization. ATFERO was transferred to the RAF and became Ferry Command in July, taking control of OAMCU, now re-named 44 Group, in the following month. The AOC-in-C was Air Chief Marshal Sir Frederick Bowhill, with his HQ at Dorval. Bowhill, who was aged sixty-one and had actually been placed on the retired list on 1 July 1942 but immediately re-employed, had enjoyed a highly distinguished career, becoming the AOC of the Fighting Area of ADGB in 1931, Air Member for Personnel in 1933 and AOC-in-C of Coastal Command in 1937.

As well as being a staging post on the route to Cairo, Malta became a destination in itself. Supplying the island during its long siege became of vital importance and, although most of the heavy goods and all the fuel went by sea, vital supplies were also carried by air, providing 44 Group for the first time with a genuine transport rather than a ferry role.

In the meantime, the Aircraft Delivery Unit (Middle East), which had handled from the outset the arrival in Egypt of all aircraft on the West African Reinforcement Route and their subsequent deployment, became 216 Ferry Group, not only taking control of all ferry operations terminating in Egypt but also operating four transport squadrons, deploying Bombays, Hudsons, Lockheed Lodestars and later Dakotas, in which role it supported the campaign in North Africa. On a smaller scale, 179 (Ferry) Wing was set up in Karachi to receive and prepare for active service the aircraft required for the campaign in India and Burma against the Japanese. At the same time it acted as the receiving unit for transport aircraft arriving from the UK and the Middle East.

With demand growing, the Air Staff produced a paper in early 1943 with the title of 'Organisation for Air Transport', which was tabled at a meeting of the Air Council on 3 March. The paper considered the current organization and the services which it was providing on either side of the Atlantic and in the Middle East and India, noting also the position of BOAC, which operated a number of air routes, including invaluable ones to neutral Stockholm and Lisbon. It proposed that a new Transport Command should be created to control all the relevant RAF operations, with its HQ in the UK, and this was duly announced by Sir Archibald Sinclair in the House of Commons on 11 March. Bowhill transferred from Canada to the UK as the first AOC-in-C, in due course setting up his HQ at Harrow with four groups under command: No. 44 in Gloucester, No. 45, formerly Ferry Command, at Dorval, No. 216 in Cairo and No. 229, formed initially on the back of 179 Wing, in Karachi.

For the remainder of the war Transport Command performed an increasingly important role. Not only did it continue with its existing ferrying and air transport activities, but it acted in support of a number of army operations, including the landings in Sicily and on the Dodecanese Islands in 1943, the invasion of North-West Europe in June 1944 and the airborne operations at Arnhem in September 1944 and over the Rhine in March 1945. It was also engaged in Italy and the Balkans, for which purpose the aircraft of 216 Group came under the operational command of Mediterranean Allied Air Forces, and in Burma, where air supply became critical to the success of operations being carried out at the end of a very long and tenuous overland line of communication.

The first new group to be formed by Transport Command was 46 Group. Equipped from the start with Dakotas, it became heavily involved in 21st Army Group's operations in 1944 and 1945. In conjunction with 38 Group, which was permanently attached to the Airborne Forces and did not become part of Transport Command until June 1945, it dropped parachutists in Normandy on D-Day and pulled gliders to Arnhem in Operation MARKET GARDEN in September 1944, during which the only VC in Transport Command was awarded posthumously to Flight Lieutenant David Lord, and in Operation VARSITY, the airborne crossing of the Rhine in March 1945. Whilst not so employed, it carried out continuous re-supply and casualty evacuation operations for the army group.

Ralph took up his appointment as AOC-in-C on 15 February 1945, a month after he had left 5 Group, with his HQ initially at Harrow before moving to Bushy Park, near Teddington, the site of Eisenhower's headquarters during the run-up to the Normandy landings. He and Hilda moved into a house in Putney, followed by one in Kingston.

The delay in the handover was due to the reluctance of Bowhill to be finally retired. When Ralph rang him to ask when it would be convenient to take over, he received a dusty answer from Bowhill to stay where he was as he had no intention of giving up his command. The Air Ministry, however, thought otherwise! Bowhill had in any event by this time become unpopular with his Deputy AOC-in-C, Air Vice-Marshal Conrad Collier, and his SASO, Air Vice-Marshal A. L. 'Fido' Fiddament. In a letter to Ralph in 1971, Fiddament wrote that the credit for the raising of 46 Group and its training in the airborne forces role in just four months could be attributed entirely to Collier but had received scant recognition from Bowhill; indeed, on occasion Collier received the reverse of recognition or understanding. It was little surprise, then, that Ralph's appointment was warmly welcomed. 'Your arrival', wrote Fiddament 'brought great changes – fresh air at last (and a sense of humour!).'[1] The regard was mutual, Ralph writing later,

'Fortunately in Conrad Collier who was Deputy C-in-C I had a first class organiser, and in Fiddament a strong backup. With this team we were able to organize the expansion.'[2]

In early 1945 Transport Command was already a very substantial organization, comprising six groups, nineteen wings, six airports and thirty-five stations and staging posts. Its expansion continued in the last few months of the war and its immediate aftermath; indeed, it was the only part of the RAF to grow after VE Day, when cutbacks took place in all other commands. A number of squadrons from Bomber and Coastal Command were fed in rather than be disbanded, but they were well utilized for a while, particularly with the formal implementation of Large Scale Trooping by air to and from the Far East.

Yet another group, No.47, had been formed shortly before Ralph's arrival and was primarily designated to operate the trunk routes, which by now spanned the world, even crossing the Pacific to Australia via the United States. One of 47 Group's five squadrons was No.24, the VIP squadron, which was largely equipped with the Avro York, a civilian spin-off from the Lancaster, and the Dakota, but also included the Prime Minister's C-54 Skymaster, allocated to him specially by General 'Hap' Arnold, Chief of Staff of the USAAF. It was used extensively by Churchill, notably to attend the Yalta Conference shortly before Ralph's arrival as AOC-in-C. Ralph was to greet Churchill at Northolt on his return from the Potsdam Conference on 25 July 1945, the day before the announcement of the general election results which were to see him lose office.

The war against Japan continued for the first six months of Ralph's appointment. At this time, 229 Group had relocated from Karachi to New Delhi, which was better suited for its major role other than receiving aircraft from the UK, which was supporting the advances of Fourteenth Army in Central Burma and XV Corps in the Arakan. Its eleven locally-based squadrons came under the operational control of Air Command South-East Asia for this purpose, but it was still responsible to Transport Command for movements into and out of India.

The repatriation of troops going on demobilization and of former prisoners of war was particularly sensitive politically. Those in Europe were to some extent handled by Bomber Command, which had brought home a very large number of PoWs from Germany in Operation EXODUS and servicemen for demobilization from Italy in Operation DODGE, although the main onus in all such exercises fell on Transport Command. On 16 September Portal wrote to Ralph to emphasise this:

> One of the most urgent, if not the most urgent, need of this country today is to increase as quickly as possible the flow of men and women from the Services into industry and commerce ...
>
> Since shipping cannot do all this at once, most important assistance is to be given by the R.A.F. and we have set ourselves the objective of carrying at least 10,000 men a month from India, beginning in October ... It is a challenge which the Royal Air Force has accepted and in which it must not fail.[3]

Transport Command could only do this by expanding its resources, and by November 1945 it deployed twenty-two squadrons of four-engined aircraft and thirty-five of twin-engined aircraft. Those who were forward-thinking realized that this could not last – indeed, many of the aircrew members were themselves hoping for demobilization – but in the meantime, crews were getting valuable experience. Jack Slessor, at the time the Air Member for Personnel, wrote to Ralph to say that the Air Council and the Ministry of Civil Aviation had agreed that Transport Command should be officially recognized as the normal outlet from the RAF to civil aviation.

By the beginning of 1946 Transport Command had established four functions. The first was the regular movement of military passengers, mails and freight along its trunk routes, and the provision of local transport in each theatre; the second was the strategic movement of personnel and equipment between and within theatres; the third was its original function, aircraft deliveries; and the fourth was transport support for military operations. Two groups had been disbanded, Nos. 44 and 45, due to the cessation of ferry services from North America, but 38 Group, still devoted to airborne operations, had joined the command, as had 4 Group, hitherto part of Bomber Command. Early in the year, both Collier and Fiddament left the HQ, the former to command 3 Group in Bomber Command, the latter to remain in Transport Command as AOC 38 Group. The role of Deputy

AOC-in-C was abolished and Fiddament was relieved by Air Vice-Marshal Gerald Gibbs, who had shared the small and stuffy office in the Air Ministry with Ralph and Portal in the early 1930s.

There was one major fly in the ointment during the period of major expansion and it concerned accidents. The number of fatal accidents was far too high, and in one particularly distressing incident an aircraft full of troops returning from Burma had crashed with no survivors. Questions began to be asked in the House of Commons, accompanied by considerable criticism in the press, which compared the recent record unfavourably with pre-war civil aviation. Ralph grasped the nettle and persuaded the Secretary of State for Air, Viscount Stansgate, himself a former RAF officer with a DSO and a DFC from the Great War, to bring down a delegation of parliamentarians from Westminster for Ralph to talk to. By the use of graphs, charts and route maps he was able to demonstrate that, whilst the accident rate was too high, it was in fact dramatically lower in terms of the rate of accidents per air miles flown than it had been for pre-war civil aviation. He then carried out the same exercise with the aviation correspondents of the press which went off very well. These sessions, together with one for a large audience from the Air Ministry, raised the profile of Transport Command considerably and resulted in it being viewed much more favourably.

Ralph had, in fact, been on top of the problem for some time. His concern at the accident rate had caused him to establish the Transport Command Examining Unit in late 1945, with the objectives of setting standards for aircrew and training and testing them. Under the leadership of Squadron Leader (later Group Captain) R. C. E. Scott, the unit's staff was drawn from Category A aircrew – those graded exceptional – and involved flying tests and classroom examinations to test technical knowledge, airmanship and route experience. Every crew was route-checked during an actual operation at least once every six months. The standard improved dramatically and accident rates fell, helped also by another decision of Ralph's, that pilots should in future specialize on one type of aircraft.

In the meantime, the Air Council was addressing another issue, and its decision on it was to lead to a substantial contraction in Transport Command. Ever since it was formed it had been responsible for transport activities not only in and from the UK, but world-wide, the main exceptions being the campaigns in the Mediterranean and Burma, which had necessarily required local control of operations against the enemy but not of any of the command's other functions. This was not true of any of the other home commands, other than Coastal Command's outposts in Iceland, Gibraltar and the Azores. In the peacetime environment the RAF commanders outside the UK naturally wanted to take full control of establishments and operations in their own areas.

Unsurprisingly, the Air Council came down in favour of a reorganization. The Air Member for Supply and Organization, Ralph's old friend from Cranwell, Leslie Hollinghurst, wrote to him with their decision on 5 February 1946, later amplified by further directives. In future Transport Command would have the following responsibilities:

- The operational control and administration of all inter-command strategic moves, trunk route scheduled services and ferry operations.
- The control of all stations and units allocated to Transport Command in the UK, together with all military transport services into and within Europe and staging posts there.
- The training of all transport crews to standards laid down by the Air Ministry and the provision of transport crews to overseas commands.
- The development of techniques of air transport.
- The command of transport and airborne assault experimental establishments.

The overseas commands would in future assume the command and administration of all transport groups and units in their theatre and of all stations and staging posts there, and would be in charge of local flying control, but would also have to provide the facilities for Transport Command trunk routes to the standards laid down by the Air Ministry. The Ministry itself would define policy, allocate resources and plan trunk routes in collaboration with Transport Command and the Ministry of Civil Aviation.

Ralph did have to head off an attempt by the Air C-in-Cs in the Middle East and India to disband 216 and 229 Groups, something which was duly stamped on by Hollinghurst, but otherwise the reorganization was very sensible and relieved him of a considerable burden. One aspect continued to concern him, that the long-term demand for trunk routes, in particular to the Far East, could not be accurately assessed and might even be negligible in normal conditions. This would leave transport squadrons underemployed in the UK and would exacerbate the existing situation in which Transport Command was already markedly less efficient than its USAAF equivalent, which operated at eleven man-hours for every hour of flying time to the RAF's twenty-four man-hours. A somewhat testy correspondence on the issue ensued with the VCAS, Air Chief Marshal Sir Douglas Evill, but the key question, that of the likely utilization of transport, remained unresolved.

Ralph had, in the meantime, a number of other issues to consider, one of which was the actual operation of the trunk routes to the Far East. These had begun with one squadron flying regularly from Lyneham to Singapore, using the 'slip crew' method, whereby each stage was flown by a different crew. With rapid expansion it was found that more and more aircraft were becoming unserviceable, clogging the whole system. The otherwise highly efficient operations room at Bushy Park, run by Air Commodore 'Mouse' Fielden,[4] the Deputy SASO, was unable to resolve it, so Ralph ordered a change to single crews, each of which took one aircraft the whole way. This restarted the flow, albeit at a much slower tempo due to the crews' requirement to rest.

Much of the unserviceability was due to perceived problems with the magnetos in the aircraft engines, and Ralph went to Derby to seek the advice of Ernest Hives, the managing director of Rolls-Royce. His advice was to seal the engines and to allow the seals to be broken only on the explicit orders of the captain of the aircraft, and this measure had an immediately beneficial effect. The overriding problem, however, lay with engineers looking at the engines at every stop, a situation similar to that of petty unserviceability which had adversely affected 5 Group three years earlier. The rules already in place required inspections after a specific number of hours and, if this point occurred during a long-distance trip, the aircraft would be grounded. The hours were accordingly reduced so that the inspection would be carried out before departure if the aircraft was likely to exceed them during a trip, or increased if by so doing it would take the aircraft to a station which was equipped to carry out the inspection.

In order to see for himself what was happening on the ground, Ralph travelled up and down the route on a number of occasions in a York or a

Lancastrian, yet another aircraft derived from the Lancaster. The first of these involved a marathon journey from late July to early September 1945, taking Ralph to Malta, Egypt, the Persian Gulf, India, Burma, Ceylon, the Cocos Islands, Australia and New Zealand. In the last of these he was met by Tom Barrow, still the Air Secretary, and Maurice Buckley, formerly CO of 75 (NZ) Squadron and now an air commodore, and was the guest of honour at a lunch hosted by Peter Fraser, who was in his sixth year as prime minister.

Ralph had spent many hours standing on the tarmac of one or other of his airfields waiting for distinguished visitors to leave and was determined to avoid any such delays when he himself was travelling. He therefore coached the crews into priming the engines for take-off as soon as they saw him coming. Once he was aboard, the engines would be started immediately and the aircraft would begin to taxi with no delay at all.

He was also determined to speed up the landing process, once again drawing on his success in 5 Group. This was largely achieved by the installation of an instrument in the cockpit of each aircraft which could read the distance and direction from a beacon in the centre of the airfield.[5] As the aircraft approached it would call out the reading to the flying controller, who would then give the radius at which to turn on to a circular course and the point at which to turn in towards the runway. This was demonstrated to the visiting members of an international civil aviation organization, who were invited to give a different course to each of two Mosquitoes, two Halifaxes and two Dakotas, between them capable of very different speeds. The aircraft then took off and flew on their given courses for five minutes before executing a 180° turn back to the airfield, where the controller sorted them out so that they landed at a rate of one a minute, impressing the audience immensely.

By September 1946 the RAF was contracting fast, although Transport Command up until then was less affected than the other commands. The command still had several hundred aircraft on charge, the majority of them Dakotas and Yorks for long-distance operations, and Avro Ansons and Airspeed Oxfords for short-range work. It was, however, to face retrenchment itself when, in the following month, a proposal was put forward to merge 38 and 46 Groups. Ralph resisted strongly, writing to Hollinghurst that he had done his utmost to reduce overheads but that, given the different types of work undertaken by each group, it was necessary to retain them all. He suggested, therefore, that the command should consist of four groups of about 4,000 personnel each. The counter-proposal from the Air Ministry was to disband 4 Group and to transfer 38 Group, which retained its commitment to the Airborne Forces, to the British Air Forces of Occupation in Germany.

The debate continued into 1947 but, with the growing demands to cut costs, something had to give. As it turned out, 4 Group was indeed disbanded, but both 38 and 46 Groups remained as separate entities in Transport Command, the former continuing to provide training and transport for the Airborne Forces and also to absorb the whole of the Transport Command Development Unit. All the short-range services were handled by 46 Group, including the Metropolitan Communications Squadron for VIPs, but it also included 24 Squadron for long distance VIP flights, while 47 Group ran all the long-distance trunk routes and trooping flights.

In the autumn of 1946 Ralph began to consider his own future. He was later to say that Transport Command was the toughest appointment that he had had in the RAF, although it had certainly not lacked interest. One of the attractions was the close relationship which he had built up with British civil aviation, which was starting a period of considerable expansion. BOAC, created as a state airline in 1939 by the amalgamation of Imperial Airways and British Airways, had played a major role in wartime civilian transport operations, latterly in conjunction with Transport Command. In 1944, for instance, it flew nearly 19 million miles and carried over 100,000 passengers, 6,500 tons of cargo and nearly 2,000 tons of mail. By the end of the war it was operating twenty-five regular routes to Europe, North America, the Middle East, South Asia, and North, West, South and Central Africa.

In the meantime, the British Government was creating two other state-owned airlines, one of which was to become British European Airways, whilst the other, British South American Airways, was set up in late 1945 with Donald Bennett as its Managing Director, following his early retirement from the RAF. A number of smaller privately owned airlines had also been formed or were in contemplation.

Ralph had had a great deal to do with BOAC throughout his time at Transport Command and knew all the other players. With considerable growth in the industry a certainty, he was greatly attracted by its potential, and his name began to be spoken of in connection with the appointment of a new Managing Director or even Chairman at BOAC. In the autumn of 1946 he made an informal approach to Jack Slessor, as Air Member for Personnel, to see if he might be able to take early retirement in order to assume one of these roles. The response was immediate and came by way of a private handwritten letter:

> I will not pretend that it would not be a considerable embarrassment to us if you were to want to retire next year. There is no present intention of relieving you in Transport Command – the two year tenure does not apply rigidly to key appointments like yours. And we are running on such a narrow margin of experienced and capable very senior officers that a premature retirement even of one is liable to set in train a whole host of consequentials and play hell with any planned scheme of appointments.[6]

Slessor went on to say that it might be possible to get the board of BOAC to extend Viscount Knollys' term as chairman, but in fact Knollys was to retire in early 1947.

There was no way in which Ralph would have rejected such an appeal to his sense of duty but, in agreeing to stay on, he said goodbye to a promising career in civil aviation. His powers of leadership and organization were such that he would certainly have made an excellent head of BOAC during the period of post-war expansion, when new aircraft were being introduced and in which passenger air transport was rapidly becoming attractive to the many and not just to the well-heeled few. In the event, he soldiered on in his current job until late September 1947, assuming a new appointment as AOC-in-C of Flying Training Command in the following month. He left behind a highly capable organization, which would distinguish itself during the Berlin Airlift in the following year.

As a pleasing coda to his service at Transport Command, he was delighted to hear in March 1948 that the Royal Aeronautical Society had awarded him the Edward Busk Memorial Prize for a paper which he had delivered to the society over a year earlier on 'Development of Air Transport during the War'.

Chapter 21

The Air Council

If there was a branch of the RAF on which Ralph was an acknowledged expert, other than bomber and transport operations, it was flying training. In addition to his own training at 4 FTS in Egypt, he had been the Training Officer at Wessex Bombing Area in the early 1930s, a senior officer on the staff of Training Command in 1936, SASO of a Bomber Command training group and then AOC of another in 1940, followed by nearly two years in the Air Ministry as Director of Flying Training. He had also been deeply concerned with all aspects of flying training whilst CAS in New Zealand and much later as AOC of two bomber groups, with heavy conversion units and a Lancaster finishing school under his direct command, and he had made flying training one of his priorities as AOC-in-C of Transport Command. There was, in fact, little that he did not know about the subject.

Flying Training Command was headquartered at Shinfield Park, near Reading. The AOC-in-C's residence had been handed over to another command, so Ralph and Hilda had to look for an alternative. They found one in the shape of Holdshott House in Heckfield, not far from the HQ, which was acquired and furnished by the Air Ministry, becoming a comfortable family home where Hilda was able to improve the garden, much as she had done at The Field House whilst Ralph was Director of Flying Training from 1940 to 1942.

By the time that Ralph took up his appointment, the command had been progressively scaled down into a much smaller organization than the one which had satisfied the requirements of war. Among other things, the distinction between elementary and service flying training schools had been abolished, and all the remaining units were designated simply as flying training schools, which followed the pre-war model of 'all-through' training.[1] The command was divided into three groups and would shortly be reduced to two. No. 21 was based at Ralph's old 5 Group HQ, Morton Hall, Swinderby and was responsible for the RAF College at Cranwell, the Empire Air Navigation School and the flying training schools in the Midlands, North of England and Scotland, whilst 23 Group was based in Leighton Buzzard and responsible for the flying training schools in the Cotswolds and the West and South of England, as well as the Aeroplane and Armament Experimental Establishment, the Central Flying School and the Empire Flying School. In April 1948, 25 Group, hitherto responsible for armament training, was disbanded and its activities absorbed into the other groups.

In spite of the cutbacks, the average aircraft strength of Flying Training Command during 1948 was 885, of which the most prolific type was the North American Harvard, used for advanced single-engine training. Initial training was still carried out on Tiger Moths, but they were in the course of being replaced by the Percival Prentice, whilst early stage multi-engine training remained on Ansons and Oxfords, both of which were to give many more years service. Advanced training took place on Lancasters, Wellingtons, Mosquitoes and Spitfires.

During the same year 3,452 aircrew passed out of flying training schools, of whom 2,319 were pilots, 808 navigators, 247 wireless operators and 63 air gunners, with 15 unspecified. The wastage figure was 937, of whom 19 had been killed or were missing.

A familiar problem raised its head before Ralph had even arrived at Shinfield. On his way down from Scotland, where he had been staying at Crawford Priory, he landed at one training unit which was flying Wellingtons and which, as he had been briefed in advance, had not satisfied its target of flying hours, largely due to maintenance problems with its aircraft. It had an establishment of twenty-four aircraft, and the CO requested a further six in order to remedy the situation. Ralph quickly ascertained that the unit actually had more aircraft than it could service with the manpower available. Instead of providing six more aircraft he took six away, telling the CO that he expected him to fulfil his quota of flying hours with the reduced number. With help from the engineering staff at Shinfield Park, the CO, who quite clearly thought that Ralph was mad at the time, was in due course able to achieve his targeted level of efficiency.

Part of the solution, as it had been at both 5 Group and Transport Command, was a rationalization of the engineering inspection regime. The first step was to replace the daily inspection of each aircraft with either a weekly or a ten-flying-hour inspection, whichever occurred sooner. The next was to increase what was called the 'minor cycle' inspection from 50 to 100 hours, at the same time cutting down on certain tasks. These changes proved to be beneficial, without any serious adverse impact, and saved both time and cost.

Much of this work was initiated by the Research Branch of Flying Training Command, which carried out a detailed programme of tasks under the leadership of Mr F. C. Watts, the Principal Scientific Officer. This covered all aspects of flying training, including the selection of students, examination and assessment techniques, monitoring of students' progress, planning and forecasting. Watts, who had first met Ralph at Syerston in 1943, was later to write of his management style:

> I believe that this was Sir Ralph's principle and forte – to take a team of men as they were and to get the best out of them, by delegating responsibility to them and integrating their efforts. His was the originality of concept and the drive, to get things done.[2]

All this was carried out in the name of maximum efficiency, which remained Ralph's holy grail. He was concerned, as he had been in Transport Command, that the USAF was able to achieve much higher levels of efficiency than the RAF. He accepted that this was to some degree a matter of scale, but he was anxious to learn more himself. In early 1950 he accepted an invitation to lecture at both the USAF's Air Command and Staff College at Maxwell Air Force Base near Montgomery, Alabama, and the National War College near Washington DC,[3] which enabled him also to visit a number of flying training establishments. His guide whilst he was there was Brigadier General Byron E. Gates, for some reason nicknamed 'Hungry', who was the Deputy Commander and Chief of Staff of the Flying Division of Air Training Command, based at Randolph Field, Texas. Ralph quickly discovered that, in the vast open spaces available to them, the Americans could very easily build a training base in an area which could be assured of good weather and surround it with satellite fields where the actual work could take place, allowing them to make economies which were impossible in the UK. Ralph had closed a number of surplus stations following his arrival at Flying Training Command, which had certainly saved costs, but non-financial efficiencies such as flying hours were more difficult to achieve.

Ralph's visit to the United States enabled him to establish valuable contacts with the USAF at a very senior level, which included Generals Muir Fairchild, the Vice-Chief of Staff, Lauris Norstad, at the time Deputy Chief of Staff for Operations and shortly to command US Air Forces in Europe, and Benjamin Chidlaw, Deputy Commanding General of Air Materials Command. He was impressed by the quality of the students at the two colleges, who asked a lot of intelligent questions and laughed freely. The same was true of the students at the Canadian Forces College, which he visited subsequently.

Back in the UK, Ralph encountered another familiar problem, the commissioning of pilots. Once again the criteria seemed to include the accents with which they spoke, in addition to the qualities which he valued much more highly, flying ability, initiative and leadership. In his desire in particular to avoid attaching too much weight to social status, he wrote a note for guidance, which successive AOCs-in-C were to use for many years afterwards.

The whole command felt the force of his personality. The influential editor of *The Aeroplane* wrote later:

> His way of doing things shook a good many people, and put the fear into some, but his way worked. A very old friend of mine in the Command admitted that there was a certain amount of trembling at first. 'But', said he, 'it's all right when you've become inCochranated.' And Training Command under him, like Transport Command, was a 'happy ship'.[4]

Ralph had believed for some time that the RAF required a practical counterpart to its Staff College. He found an enthusiastic ally in Basil Embry, now ACAS (Training) at the Air Ministry, with whom Ralph had visited Southern Rhodesia in September and October 1948 to inspect training facilities there. Embry was to write subsequently:

Ralph Cochrane, the exceptionally able Commander-in-Chief of Flying Training Command and I were both anxious to establish a college of advanced study into the practicable problems of all aspects of modern Service aviation ... The professional side of an officer's training had become far more complex and assumed much greater importance than in the pre-war era, when a keen officer could keep abreast of current developments comparatively easily. But now we believed that a college with at least equal status to that of the Staff College was a pressing requirement if the R.A.F. was to maintain its professional standards and obtain maximum results from its equipment.[5]

Ralph had just the site in mind, RAF Manby in Lincolnshire, an Expansion Period airfield with a good number of large brick buildings, whose sole occupant was the Empire Air Armament School, part of 21 Group. He and Embry put up a proposal to the Air Council, which was accepted, and the RAF Flying College, into which the Armament School was folded, opened on 1 June 1949. In addition to familiar aircraft from the war years, the school acquired a number of post-war types, including the Avro Lincoln, successor to the Lancaster, the de Havilland Vampire, which followed the Gloster Meteor as the second jet aircraft in operational use with the RAF, and two transport aircraft, the Vickers Valetta and the Handley Page Hastings, designed to replace the Dakota and the York respectively.

Ralph used the RAF Flying College as the venue for the annual Flying Training Command Conference. One or more stations were usually persuaded to write and perform a play on a topical subject, some of which were extremely witty. At the first conference held at the college, shortly after it opened, the principal guest speaker was Major General Robert W. Harper, Commanding General of the USAF Air Training Command.

A very much more demanding conference, from Ralph's perspective at least, was held at the Royal Empire Society's building in Northumberland Avenue on 16–20 May 1949 on the initiative of Tedder, who had succeeded Portal as CAS on 1 January 1946. Ralph was given the task of organizing what was codenamed Exercise ARIEL, whose purpose was to debate many of the problems of an air force in peacetime. Ralph arranged a very ambitious programme, which nearly came to grief when the Prime Minister,

Clement Attlee, got wind of it and then vetoed it on the grounds that some of the subjects to be discussed impinged on ministerial responsibility. After Tedder and Ralph had explained more fully what was to be involved, and a few small adjustments had been made to the programme, Attlee relented and the conference went ahead, accompanied by a concurrent exhibition on 'Why the Royal Air Force wants quality in its men' at the nearby Victoria Hotel.

The first two days were reserved for 162 senior RAF and civilian Air Ministry personnel and covered policy and organization on the first afternoon and then manning and training on the next full day, with presentations from the relevant members of the Air Council and the Air Staff and an opening address and closing summary by Tedder, who throughout the conference sat with Ralph at a table on the platform.

For the next two and a half days those already present were joined by 190 representatives of the other two services and people from many other walks of life, including leading civil servants, industrialists, educationalists, trades unionists, journalists, scientists and representatives of professional bodies and business organizations. The theme was the harmonization of the RAF's requirements for high quality intelligence and technical skill in its personnel with those demanded by civilian careers. Among the questions asked were how the nation could reap the benefit of the training, skill and experience gained in the RAF, and how an individual could make an initial career in the RAF and then move on seamlessly to another outside the service. One session involved a panel of representatives from industry and the trades unions, chaired by the historian Sir Arthur Bryant, and the last afternoon was devoted to discussion, led by an RAF chairman with representatives of management, labour, education and the professions.

Ralph's conclusion was that it had proved to be a very useful exercise albeit, on occasion, a controversial one. He later contrasted it favourably with a conference held by Montgomery at the Army Staff College at Camberley, writing:

> With typical Monty showmanship he made his entrance into the arena carrying under his arm a green book. This he then held aloft saying, 'This is the green book – this is the tactical doctrine which the Army is

to be taught – and there will be no argument.' I was sitting with Tedder. I could feel him squirming at the thought that in a period when the first atom bomb had been dropped anyone could be so foolish as to wish to stifle argument, or to think that it was possible to produce a doctrine.[6]

Tedder loathed Montgomery and vice versa, but it is difficult to disagree with the former's sentiment. Ralph was later to find that when lecturing at Camberley it was difficult to raise more than a few superficial questions, whilst at the RAF and Royal Navy Staff Colleges he could always get a decent argument going.

In March 1949 Ralph was once again appointed Air ADC to the King. As before, this was not a particularly onerous duty, but he was required to attend a number of specifically RAF events alongside the monarch, an example being the presentation of a new King's Colour to the service in May 1951, following which he received a signed copy of the address as an expression of thanks. He had become a Knight Commander of the Order of the Bath in the Birthday Honours of 1948 and, two years later, was to be advanced to Knight Grand Cross in the Order of the British Empire. Following the King's untimely death in 1952, Ralph was reappointed as Air ADC to the Queen.

In October 1949 Ralph read an article in the *Evening News* which revealed that Tedder was to retire as CAS and forecast that he was to succeed him. Tedder, whom he saw on the following day, confirmed that Ralph was indeed his personal choice[7] and that he had recommended him as such to Attlee, in whose effective gift the appointment lay, subject only to confirmation by the King. Ralph, who had been promoted to air chief marshal on 1 March, possessed all the qualifications, but Attlee had another officer in mind, Jack Slessor, and it was Slessor who succeeded Tedder on New Year's Day 1950.

Why Slessor should have been preferred to Ralph is a matter of conjecture.[8] Ralph has frequently been described as having the best brain in the RAF during his later years in the service, but he was almost certainly less well known outside it than Slessor. The latter had enjoyed a stellar career, notably as AOC-in-C of Coastal Command during the period when the Battle of the Atlantic was effectively won, and had held a series of appointments during the war which brought him into close contact with the other two British services and with senior American commanders, latterly as C-in-C of the RAF in the Mediterranean and Middle East and Deputy Air C-in-C of the Mediterranean Allied Air Forces. In the early 1930s he had spent four years on the Directing Staff at Camberley, making numerous friends in the Army. Moreover, for the two years before his appointment as CAS, he had been Commandant of the Imperial Defence College, in which appointment he had followed General Sir William Slim, who had himself just been appointed to succeed Montgomery as Chief of the Imperial General Staff. At the IDC Slessor had enjoyed unparalleled exposure to politicians, senior civil servants, industrialists, bankers, trades unionists and representatives of Great Britain's allies, whilst Ralph, at the same time, remained relatively unknown on a personal level to the non-RAF community.

This unquestionably came as a very deep disappointment to Ralph, but there was a consolation prize when Slessor immediately asked him to become his Vice-Chief.[9] He accepted because he had always liked Slessor and knew that he could work well with him, but he was in any event probably better suited to a role which was facing inward towards the RAF rather than outwards towards politicians and the public. The Air Council, moreover, numbered many friends amongst its members, notably Hollinghurst as Air Member for Personnel and his old friend from the airship service, Victor Goddard, as Air Member for Technical Services, whilst Alex Coryton, now the Controller of Supplies, sat as an additional member.

There had been a Deputy Chief of the Air Staff since 1920, but the position of VCAS was a much more recent one, the first being appointed in 1940 in response to the demands of world war. The VCAS became perceived, if anything, as senior to the DCAS, with men like Wilfrid Freeman becoming very much the right hand man of the CAS. During the war and for some time afterwards, including throughout Ralph's tenure, the vice-chiefs of the three services had their own committee, which had certain continuing functions but also acted for the chiefs when they were out of the country, notably at the major wartime Allied conferences.

Ralph's predecessor as VCAS, Air Marshal Sir Arthur Sanders, now became the DCAS, at the same time holding on to his existing portfolio of responsibilities. These included operations and intelligence, which were no longer the priority that they had been in wartime, but also strategic and inter-service policy, the RAF's roles in NATO and the Western Union[10] and relationships with Commonwealth and foreign air forces. Ralph's own duties, held hitherto by the DCAS, consisted of the strength and the fighting efficiency of the RAF, the requirement for and the development and production of new aircraft, air training, organization and communications. It is clear that, on the one hand, Slessor wanted Ralph as his right-hand man, but on the other believed that he was better suited to a different portfolio of responsibilities than those of his predecessor.

Reporting to Ralph were three Assistant Chiefs of the Air Staff, responsible respectively for training, operational requirements and signals, and the Scientific Adviser to the Air Ministry. The ACAS (Signals) was responsible not only for communications but also for all the electronic navigation systems and counter-measures employed by the RAF, and the incumbent was Edward Addison, who had been AOC of 100 (Bomber Support) Group during the latter stages of the war and was well known to Ralph.

The Scientific Adviser, Dr Robert (later Sir Robert) Cockburn, had played a key role in the development of electronic counter-measures. He was responsible for briefing Ralph in respect of his membership of the Defence Policy Research Committee, which was chaired initially by Sir Henry Tizard, who had so strongly supported Barnes Wallis in the development of UPKEEP. Unfortunately, Tizard had never seen eye to eye with Lord Cherwell, and when Churchill returned to office as Prime Minister in October 1951 and appointed Cherwell as Paymaster General, Tizard stood down from the chairmanship. He was replaced by Sir Frederick Brundrett, the Deputy Scientific Adviser to the Ministry of Defence. In Ralph's opinion, the Defence Policy Research Committee never achieved much in any event, largely because the Royal Navy effectively opted out of much of its business, although the representatives from the Admiralty were personally well disposed.

Whilst the inter-service relationships in general were better than they had been before the war, the Royal Navy kept up its long campaign to take over Coastal Command. Slessor, a former AOC-in-C of the Command, who had worked harmoniously with the Navy during the war, made what Ralph considered to be a very generous offer of what would effectively have been a joint venture, putting the Royal Navy in an even better position than the nominal operational control that it had secured from 1941 to 1945. The Navy, however, wanted all or nothing and got nothing!

If relations with the Royal Navy were not always harmonious, those with the USAF were excellent, and Ralph visited the USA and Canada on two further occasions. On the first of these, in company with Cockburn and with Air Vice-Marshal Claude Pelly, the ACAS (Operational Requirements), who had served under him at the Air Ministry in 1939, he went primarily to discuss the requirements for coordinating air defence with the British Combined Services Committee in Washington, which was chaired by Tedder, and with the Americans. This visit included a tour of experimental establishments and, whilst doing so on the West Coast, Ralph and his colleagues were the guests of Howard Hughes. Landing at Hughes' airfield, Ralph was told that a figure in grubby overalls working on the engine of a light aircraft was the great man himself. He asked if he should go across to speak to him, but was advised not to do so and, indeed, this was the last that the party saw of him. There was, however, nothing wrong with their host's hospitality, with Ralph accommodated in Marilyn Monroe's vast bedroom in one of his hotels.

On their way back they paid a visit to an experimental station which, for Ralph, was notable for three things. One was hearing his first supersonic boom; the second was meeting a young man in whose work nobody appeared to be taking any interest, but whom Ralph was able to reassure from his own experience that he was working on exactly the right lines; and the third was winning the jackpot of 25 cent pieces in the officers' club and spending the rest of the evening putting them back in!

The geopolitical background to Ralph's term of appointment as VCAS was dominated by the growing threat from the Communist powers, the USSR and China. The RAF had performed magnificently during the Soviet blockade of Berlin, when Transport Command had carried over half a million tons of supplies to the beleaguered city. Even more ominously than this confrontation, the Russians had exploded a nuclear device in the summer of 1949, years ahead of the experts' predictions. The emphasis of defence was thus firmly fixed on the border between Western and Eastern Europe and, in September 1951, the British Air Forces of Occupation in Germany were placed at the disposal of the NATO Supreme Allied Commander.

In the meantime, operational requirements, which were in many ways the most significant element of Ralph's responsibilities, now included the introduction of not only a whole new generation of jet aircraft, beginning with the English Electric Canberra, which entered service in January 1951, and continuing with the V-Bombers and the Hawker Hunter, but also a variety of missiles, air-to-air, air-to-ground and ground-to-air. Ralph was in favour of building up and maintaining a 24-hour response force capable of very rapid deployment and making sure that the Russians were well aware of the UK's ability to counter any attack.

The focus on European defence meant that the United Kingdom was unable to provide a major air force front-line commitment to the United Nations during the Korean War, although it despatched a squadron of Sunderland flying boats, provided volunteer pilots for the USAF and the RAAF and transported large amounts of supplies and personnel for the British and Commonwealth ground forces. The RAF was, however, heavily engaged in countering the communist insurgency in Malaya, carrying out both strikes against the guerillas and supply drops in the jungle to those fighting them.

On the domestic front, Ralph and Hilda had bought the end of the lease of a large flat in Bradbrook House, Kinnerton Street, Belgravia. This was an extraordinary dwelling, whose walls had reputedly been panelled by an eccentric Canadian millionaire from villas in Italy. It contained a magnificent room with an enormous fireplace and a minstrel's gallery, where John had to sleep as there were not enough bedrooms, and which was highly suitable for entertaining, especially as Grizel was by this time beginning to attract attention. The floor, however, which had appeared to be beautifully sprung, was not up to the demands of an eightsome reel, which had the occupants of the flat below rushing up to say that the ceiling was about to collapse!

In 1951, the first of what would be a multitude of books was published on Operation CHASTISE and, indeed, on the further wartime exploits of 617 Squadron. The initiative for this came from the Air Historical Branch of the Air Ministry, which first approached Leonard Cheshire to write it; but he declined due both to ill-health at the time and the demands made on him by running a hospice. The choice of author eventually fell on Paul Brickhill, a former RAF fighter pilot who had been shot down and made a prisoner-of-war. A journalist by profession both before and after the war, Brickhill was already writing a book on the mass break-out from Stalag Luft III which was published in 1950 as *The Great Escape*, but he agreed to take on the second project at the same time. *The Dam Busters* came out in 1951 and was an immediate best-seller. Ralph had been involved from the outset and was highly supportive, making himself readily available to the author.

The book's publication came shortly after Barnes Wallis had received an award of £10,000 from the Royal Commission on Awards to Inventors for his work on the development of UPKEEP. This had been at the instigation of his long-time supporter Wilfrid Freeman, and Wallis had initially turned down the idea. However, he changed his mind after deciding to settle any sum received on a foundation at his old school, Christ's Hospital, for the education of the children of RAF personnel. He was appalled when the Ministry of Supply opposed his application on a number of specious grounds. He was, however, strongly backed by a number of others, notably Freeman himself, but also Ralph and many who had been involved in CHASTISE, and the award went through, albeit that it was less than Wallis had hoped for.

It was in the aftermath of these events that the first reunion of 617 Squadron was held at the Connaught Rooms in London on 19 October 1951. Tait was in the chair, and Ralph was the guest of honour and made a short speech before proposing a toast to the squadron. Wallis was loudly applauded for setting up the new foundation, and Cheshire was called upon to speak by those present, followed by Micky Martin, who had made the arrangements. A number of others associated in the past with the squadron were present as guests, including Mutt Summers, Harry Satterly and Bobby Sharp.

On 29 November 1952 Ralph's thirty-seven-year career in the RNAS and the RAF came to a close. As both he and Slessor had taken up their appointments on the Air Council at much the same time, they agreed that Ralph, who would be reaching retirement age first, should go six months ahead to allow his successor to bed himself in before a new CAS was installed. The reverse of what had happened on Ralph's appointment now took place. John Baker, who had succeeded Sanders as DCAS in March 1952, became VCAS but retained his portfolio of responsibilities, whilst Ronald Ivelaw-Chapman took over Ralph's duties, but with the title of DCAS.

There were many who were sorry to see him go, and not just from his own service. Admiral Sir Michael Denny, the Third Sea Lord and Controller of the Navy, spoke of the 'wise comment and shrewd counsel which has always been your contribution',[11] whilst Air Chief Marshal Sir William Dickson, the Air Member for Supply and Organization and recently nominated to succeed Slessor as CAS, wrote that Ralph's 'clear and far-seeing mind has done immense things for the service and it seems madness to be losing you just when you are beginning to see general respect and acceptance of your views'.[12] Slessor himself went further: 'If there is any gratitude going between us two I promise you that it is you who should be at the receiving end! You have never been one for personal publicity and I doubt whether the service will ever realize what it owes to you, both as a Commander-in-Chief and as VCAS.'[13]

Chapter 22

Into Industry

Ralph had never intended that his retirement from the RAF should lead to a life of ease, but his immediate action was nevertheless to take several weeks holiday. This included some skiing, a sport which he had taken up again with great enthusiasm; indeed, he had led a large party, including members of the family, to Zweisimmen in Switzerland during the first winter after the war. He had not been able to spend a great deal of time with his parents or siblings during the war, although visits to Crawford Priory had become more frequent subsequently. Both of his parents had died whilst he was still in the service, his mother in 1950 at the age of eighty-nine and his father in the following year at a remarkable ninety-three. Tom had inherited the title and taken over Crawford Priory and the management of the lime works and farm. A widower since Nellie was killed in Egypt in 1934, he had married Mary Duckham in 1948.

Ralph's brother Archie had sat as a Unionist Member of Parliament for East Fife from 1924 to 1929, when he lost narrowly to the Liberal candidate in a general election, and for Dunbartonshire between 1932 and 1936, stepping down when he was appointed Governor of Burma. He retired from the governorship in 1941, narrowly avoiding the fate of his successor, who in early 1942 was forced out of the country in humiliating circumstances by the Japanese invasion. Archie offered his services once again to the Royal Navy and, with the rank of acting captain, spent much of the rest of the war in command of an armed merchant cruiser on convoy duty in the Atlantic. His wife Dorothy, née Cornwallis, was a formidable woman who had been until very recently the Chief Commissioner for England of the Girl Guides and was now their President.

Ralph's only surviving sister, Kitty, Countess of Elgin and Kincardine, had been appointed a Dame of the British Empire in her own right in 1938 for good works in Scotland. Ralph had always been close to Kitty, and he and

Hilda were frequent visitors to the Elgins' house, Broomhall, on the north bank of the Firth of Forth near Dunfermline.

At the time of Ralph's retirement from the RAF Grizel had recently become engaged. Her fiancé, Bobby Stewart, had served as a subaltern in the Scots Guards during the war and its immediate aftermath before going on to take a BA in Agriculture at Oxford, with a view to running his family estate, Arndean, by Dollar in Clackmannanshire. He retained his commission as an officer in the 7th (Territorial) Battalion of the Argyll and Sutherland Highlanders, which he was to command a decade later. He and Grizel were married in May 1953 and produced Ralph and Hilda's first grandchild, Catriona, in the following year, to be followed in due course by four others, a second daughter, Sara, and three sons, Alexander, John and David. Bobby was to achieve prominence in local affairs, becoming in due course Lord Lieutenant of Kinross-shire and later of Clackmannanshire.

John had received his secondary education at Eton, which he left in 1953. He decided to follow his father into the RAF for his two years of National Service and was selected initially for navigator training on the Canberra; but there was an excess of applicants, so he opted instead for the RAF Regiment, serving in Germany. After his National Service ended he accepted a temporary job offer in Tema, Ghana, building a harbour. He travelled there overland by motorbike, other than on a short stretch of the journey when both he and the bike travelled on an ancient lorry with five other passengers and a goat that became dinner that evening; Ralph was most impressed by his initiative. On his return, John went up to Balliol College, Oxford to read Politics, Philosophy and Economics, graduating in 1959 and joining the accountancy firm of Peat, Marwick and Mitchell as an articled clerk. Shortly after he arrived at the firm he was given permission to take a month off for a project to which he had committed himself earlier. This involved taking a party of thirty graduates and undergraduates to Moscow in an old London Transport double-decker bus, an epic journey which, for a short time, grabbed the attention of the British and European press and also pleased his father enormously.

Malcolm followed John to Eton in 1952. On leaving in 1956, he spent a gap year in France before undertaking his National Service in the Scots Guards. In 1959 he went up to Balliol, once again in his brother's footsteps.

Whilst there he won a Pathfinder Scholarship to study Fine Art in the USA, which was extended from the customary eight weeks to a full year.

It was a deep disappointment to Ralph that he had been unable to follow up the feelers which had been put out to him in 1946 by BOAC to assume a role in the company for which he was exceptionally well suited at the time, but which was now firmly occupied. He had been in touch more recently with Sholto Douglas, whom he had known well as a member of the Directing Staff at the IDC in 1935 and who was now the chairman of British European Airways. However, the managing director of BEA was well entrenched in his job and, although the possibility of Ralph becoming deputy chairman was mooted, this would have been a non-executive role, and Ralph was determined from the outset to pursue a full-time second career.

As it happened, what seemed like a suitable opportunity emerged early in January 1953, when he was approached by a former RAF colleague, Group Captain George Bailey. Bailey was the son of the founder and now himself the chairman and managing director of C. H. Bailey Ltd., which was engaged in ship repairing, heavy engineering and the operation of docks in Newport, Monmouthshire. He also introduced Ralph to Sir John Howard, the founder, chairman and managing director of John Howard & Co. Ltd., civil engineers. After a few meetings Ralph was invited to become the managing director of a new company which they proposed to set up to build ships on the bank of the River Usk at Newport, in newly constructed dry docks rather than on traditional slipways. These docks, due to the very high rise and fall of the tide in the Severn Estuary, could be filled on the flood and drained on the ebb. The hull and basic superstructure of the vessels could thus be built in a dry dock and floated out on the high tide for fitting out in the Newport docks. Ralph was impressed by the vision of the two men and agreed to join them as the new company's managing director.

Bailey Shipbuilding Development Company Ltd. had been registered in July 1952 and, early in the following year, Atlantic Shipbuilding Company Ltd. was formed to acquire the whole of its undertaking, assets and liabilities. Bailey, Howard and Ralph were joined on the board by Colonel Sir Godfrey Llewellyn, a prominent figure in South Wales, Bernard Sunley, the founder of the eponymous property development company, which had among other projects constructed numerous RAF airfields during the war, and Yusuf Alghanim, the owner of one of the largest companies in Kuwait and a potential ship buyer. Ralph became involved immediately in raising working capital from the City of London to repay loans from C. H. Bailey and John Howard & Co.

It was decided very quickly that it would help in raising further permanent capital if orders could be obtained before the docks were constructed. The new company bid for and was awarded the contracts to build two 3,000-ton Great Lakes pulpwood carriers for the Quebec and Ontario Transportation Company, one for delivery in fifteen months, the other six months later. An option had already been obtained on the land on which the first dry dock was to be situated, and John Howard & Co. built the adjacent offices very quickly. A general manager with considerable experience of shipbuilding was recruited from Tyneside, and wages were agreed with the two unions in the industry, the Ship Constructive and Shipwrights Association and the United Society of Boilermakers, Shipbuilders and Structural Workers. As a harbinger of problems which were to arise later, the management of Atlantic Shipbuilders was surprised to find that the two unions were not prepared to sit at the same table but insisted on separate meetings at all times. This behaviour had its origin in a wartime local agreement in the Bristol area whereby the Boilermakers took over some of the Shipwrights' work, which they then refused to hand back once hostilities were at an end.

Before the difficulties arising out of this inter-union dispute grew more serious, construction began on the dock itself, which was completed in the time agreed and opened with due ceremony on 27 November 1953 by the Home Secretary and Minister for Welsh Affairs, Sir David Maxwell Fyfe. Work began immediately on the first two ships, whilst orders were sought and obtained for two more 'Canallers', as the Great Lakes vessels were called. Even before that, contact had been made with the Russian Government, which was in the market to acquire a fleet of fish factory ships and, an initial proposal having been made by Atlantic, Ralph and the company's chief estimator were invited to Moscow to discuss the specifications and negotiate a price. It appeared that a German shipyard was also bidding for the work, and Ralph and his colleague were forced to wait in Moscow whilst some parallel negotiations were taking place. In the end, the Russians stipulated a maximum price which Atlantic was unable to meet. Discussions continued, however, but eventually came to a halt when the British Government refused an export licence on the grounds that the vessels might be converted into submarine depot ships in wartime.

Ralph and Hilda had by this time moved to Wales, having sold the remainder of the lease on their flat in London. Whilst looking for somewhere to live close to his new place of work, they were introduced to Baron Harry van Moyland, who suggested that they might like to rent the original red brick Queen Anne part of his own house, Pant-y-Goitre, which was very pleasantly situated between Abergavenny and Raglan and thus only about 20 miles from the dockyard. It came with three miles of fishing on the River Usk, which suited Ralph admirably.

The initial success of Atlantic Shipbuilders allowed it to be floated on the London Stock Exchange in 1954, raising additional capital in the process. Thereafter, however, its situation became increasingly bedevilled by industrial relations, not between the company and the trades unions, but between the unions themselves. The demarcation of work between the Shipwrights and the Boilermakers proved to be impossible to agree and, in July 1955, the Shipwrights walked out. This meant that any work requiring wood, which was the preserve of the Shipwrights, had to be converted to metal, far from easy from a technical point of view. Particularly when it came to undocking, the involvement of the Shipwrights was vital. An appeal was made to the general secretaries of the two unions, Ted Hill of the Boilermakers and Syd Ombler of the Shipwrights. However, the former maintained that this was a local matter and that he had instructed his local committee to deal with it, whilst the latter declared that it was a national matter and that his local committee should stay out of the debate. Although both men lived in Newcastle, they had not spoken to each other for months.

Ralph determined to bring them together and travelled up to Newcastle, where he persuaded Hill to meet him for lunch in a private room in the Station Hotel. The lunch was successful, and Hill said that he was prepared to help. Ombler had been invited to join them but declined, although he agreed to drop in afterwards. All seemed to go well, and Ralph believed that agreement had been reached. However, when Hill sent details of the draft agreement to his local committee in Monmouth, the members repudiated it on the grounds that it interfered with local custom and practice.

The local Shipwrights then declared that they would be prepared to take on woodwork, but they were instructed not to do so by their union. The dispute dragged on for many months, with a potentially disastrous effect on Atlantic's fortunes. A particularly difficult issue was the inability to get anyone to line up the keel blocks supporting the ships, traditionally the work of the Shipwrights. The Boilermakers were not prepared to touch it, and neither were the Amalgamated Engineering Union, who had been approached for help, for fear of offending the Shipwrights. An appeal was made to Sir Vincent Tewson, General Secretary of the Trades Union Congress, who was prepared to assist, but the unions concerned remained obdurate.

Matters were not helped by a number of additional problems, some of the company's own making – it had, for instance, proved very difficult to attract an adequate number of draughtsmen, and taking them on secondment from third parties was very expensive – but others due to failures on the part of technical advisors and contractors. In general, the cost of labour in the Newport area was rising sharply due to the formation of a number of new businesses there and this, combined with the other issues, meant that the company was heading for a financial loss in 1955. There were three options for the future: to continue with just the initial dock for building small vessels, to build a second dock to take ships up to 15,000 tons or to proceed with a scheme for a dock to take large tankers. Ralph felt that only the first would be practicable until the demarcation dispute was resolved, but even that would require the raising of further capital. In the meantime, he was very much involved in the sales process, travelling to Canada, Sweden and Germany, among other countries.

In the spring of 1956 the Boilermakers at last agreed to accept the company's ruling on demarcation, but by this time the financial position had become very difficult. Ralph, moreover, had one other major problem of a more personal nature. George Bailey's son, Christopher, had been brought into the business at the outset as Ralph's assistant. A young man of undoubted ability and strong opinions, which Ralph considered were not always well balanced, he now began to make it clear to Ralph that he felt their roles should be reversed. The atmosphere deteriorated to such a state that, by the summer of 1956, Ralph felt that he could no longer continue as managing director and resigned.[1]

He was not to be idle for long. Whilst Vice-Chief of the Air Staff, and specifically because of his responsibility for Operational Requirements, he had had frequent contact with Rolls-Royce, the leading manufacturer of aero engines for the RAF's aircraft. He had, as a result, formed a good relationship with Lord Hives, whom he had first encountered at Transport Command and who was now the chairman of the company, and Hives had told him to get in touch if he ever wanted a job. This Ralph now did and was immediately invited to the company's headquarters in Derby. Hives told him that his approach was very well timed, as he was proposing to set up an advanced research organization at The Old Hall, which was situated in Littleover on the outskirts of Derby, and needed someone to run it. Ralph suggested that a scientist might be more appropriate, but Hives countered that a senior scientist was likely to lack the necessary management skills and would perhaps seek to influence younger men, whose ideas were what he wanted. He believed that someone with a strong background in organization, combined with experience of technical problems, was what was needed. Ralph agreed and was appointed to the position on 7 June.

The Old Hall had been a large suburban house, whose extensive gardens and greenhouses were looked after by a staff of four. Its stables had been converted into laboratories, much to the dismay of the neighbours, who had opposed the planning application, especially when they realized that the conversion would cause the height of the buildings to be raised to that of a spire at one end. It took some time for Ralph to overcome their resentment and restore friendly relations.

The Chief Scientist was Dr A. A. Griffith, who had had a highly distinguished career, both in identifying the causes of metal fatigue and in designing turbojet engines. He had joined Rolls-Royce in 1939, having previously been the principal scientific officer at the Air Ministry and then head of the engine department at the Royal Aircraft Establishment at Farnborough. He had led the work on the Rolls-Royce Avon engine which powered both the English Electric Canberra, the UK's first jet bomber, and the De Havilland Comet, its first jet airliner. By the time that Ralph was appointed, however, he was focusing on vertical take-off and landing technology.

The Chief Engineer was Adrian Lombard, who had become one of the world's leading jet engine designers without having had any formal training beyond technical college. He had been responsible for the team designing the Derwent engine for the UK's first jet fighter, the Gloster Meteor, and was now heavily involved in the development of the Conway engine which would power the Vickers VC10 and some versions of the Boeing 707 and the Douglas DC8, as well as one of the RAF's V-Bombers, the Handley Page Victor.

Relations between the various scientists were by no means always harmonious. One of the major avenues of research and development was atomic power for ships and aircraft. This was led by Dr S. G. Bauer and Dr C. D. Boadle, both of whom had come to Rolls Royce from the Atomic Energy Research Establishment at Harwell. Boadle, who was an Australian of somewhat pugnacious disposition, had accused Bauer of adopting some of his ideas without due acknowledgement, and when both transferred to The Old Hall they brought their feud with them. This grew in bitterness, and others began to take sides, so Ralph had to act. He eventually persuaded Boadle to resign, but not before the latter produced a long paper accusing Bauer of all sorts of malpractice.

Another leading character was Arthur Rubbra, who had a long history on the aero engine side; he had played a key role in the development of pre-war engines such as the Kestrel and the outstanding wartime engine, the Merlin, versions of which powered the Spitfire, the Mosquito and the Lancaster. By this time he was the technical director on the main board of Roll-Royce and nominally in charge of the programmes at the Old Hall, but in practice he ceded that responsibility to Ralph, to whom he was a ready source of advice.

Along with all the other heads of department at Rolls-Royce, some twenty in all, Ralph attended the monthly 'Policy' meetings of the company. These were chaired by Hives initially and then, following his retirement in 1957, by his successor as chief executive, Denning Pearson, who had previously headed the aero engine division. Ralph deplored the way in which, instead of discussing policy, the meetings almost inevitably focused on the latest defect in a particular engine, sparking off a tedious and rather ineffective technical discussion.

This approach ran through the whole organization, including The Old Hall. If Lombard encountered a problem with an engine he would instruct his secretary to convene a meeting at which some twenty to thirty individuals would appear and a rambling discussion would take place, with little actually resolved. With a proper staff to carry out the preparatory work Ralph believed that decisions could be reached much more expeditiously, but it was next to impossible to get men of science to operate in such a way.

For the first few months of Ralph's appointment at Rolls-Royce, Hilda had remained at Pant-y-Goitre, but it was clearly essential for them to live much closer to Derby. In the course of looking for somewhere suitable, Ralph was introduced to a Mrs Ratcliffe, who wished to sell her house at Newton Solney on the Derby side of Burton-on-Trent. He was invited to tea with her and her trustees, but when he arrived he realized that her Victorian mansion would be far too large. However, she suggested that he might like to have a look at Bladon Castle, which lay in the grounds. At first sight the edifice looked enormous, but in this case looks were deceptive. The castle was actually a folly, commissioned by a wealthy lawyer-turned-businessman at the end of the eighteenth century. Most of its imposing frontage was, in fact, a single wall, and it was generally in poor condition.

When Ralph looked more closely, however, he could see that there was a building of more substance behind part of the wall, housing a large kitchen, scullery and bakehouse, with bedrooms above. It would be possible, once blocked-up windows had been restored, to convert the kitchen into a splendid drawing room and move cooking to an adjacent stable. The building had a magnificent view, a good garden and 17 acres of woodland. Ralph agreed with Mrs Ratcliffe's trustees that he would pay a nominal £250 for the freehold, spend £4,000 on the conversion and, when his time came to leave Rolls-Royce, offer it back to them for what he had paid. This was duly agreed, and work began on what turned out to be a delightful house, with John putting together a work party of Balliol undergraduates to carry out some of the repairs. To make Ralph's happiness with domestic arrangements complete, he also acquired fishing rights on the nearby River Dove.

Ralph's other major sporting interest remained skiing, and he went as often as he could to the Alps during the season, on one occasion joining a party of John's friends, to whom he demonstrated exquisite Telemark turns whilst they floundered about in soft snow! He had joined the Ski Club of Great Britain in 1920 and served as President from 1959 to 1961. Whilst in the post he took a great interest in the training of the UK's representative skiers and was particularly keen to promote Scotland as a future destination, although the facilities available there at that time were still very poor.

From the date of his appointment to the Board of Atlantic Shipbuilders until he eventually stepped down from his job at Rolls-Royce in 1961, Ralph's primary focus was on his two employers' businesses, but he was nevertheless able to give time to other matters. His reputation as a thinker on strategic military issues stayed with him, and his views remained much in demand. He lectured twice at the USAF Air Command and Staff College, once in 1953, shortly before taking up his position at Atlantic Shipbuilding, and again in 1955, taking advantage of the latter trip to carry out some marketing in Canada. He also spoke at the RAF Staff College at Andover and the IDC and wrote articles on defence for national newspapers, among other things contributing to *The Times Survey of British Aviation*. In 1954 he appeared on the BBC Home Service on Trafalgar Day, discussing the future of the Royal Navy alongside Captain S. W. Roskill, the author of *The War at Sea*,[2] and Rear Admiral Adam Nicholl, with both of whose views he did not always agree. He participated in another debate on the Home Service in April 1957 under the chairmanship of the historian Alan Bullock, this time on British defence policy in the thermo-nuclear age, was interviewed on the same programme on the Defence White paper later that year and gave a talk on nuclear missiles in 1958.

Perhaps the most significant overseas journey which Ralph made in the decade following his retirement from the RAF was to New Zealand in March and April 1958, his first visit there since 1945. This was on the occasion of the twenty-first birthday of the RNZAF, and he was there at the invitation of the New Zealand Government as the principal guest of honour. He was welcomed on his arrival at Ohakea by the current CAS, Air Vice-Marshal Cyril Kay, whom he had known in the early 1950s as the RNZAF representative in London and who had been one of the founder members and later the CO of 75 (NZ) Squadron; Ralph was the guest of honour at a reunion of the squadron in Palmerston North.

Ralph travelled all over the country, from Auckland in the north to Invercargill in the south, and met numerous old friends. They included Sir Robert Clark-Hall, with whom he had stayed in Christchurch on his very first visit there, Les Munro, the only New Zealand pilot on the Dams Raid, and Fred Jones, Tom Wilkes, Leonard Isitt, Arthur Nevill[3] and Tom Barrow, the original members, with himself, of the Air Board.

Ralph was particularly pleased with Ohakea, which he had selected personally as one of the RNZAF's new airfields and which on 29 March hosted the largest flying display ever seen in the country. There were numerous other important guests, including General Curtis Le May, the Vice-Chief of the USAF, and Air Marshal the Earl of Bandon, AOC-in-C of the Far East Air Force. Ralph left Auckland to fly back to the UK on 1 April, the twenty-first anniversary of his appointment as New Zealand's first Chief of the Air Staff.

Ralph maintained close contact with many of his former RAF colleagues, mostly at a senior level, but also in particular with those who had served in 617 Squadron. One of these was Cheshire, who had become a personal friend, although to the end of Ralph's life his former subordinate never ceased to address him as 'Sir Ralph'. Cheshire had been the official British observer of the destruction of Nagasaki by the second atomic bomb, an event which had affected him deeply. After the war he had suffered poor health for some time and resigned his commission in 1946. Shortly afterwards, he set up the 'Vade in Pacem' (Go in Peace) colony for veterans and war widows at Gumley Court in Leicestershire and then at Le Court in Hampshire. At the latter he began to admit a number of terminally ill men and women, his first step towards the formation of the Cheshire Homes, which were to become renowned for their support of the disabled. Cheshire's organization grew fast but was perennially short of money. He turned to Ralph frequently for advice and support, which the latter provided very willingly. Ralph also gave a lot of time to Andrew Boyle, who was writing a biography of Cheshire, published as *No Passing Glory* in 1955.

At much the same time Ralph provided Boyle with an introduction to Lord Trenchard, whose biography the author was also hoping to write. Ralph had remained in touch with the 'Father of the RAF', from whom a letter which he had written in May 1953 to the *Naval Review* on an article debating the independence of the RAF had provoked a particularly enthusiastic response. When Trenchard died in 1956, Ralph was selected to walk in the funeral procession as one of three insignia-bearers alongside representatives of the Army and the Metropolitan Police.[4]

With the release of *The Dam Busters* film, based on Brickhill's book following the acquisition of the rights by the Associated British Picture

Corporation, 617 Squadron was exposed to the public gaze once more. One of the leading playwrights of the day, R. C. Sherriff, was selected as screenwriter, and it was decided that the film should focus exclusively on the Dams Raid itself. Michael Anderson directed and an excellent cast was recruited, with Richard Todd as Gibson and Michael Redgrave as Wallis. Ralph was played by Ernest Clark, a versatile stage, screen and television actor.[5] The memorable theme tune was composed by Eric Coates.

The film was released on 16 May 1955, the twelfth anniversary of the raid, at a Royal Premiere attended by Princess Margaret and hosted by Tedder and Lord de L'Isle, the Secretary of State for Air. Among those presented to the princess were Eve Gibson, Gibson's father and some of the mothers of those who died on the raid. Wallis was accompanied by boys from Christ's Hospital who had benefited from his Foundation. *The Dam Busters* was an instant hit with the public, becoming the most successful British film of the year at the box office. It contained, inevitably, a very large number of historical inaccuracies, but these did not detract in any way from the overall thrust of the narrative, and the film was widely applauded by the critics.

The premiere was preceded by a 617 Squadron reunion, the first since 1951, in spite of the demands of those present at that event that there should be another in the following year. Ralph was present at both the reunion and the premiere, accompanied to the latter by Hilda.

A rather less happy event was the publication in late 1958 of Donald Bennett's memoirs, *Pathfinder*. Ralph took exception to a number of the assertions made by Bennett. These included: Bennett's contention that higher losses of aircrew were caused by the decision to drop the second pilot on heavy bombers when Ralph was Director of Flying Training; Ralph's apparent willingness to send out bombers on a raid to Berlin, whilst Coryton refused and was sacked by Harris as a result; the supposed grounding of 3 Group aircraft for training; the alleged failure of Cheshire's low-level marking at Munich on the night of 24/25 April 1944; Ralph's apparent insistence on fitting the Mark IX bomb sight in 617 Squadron, when in fact it was the far superior Mark II SABS; and his supposed advocacy of highly dangerous low-level marking at 50ft, whereas it actually took place at between 500 and 1,000ft.

Ralph entered into correspondence with the publishers, Frederick Muller Ltd., with the objective of having appropriate changes made in any subsequent reprint, suggesting that these assertions were not only inaccurate but libellous to the extent that they called into account his fitness to manage bomber operations. He referred not only to W. J. Lawrence's history of 5 Group, which had been published in 1951, and to Boyle's biography of Cheshire, but also to the Air Ministry's records, which he had had independently examined. The publisher agreed in principle to making a number of alterations, subject only to Bennett's approval. Bennett's response spoke volumes:

> I am sorry to hear that Sir Ralph Cochrane has some objections to passages in 'Pathfinder'. Although he and I have sometimes disagreed professionally, he is a friend and I am therefore perfectly happy to make any reasonable amendments or omissions.
>
> I suggest that you proceed on the lines which you and Cochrane have discussed. Although agreeing to the various deletions you have made, I would of course like to make it clear that I do not agree for a moment with Cochrane's memory of the events in question and indeed I have corroborations for my own versions from many sources. I do, however, value my relationship with Cochrane and I am therefore happy to agree to the deletions.[6]

At least in the letter he spelt Ralph's surname correctly, having failed to do so throughout the book! As to the suggestion of friendship, this had not been readily visible at any time since 1943.

The changes were duly made for the Panther paperback edition published in 1960, which also spelt Ralph's name correctly. However, when the book was republished in 1983, six years after Ralph's death, it reverted to the text of the first edition, bringing back not only all those sections which had previously been excluded, but also the misspelling of Ralph's name. Since the law holds that only living people can sue for defamation, it was not possible to address this injustice.

Chapter 23

Family Business

Ralph retired from Roll-Royce in 1961. At the age of sixty-six, however, he was by no means prepared to become economically inactive and had already lined up something to keep him busy, at least for the time being. His brother Tom had taken over the lime works on the Crawford Priory estate from their father before the latter's death, but was himself now not far short of his eightieth birthday. Tom's eldest son and heir, Anthony, much loved throughout the family, had been born with cerebral palsy. Although he had a fine brain, he was confined to a wheelchair and was unable to accept such a responsibility, whilst Vere, the second son, was out of favour with his father at the time. Tom therefore decided that his third son, Julian, should take over the business in due course. Julian, however, after two years of National Service, needed to build up much more business experience before so doing. He joined first De Havilland on an apprenticeship scheme, recommended by Ralph, and then another major engineering group, but it would be some time before he was ready. Ralph therefore agreed to fill the gap after leaving Rolls-Royce and, during his last few years at The Old Hall, paid a number of visits to Scotland to understudy Tom. Now he was to become much more deeply involved.

Cults Lime's origins lay back in the fourteenth or fifteenth century. The seam of lime had been intensively worked over the centuries and, at its peak in the 1920s, there were some ninety employees, of whom the great majority were miners. However, by the mid-1950s, just after the business had been incorporated as a limited company, the geology began to prove difficult due to a fault cutting across the limestone bed. By the time that Ralph became involved a decision had already been taken to drive a tunnel through the fault and pick up the limestone bed on the other side. Whilst this was taking place, production was very limited, and the company began to incur losses, whilst the cost of additional equipment required to move the material ate into its finances. When the new seams were worked, one of them proved prone to flooding, whilst the other produced limestone with a high magnesium content which could not be burnt in the kilns. Moreover, cement was by that time replacing burnt lime as a building material.

As a result of these problems Ralph persuaded Tom that he needed to move on from purely producing limestone, and a decision was taken in 1960 to start a brickworks, which was incorporated as Cults Bricks Limited in 1962. The bricks were a combination of cement, sand and limestone, which could be made into a common brick for general building purposes or a facing brick for cladding. The works were housed in former aircraft hangars.

In the mid-1960s contact was established with the Balfour family, who owned a large sandpit at Kirkforthar, near Glenrothes. It was decided to set up a new brickworks using the Balfours' sand and the burnt limestone from Cults. However, a number of problems emerged, some of them mechanical – the machinery required a level of maintenance of which neither the Balfours nor the team at Cults were capable – whilst the Cults burnt lime and the Kirkforthar sand produced a brick which lacked the 'green strength' to make it resistant to crumbling. Even when a new type of felsite sand was added to the mix, the problem remained unresolved. Kirkforthar Brick had to obtain both its sand and lime elsewhere, and the joint venture between Cults and the Balfours collapsed in 1967, to the accompaniment of a certain amount of acrimony. Cults Lime and Cults Brick were by that time heavily indebted to their bank, but the new mine which had been opened some hundreds of yards to the east of the existing workings eventually proved to be satisfactory and began to generate profits again.[1] In due course Ralph handed over the management to Vere, who ran the business until Julian was ready to assume the role.

Tom died in 1968, and Crawford Priory was immediately abandoned. For years it had been something of a white elephant and it was now to become a ruin. Ralph and Hilda themselves never seem to have had any intention of settling in Scotland although, whilst he was involved with Cults Lime and Cults Brick, they stayed at Crawford Priory whenever Ralph needed to be there. In 1963 they sold Bladon Castle back to Mrs Ratcliffe's trustees on the terms agreed and moved to Great Rollright Manor, near Chipping Norton in the Oxfordshire Cotswolds. This was a part of the world very familiar to Hilda from her years of living in Cheltenham; indeed, her family had originally come from Oddington, not many miles away. The Manor was a substantial house, with a small lake and a walled garden, but it was larger than they needed. Ralph's personal financial position was adversely effected by the collapse of Kirkforthar Brick, and he and Hilda decided that it would make more sense to move to somewhere smaller. They sold Great Rollright in late 1967 and moved on a temporary basis into Glebe House in Coln Rogers, not too far away in Gloucestershire.

In the spring of 1968 Ralph and Hilda were driving between Burford and Chipping Norton when they saw a 'For Sale' sign up outside a building in Shipton-under-Wychwood. Grove Farmhouse was a property of some character in the right part of the world, so they made an offer, which was accepted. The place required a lot of refurbishment, but became a very comfortable home.

In 1962, after leaving Rolls-Royce, Ralph had set up a new company called RJM Exports (RJM for Ralph John Malcolm and Exports as it was proposed that 50 per cent of sales should be made abroad in response to a recent 'Export or Die' appeal by the Labour government). The company, however, was initially inactive whilst Ralph was heavily involved with Cults Lime and Cults Brick. Now he proposed to make a serious business out of it and began to look for suitable products. His first choice was a sharpener for carbon steel razor blades, but this was overtaken almost immediately by the introduction of stainless steel blades, which were not only much more difficult to sharpen than the old carbon steel variety but remained sharp for a considerable time, after which they tended to be thrown away. Notwithstanding some heavy development costs, it became, at a stroke, no longer a profitable business proposition.

It was Hilda, whilst on holiday with Ralph in Canada, who first became aware of a American toy called Construct-o-Straws, consisting of multi-coloured plastic straws and connectors which could be made into all sorts of shapes. Ralph agreed that it had great potential and succeeded in negotiating the rights to manufacture and sell the toy outside North America. After a false start using agents who were unable to persuade retailers to stock it, he turned to a wholesaler, with much greater success.

At about this time Ralph received a letter from a mathematics lecturer at Exeter University who pointed out that, with a few refinements and additions, it would be possible to use Construct-o-Straws to teach three-dimensional geometry, whilst an academic wrote from London University to say that, once again with the addition of more pieces, it could be used for research into complex biochemical structures. The company quickly expanded into the far larger market of teaching structural chemistry in schools and universities and became recognized as a source of applicable and practicable teaching aids, going on to develop a wide range of new products. In the meantime, the original Construct-o-Straws found a ready market in playgroups and primary schools.

As sales grew, other members of the family began to become involved. John had qualified as a Chartered Accountant in 1962, after which he joined a small company engaged in industrial market research, but from 1966, in which year he married Margaret Rose, whom he had met in his first week at Oxford, he began to take some interest in RJM and four years later resigned from his job to work there full-time as Sales Director. He and Margaret bought Fairspear House in Leafield, three miles from Shipton-under-Wychwood, which subsequently became the headquarters of the business. They went on to have four children, Phoebe, Alexandra, Thomas and Katherine.

John also became involved, at an early stage, with the financing of the business. The clearing banks at the time had little appetite for lending to small family companies and required personal guarantees as part of their security. The only way to obtain the required overdraft was to change banks, which happened three times. John eventually joined the Association of Independent Businesses, which began to lobby the government and which was, in due course, instrumental in setting up a scheme by which the government acted as guarantors of selected loans.

Malcolm, who had gone into industrial design after leaving Oxford and became in due course the Secretary of the Design Panel of British Rail, also decided to join the business in 1973, assuming the position of Production Director. He had married Mary Scrope in the previous year,[2] and the two of them now began to look for somewhere suitable to live nearby, but without success. They were staying at Grove Farmhouse whilst they did so, and Ralph and Hilda suggested that they might like to turn the empty top floor into a flat for themselves. This they did, creating in the process an excellent home and producing three children, William, Alice and Harriet.

John, who handled sales, much of which were to overseas buyers, began to realize that the name of the company was proving to be unhelpful, as it suggested an export agency rather than a manufacturer. It was decided to change it to Cochranes of Oxford. In 1975, many years into the company's history, Ralph saw a unique and precisely controllable kite being demonstrated in a television programme. When he heard that the designer was a certain Squadron Leader Don Dunford, who lived in Oxford, he made contact to enquire whether he needed help with sales. It turned out not only that Dunford had no sales organization of his own and would very much welcome an association, but also that he had served under Ralph during the war. The kites, one of which in particular was used for bird scaring, became an important part of the company's product range.

Ralph found much to engage his attention apart from Cochranes of Oxford. Throughout the 1960s and well into the 1970s he was recognized as a leading authority not only on air warfare, but on all aspects of defence, and was accordingly frequently approached by 'think tanks' such as such as the Royal United Services Institution and the International Institute for Strategic Studies, to write articles or address meetings, and he lectured at the IDC, on one occasion with his successor at 5 Group, Hugh Constantine, in the chair as Commandant. He also wrote articles for leading newspapers.

On a number of occasions he was invited to appear on BBC Radio and Television. Two were particularly notable. The first, in October 1961, was a radio interview in the immediate aftermath of the publication of the four volumes comprising *The Strategic Air Offensive*, part of the *Official History of the Second World War*. Co-authored by Sir Charles Webster, who died shortly before it was published, and Noble Frankland, who had served as a navigator in Bomber Command and been awarded the DFC, the work was highly critical of certain aspects of the bombing campaign. This Ralph accepted, but he emphasised the overall conclusion to his listeners, which was that the campaign had made a decisive contribution to eventual victory.

Eleven years later, in November 1972, Ralph appeared on BBC TV in a series called *The Commanders*, which examined the ways in which a number of exceptional men had risen to high command in the war. This time the subject was Harris. The framework was put together by the historian Corelli Barnett, who was already known to Ralph, and there was also participation by Jack Slessor, Noble Frankland and, on the German side, Albert Speer and Adolf Galland.[3] Harris had been invited to appear himself but wrote to Ralph to say that he had 'had it' with the corporation for going out of its way to smear him and Bomber Command, and that he believed that Barnett's reputation rested mainly, if not entirely, on his 'sneering account of Monty's Alamein battles'.[4] Ralph was himself somewhat concerned about Barnett's original script and suggested a number of changes, which were accepted, resulting in a moderation of some of the views expressed. Most of those who knew Harris and saw the programme felt that it was a fair reflection of both the man and the campaign. Ralph was able to make a significant contribution, not only on the war years, but also on Harris at 45 Squadron in the 1920s and in the Air Ministry in the 1930s.

In the early 1970s Ralph was invited to join the Advisory Panel on the Official Military Histories of the War, which worked under the auspices of the Cabinet Office. The chairman was Professor Sir James Butler, formerly the Regius Professor of Modern History at Oxford and at that time the editor of the UK Military Series of the Official History. Ralph's fellow panel members were all distinguished retired officers, Admiral Sir Charles Daniel, General Sir William Stirling and Lieutenant General Sir Ian Jacob.

The Panel during Ralph's term of appointment considered three volumes of the Official History, *Grand Strategy Volume I* by Professor N. H. Gibbs, the Chichele Professor of History at Oxford, *Grand Strategy Volume IV* by Professor Michael Howard, formerly Professor of War Studies at King's College London and at the time a Fellow of All Souls, Oxford, and *The Mediterranean and Middle East Volume V*, dealing with the campaigns in Sicily and Italy up to March 1944, by Brigadier C. J. C. Molony and a number of others.

During the 1960s and the 1970s Ralph was approached by a number of authors, not only for his personal reminiscences but also for his opinions on their subject matter. Among them was Wing Commander 'Jimmy' Trevenen James, who was writing a history of the RAF from 1946 onwards, subsequently published in 1976 as *The Royal Air Force – The Past 30 Years*, which included the last few years of Ralph's own service career, although he had views on the subsequent period as well. Others he helped included Robert Wright, the author of *Dowding and the Battle of Britain* and co-author with Sholto Douglas of Douglas's own memoirs, Henry Cord Meyer, an American historian specializing in modern European history, who was about to embark on a study of airships which led to a number of books on the subject, and Donald Cameron Watt, whose book *Too Serious a Business* looked at the events leading up to the Second World War.

In August 1971 Ralph was contacted by Dudley Saward, who had two weeks earlier been authorized by Harris to write his biography, albeit on condition that it would not be published until after his death. Harris had published his own memoirs in 1947, which were inevitably slanted in the author's favour, but although he may well have had other approaches, this was the first time that he had entertained a work on his life by a third party. Saward had served at Bomber Command HQ as Group Captain Radar between 1942 and 1945, where Ralph had met him, and he could be relied upon to deliver a favourable impression of his former chief. Harris himself had suggested a few people to contact, notable Saundby and Ralph, although Saward would in due course speak to many more. Harris died in 1984, and the book was published shortly afterwards.

In September 1976 Ralph was approached by a young journalist and author, Max Hastings, who had been commissioned by Michael Joseph in the UK and the Dial Press in the USA to write a book on Bomber Command. This was Hastings' first book on the Second World War and he had been advised to approach Ralph by Anthony Verrier, who had been helped by Ralph in the writing of his own book, *The Bomber Offensive*, published in 1968. Ralph was seriously ill at the time but was sufficiently recovered in the New Year of 1977 to invite Hastings to meet him. *Bomber Command*, which was not published until after Ralph's death, was a seminal work on the campaign, its message achieved by a focus not only on Bomber Command HQ and some more general topics such as area bombing, but also on the activities of a small number of individual squadrons at periods in their wartime history which were representative of the command as a whole. A whole chapter was devoted to 5 Group's devastating raid on Darmstadt on the night of 11/12 September 1944. Hastings received help from a very large number of those who had been involved in the events he described, but Ralph, along with Harris himself, Bennett, Edward Addison of 100 (Bomber Support) Group and Bufton, was the recipient of his particular appreciation.

Unsurprisingly, Ralph kept his old service contacts very warm during his last two decades. He was a regular attendee at the twice-yearly Air Marshals' Lunch and at the RAF Dinner Club. He was present at Scampton on 28 April 1968 for an event to mark the end of Bomber Command, whose groups were incorporated into the newly formed Strike Command alongside those of Coastal, Fighter and Transport Commands, and he visited other RAF establishments, notably Cranwell and Halton, which continued to house the School of Technical Training. In July 1975 he was interviewed by Group Captain Edward Haslam, the Head of the Air Historical Branch, who was in the course of recording the memories of a number of distinguished commanders and airmen for the AHB's oral history archives.

On 4 October 1975 the first reunion of 5 Group was held at RAF Brize Norton, conveniently close to Grove Farmhouse. Ralph himself was the inspiration and driving force behind the event, which was attended by 307 former members of the group, with 176 still on the waiting list. The tables were arranged by squadrons, with every single one which had served in the group represented. Three of the group's four surviving VCs, Roderick Learoyd, Bill Reid and Norman Jackson, attended, but Cheshire was abroad at the time. Even those of air rank, including Tony Heward, now an air chief marshal, sat at the squadron tables, whilst Ralph and Hugh Constantine sat at the HQ table. Harris was invited but was unable to attend, on doctor's orders. The toast to the group was proposed by one of the distinguished guests, the former Chief of both the Air Staff and the Defence Staff and Ralph's one time colleague on the Air Council, Marshal of the Royal Air Force Sir William Dickson.

After the premiere of *The Dam Busters*, there were no further 617 Squadron reunions for many years. However, 1968 was the twenty-fifth anniversary of Operation CHASTISE and it was celebrated in style on 18 May with a dinner at the RAF Club. So many applied that, in addition to the 120 participants in the private dining room, arrangements had to be made for an additional forty, largely those who had joined the squadron in the last few months of the war, to be accommodated for the meal in the main dining room of the club, although they were all present together at the reception and for the post-prandial festivities. The hosts were Cheshire, Tait, Fauquier and Martin, and the guests were Harris, Ralph, Wallis, Sir

Arnold Hall, Chairman of Hawker Siddeley, by which company Avro had been acquired, and the current commanding officers of both RAF Scampton and the squadron. The toast to the squadron was followed by one to 'The Lancaster'.

The year 1972 saw two reunions. The first, held on 28 April at a dining-in night at Scampton with about fifty former squadron members present, led by Cheshire and Tait, was specifically arranged to wish Wallis well in retirement. He had been knighted, very belatedly, only a few weeks after the 1968 reunion and was also being congratulated on that score. Ralph proposed the toast to Wallis, whilst the C-in-C Strike Command, Air Chief Marshal Sir Andrew Humphrey, proposed the one to the squadron.

The second event of the year, in which Ralph also participated, was a reunion in Canada. The UK party of forty-nine aircrew, led once again by Cheshire and Tait and many with their wives, departed from Gatwick to fly to Montreal on 17 June and then travelled on to Ottawa and Toronto, arriving at the latter city on 20 June. They had by then been joined by about twenty-five Canadian aircrew, three more from the UK, two from Australia and one from New York. The main event of the trip was a dinner at the Royal Canadian Military Institute, where the guest speaker was John Diefenbaker, a former prime minister of Canada, whilst on 25 June there was a reception at the Canadian Forces Staff College. The UK party arrived back home on 25 June.

By this time the 617 Squadron Association had been formed, with Geoff Rice of the original squadron as Chairman and Tony Iveson, who had joined the squadron in August 1944 and was second-in-command to Tait on the successful operation to sink the *Tirpitz*, as the indefatigable Secretary. In 1974 there was a reunion to celebrate the thirtieth anniversary of the sinking of the great battleship. Ralph replied to Tait's toast to the guests, as did Rear Admiral Godfrey Place, who had won the Victoria Cross for his successful attack on the *Tirpitz* in command of the midget submarine X7.

Ralph had a great deal of contact with both Wallis and Cheshire in the 1960s and 1970s. Wallis, of course, was a longstanding personal friend, and he and his wife, Molly, stayed with the Cochranes on many occasions, with Ralph and Hilda going likewise to them. Ralph, however, had no involvement with Wallis's work, although Wallis would sometimes write to him about the various problems he was encountering. Cheshire and his second wife, Sue Ryder, had also become personal friends. By now the Cheshire Homes were an established institution, with homes in many countries other than the UK; indeed, Ralph had been at the opening of one of them during the 617 Squadron reunion in Canada. As one of the most consistent and high-profile supporters of the Cheshire Homes, he believed that Cheshire had not been adequately recognized and, in 1972, he wrote to Keith Joseph, then the Secretary of State for Health and Social Security, arguing that some kind of honour was long overdue. Nothing happened, but Cheshire himself became embarrassed by any lobbying on his behalf and asked that it should cease.[5]

During these years Ralph and Hilda went on a number of foreign holidays, mostly in Europe and on several occasions to a favourite destination at Bormes-les-Mimosas in Provence, a villa owned by his brother Tom's second wife, Mary. Ralph continued to ski late into his life, spending his seventieth birthday with the family in Klosters, one of his favourite Alpine resorts, and he also managed to get away to Scotland to fish from time to time. In 1966 Ralph and Hilda visited Iran, retracing some of his journey of 1923 on leave from his posting at Hinaidi, notably to Kasvin, Teheran, Isfahan and Shiraz, but also to the Lar Valley, close to where he and Percy Maitland had so conspicuously failed to shoot any big game.

In the mid-1970s health began to become an issue for both Ralph and Hilda. Ralph had an attack of angina in early 1974, whilst Hilda was diagnosed with early-onset dementia. On 6 June 1976 Ralph suffered a stroke, coming to on the floor beside his bed with his left side paralysed and unable to move. Luckily Malcolm heard his calls for help and got him back into bed; on the next day he was taken to the cottage hospital in Burford, where he stayed for a fortnight before being moved to the Churchill Hospital in Oxford. One of his drugs was mistakenly cut off on his first night there and, unable to breathe, he very nearly died. After a month he and Hilda went to the RAF's Princess Alexandra Hospital at Wroughton, near Swindon, where they shared a room for another month, following which they returned home. Although Malcolm and Mary helped as much as they could, it was clear that his parents needed more expert care and they moved again, this time to the RAF Sussex Down Nursing Home near Storrington, but the thick pile carpets there caused Ralph to suffer badly from asthma and they had to move back to Wroughton.

It was now evident that Hilda would be unable to manage at home, even with family help, so with the assistance of Leonard Cheshire, Malcolm found a place for her in the Lilian Faithful Nursing Home in Cheltenham, where the RAF Benevolent Fund had two beds. No bills arrived for her stay there, and Cheshire later told the family that they had been waived in recognition of all that Ralph and Hilda had done for the service during the war.

Ralph himself was still far from fully recovered, but he accepted an invitation from his sister Kitty to stay at Broomhall for that Christmas. There he began to recuperate by taking longer and longer walks, but his recovery was set back first by pulling a muscle in one leg and then by cracking three ribs in a fall on the staircase. It was 7 January 1977 before he was able to return home.

Ralph had recovered sufficiently to be able to attend the Bomber Command Reunion Dinner on 30 April, where he met a number of friends, including Martin, Tait and Constantine, whilst Harris was in ebullient form, making a long and very well received speech on how the command had won the war in Europe. Ralph was also able to attend the dinner at Thatcher's Hotel in East Horsley, Surrey on 24 September, given by the former aircrew of 617 Squadron to celebrate Wallis's ninetieth birthday. Cheshire was in the chair, Fauquier and many others had come from overseas and the guests included Molly Wallis, Eve Gibson and Harris, with his very popular wife, Jill. On this occasion Malcolm accompanied Ralph and was astonished by the overwhelming standing ovation which his father received from the assembled veterans as they left the dinner. In the words of the 617 Squadron Association newsletter, 'We who were present will long remember the pleasure that lit his face as he moved between the tables and the lines of applauding guests.'

'I am rather pleased that you now know what my wartime aircrew thought of me', said Ralph to Malcolm as they walked to their car.

On the orders of his doctor, Ralph was not well enough to accept another invitation, this time to visit New Zealand once again. It came from the Museum of Transport and Technology of New Zealand, which was proposing to induct him into its Hall of Fame. Ralph was bitterly disappointed, but nevertheless wrote the speech which he would have given himself, had circumstances permitted, and went on 4 October to Brize Norton to hand it to his former SASO at 5 Group and subsequent good friend, now Marshal of the RAF the Lord Elworthy.[6] Elworthy was actually flying to New Zealand for a completely different purpose. A new colour had been presented to the Queen's Colour Squadron of the RAF, and it had been decided that the old colour should be laid up at St Paul's Cathedral in Wellington, with Elworthy, himself a New Zealander, selected to accompany it there on behalf of Her Majesty.

The induction ceremony took place at the Museum in Wellington on 7 October, with Elworthy first unveiling a portrait of Ralph and a description of his role in the formation of the RNZAF. The speech was then read out on Ralph's behalf by another New Zealander, Air Marshal Sir Rochford Hughes, who had been in the first draft of trainees selected by Ralph for the new RNZAF at Wigram, had commanded 511 Squadron, flying Avro Yorks in Transport Command in 1945/6, and had served again under Ralph in the Air Ministry whilst he was VCAS. Two days after his return to the UK, Elworthy had lunch with Ralph to describe the occasion, saying later, 'Though clearly his body was failing his mind was as active, sharp and inquisitive as ever.'[7]

Ralph had been intending to spend Christmas in Scotland with Grizel and her family. However, shortly before he was due to travel, he became seriously ill, this time with bronchopneumonia and cardiac asthma. He was admitted once again to Burford Cottage Hospital, where he died on 17 December 1977.

Ralph's funeral was held for the family and local people in the old parish church at Cults. Condolence letters and telegrams poured in from far and wide, and a Service of Thanksgiving was held at St Clement Danes, the Central Church of the RAF, on 28 February 1978. The church was packed, with the RAF providing the strongest contingent. Serving and retired senior officers, one of whom represented the Queen, were headed by the Chief of the Defence Staff, Marshal of the Royal Air Force Sir Neil Cameron, whilst Cheshire and Tait led over thirty wartime veterans of 617 Squadron, some accompanied by their wives, with Eve Gibson and the current commanding officer of the squadron seated amongst them. The lessons were read by Cheshire and John, and the address was given by Elworthy.

Chapter 24

Reflections

Although Ralph had been born into the aristocracy, as a third son he had always been expected to make his own way in the world. For someone who was considered by many to possess the best brain in the RAF in the later stages of his career, he showed no signs of outstanding academic prowess in his early years, although he passed out of Dartmouth comfortably above the average. It is said that luck usually plays a role in the life of any great man, and in Ralph's case it determined the direction of his future career on two occasions. The first was his presence on the bridge of HMS *Colossus* when the telegram arrived calling for volunteers for special duties which resulted in his joining the Royal Naval Air Service. The second was his meeting with Trenchard in Egypt in 1921, which led to his transfer from what would prove to be a blind alley, the airship service, into the mainstream RAF.

The career which followed between the two world wars was a typically varied one, but by 1939 Ralph had established himself as a specialist in both bombing and training. Moreover, during the late 1920s and the 1930s he became recognized for his intellect, evidenced not only by his appointment to the Directing Staff at the Staff College and later by his selection to be a student at the Imperial Defence College, but also, both inside and outside the service, by his winning prizes for essays on defence subjects. His selection, as a mere wing commander, to advise the Government of New Zealand on its requirements for air defence was a recognition of his ability to think well beyond the day-to-day demands of his rank.

During the inter-war years Ralph was able to attract the attention of a number of officers who would be instrumental in furthering his career, but two were particularly important. As a flight commander of 45 Squadron in Iraq he was one of Harris's two deputies, whilst he came into close contact not only with Harris but also with Portal whilst serving in the Wessex

Bombing Area and later at the Air Ministry. His appointment as Director of Flying Training in 1940 was engineered by Portal, and both Portal and Harris were behind his subsequent move to command a bomber group. Portal rated Ralph highly enough to ask for him to be one of his assistant chiefs of staff in the summer of 1944. Although this was vetoed by Harris at the time, remaining where he was allowed Portal to have him appointed commander-in-chief of Transport Command in early 1945, by which time the outcome of the war was certain. Portal realized that the RAF's peacetime priorities would be quite different and he wanted a trusted associate in the only arm of the service likely to experience expansion.

In spite of his more senior appointments in the last eight years of his career, Ralph's name has become inextricably linked with 5 Group and with one of its squadrons in particular, No.617. Whilst his achievements at other times were considerable, it is on the period between March 1943 and January 1945 that his reputation largely rests.

The transformation of Bomber Command from a formation which, in mid-1941, was incapable of dropping more than one-third of its bombs within five miles of its target, to one which, by early 1945, could wreak material destruction almost at will on German cities, was due to a number of factors, amongst which the introduction of new aids to navigation and the creation of the Pathfinder Force were arguably the most important. Within the command, however, 5 Group was something special, and this was particularly so for the last year of the war. Harris recognized this – it must be said that it suited his own purposes to do so, as it provided some loosening from what he regarded as the shackles of the Air Ministry – and he let it operate substantially on its own. This was entirely due to Ralph, who was determined to do things differently, but only as long as they were better. Some of his innovations, such as the 5 Group corkscrew, the ban on weaving when approaching the target, the 5 Group landing system, time-and-distance bombing and offset marking attracted widespread attention; others – the changes to the aircraft maintenance regime, the conference calls with base and station commanders, the insistence on captains being commissioned, the method of briefing the aircrews before operations – were less obvious to an outside observer but were just as important to the creation of what was regarded, not least by his superiors, as the most effective formation in Bomber Command.

Association with 617 Squadron came as a gift to Ralph. From an operational perspective, CHASTISE was by no means the most important of its activities, particularly as it proved incapable of repetition. What it did do, however, in addition to raising the public profile of Bomber Command when it needed it most, was to present Harris with a test bed for alternative methods of hitting the enemy, and he remained its strong supporter even whilst others were questioning its value. This took time, and it was only with the arrival of Cheshire in the aftermath of the disastrous raid on the Dortmund–Ems Canal that it began to realize its full potential.

Ralph was at the heart of this. His role in the Dams Raid itself, whilst generally acknowledged by all subsequent historians, has been subordinated in the public mind to those of Gibson and Wallis. Along with Douglas Bader, Gibson is the name which will most readily spring to the lips of anyone asked to name a pilot of the Second World War, whilst even today Wallis retains his reputation as an extraordinarily talented engineer and inventor. Both conform to heroic stereotypes, the daring military leader and the brilliant scientist. Ralph, on the other hand, has been overshadowed, yet it was he who led the team putting the operation together, taking on the planning, when this would normally have been carried out at High Wycombe, supervising the formation of the new squadron and its training and carrying the overall burden of responsibility for its success. As an essentially modest and rather private man, this is probably what he himself would have wanted.

It was the advent of Cheshire as CO which provided the impetus for 617 Squadron's further exploits and the developments of new methods of low-level marking and high-level precision bombing, the latter with Wallis's highly effective new weapons. Cheshire later described how Ralph worked:

Arguably, he had the finest and the clearest mind in Bomber Command, if not in the entire Royal Air Force of the day. Above all he had the ability to think for himself and from a wholly new perspective, instead of accepting current strategy, and seeing how it could be improved. But for this, there would probably have been no 617 Squadron, as built up by Guy Gibson and then developed throughout the remaining phases of the war. When you presented him with a new idea for precision-bombing, he looked at it rather as something the cat had brought in the door. But you knew that, beneath the mask, the brain was working, digesting the various elements and sorting the less from the more important. It might take you three weeks of continuous, concentrated argument and visual results to convince him. But you knew that, once convinced, he would back you totally and irrespective of the cost to himself. More than this, he would usually come up with his own suggestions for improving the basic idea which the Squadron had developed. On the other hand, woe betide you if the proposal did not stand and you had wasted your time and his.[1]

Without 617 Squadron and its low-level marking, there would have been no 'Independent Air Force'. There is something of an irony here. If Bennett had embraced the new marking methodology for the Pathfinders, Harris would have found it very much more difficult to remove three of his squadrons and 'lend' them to 5 Group.

Ralph was said by his family to have been heartbroken not to have been appointed Chief of the Air Staff. Exactly why Attlee rejected Tedder's recommendation in favour of Slessor will never be known for certain, but it is likely that it was to some extent a matter of personal chemistry. Slessor was certainly just as well qualified for the job, but he was also a man of notably outgoing character. Ralph was much more difficult to get to know, as Cheshire had been warned prior to their first meeting:

I was told that Air Vice Marshal Cochrane was probably the most efficient of all Bomber Commands AOCs, but totally humourless, devoid of any human feeling, and that I would not enjoy working for him …

From the word go, I knew that here was a man to be respected, perhaps even feared. But he was also a man I knew that I could get on with. He clearly knew exactly what he wanted and, if I had any prepared arguments in my mind, I soon dismissed them, knowing that he would quickly see through anything that he thought was not genuine. Contrary to what I had been told, I had the impression of a slight smile about his lips every now and then, though from the content of what he was saying you would not have thought so. Still, it was definitely there; and in the months that were to follow I came to admire, even at times to love, his moments of real wit and humour. Yet, I suspect that one had to know him and gain his confidence before he let it shine through.[2]

Relative to his thirty-seven-year service career, Ralph's subsequent employment seems in retrospect to have been less satisfactory. It was a great misfortune that his sense of duty meant that he was unable to respond to the approach by BOAC in 1946 to join the corporation at the top level, probably as managing director; his organizational skills and his experience of running Transport Command would have been immensely valuable during the years of the corporation's post-war expansion. On his retirement he was approached by BEA to join them on a non-executive basis, but it was clear that he wanted a full-time job. As a start-up in an industry of which Ralph had no previous experience, however, Atlantic Shipbuilders was always going to be a risk for him, exacerbated by the damaging dispute between its two unions which was, to his mind, deeply frustrating and totally unnecessary, although it was not the reason for his resignation. He was on stronger ground with Rolls-Royce and found his role there more enjoyable, but one is still left with a strong impression that the job was unworthy of his talents.

Ralph's family was always very important to him; he had a good relationship with his father and mother and, amongst his siblings, was particularly close to Archie and Kitty. He did not hesitate, therefore, to step into the breach at Cults Lime and Cults Brick during the management interregnum between his eldest brother, Tom, and the next generation, although this, too, turned out to be a frustrating assignment. Ralph does, however, appear to have enjoyed very much running his own family business, in which, although joined in due course first by John and then by Malcolm, he continued to play an active role until shortly before his death.

From 1930 onwards the anchor to Ralph's family life was Hilda. Their relationship had taken nearly a decade to mature following their initial meeting and it was conducted for most of that time by letter. Hilda had a very different character to his, inwardly shy and sensitive, whilst outwardly kind and gentle. The possessor of no mean intellect herself, she knew many of the leading figures in the art world, partly as a result of owning and then co-owning a gallery, as well as being a fine sculptress.

Far from being overwhelmed by Ralph, Hilda was very much a strong person in her own right. Her primary objective was to be a homemaker, never easy for a service wife due to the numerous moves as one posting followed another. In fact, they were to live in no fewer than twenty-four homes and it was only the last of these, Grove Farmhouse, which had any real permanence. Hilda was determined nevertheless to give their daughter and two sons a stable childhood. Although they went away to boarding school, as was traditional in their social group, when they came home for their holidays she always put them first. She was, among other things, an enthusiastic gardener and enjoyed making small gardens for each of them.

The heaviest burden placed on Hilda came during the war, when she was deputed on many occasions to break the news of the death of the married aircrew to their wives. Although she hated this duty, she performed it without complaint as the least she could do. After the war she was delighted to be able to serve on the committee of the RAF Benevolent Fund, which disbursed financial assistance.

Outside the family, although he was far from extrovert, Ralph was in no way anti-social; indeed, during his last twenty-five years he very much enjoyed the bi-annual lunches and dinners of the Air Marshals' Club and similar events and he took great pleasure in service reunions. On the other hand, he had relatively few close friends, but amongst them were Victor Goddard from the airship service, Roderic Hill, who had succeeded Harris at 45 Squadron after Ralph's time there and had written a book about the Baghdad Air Mail subsequently, and Hugh Walmsley, who had served alongside Ralph on the Boy's Wing at Cranwell. Harris lived for the early years of his retirement in South Africa, but corresponded regularly with Ralph throughout that time, invariably addressing him as 'Dear Cocky', and saw more of him after his return. Other good friends included Francis Chichester from Ralph's New Zealand days and his time as Director of Flying Training, whilst Wallis was also in frequent contact, as were Cheshire and Elworthy from a younger generation.

Some of those who did not know him well described Ralph as austere and humourless. It is certainly true that he took the prosecution of the war by his squadrons extremely seriously and that he was not given to undue levity as a result. However, he was admired by his subordinates; indeed, it is difficult to find any serious criticism of him as a professional, other than by Bennett and during a brief period when he first arrived at 3 Group with some preconceived ideas which were rapidly discarded. Those who got to know him better could see beneath the cloak, not least the perceptive Cheshire:

> I think that I remained until the very end somewhat in awe of his mental sharpness and his insistence on correct behaviour, total commitment and professionalism. But it was the caring, human side of him that left his mark on me more than anything else. Perhaps it was the depth of this side of his character, added to a natural shyness, that made him feel that he must conceal what was going on inside by a slightly stern exterior. During the war itself, he drove himself mercilessly and was forever thinking of how he could better discharge his responsibilities, both as to the welfare of the men under his command and to the prosecution of the war effort. But, once this was all behind, it was easier for him to display his true nature. On many occasions I was touched to discover how interested he was in all my activities and by the trouble he would go to in helping or advising me. On my side I felt that he was never really acknowledged in the way he should have been and that the RAF was the loser in consequence.[3]

Although the last sentence seems to have been true as far as public acknowledgement was concerned, there was never any doubt about the respect in which he was held by his colleagues. Of the many letters addressed to his immediate family after Ralph's death, one came one from Air Chief Marshal Sir Michael Beetham, at the time the CAS, but formerly a pilot in 50 Squadron, in which he had served under Ralph in 5 Group:

> During his long and distinguished career in the service of his country, spanning as it did the two World Wars, Sir Ralph's achievements, to the benefit of the Royal Air Force in particular and aviation in general, have justly marked him out as one of the great men of our time. The Royal Air Force will of course remember him as the man who organized the epic raids on the Mohne and Eder Dams in 1943, but we will

remember him too as one of our greatest planners and organizers, not just during World War II but through the difficult years of adjustment that followed. We were fortunate then to have men of his strength and calibre to call upon to shoulder the heavy responsibilities.[4]

Johnny Fauquier, the last of 617 Squadron's wartime commanding officers to serve under Ralph, encapsulated the regard of many at a more personal level:

To me and all Canadians who served under him he was looked up to as a gentle man, a great leader, an inspiring commander.[5]

Abbreviations

AAD	Aerial Attack on Dams
ACAS	Assistant Chief of the Air Staff
ACM	Air Chief Marshal
ADC	Aide-de-Camp
ADGB	Air Defence of Great Britain
AFC	Air Force Cross
AHB	Air Historical Branch
AM	Air Marshal
AOC	Air Officer Commanding
AOC-in-C	Air Officer Commanding-in-Chief
ATFERO	Atlantic Ferry Organization
AVM	Air Vice-Marshal
BBC	British Broadcasting Corporation
BEA	British European Airways
BOAC	British Overseas Airways Corporation
CAS	Chief of the Air Staff
CBE	Commander of the Order of the British Empire
CFS	Central Flying School
CGM	Conspicuous Gallantry Medal
C-in-C	Commander-in-Chief
CO	Commanding Officer
DCAS	Deputy Chief of the Air Staff
DDI(2)	Deputy Director of Intelligence (2)
DDI(3)	Deputy Director of Intelligence (3)
DFC	Distinguished Flying Cross
DFM	Distinguished Flying Medal
DH	De Havilland
DSO	Distinguished Service Order

FTS	Flying Training School
GOC	General Officer Commanding
HC	High Capacity
HCU	Heavy Conversion Unit
HMA	His Majesty's Airship
HMS	His Majesty's Ship/Her Majesty's Ship
HQ	Headquarters
IDC	Imperial Defence College
MAP	Ministry of Aircraft Production
MC	Military Cross
MP	Member of Parliament
MRAF	Marshal of the Royal Air Force
NATO	North Atlantic Treaty Organization
NCO	Non-commissioned Officer
NZ	New Zealand
OAMCU	Overseas Air Movements Control Unit
OTU	Operational Training Unit
PA	Personal Assistant
PAF	Permanent Air Force
PFF	Pathfinder Force
PoW	Prisoner of War
RAF	Royal Air Force
RAAF	Royal Australian Air Force
RAFO	Reserve of Air Force Officers
RAFVR	Royal Air Force Volunteer Reserve
RAuxAF	Royal Auxiliary Air Force
RCAF	Royal Canadian Air Force
RFC	Royal Flying Corps
RMS	Royal Mail Ship
RN	Royal Navy
RNAS	Royal Naval Air Service
RNZAF	Royal New Zealand Air Force
RT	Radio Telephone
RUSI	Royal United Services Institution
SASO	Senior Air Staff Officer

SFTS	Service Flying Training School
S/O	Section Officer (WAAF)
SR	Semi-rigid
SS	Steam Ship
UK	United Kingdom
US	United States
USA	United States of America
USAAF	United States Army Air Force
USAF	United States Air Force
USSR	Union of Soviet Socialist Republics
VC	Victoria Cross
VCAS	Vice-Chief of the Air Staff
VE-Day	Victory in Europe Day
VHF	Very High Frequency
VIP	Very Important Person
VTOL	Vertical Take-off and Landing
WAAF	Women's Auxiliary Air Force

Acknowledgements

I could not have written this book without the help of the Cochrane family. Grizel is the eldest of Ralph's children and her memory stretches back the furthest. She was particularly helpful to my understanding of her mother, Hilda, but had much else to contribute, both in a telephone interview and when my wife and I visited her in Scotland. We were very privileged to meet her husband, Bobby, shortly before his death.

John Cochrane holds the majority of the material relating to his father, which he very generously allowed me to take away to review at my leisure. It proved to be much more copious than I had expected and made the most significant single contribution to the writing of the book. John is also extremely well informed not only on the years after Ralph's retirement from the RAF, but also on his service history. He came up with a number of most useful corrections on the book in draft. He also provided the photo albums and loose photos which have provided the substantial majority of the illustrations for the book.

Malcolm also held some papers and was the closest to his father and mother in the last years of his life as he and his wife, Mary, lived in the same house. They granted me a most useful interview.

Julian Cochrane, the youngest son of Ralph's brother Tom, the 2nd Lord Cochrane of Cults, whom I both corresponded with and met at his home in Scotland, had some very useful observations, not only on Ralph's involvement with Cults Lime, but also on the family background.

I must also thank Air Commodore Sir Timothy Elworthy, who provided me with the introduction to John Cochrane which led to my writing the book. Some of the material which Tim lent me whilst I was writing a biography of his father, Marshal of the RAF the Lord Elworthy, proved to be of continuing interest, and I am grateful for his permission to hold on to it during my research.

I am most appreciative of the help provided by Simon Moody, the Research Curator of the Air Force Museum of New Zealand. The Museum holds the originals of Ralph's papers regarding his appointment there, although John Cochrane retained copies of everything. I would also like to thank Cherie Cooper, who runs the museum's shop and who sent me a copy of Brian Lockstone's short but highly relevant book on the birth of the RNZAF; to my utter astonishment, it arrived three days after being posted!

As far as Ralph's service in Bomber Command was concerned, I had an immense amount of help from Dr Robert Owen. Rob is the Official Historian of 617 Squadron and the acknowledged expert on the activities of the squadron from its formation in 1943 until today, two years after it both celebrated its seventy-fifth Anniversary and was re-formed to fly the new Lockheed Martin F-35 Lightning. Rob provided me with a copy of his doctoral thesis on the squadron, which focused on its operations after the Dams Raid and which I found exceptionally helpful, answered all my queries very promptly and read and commented on the drafts of all the chapters relating to Ralph's service in Bomber Command. He has earned my deep gratitude.

As always I have been deeply impressed by the efficiency of the National Archives. I found that the files on 617 Squadron had to be read in a secure room, not, I understand, because they are in any way confidential or sensitive, but because they are thought to be vulnerable to vandalism or even theft.

The RAF Museum at Hendon, where Sir Arthur Harris's papers are deposited, was also very helpful, with those papers relating to Cochrane swiftly identified for my perusal.

I have been exceptionally fortunate in retaining the same team at Pen & Sword for many years. Henry Wilson, the commissioning editor, is invariably my first point of contact and has, as always, been highly supportive. George Chamier has edited my draft with his usual deft touch, whilst Matt Jones, the production manager, has been as efficient as ever.

As always, I could not have done without the support of my immediate family, my wife Sheelagh, my elder son Tim and my younger son Rupert, the last of whom has been once again the first to see, correct and comment on all the draft chapters.

Notes

Chapter 1
1. This was the ship which, fourteen years later, was to take Napoleon into exile on St Helena.
2. Patrick O'Brian based his fictional hero Jack Aubrey to a large extent on Cochrane, and the first book of the series, *Master and Commander*, includes this exploit, with Aubrey's brig *Sophie* taking the Spanish frigate *Cacafuego*. Another book in the series, *The Reverse of the Medal*, is based on Cochrane's later trial and disgrace.
3. Whilst in exile on St Helena, Napoleon told his physician, Dr O'Rourke, 'He [Cochrane] could not only have destroyed them, but he might and could have taken them out had your Admiral supported him as he ought to have done.'

Chapter 2
1. Report dated 2 August 1911.
2. The history is far from clear, but it seems likely that the company, or its assets, was acquired by a subsidiary of the Shell Oil Company not long afterwards.
3. Now called Castletown Bere.

Chapter 3
1. Memoirs.
2. Ralph supervised the erection of the airships at Wormwood Scrubs and flew one of them up to Scapa Flow himself.
3. Nobile is best known for his Arctic airship expeditions, the first of which, in the *Norge*, was the first flight over the North Pole from Europe to America. The second flight, in the *Italia*, came to grief on the polar ice cap, for which Nobile, who was later found and evacuated, was forced to take the blame.
4. The site of what is now Rome's second international airport.
5. Two of Archie's companions, Captains Andrew Johnston and Kenneth Yearsley, wrote an account of the escape, published in 1919 as *Four-Fifty Miles to Freedom*.
6. It is now awarded for 'an act or acts of exemplary gallantry while flying, though not in active operations against the enemy'.
7. Dorothy was to marry Sir Thomas Burton in 1923, but died in 1927, shortly after giving birth to her second child.

Chapter 4
1. The station was called RAF Almaza for part of this time.
2. One of the delegates was T. E. Lawrence, to whom Ralph was introduced and who he thought was 'marvellous', albeit that he had no presence of any sort until he started to talk about the Arabs, when he was most impressive.
3. Memoirs.
4. Wood was suffering from tuberculosis, from which he was to die not very long afterwards.
5. 45 Squadron had been formed as a fighter-reconnaissance squadron in 1916 and served in both France and Italy, but was disbanded at the end of 1919.
6. Later MRAF Sir Edward Ellington, Chief of the Air Staff 1933–7.
7. Later MRAF Sir John Salmond, Chief of the Air Staff 1930–3.
8. Harris, *Bomber Offensive*, p.22.
9. Diary 3.2.1923.
10. Ibid.
11. The IBP, in spite of being the note-issuing bank for Persia, was British-owned at this time.
12. Diary of a trip to Persia 24.8.1923.

Chapter 5
1. Major George Scott, one of the leading airship pilots, captained R.34 on its round trip to North America in 1919 and R.100 on its maiden flight in 1929. He was killed, with forty-seven others, in the crash of R.101 on 5 October 1930, which spelt the end of the British airship programme.
2. Diary 1.11.1924.
3. Diary 2.3.1926.
4. Diary 30.3.1926.
5. Diary 28.5.1925.
6. Diary 6.4.1926.
7. Park was to die in October 1928 following a hospital operation.
8. Memoirs.
9. Diary 21.4.1926.
10. Kitty had worked in the Foreign Office prior to her marriage and was included in the delegation at the Peace Conference in Versailles.
11. Flying Log 10.8.1927.

Chapter 6
1. Memoirs
2. The formal division into the Eastern and Western Protectorates did not come until 1940.

Chapter 7

1. The prize was one of a number set up in memory of Air Commodore R. M. Groves, who died in an aircraft accident in Egypt. Some were for flying, navigation and research, others for essays. The Special Prize was for the essay considered to be the most striking and original.
2. Memoirs.
3. Norman would be closely associated with the Airborne Forces in the Second World War, initially as CO of the Central Landing Establishment and latterly as AOC of 38 Group, the RAF formation dedicated to airborne operations. He was to die when his plane crashed in 1943 whilst taking off for North Africa.
4. At the time Ralph's own time on fixed-wing aircraft amounted to 767 flying hours.
5. The aircraft which Ralph saw eventually became a museum piece in Berlin; it was destroyed in a bombing operation, which included many aircraft from Ralph's 5 Group, on the night of 23/24 November 1943. The group also inflicted serious damage on Friedrichshafen on the night of 20/21 June 1943.
6. Loerzer was a close friend of Herman Goering, under whom he was to rise to the rank of lieutenant general in the Luftwaffe.
7. Arthur was also to die relatively young, aged only forty-three, whilst serving as Counsellor at the British Embassy in Tokyo in 1935. His son, later Sir Charles Wiggin, was to earn a DFC in March 1944 flying with 44 Squadron in 5 Group.
8. Private Flying Diary 11.4.1931.
9. He was to serve for a time as Ralph's SASO at Transport Command and later retire as an air marshal.
10. Tom had married Elin Douglas-Pennant, always known as Nellie, in 1920 and they had three children. Tom married his second wife, Mary Duckham, in 1948.
11. Memoirs.
12. Air Historical Board Interview 30.7.1975.
13. Ibid.
14. The new footbridge on the site of Martel's temporary structure is called the Passerelle des Anglais.
15. Memoirs.

Chapter 8

1. New Zealand Diary 23.11.1936.
2. Isitt and Nevill were both numbered amongst Ralph's successors as CAS of the RNZAF, the former from 1943 to 1946, the latter from 1946 to 1951.
3. Although by the late 1930s the New Zealand Division of the Royal Navy was substantially manned by New Zealanders, the Royal New Zealand Navy was only established as an independent component of the country's armed services in 1941.

4. This was the Vickers Wellington, whose prototype had flown for the first time in June 1936 and which had been ordered by the RAF two months later. It was to enter squadron service in the RAF in October 1938.
5. The eventual order was for thirty aircraft, including six 'spares'.
6. Clark-Hall had asked for early retirement in 1934, after achieving command of the Coastal Area. He rejoined the armed services as a wing commander in the RNZAF in 1940, rising in due course to air commodore.
7. Maurice Buckley, who was about to be promoted to squadron leader, was the same age as Ralph and had served in the RNAS in the Great War. He had been an instructor in the PAF and was to become the first CO of 75 Squadron, the New Zealand-manned unit which flew the Wellingtons ordered on Ralph's advice. The advent of war in 1939 meant that the Wellingtons never operated in New Zealand, but were donated by the New Zealand Government to the RAF.
8. One of the other passengers was the artist Augustus John, whose agent Hilda subsequently became.
9. They included Air Chief Marshal Sir Keith Park, AOC 11 Group Fighter Command during the Battle of Britain and later AOC Malta and Allied Air C-in-C South East Asia, and Air Marshal Sir Arthur 'Maori' Coningham, AOC of the Desert Air Force and then the Second Tactical Air Force.
10. On a visit to Australia and New Zealand in 1945 Ralph was told by Vice-Admiral James Rivett-Carnac, who had been captain of the *Leander* at the time, that it was generally accepted that these airfields had played a major role in preventing the Japanese from expanding their territory further east and south in late 1941 and early 1942.
11. Letter from Lord Galway to Sir Thomas Inskip 5.4.1939.

Chapter 9
1. Memoirs.
2. At the time Goddard was one of Ralph's fellow Deputy Directors as DDI(3).
3. The Handley Page Hereford had the same airframe as the Hampden, but different engines, which proved to be unreliable. It was quickly moved from an operational role and relegated to training, although some were re-engined.
4. Interview of MRAF the Lord Elworthy by the Air Historical Board 21.3.1975
5. Memoirs.
6. 4 FTS was subsequently disbanded and its instructors were relocated to Southern Rhodesia.
7. Memoirs.
8. Anthony Armstrong was a pseudonym of Anthony Armstrong Willis, a well known novelist and playwright.
9. Prune's crew consisted of Sergeant Straddle (Air Bomber), Flying Officer Fixe (Navigator), Sergeant Backtune (Wireless Operator) and Sergeant Winde (Air Gunner).

278   Dambuster-in-Chief

10. AIR/20/1638 Notes on aircrew training.
11. Bennett, *Pathfinder*, pp.174–5.
12. AHB Interview 10.7.1975.
13. Harris, *Bomber Offensive*, p.97. Jack Slessor, in *The Central Blue*, p.384, attributed the initiative for the decision to MacNeece Foster at 6 (Training) Group.

Chapter 10
1. XV Squadron was one of very few which used Roman rather than Arabic numerals, one way of denoting their RFC heritage.
2. 90 Squadron had earlier been equipped with the Boeing B.17 Flying Fortress, but this proved to be an unsuitable aircraft for Bomber Command's night-time bombing campaign. It never flew its Blenheims operationally.
3. Memoirs.
4. Because of their high ceiling and relative immunity to night fighters and flak, Mosquitoes became the most usual platform for Oboe, although it was also installed on occasion in Lancasters.
5. Memoirs.
6. AIR 14/3544.
7. K. S. Batchelor, IWM interview. Gray himself was a remarkable man who had won a George Medal for pulling two members of the aircrew out of a plane which had crashed into a bomb dump, incurring severe burns in the process.
8. Memoirs.

Chapter 11
1. AIR 14/3544.
2. Lawrence, *No 5 Group RAF*, p.13.
3. Slessor, *The Central Blue*, p.380.
4. Harris Papers – Correspondence with AOC 5 Group February 1942 to December 1944.
5. Bennett, *Pathfinder*, p.204.
6. Coryton went on to have a distinguished career, initially at the Air Ministry and then in command of the RAF in India and Burma for the last year of the war against Japan. He subsequently held senior roles at the Ministry of Supply.
7. This was the house whose garden was immortalized by T. S. Eliot in the first of his *Four Quartets*.
8. The name was changed back from Grantham to Spitalgate in 1944.

Chapter 12
1. Here Harris inserted a rough drawing of what appears to be a toboggan shape.
2. The Toraplane was an air-launched glided torpedo designed by Sir Dennistoun Burney and Nevil Shute. It never got off the ground.
3. AIR 14/840.

Notes 279

Chapter 13
1. AIR 14/840.
2. Ibid.
3. The Station Commander at Syerston had put Gibson in for a bar to the DSO, only to have it rejected by Ralph in favour of a second bar to his DFC. Harris had then overturned Ralph's recommendation, on the grounds that anyone who had completed as many sorties as Gibson deserved at least a bar to the DSO, if not a VC.
4. Gibson, *Enemy Coast Ahead*, p.238.
5. Ibid.
6. Memoirs. In fact Gibson had not been a head prefect at any of his schools.
7. In the film *The Dambusters* the idea comes to Gibson whilst watching the spotlights on the stage during a London theatre production. This is, sadly, complete fiction!

Chapter 14
1. Wallis must have assumed that it was actually fifty-six men who had died, as the survival of Burcher, Fraser and Tees was not known about until much later.
2. Only 111 CGMs were awarded to RAF personnel during the Second World War.
3. To ensure balance, Their Majesties also visited 57 Squadron. Moreover, they later moved on to Binbrook.

Chapter 15
1. Memorandum C.C.S. 166/1/D by the Combined Chiefs of Staff, 21 January 1943.
2. Memoirs.

Chapter 16
1. AIR 14/2062.
2. Memoirs.
3. He and his crew were lost in a raid on Mannheim on 23/24 September 1943.
4. AIR 14/717.
5. The operation was successful, but everyone in the party was captured.
6. The exceptions were Flight Lieutenant Richard Trevor-Roper, the rear gunner and a close friend of Gibson's, who went to a training unit before joining another squadron, and Sergeant John Pulford, the flight engineer, who was frequently disparaged by Gibson; both men were to be killed on operations later in the war.
7. Memoirs.
8. AIR 14/2062.
9. Ibid.

10. Memoirs. Ralph later told his nephew Julian that when he told the other bomb aimers that if he could do it, so could they, a voice at the back of the room was heard to mutter, 'If we could do it we'd all be air vice-marshals'!
11. Townsend had left to become an instructor at a HCU in early October.
12. Cheshire, *The Face of Victory*, p.30.

Chapter 17
1. It was later estimated that FIDO had saved the lives of some 10,000 aircrew.
2. In fact, one per minute was never achieved on average, but the rate did fall to one per 1.29 minutes.
3. Memoirs.

Chapter 18
1. Bennett, *Pathfinder*, p.214.
2. Sharp was criticised by his new aircrews for his lack of operational experience, a common complaint against senior officers. He subsequently persuaded Ralph to get Harris to allow him to go on some operations, almost unprecedented amongst base commanders, and was in due course awarded a DSO.
3. Article by Group Captain J. R. Goodman on 627 Squadron website.
4. Bennett was later to claim in *Pathfinder* (1958 edition) pp.216–7 that Cheshire had failed to drop his markers and had to leave due to lack of fuel, calling in the Pathfinders to mark using the Newhaven technique. This was completely untrue. The raid was subsequently specifically referred to in his VC citation.
5. Memoirs.
6. Harris Papers – Correspondence with AOC 5 Group February 1942 to December 1944.
7. The Mustang was apparently acquired by Cheshire as a direct result of the visit by Spaatz and Doolittle to Woodhall Spa on 31 March 1944; with true American generosity they had told Cheshire to ask for anything he wanted.
8. Cheshire, *The Face of Victory*, p.44.
9. Four specialized Master Bomber posts were established in 54 Base Flight at Coningsby, those appointed all holding the rank of wing commander.
10. Memoirs.
11. Harris Papers – Correspondence with AOC 5 Group.
12. Harris Papers – Correspondence with CAS.
13. Ibid.

Chapter 19
1. Two months later, Satterley succeeded Sharp as Commander of 54 Base, thus maintaining his association with 5 Group.
2. Interview by Air Historical Branch 7.3.1975.
3. 5 Group News September 1944.

4. The 'Johnny Walker' mine was designed to sink 30ft and then rise to the surface, hopefully to strike the hull of a vessel, and to do this again and again until it exploded; it was not a success!
  5. The Oboe system was reversed in Gee-H, with the aircraft transmitting to the ground station rather than vice versa.
  6. Memoirs.
  7. In the event, the Japanese surrender in August 1945 meant it was disbanded before it could begin operations.
  8. Memoirs.
  9. Ibid.
  10. Ibid.

Chapter 20
  1. Letter from Fiddament to Ralph 4.8 1971.
  2. Memoirs.
  3. AIR 20/3102.
  4. Fielden was well known to Ralph; he had commanded 161 (Special Duty) Squadron at RAF Tempsford and then Tempsford itself whilst Ralph was AOC 3 Group and RAF Woodhall Spa shortly before Ralph left 5 Group.
  5. This was known as the Beam Approach Beacon System or BABS.
  6. Letter from Slessor to Ralph 30.11.1946.

Chapter 21
  1. Advanced flying schools and operational conversion units remained the responsibility of the individual operational commands.
  2. Letter from F. C. Watts to John and Malcolm Cochrane 1.1.1978.
  3. The Air War College sits at the senior level of military education in the USA, with the Air Command and Staff College at the intermediate level.
  4. C. C. Grey, *The Aeroplane*, 7.11.1952.
  5. Embry, *Mission Completed*, p.286.
  6. Memoirs.
  7. In a letter to Hilda after Ralph's death, Tedder's son John confirmed that his father had always hoped that Ralph would become CAS.
  8. There is no evidence to support any undue bias on Attlee's behalf, but both Slessor and his successor, William Dickson, were alumni of his own school, Haileybury.
  9. Slessor admired Ralph, describing him in his own memoirs as 'the best group commander that Bomber Command ever had' (Slessor, *The Central Blue*, p.373).
  10. The Western Union was the post-war treaty between the UK, France and the Benelux countries; it was later rolled into NATO.
  11. Letter from Denny to Ralph 31.10.1952.
  12. Letter from Dickson to Ralph 31.5.1952.
  13. Letter from Slessor to Ralph 10.11.1952.

Chapter 22

1. Atlantic Shipbuilders managed to overcome its various difficulties and continued to build ships into the 1960s, when it was restructured under new ownership as the Newport Shipbuilding Company.
2. The Official History of the Royal Navy between 1939 and 1945.
3. Isitt was the first New Zealander to become New Zealand's CAS in 1943 and was followed by Nevill in 1946.
4. Trenchard had been Commissioner of the Metropolitan Police from 1931 to 1935.
5. Clark became best known for playing the irascible Professor Geoffrey Loftus in the television comedy series of the late 1960s, *Doctor in the House*.
6. Letter dated 30.6 59 from Bennett to J. C. Reynolds of Frederick Muller.

Chapter 23

1. The limeworks ceased production in 2002, and the brickworks were closed two years later.
2. The ceremony at Ampleforth Abbey was conducted by the Abbot, Dom Basil Hume, later Archbishop of Westminster.
3. Galland was Germany's most famous fighter ace and had held high command in the Luftwaffe's fighter force against the Allied bombers in 1944–5, before being sacked by Goering.
4. Letter from Harris to Ralph 24.4.1972. Harris was referring to *The Desert Generals*, an account of the war in North Africa which was highly critical of the then General Montgomery. Harris was an admirer of Monty, whom he had known as a member of the Directing Staff at the Army Staff College in 1928/9.
5. It would be 1981 before Cheshire was admitted to the Order of Merit, an honour in the personal gift of the Queen, and 1991 before he was created a life peer.
6. Sam Elworthy had gone on to be Chief of the Air Staff and the Defence Staff and was by this time the Constable and Governor of Windsor Castle, a peer of the realm and a Knight of the Garter. He had, throughout his distinguished career, kept in close contact with Ralph, whom he admired more than any other officer under whom he had served, and he and his wife Audrey had become close friends of the family.
7. Elworthy's address at the Service of Thanksgiving for Ralph on 28 February 1978.

Chapter 24

1. Article written by Cheshire in 1988.
2. Ibid.
3. Ibid.
4. Letter from Michael Beetham to Hilda 20.12.1977.
5. Undated letter from Fauquier to John or Malcolm.

Sources and Bibliography

Interviews
Mr John Cochrane
Mr Malcolm Cochrane
The Hon. Julian Cochrane
Grizel, Lady Stewart

Primary Sources

National Archives
ADM 1/8488/97	Employment of airships against submarines
AIR 1/306/15	Memo on use and control of airships
AIR 1/308/15	Organization of Airship Branch, Admiralty
AIR 1/645/17	Allocation of airships to Kingsnorth
AIR 1/672/17	Airship station at Capel, Folkestone
AIR 1/2103/207	Complements of Airship Stations 1918
AIR 2/8395	Operation Chastise
AIR 2/9726	Harris despatch on Bomber Command February 1942–May 1945
AIR 8/377	Flying Training 1940–41
AIR 14 717	617 & 619 Squadron Operations
AIR 14/842	Upkeep progress reports
AIR 14/840	Operation Chastise
AIR 14/844	Operation Chastise
AIR 14/994	Sinking of Tirpitz
AIR 14/2008	High level night bombing by 617 Squadron
AIR 14/2011	'Tallboy' and 'Grand Slam' bombs – trials and development
AIR 14/2062	Operational Role of 617 Squadron
AIR 14/2036	Operation Chastise
AIR 14/2040	Operation Crossbow
AIR 14/2057	Attack on Saumur Tunnel June 1944
AIR 14/2052	Attack on Antheor Viaduct November 1943
AIR 14/2062	Operational Role of 617 Squadron
AIR 14/2087	Report on Chastise
AIR 14/2088	Operation Chastise

AIR 14/3544	C-in-C correspondence with AOC 3 Group 1942–43
AIR 19/220	Notes on Flying Training 1940–41
AIR 20/1368	Air crew training notes 1940–45
AIR 20/1370	Empire Air Training Scheme May 1941–January 1942
AIR 20/1374-1376	Empire Air Training Scheme Committee
AIR 20/3102-3106	Transport Command Organization September 1944–October 1946
AIR 24/1	Operational Record Book Air Staff Aden Command 1928–1939
AIR 24/1617-1618	Transport Command Organization January–May 1945
AIR 24/1634-1635	Transport Command Operations January–May 1945
AIR 24/2035-2040	HQ Transport Command January 1946–May 1947
AIR 25/52	3 Group Operational Record Book January 1941–December 1943
AIR 25/109A	5 Group Operational Record Book September 1937–December 1943
AIR 25/110	5 Group Operational Record Book January 1944–December 1945
AIR 25 119-125	5 Group Operational Record Book Appendices July 1943–March 1945
AIR 25/149	7 Group Operational Record Book
AIR 25/150	7 Group Operational Record Book Appendices
AIR 27/112/20-30	8 Squadron Operational Record Book 1929
AIR 29/554	4 FTS Operational Record Book
AIR 32/64	CAS conference 1949 Exercise 'Ariel'
AIR 32/70	Flying Training Command navigator training policy
AIR 32/72	Statistical summary Flying Training Command 1948
AIR 32/110	Summary of training of all flying personnel 1948
AIR 32/118	Flying Training Command Research Branch
AIR 32/120	Flying Training Command programme of work
AIR 32/185	Reduction of servicing in Flying Training Command
AIR 32/252	Methods of selection & training of aircrew Flying Training Command
AIR 692/21/20/45	History of 45 Squadron
AIR 8530/197	Ordering of further rigid airships
DSIR 23/806	Visit to RN Airship Station, Kingsnorth

RAF Museum London
The Papers of MRAF Sir Arthur Harris

Imperial War Museum
Recorded interviews with K. S. Batchelor, P. D. Bird, A. R. Eastman, J. C. Elliott, J. R. Goodman, G. King and R. E. Knights

Private Cochrane Records
Ralph's Memoirs written in 1974 & 1976
Diaries 1921–26, 1953, 1963, 1966–70, 1972–74
Diary of a trip to Persia, 1923
Diary of a trip to Yugoslavia, 1925
Diary of a tour in Europe, 1928
Private Flying Diaries, 1930 & 1931
New Zealand Diary, 1936–37
Diaries of trips to the USA and Canada, 1950 & 1952
Midshipman's Journal HMS *Colossus*, 1912–14
Airship Flying Log Book, 1916–17
Pilot's Flying Log Books, 1921–44
New Zealand Flying Log, 1937–39
RAF Staff Interview conducted on 30 July 1975
Prize essays and articles written by Ralph
Letters from Ralph to Hilda
Letters, articles and other papers collected by Ralph
Photograph albums
RAF Service Record

Secondary Sources
5 Group News, February 1943–February 1945
5 Group Tactical Notes

Other Sources
Air Force List
Dictionary of National Biography
London Gazette
The Times Digital Archive
Who's Who
Wikipedia and other websites, notably Air of Authority – A History of RAF Organization

Books
Austen, R. L., *High Adventure – A Navigator at War*, Chichester 1989
Bennett, Donald, *Pathfinder*, London 1958, 1960 & 1983
Bentley, Geoffrey, *RNZAF – A Short History*, Wellington, New Zealand, 1960
Bishop, Patrick, *Target Tirpitz*, London 2012
Bowyer, Chaz, and Turner, Michael, *Royal Air Force – The aircraft in service since 1918*, Feltham 1981
Brickhill, Paul, *The Dam Busters*, London 1951
Castle, Ian, *British Airships 1905–30*, Oxford 2009
Charlwood, D. E., *No Moon Tonight*, London 1956

Cheshire, Leonard, *Bomber Pilot*, London 1943
Cheshire, Leonard, *The Face of Victory*, London 1961
Churchill, Winston S., *The Second World War*, Volumes I–VI, London 1949–54
Cochrane, Alexander, *The Fighting Cochranes – A Scottish clan over six hundred years of naval and military history*, London 1983
Cole, Christopher & Grant, Roderick, *But Not In Anger – The RAF in the Transport Role*, Shepperton 1979
Embry, Basil, *Mission Completed*, London 1957
Falconer, Jonathan, *Bomber Command Handbook 1939–1945*, Stroud 1998
Gibson, Guy, *Enemy Coast Ahead*, London 1946
Harris, Arthur, *Bomber Offensive*, London 1947
Hasting, Max, *Bomber Command*, London 1979
Hastings, Max, *Chastise – The Dambusters Story 1943*, London 2019
Hill, Roderic, *The Baghdad Air Mail*, London 1929
Holland, James, *Dam Busters – The Race to Smash the Dams, 1943*, London 2012
Lawrence, W. J., *No. 5 Bomber Group RAF*, London 1951
Lockstone, Brian, *Into Wind … The birth of the RNZAF*, Christchurch, New Zealand, 2007
Mead, Richard, *'Sam' – Marshal of the Royal Air Force The Lord Elworthy – A Biography*, Barnsley 2018
Meager, George, *My Airship Flights 1915–1930*, London 1970
Melinsky, Hugh, *Forming the Pathfinders – The Career of Air Vice-Marshal Sydney Bufton*, Stroud 2010
Messenger, Charles, *'Bomber' Harris and the Strategic Bombing Offensive, 1939–1945*, London 1984
Middlebrook, Martin & Everitt, Chris, *The Bomber Command War Diaries – An Operational Reference Book 1939–1945*, Harmondsworth 1985
Mondey, David, *The Hamlyn Concise Guide to British Aircraft of World War II*, London 1994
Mondey, David, *The Hamlyn Concise Guide to American Aircraft of World War II*, London 1996
Mondey, David, *The Hamlyn Concise Guide to Axis Aircraft of World War II*, London 1996
Morpurgo, J. E., *Barnes Wallis – A Biography*, London 1972
Morris, Richard, *Cheshire – The Biography of Leonard Cheshire VC, OM*, London 2000
Price, David, *The Crew – The Story of a Lancaster Bomber Crew*, London 2020
Probert, Henry, *High Commanders of the Royal Air Force*, London 1991
Probert, Henry, *Bomber Harris – His Life and Times*, London 2001
Richards, Dennis, *Portal of Hungerford – The Life of MRAF Viscount Portal of Hungerford KG, GCB, OM, DSO, MC*, London 1977
Saundby, Robert, *Air Bombardment – The Story of its Development*, London 1961

Saward, Dudley, *Bomber Harris: The Authorized Biography*, London 1984
Slessor, John, *The Central Blue – Recollections and Reflections*, London 1956
Sturtivant, Ray, with Hamlin, John, *Royal Air Force Flying Training and Support Units since 1912*, Staplefield 2012
Sweetman, *The Dambusters Raid*, London 1982 & 1990
Tedder, Arthur, *With Prejudice – War Memoirs*, London 1966
Trevenen James, A. G., *The Royal Air Force – The Past 30 Years*, London 1976
Turpin, Brian, *Coastal Patrol – Royal Naval Airship Operations during the Great War 1914–1918*, Stroud 2016
Ward, Chris, *5 Group Bomber Command – An Operational Record*, Barnsley 2007
Ward, Chris & Smith, Steve, *3 Group Bomber Command – An Operational Record*, Barnsley 2008
Ward, Chris, Lee, Andy & Wachtel, Andreas, *Dambusters – The Definitive History of 617 Squadron at War 1943–1945*, Walton-on-Thames 2003
Wynn, Humphrey, *Forged in War – A History of Royal Air Force Transport Command 1943–1967*, London 1996

Index I

Individuals
Organisations, Institutions and Businesses
Military Operations, Formations and Units

Abdullah, King of Transjordan 32
Addison, Air Vice-Marshal E. B. 207, 231, 255
Alexandria, Royal Yacht 19
Alghanim, Yusuf 238–9
Allsebrook, Flight Lieutenant Ralf 165, 167, 255
Anderson, Pilot Officer Cyril 136, 149, 150, 165
Anderson, Michael 247
Archer-Shee, George 15
Ardvreck School 13–14
Argyll, John, 1st Marquis of 2
ARIEL, Exercise 227–8
Army, British
   Army
      British Expeditionary Force 23
   Brigade
      Aden 58
      2nd Cavalry 50
      Natal Mounted 9
   Regiment / Battalion
      Argyll & Sutherland Highlanders 9, 237
      Black Watch 10
      Scots Guards 9, 237
   Colonial Troops
      Aden Protectorate Levies 57–8
      Assyrian Levies 39
   Other
      School of Chemical Warfare 50
      Staff College, Camberley 49, 50, 228–9, 230

Army, French
   Army
      First 203
Army, German
   Division
      17 SS Panzergrenadier 193
Army, United States
   Army
      Seventh 203
Arnold, General of the Air Force Henry H. 215
Association of Independent Businesses 252
Astell, Flight Lieutenant William 135, 145, 146
Atlantic Ferry Organisation 109, 171, 212
Atlantic Shipbuilding Company Ltd 238–41, 245, 256, 282
Atomic Energy Research Establishment 243
Attlee, Earl (Clement) 228, 229, 264, 281
Attwood, Group Captain C. W. 58
Avro (A. V. Roe & Co. Ltd) 118, 129, 257

Bader, Group Captain Sir Douglas 263
Bailey, Christopher 241
Bailey, Group Captain George 238, 241
Bailey Shipbuilding Development Company Ltd 238
Baker, Air Chief Marshal Sir John 64, 108, 128, 234
Baldwin, Air Marshal Sir John 103, 109, 111
Baldwin, Earl (Stanley) 54

Balfour, Earl of (Arthur) 10, 13
Balfour family 250
Balliol College, Oxford 237, 244
Bandon, Air Chief Marshal the Earl of 246
BANQUET, Operation 94–5
BANQUET TRAINING, Operation 94
Barker, Wing Commander William 49
Barlow, Flight Lieutenant Norman 136, 145, 146
Barn School 122
Barnett, Correlli 253–4
Barratt, Air Chief Marshal Sir Arthur 63
Barrow, Tom 83, 85, 220, 245
Barton, Group Captain R. J. F. 46
Barzanji, Sheikh Mahmud 38
Batchelor, Group Captain K. S. 113, 278
Batten, Jean 83
Batterbee, Sir Harry 89
Bauer, Dr S. G. 243
Bazin, Wing Commander J. M. 201
Beardsworth, Air Vice-Marshal H. I. T. 36
Beetham, Marshal of the Royal Air Force Sir Michael 267–8
Beg, Karim Fatteh 38
BELLICOSE, Operation 158
Belvoir Hunt 46
Bennett, Air Vice-Marshal Donald 156, 172, 207, 212, 221, 255, 267, 282
 blames Ralph for loss of second pilot 101
 chosen to form Pathfinders 109
 relations with Ralph at 3 Group 110–11
 on Ralph and Coryton 121
 opposition to low-level marking 157, 174–5, 185, 264
 reaction to transfer of squadrons to 5 Group 187–8, 197
 criticises Ralph in memoirs 247–8
 on Cheshire in Munich raid 280
Bettington, Colonel Arthur 77
Binney, Constance, *see* Cheshire
Bird, Group Captain P. D. 161
Blackett, Lord 126
Blair, Alexander, *see* Cochrane, Alexander
Blankney Hunt 46

Boadle, Dr C. D. 243
Bonaparte, Emperor Napoleon 274
Boothby, Captain RN Frederick 29
Borthwick-Clarke, Group Captain E. S. 58
Bottomley, Air Chief Marshal Sir Norman 63, 117, 127, 140, 144, 166, 208
Bowhill, Air Chief Marshal Sir Frederick 212, 213, 214
Boyle, Andrew 246, 248
Boyle, (George) Earl of Glasgow 10, 11
Boyle, Gertrude, *see* Cochrane, Gertrude
Breguet, Louis 64
Brickhill, Paul vii, 233–4, 246
British Airways 221
British Commonwealth Air Training Plan 98–9
British European Airways 221, 238, 265
British Overseas Airways Corporation 212, 213, 221–2, 238, 265
Brooke-Popham, Air Chief Marshal Sir Robert 49, 50, 63
Brown, Squadron Leader Ken 136, 149, 150, 151, 153
Bruce, (Edward) Earl of Elgin and Kincardine 54
Bruce, Katherine (Kitty), Countess of Elgin and Kincardine 12, 13, 54, 236–7, 259, 265, 275
Brundrett, Sir Frederick 231
Bryant, Sir Arthur 228
Buckley, Air Commodore Maurice 83, 220, 277
Bufton, Air Vice-Marshal Sidney 108–9, 110, 127, 140, 184, 255
Burcher, Pilot Officer A. F. 146–7, 279
Burford Cottage Hospital 258, 260
Burnett, Air Chief Marshal Sir Charles 76
Burney, Sir Charles Dennistoun 47, 278
Burpee, Pilot Officer Lewis 134, 149
Buss, Air Commodore K. C. 90, 91
Butler, Professor Sir James 254
Butt, D. M. 107
Buxton, The Hon. Dorothy, Lady 12, 13, 31, 274

Buxton, Sir Thomas 274
Byers, Pilot Officer Vernon 136–7, 145, 146

Callaway, Air Vice-Marshal W. B. 115–16
Cameron, Marshal of the Royal Air Force Lord 260
Canadian Forces Staff College 257
Carr, Air Marshal Sir Roderick 110, 172
Carson, (Edward) Lord 15
Casablanca Conference 155
Castoldi, Mario 56
CATECHISM, Operation 205–6
Cave-Brown-Cave, Wing Commander T. R. 23
Chadwick, Roy 118, 129, 152
Chamberlain, Joseph 10
Charles I, HM King 1–2
Charles II, HM King 2
CHASTISE, Operation 144–54, 136, 159, 165, 166–7, 169, 172, 173, 186, 194, 233, 234, 256, 263
C. H. Bailey Ltd 238, 239
Cherwell, Frederick Lindeman, Viscount 125, 126–7, 231
Cheshire, Flight Lieutenant Christopher 171
Cheshire, Constance (née Binney) 171
Cheshire Homes 246, 258
Cheshire, Group Captain Leonard, Lord 173, 178, 207, 233, 234, 247, 248, 256, 257, 259, 266, 280, 282
  early RAF career 171–2
  Ralph selects to command 617 Squadron 172
  and low-level marking 174–5, 185, 187, 189–90, 263
  early impact on 617 Squadron 176
  and first use of TALLBOY 193
  uses Mustang for marking 194, 280
  steps down from 617 Squadron 194
  awarded VC 195
  post-war career 246, 258
  at 617 Squadron reunions 256–7, 259
  reads lesson at Ralph's funeral 260
  opinion of Ralph 263–4, 264–5, 267
Cheshire, Lady (Sue), *see* Ryder, Sue
Chichester, Sir Francis 100, 266
Chidlaw, General Benjamin W. 226
Christ's Hospital 234, 247
Churchill Hospital 258
Churchill, Sir Winston 32, 33, 73, 107, 125, 142, 148, 150, 215, 231
Clark, Ernest 247, 282
Clark-Hall, Air Marshal Sir Robert 82, 245, 277
Clayton, Flight Lieutenant B. W. 165
Coates, Eric 247
Cochrane, Alexander (formerly Blair) 1
Cochrane, Admiral Sir Alexander 3–5, 6
Cochrane, Alexandra 252
Cochrane, Alice 252
Cochrane of Cults, Anthony, 3rd Lord 72, 249
Cochrane, Archibald, 9th Earl of Dundonald 2–3
Cochrane, The Hon. Sir Archibald 6
Cochrane, Captain Sir Archibald 12, 14, 28–9, 38, 45, 51, 56, 236, 265, 274
Cochrane, Admiral Sir Arthur 9
Cochrane, The Hon. Dorothy, *see* Buxton, the Hon. Dorothy
Cochrane, Dorothy the Hon. Lady (wife of Captain Sir Archibald) 51, 236
Cochrane, Lieutenant General Douglas, 12th Earl of Dundonald 9
Cochrane, The Hon. Elin ('Nellie') 72, 276
Cochrane, Elizabeth 1
Cochrane, Gertrude, Lady Cochrane of Cults 10, 11, 236, 265
Cochrane, Grizel, *see* Stewart, Grizel, Lady
Cochrane, Harriet 252
Cochrane, Hilda, Lady ix, 71, 75–6, 91, 93, 95, 121, 214, 233, 237, 240, 244, 250, 251, 252, 257, 277
  Personal
  family background 67
  character 67, 255–6

love of art and friendship with
    artists 67, 88, 265
love of gardening 96, 223, 266
1930–39
    meeting Ralph 66
    wedding 66
    honeymoon 67–8
    Ralph flies around Europe 68–9
    Wednesday–Thursday/Storran
        Gallery 69
    in New Zealand 83, 85, 88, 89
1939–45
    and RAF Benevolent Fund 180, 266
    conveys news of casualties 180, 266
1945–1977
    at premiere of *The Dambusters* 247
    discovers Construct-o-Straws 251
    illness 258–9
    moved to nursing home 259
Cochrane of Cochrane, Colonel Sir
    John 1–2
Cochrane, John 75, 85, 88, 121–2, 233,
    237, 244, 252, 253, 260, 265
Cochrane, The Hon. Julian 249, 250
Cochrane, The Hon. Katherine, *see* Bruce,
    Katherine
Cochrane, Katherine (Ralph's
    granddaughter) 252
Cochrane, Lady Louisa, *see* O'Neill, Louisa
Cochrane, The Hon. Louisa 11–12
Cochrane, Malcolm 88, 121–2, 237–8, 258,
    259, 265
Cochrane, Margaret (Ralph's daughter-in-
    law) 252
Cochrane, The Hon. Marjorie 12
Cochrane, Mary (Ralph's daughter-in-
    law) 252, 258
Cochrane of Cults, Lady (Mary) 236, 258
Cochrane, Phoebe 252
Cochrane, Air Chief Marshal the Hon. Sir
    Ralph
    Personal
        birth 10, 11
        health 37–8, 59, 72–3, 75, 258–9
        death 260

Family
    Cochrane family background 1–10
    Parents, *see* Cochrane of Cults,
        Thomas, 1st Lord and Cochrane,
        Gertrude
    Wife, *see* Cochrane, Hilda
    Children, *see* Stewart, Grizel and
        Cochrane, John and Malcolm
Childhood and education
    childhood 11–14
    prep school 13–14
    Osborne 14–15
    Dartmouth 15–16
Sporting interests
    fishing 34, 38, 83, 87, 240, 244, 258
    golf 71, 76, 87
    hunting 46–7, 51
    polo 43, 62
    sailing 15, 18, 34, 61–2, 66
    shooting 38, 44, 46, 62, 258
    skiing 31, 45, 51, 56, 65, 69, 88, 236,
        244
    squash 32, 46
Orders and Decorations
    AFC 30
    CBE 89
    CB 152
    KBE 207
    KCB 229
    GBE 229
Royal Navy career
    appointed midshipman 15
    serves on HMS *Colossus* 16–20
    in RNAS airship service 21–7
    promoted to flight sub-lieutenant 21
    promoted to acting flight
        commander 27
RAF Career 1918–39
    in RAF airship service 27–30
    serves in Egypt 32–5
    learns to fly aircraft 33–5
    in 45 Squadron 35–44
    commands 3 Squadron, Boys' Wing,
        Cranwell 45–7

attends RAF Staff College 48–51
promoted to squadron leader 51–6
at HQ Wessex Bombing Area 51–5
on staff of Aden Command 57–9
commands 8 Squadron 59–62
on Directing Staff at RAF Staff
College 63–9
serves at Air Ministry 69–71, 73
promoted to wing commander 71
temporarily attached to AOC Middle
East 71–3
attends IDC 73–5
on staff of Inland Area/Training
Command 75–6
seconded to Government of New
Zealand 77–82
promoted to group captain 83
CAS RNZAF 83–9
RAF Career 1939–45
Deputy Director of Intelligence 90–1
CO Abingdon 90–3
SASO 6 Group 93
promoted to air commodore 93
AOC 7 Group 93–5
Director of Flying Training 95–102
AOC 3 Group 103–14
AOC 5 Group 115–23, 131–210
and Operation CHASTISE 131–54
RAF Career 1945–52
AOC-in-C Transport Command 211–22
AOC-in-C Flying Training Command 223–30
Vice-Chief of the Air Staff 230–5
Post-war career
Atlantic Shipbuilding 238–41
Rolls-Royce 241–4
Cults Lime and Cults Brick 249–50
RJM Exports/Cochrane's of Oxford 251–3
Cochrane, Robert, Earl of Mar 1
Cochrane, The Hon. Roger 12
Cochrane, Admiral Thomas, 10th Earl of Dundonald 5–9

Cochrane, Thomas, 11th Earl of Dundonald 9
Cochrane. Admiral of the Fleet Sir Thomas 5
Cochrane of Cults, Thomas, 1st Lord 9–10, 11, 12–13, 14, 15–16, 46, 88, 236, 240, 265
Cochrane of Cults, Thomas, 2nd Lord 12, 72, 236, 249, 250, 258, 265, 276
Cochrane, Thomas (Ralph's grandson) 252
Cochrane of Cults, Vere, 4th Lord 249, 250
Cochrane of Cochrane, William 1
Cochrane, William (Ralph's grandson) 252
Cochrane, William, 1st Earl of Dundonald 2
Cochranes of Oxford Ltd 253
Cockburn, Admiral of the Fleet Sir George 4
Cockburn, Sir Robert 231, 232
Codrington, Admiral Sir Edward 9
Collier, Air Vice-Marshal Sir Conrad 64, 214–15, 216
Collingwood, Vice-Admiral Cuthbert, Lord 6
Colossus, HMS 18–20, 30, 82, 261
COLOSSUS, Operation 166, 195
Colville, Admiral Sir Stanley 17
Coningham, Air Marshal Sir Arthur 277
Constantine, Air Chief Marshal Sir Hugh 209, 253, 256, 259
Coryton, Air Chief Marshal Sir Alec 119, 120–1, 122, 208, 230, 247, 278
Courtney, Air Chief Marshal Sir Christopher 49, 50
Craven, Sir Charles 128, 129
Crawford, Mrs A. D. 85, 88
Crawford, George Lindsay, 21st Earl of 11
Crawford, Lady Mary Lindsay 11
CROSSBOW, Operation 173, 175, 190, 193–4, 196
Cults Brick Ltd 250, 251, 265
Cults Lime Ltd 249, 250, 251, 265, 272
Cunningham, Air Vice-Marshal A. D. 23, 30, 38, 48

Index I   293

D'Albiac, Air Marshal Sir John 41
Daniel, Admiral Sir Charles 254
Dann, Air Commodore C. L. 139
De L'Isle, Viscount 247
Denny, Admiral Sir Michael 234
De Havilland, Captain Sir Geoffrey 66
Derain, André 69
Dickson, Marshal of the Royal Air Force Sir William 234–5, 256, 281
Diefenbaker, John 257
Divall, Flying Officer William 135, 144, 165, 167, 168
DODGE, Operation 216
Donald, Air Marshal Sir Grahame 49
Doolittle, General James H. 176, 186, 280
Douglas of Kirtleside, Marshal of the Royal Air Force the Lord 73, 238, 255
Drew, Group Captain H. V. 54–6
Drummond, Vice-Admiral the Hon. Edmund 80
Duckworth, Admiral Sir John 4
Dundonald, Earls of, *see* Cochrane
Dunedin, HMS 82
Dunford, Squadron Leader Don 253
Dunn, Wing Commander W. E. 144, 145, 147, 152
Dunville, Colonel John 21
Durrant, Flight Officer Carol 113, 122

Eaker, General Ira C. 155
Edward VIII, HM King 15
Eisenhower, President/General of the Army Dwight D. 186, 196, 199, 200, 214
El Gamo, Spanish frigate 6
Elgin and Kincardine, Earl of, *see* Bruce
Eliot, T. S. 278
Elizabeth II, HM Queen 229, 260, 282
Elizabeth the Queen Mother, HM Queen 152
Ellen, Air Commodore C. N. 36, 37
Ellenborough, Edward Law, Earl of 7–8
Ellington, Marshal of the Royal Air Force Sir Edward 36, 71, 275
Elworthy, Audrey, Lady 282

Elworthy, Marshal of the Royal Air Force Lord viii, ix, 95, 127, 128, 159, 162, 179, 199, 200, 206, 260, 266, 282
Elworthy, Air Commodore Sir Timothy viii
Embry, Air Chief Marshal Sir Basil 109, 206, 226–7
Epstein, Sir Jacob 69
Esmeralda, Spanish frigate 8
Eton College 237
Evans-Evans, Group Captain A. C. 176
Evill, Air Chief Marshal Sir Douglas 49, 143, 219
EXODUS, Operation 216

Fairchild, General Muir S. 226
Fauquier, Air Commodore J. E. 206–7, 256, 259, 268
Fawke, Squadron Leader G. E. 189, 193, 196, 203
Feisal, King of Iraq 32
Fellowes, Air Commodore P. F. M. 47, 48
Fiddament, Air Vice-Marshal A. 214–15, 216–17
Fielden, Air Vice-Marshal Sir Edward 219, 281
Fisher, Admiral of the Fleet Lord 21
Fitzherbert, Admiral Sir Edward (13th Lord Stafford) 20
FORTITUDE, Operation 191–2
Foster, Air Chief Marshal Sir Robert 49
Foster, Air Vice-Marshal W. F. MacNeece 93, 278
Frankland, Noble 253, 254
Fraser, Pilot Officer J. W. 146–7, 279
Fraser, Peter 79, 83, 89, 220
Freeman, Air Chief Marshal Sir Wilfrid 109, 130, 143, 230, 234
Freyberg, Captain RN Geoffrey 18
Frost, Katie 13
Frost, W. E. 13

Galland, General Adolf 254, 282
Galway, George Monckton-Arundell, Viscount 80, 89

Gambier, Admiral James, Lord 7
Garner, Wing Commander 140
Garrod, Air Chief Marshal Sir Guy 49, 97, 101
Gates, Major General Byron E. 225
Gatty, Harold 87
Généreux, French ship of the line 5
George V, HM King 19
George VI, HM King 15, 96, 152, 229
Gibbs, Air Marshal Sir Gerald 69, 217
Gibbs, Professor N. H. 254
Gibson, Esmond 83, 84, 87
Gibson, Eve 133, 247, 259, 260
Gibson, Wing Commander Guy vii, viii, ix, 135, 152, 154, 157–8, 164, 165, 166, 168, 172, 195, 207, 247, 263, 279
  early RAF career 131
  first meetings with Ralph 132–3
  Ralph's opinion of 134
  selects 617 Squadron personnel 134–7
  meets Wallis 137–8
  watches UPKEEP trials 138, 139, 141
  and security breach 140
  and plan for CHASTISE 142
  leads CHASTISE 144–9
  awarded VC 151, 279
  death of 200–1
Glanville, Sir William 140
Glasgow, Earl of, *see* Boyle
Glengorm Castle, SS 44
GLIMMER, Operation 192
Gneisenau, German battleship 103, 118
Goddard, Air Marshal Sir Victor 90, 230, 266, 277
Goebbels, Joseph 121
Goering, Herman 121, 271, 282
Gomm, Wing Commander C. L. 158
Goodenough, Admiral Sir William 18
Goodman, Group Captain J. G. 'Benny' 188–9, 280
GOODWOOD, Operation 196
Government Code and Cypher School 91
Grant, Duncan 69
Gray, Group Captain J. A. 113, 278

Green, Sergeant 32, 34
Griffith, Dr A. A. 242
Groves, Air Commodore R. M. 63–4, 276

Haining, General Sir Robert 73
Hall, Sir Arnold 256–7
Handasyde, Robert 126
Hankey, Maurice, Lord 70
Hannah, Flight Sergeant John 117
Harper, Lieutenant General Robert W. 227
Harris, Marshal of the Royal Air Force Sir Arthur 63, 70, 76, 77, 101, 106, 111, 115, 119–20, 135, 139, 142, 151, 160, 162, 167, 176, 180, 186, 194, 196, 199, 204, 205, 206, 208, 209–10, 253–4, 255, 256, 259, 266, 278, 279, 280, 282
  commands 45 Squadron 39–42, 261
  in Wessex Bombing Area 53, 261–2
  shares office with Ralph 73
  asks for Ralph to command 3 Group 103–4, 262
  and formation of Pathfinders 109–10
  on time-and-distance bombing 113–14
  as AOC 5 Group 116–17
  replaces Coryton with Ralph 120–1
  briefs Ralph on CHASTISE 123–4
  and UPKEEP 127–30
  selects Gibson to command 617 Squadron 131–3
  at Grantham and Scampton during CHASTISE 145–6, 147, 148, 149–50
  employs 617 Squadron for precision bombing 154, 164–5, 169, 188, 191, 263, 264
  and POINTBLANK 155
  and Battle of the Ruhr 156–7
  and Battle of Berlin 177–8, 183–4
  transfers Pathfinder squadrons to 5 Group 187–8, 197
  recommends Cheshire for VC 195
  rejects Portal's request for Ralph as ACAS 197–8, 262
Harris, Lady (Jill) 259
Harrison, Air Vice-Marshal R. 207

Harvey, Robert 74
Haslam, Group Captain Edward 256
Hassan, Mohammed Abdullah 33
Hastings, Sir Max 255
Hawker Siddeley Aircraft Co. Ltd 257
Hay, Flight Lieutenant Bob 136, 138, 139, 140, 144, 151, 175, 194
Hayes, Lieutenant Colonel R. C. 26
Hazell, Squadron Leader T. F. 39
Hermes, Gertrude 69
Heward, Air Chief Marshal Sir Anthony 188, 256
Hill, Edward (Ted), Lord 240
Hill, Air Chief Marshal Sir Roderic 63, 266
Hitler, Adolf 55, 69, 74, 162, 173
Hives, Lord (Ernest) 219, 242, 243
Holden, Wing Commander G. W. 166, 167, 168, 171, 172, 195, 202
Hollinghurst, Air Chief Marshal Sir Leslie 46, 47, 218, 220, 230
Hooper, W. J. ('Bill') 100
Hopgood, Flight Lieutenant John 134, 144, 145, 146–7
Howard, Sir John 238
Howard, Professor Sir Michael 254
Hughes, Howard 232
Hughes, Air Marshal Sir Rochford 260
Humphrey, Marshal of the Royal Air Force Sir Andrew 257
Humphries, Flight Lieutenant Harry 137, 151
Hussein, President Saddam vii

Imperial Airways 51, 71, 87, 109, 221
Imperial Bank of Persia 43
Imperial Defence College 73–5, 230, 262
Inglis, Air Vice-Marshal F. F. 91
International Institute for Strategic Studies 253
Isitt, Air Vice-Marshal Sir Leonard 79–80, 85, 245, 276, 282
Ivelaw-Chapman, Air Chief Marshal Sir Ronald 234
Iveson, Squadron Leader Tony 257

Jackson, Warrant Officer Norman 256
Jacob, Lieutenant General Sir Ian 254
James III, HM King of Scotland 1
James, Wing Commander A. G. Trevenen 254
Jellicoe, Earl (John) 17
John Howard & Co. Ltd 238, 239
Johnson, Group Captain P. W. 176
Johnston, Captain Andrew 274
Joseph, Sir Keith 258
Joubert de la Ferté, Air Chief Marshal Sir Philip 63

Kay, Air Vice-Marshal Cyril 245
Kearns, Squadron Leader R. S. D. 189
Keith, Admiral Viscount 3, 5
Kellaway, Squadron Leader W. H. 165
Kirkforthar Brick Ltd 250
Knight, Flight Lieutenant Les 136, 145, 147, 148, 167, 168
Krupp (company) 156, 161

Lake, Colonel M. C. 58, 61
Lamplugh, Captain A. G. 66
Lancaster, Flight Sergeant George 135
Lawrence, T. E. 275
Lawrence, W. J. 248
Learoyd, Wing Commander Roderick 117, 167, 256
Lee, John A. 82
Leggo, Flight Lieutenant Jack 136, 151
Leigh-Mallory, Air Chief Marshal Sir Trafford 49–50, 131, 186
Le May, General Curtis E. 176, 246
Lilian Faithful Nursing Home 259
Linnell, Air Marshal Sir Francis 129
Llewellyn, Colonel Sir Godfrey 238
Lloyd, Air Chief Marshal Sir Hugh 49, 208
Lockspeiser, Sir Ben 127, 129, 139
Loerzer, Colonel General Bruno 65, 276
Lombard, Adrian 242–3
Lord, Flight Lieutenant D. S. A. 214
Lovell, Pilot Officer Ray 135

Ludlow-Hewitt, Air Chief Marshal Sir
  Edgar 63, 69, 199
Lufthansa 55
Luftwaffe
  Jagdgeschwader
    5 205
  Staffel
    9 205

McCarthy, Wing Commander Joe 136, 145,
  146, 148, 149, 153, 187, 194
McEntegart, Air Vice-Marshal B. F. 140,
  141
McEwen, Air Vice-Marshal Clifford 64,
  207
McKean, Air Vice-Marshal Sir Lionel 76,
  99
McMullen, Air Commodore C. C. 201
Madden, Admiral Sir Alexander 16
Maitland, Air Commodore E. M. 30, 47
Maitland, Air Vice-Marshal P. E. 43–4, 258
Maltby, Squadron Leader David 136, 145,
  147, 148, 165, 166, 167, 168
Manser, Flying Officer Leslie 120
Margaret, HRH Princess 247
MARKET GARDEN, Operation 214
Markham, Flight Lieutenant Bill 72
Martel, Lieutenant General Sir Giffard 74,
  75, 276
Martin, Air Marshal Sir Harold 135–6,
  145, 147, 168, 170, 173, 175, 194, 234,
  256, 259
Marwood-Elton, Group Captain N. W.
  D. 174
Mataroa, RMS 78, 85
Matthews, R. H. 122
Maudslay, Squadron Leader Henry 135,
  144, 145, 146, 147, 148, 149
Maxwell Fyfe, Sir David (*later* Earl
  Kilmuir) 239
Meager, Captain George 28, 29
Medhurst, Air Chief Marshal Sir
  Charles 49, 63
Mediterranean Allied Air Forces 214, 230

Mediterranean Allied Coastal Force 208
Melville, Robert Dundas, Viscount 6
Meyer, Henry Cord 255
Minchin, Sergeant J. W. 146
Mitchell, Reginald 56
Mitchell, Air Chief Marshal Sir
  William 58, 59
Molony, Brigadier C. J. C. 254
Monroe, Marilyn 232
Montgomery, Field Marshal Viscount 196,
  228–9, 230, 254, 282
Moore, Henry 69
Moore, Lieutenant General Sir John 3
Mostyn, Sir Pyers 72
Moyland, Baron Harry van 240
Munro, Squadron Leader Les 136, 145,
  146, 187, 194, 245
Murray, Squadron Leader E. M. 35, 36,
  27, 39
Museum of Transport and Technology
  (NZ) 78, 259, 260

Nash, Paul 93
Nash, Sir Walter 79
National Covenant 1–2
National Physical Laboratory 126
Nettleton, Wing Commander John 119
Nevill, Air Vice-Marshal Sir Arthur 80, 83,
  85, 245, 276, 282
Newall, Marshal of the Royal Air Force Sir
  Cyril 71, 72–3
New Zealand Railways Department 86
Nicholl, Rear Admiral Angus 245
Nobile, General Umberto 28, 274
Norman, Air Commodore Sir Nigel 64, 65,
  66, 276
Norstad, General Lauris 226
North Atlantic Treaty Organisation
  (NATO) 231, 232, 281

O'Brian, Patrick 274
OBVIATE, Operation 205–6
O'Connor, General Sir Richard 74
Oddie, Air Commodore G. S. 76

O'Higgins, General Bernardo 8
O'Higgins, Chilean warship 8
Olaf, Crown Price, *later* King of Norway 206
Oliver, Vice-Admiral R. D. 16, 80
Ombler, Sydney 240
O'Neill. Edward, 2nd Lord 13
O'Neill, Lady (Louisa) 13
Ottley, Pilot Officer Warner 136, 148–9
Oxland, Air Vice-Marshal R. D. 174, 207–8

Pan American Airways 87
PARAVANE, Operation 201–2
Park, Air Chief Marshal Sir Keith 277
Park, Squadron Leader Walter 51
Parry Jones, Captain 28
Pearson, Sir Denning 243
Pedro I, Emperor of Brazil 8
Pelly, Air Chief Marshal Sir Claude 90, 232
Peirse, Air Chief Marshal Sir Richard 103, 117
Percival, Lieutenant General Arthur 74
Petwood Hotel 174, 194
Philpott, Group Captain M. G. 194
Pidcock, Air Vice-Marshal G. A. H. 127
Pilcher, Flying Officer G. N. 62
Pirie, Air Chief Marshal Sir George 64
Place, Rear Admiral Godfrey 257
POINTBLANK, Operation 155, 186
Pollock, Lieutenant Colonel C. F. 21
Portal of Hungerford, Marshal of the Royal Air Force Viscount 73, 107, 117, 121, 125, 128, 148, 184, 188, 208, 216, 227
   in Wessex Bombing Area 53, 261–2
   Ralph shares office with 69, 70–1, 217, 262
   appoints Ralph to command at Abingdon 91
   selects Ralph as Director of Flying Training 95, 262
   appoints Ralph AOC 3 Group 103, 262
   orders formation of Pathfinders 109
   backs raid on dams 128–30, 143
   asks for Ralph as ACAS 197–8, 262

Pound, Admiral of the Fleet Sir Dudley 128
Powell, Flight Sergeant George 137
Power, Admiral of the Fleet Sir Arthur 73
Pratt, H. B. 26
Prinz Eugen, German cruiser 103
Pulford, Sergeant John 279
Pye, Sir David 125

Quebec & Ontario Transportation Company 239

Ratcliffe, Mrs 244, 250
Rattigan, Sir Terence 15
Redgrave, Sir Michael 247
Reid, Flight Lieutenant William 256
Rice, Air Vice Marshal Sir Edward 208
Rice, Flight Lieutenant Geoff 135, 145, 146, 167, 168, 173, 257
Rickards, Wing Commander A. R. M. 58–9, 61
Rising Star, Chilean warship 8
Ritchie, Professor A. D. 28
Rivett-Carnac, Vice-Admiral James 277
RJM Exports Ltd 251, 252
Rodney, Admiral Lord 3
Rolls-Royce Ltd 219, 242–5, 249, 251, 265
Rongotai Airfield 85, 88
Rope, Captain F. M. 28
Rose, Pilot Officer 140
Roskill, Captain S. W. 245
Ross, Major General Robert 4
Royal Aircraft Establishment 50, 76, 242
Royal Air Force
   Overseas Air Forces
      Advanced Air Striking Force 91
      Air Forces of Occupation 221, 232
      Allied Expeditionary 187
      Desert 210, 277
      Second Tactical 277
   Home Commands
      Air Defence of Great Britain 50, 52, 75, 212
      Army Co-operation 97

Bomber viii, 40, 64, 75, 91, 94–5, 97, 100, 102, 103–210, 215–16, 223, 253, 254–6, 259, 262–4, 273, 278, 281
Coastal 63, 75, 91, 97, 98, 102, 135, 181, 212, 215, 218, 229, 231, 256
Ferry 212, 213
Fighter 75, 97, 98, 131, 141, 184, 256, 277
Flying Training 92, 94, 95, 97, 222, 223–9
Maintenance 49
Strike 256
Technical Training 97
Training 75–6, 89, 92, 97, 223
Transport ix, 64, 209, 211–22, 223, 225, 226, 232, 242, 256, 260, 262, 265, 276

Areas
Central 91
Coastal 75
Fighting 52, 212
Inland 75
Wessex Bombing 51–2, 56, 63, 91, 112, 122, 223

Groups
1 91, 104, 111, 162, 179, 181, 183, 189, 190, 193, 204, 207, 208
2 199
3 102, 113–15, 121–2, 142, 157, 159, 162, 175, 178, 192–3, 204, 207, 216, 247, 267, 281
4 102, 110, 111, 116, 162, 166, 171, 172, 195, 204, 207, 216, 221
5 viii, 102, 110, 112, 114, 115–210, 214, 219–20, 224–5, 248, 253, 255–6, 260, 262, 264, 267, 276, 281
6 91, 93, 278
7 93–7, 112–3, 117, 179, 208
8 101, 107, 134, 156, 162, 172–3, 174–5, 181, 184–5, 187–8, 190, 193, 196–7, 205, 207
11 277
12 131

21 224, 227
23 75, 224
24 75
25 224
38 214, 216, 220, 221, 276
44 212, 213
45 213
46 214, 220, 221
47 215, 221
100 184, 194, 205, 207, 231, 255
216 213, 214, 218
229 213, 215, 218
Armament 75

Bases
51 179
52 179
53 179, 195
54 179, 186–7, 188, 201
55 179
56 179

Wings
179 213

UK Stations
Abingdon 91–3
Andover 52
Balderton 179, 204
Bardney 179, 196, 201, 203
Bicester 93, 95
Binbrook 279
Bircham Newton 52, 53
Boscombe Down 139, 145
Bottesford 104, 123, 179, 180
Bourn 104
Brize Norton 256, 259
Chedburgh 104
Coningsby 132, 167, 168, 174, 176, 179, 187, 188, 189, 201, 280
Cottesmore 93
Cranfield 132
Digby 132
Downham Market 104
Dunholme Lodge 158, 179, 204
Eastchurch 52
East Kirkby 179

East Wretham 104
Feltwell 104, 107
Fiskerton 123, 179, 181, 204
Fulbeck 179, 204
Halton 46–7, 48, 75, 122, 256
Harwell 106
Grantham/Spitalgate 52, 122, 278
Lakenheath 104
Langar 123, 179, 180
Leuchars 76
Lossiemouth 181, 205
Ludford Magna 181
Lyneham 219
Manby 227
Manston 52, 76, 138, 139, 141, 203
Marham 104
Marston Moor 171, 172
Metheringham 179, 181, 187
Mildenhall 104
Montrose 76
Netheravon 52, 76
Newmarket 104, 107
Northolt 215
Portreath 212
Prestwick 212
Ridgewell 104
Scampton 122, 131, 133–4, 136, 138, 142, 144–5, 148–52, 154, 167, 179, 204, 256–7
Skellingthorpe 123, 179
Spilsby 179
Stradishall 104, 107
Strubby 179, 180
Sturgate 181
Swinderby 122, 123, 179, 180
Syerston 121, 132, 133, 179, 225, 279
Tangmere 104
Tempsford 104, 173, 281
Upper Heyford 93
Upwood 93
Waddington 118, 123, 159, 179, 195, 199
Wellingore 132
West Malling 132

Wigsley 179
Winthorpe 179
Woodhall Spa 123, 156, 174, 176, 179, 187, 188, 194, 206, 280, 281
Worthy Down 52, 53, 116
Wyton 110
Overseas Stations
Abu Sueir 34, 35, 37, 99
Blida 159, 166, 171
Dorval 212, 213
Habbaniya 99
Heliopolis/Almaza 32, 33, 35, 36, 275
Hinaidi 36, 37, 38, 41, 42, 44, 60, 61, 116, 212, 258
Khormaksar 59
Squadrons
1 38, 39
7 52, 53, 103, 110–11
8 38, 39, 58, 59–62, 112, 170
9 52, 196, 201–2, 203, 205–6
10 101, 109
11 52
12 52
13 52
15 (XV) 104, 199, 278
24 221
29 131–2
30 42
31 39, 119
39 52
44 118, 119, 135, 136
45 35–42, 63, 104, 109, 112, 116, 170, 211, 254, 261, 266, 275
49 117, 134, 136, 158, 165, 204
50 122, 135–6, 188, 267
51 195
55 39
57 123, 134, 135, 137, 279
58 52, 53, 116
61 123, 136, 188
70 34, 35, 38, 39, 211
75 104, 105, 106, 107, 220, 245, 277
76 171, 172
78 166, 195

82 199
83 110, 119, 122, 131, 134, 187, 188, 190, 191
90 104, 105, 278
97 92, 119, 123, 136, 156, 157, 158, 187, 188, 190, 191
99 52
100 52
101 104
102 135, 166, 171
106 123, 132, 134, 137
108 199
109 110
115 104, 105
138 104, 173
149 104
156 110
158 166
161 104, 281
166 91
189 204
207 52, 118, 123, 136
210 139
214 104
216 32
218 104, 192
227 203–4
405 166, 207
511 260
617 vii, viii, ix, 134–151, 155, 157–8, 164–176, 178, 185, 186–90, 192–6, 201–3, 205–7, 233–4, 246–7, 256–60, 262–4
619 156, 178, 188, 204
627 187, 188–9, 190, 191, 280
630 179
Metropolitan Communications 221
Training Units
　Air Armament School 75
　Air Observers School 75
　Central Flying School 75, 76, 224
　Empire Air Armament School 227
　Empire Air Navigation School 224
　Empire Flying School 224

RAF College, Cranwell 45, 75, 194, 195, 224, 256
RAF Flying College 227
RAF Staff College, Andover 46, 47, 48–51, 63–4, 69, 97, 117, 186, 226–7, 245, 262
School of Air Navigation 75
1 FTS 36
2 FTS 63
3 FTS 39, 76
4 FTS 34–5, 99, 223, 277
6 FTS 76
7 FTS 76
8 FTS 76
9 FTS 76
10 FTS 76
11 FTS 76
1652 HCU 171, 172
1654 HCU 122, 179
1660 HCU 122
1661 HCU 179
5 Lancaster Finishing School 179
10 OTU 92
13 OTU 93, 94, 95, 199
14 OTU 93, 94, 117, 131, 132
16 OTU 93, 94, 117, 131, 132
17 OTU 93, 94
51 OTU 132
Other
　Aeroplane & Armament Experimental Establishment 139
　Boy's Wing, Cranwell 45–6, 266
　Overseas Air Movements Control Unit 212
　Oxford University Air Squadron 91, 171
　RAF Benevolent Fund 180, 259, 266
　RAF Princess Alexandra Hospital 258
　RAF Regiment 237
　RAF Sussex Down Nursing Home 258
　Reserve of Air Force Officers 75, 76, 198
　Tiger Force 208
Royal Air Force Club 96, 256

Royal Air Force Volunteer Reserve 171
Royal Airship Works 47
Royal Australian Air Force
  Squadrons
    455 122, 136
    463 178–9, 201, 206
    467 123, 137, 158, 179
Royal Auxiliary Air Force
  Squadrons
    600 199
Royal Canadian Air Force
  Group
    6 (RCAF) 163, 173, 204, 206, 207
Royal Canadian Military Institute 257
Royal Commission on Awards to
  Inventors 234
Royal Empire Society 227
Royal Geographical Society 62
Royal Navy
  Fleet
    Home, later Grand 17, 19–20
  Squadron
    First Battle 17
    Second Battle 17–19
  RNAS Airship Stations
    Capel-le-Ferne 23, 30, 38
    Howden 26, 47
    Kingsnorth 22–3, 25, 26, 27, 29
    Pulham 29, 47
    Scapa 25–6, 274
    Wormwood Scrubs 274
  Fleet Air Arm Station
    Gosport 50
  Ships
    Arab 6
    Ajax 3–4
    Barfleur 5
    Carysfort 24
    Centurion 70
    Colossus 16–20
    Cornwall 15–16
    Dunedin 82
    Hind 5
    Impérieuse 6

    Leander 87
    Northumberland 4
    Pacahunter 3
    Queen Charlotte 5
    Speedy 5–6
    Thetis 3
    Warrior 9
  Submarines
    E-7 29
    X7 257
  Shore Establishments
    No. 1 Balloon Training Wing 21
    Royal Naval College, Dartmouth 14,
      15–16
    Royal Naval College, Osborne 14–15
    Royal Naval Staff College,
      Greenwich 48–9, 50
Royal New Zealand Air Force
  Bases
    Hobsonville 83, 84, 89
    Ohakea 84, 245, 246
    Whenuapei 84
    Wigram 81, 82, 83, 86, 260
  Squadrons
    75 104, 105, 106–7, 220, 245, 277
Royal United Services Institution 62
Royal Yugoslav Army Air Force 51
Royal Yugoslav Navy 51
Rubbra, Arthur 243
Ryder, Sue (Lady Cheshire) 258

St Clement Danes 260
St Nicholas, fishing boat 34–5
St Vincent, Admiral of the Fleet, John, Earl
  of 6
Salmond, Marshal of the Royal Air Force
  Sir John 40, 44, 50, 70, 77, 275
Salote, Queen of Tonga 87
Sanders, Air Chief Marshal Sir
  Arthur 230, 234
San Martin, General José de 8
Satterly, Air Vice-Marshal H. V. 122, 124,
  133, 137, 139, 142, 144, 145, 151, 154,
  179, 194, 234

Saundby, Air Marshal Sir Robert 36, 37, 40, 42, 53, 104, 127, 129, 140, 174, 188, 255
Saunders, Air Chief Marshal Sir Hugh 88–9
Saward, Group Captain Dudley 255
Sayer, Wing Commander E. J. 58
Scharnhorst, German battleship 103, 118
Schneider Trophy 55–6
Scott, Major George 48, 275
Scott, Group Captain R. C. E. 217
Scroggs, Group Captain H. S. 44
Searby, Air Commodore J. H. 162–3
Shand, John 65, 66
Shannon, Squadron Leader David 134, 145, 147, 148, 167, 168, 170, 189, 193, 194
Sharp, Air Vice-Marshal Bobby 188, 194, 234, 280
Sherriff, R. C. 247
Ship Constructive & Shipwrights Association 239, 240–1
Shute, Nevil 278
Sinclair, Sir Archibald, *later* Viscount Thurso 103, 206, 208, 213
Sinclair-Burgess, Major General Sir William 80
Ski Club of Great Britain 244
Slee, Group Captain L. C. 158
Slessor, Marshal of the Royal Air Force Sir John 96, 117, 118–19, 132, 208, 216, 222, 229–30, 231, 234–5, 254, 264, 278, 281
Slim, Field Marshal Viscount 230
Sorley, Air Marshal Sir Ralph 127
South-West Wiltshire Hunt 51
Spaatz, General Carl A. 176, 186, 280
Special Operations Executive 104
Speer, Albert 153, 254
Spyway School 122
Standard Oil Company 16
Stansgate, William Wedgwood Benn, Viscount 217
Steele, Air Chief Marshal Sir John 52–3

Stewart, Alexander 237
Stewart, Catriona 237
Stewart, David 237
Stewart, Grizel, Lady 72, 76, 85, 88, 122, 233, 237, 260
Stewart, John 237
Stewart, Colonel Sir Robert 237
Stewart, Sara 237
Stirling, General Sir William 254
Story, Ala 69
Suggitt, Squadron Leader W. R. 173
Summers, Captain Joseph 'Mutt' 126, 129, 138, 144, 152, 234
Sunley, Bernard 238
Sutton, Air Chief Marshal Sir Bertine 49

Tait, Group Captain J. B. 195, 196, 201, 203, 206, 207, 234, 256, 257, 259, 260
TAXABLE, Operation 192
Tedder, Marshal of the Royal Air Force Lord 63, 73, 186, 199, 227, 228, 229, 232, 247, 264, 281
Tees, Flight Sergeant F. 149
Tewson, Sir Vincent 241
Thatcher's Hotel 259
Thomas, Flight Lieutenant Godfrey 30
Tidworth Forest Hunt 51
Tirpitz, German battleship ix, 138, 201–2, 205–6, 257
Titanic, RMS 16
Tizard, Sir Henry 125, 126, 231
Todd, Richard 247
Todt Organisation 153
TORCH, Operation 111
Townsend, Flight Lieutenant Bill 136, 149, 150, 151, 280
Transportation Plan 186, 190, 196
Trenchard, Marshal of the Royal Air Force Viscount 32–3, 38, 40, 45, 48, 49, 52, 142, 246, 261, 282
Trevor-Roper, Flight Lieutenant Richard 279
Trinidad Oilfields 16
Troubridge, Admiral Sir Thomas 16

Tudor Hall 122
Turner, Charles 84

United Society of Boilermakers, Shipbuilders & Constructive Workers 239, 240–1
United States Army Air Force/United States Air Force
Air Force
Eighth 155, 176, 186
Command
Air Materials 226
Air Training 225
Air Force Base
Maison Blanche 158–9
Maxwell 225
Randolph 225
Other
Air Command and Staff College 225, 245, 281
National War College 225

VARSITY, Operation 214
Verrier, Anthony 255
Vickers 26, 27, 47, 51, 81, 126, 128, 129, 137
Victoria, HM Queen 9, 13, 14
Vinchon-Bolland, Adrienne 65
Von Schiller, Captain Hans 65

Wallis, Sir Barnes viii, 141, 148, 152, 154, 166–7, 199, 231, 234, 247, 256, 257–8, 259, 263, 265
Ralph works with on airships 26
Ralph meets in 1924 47
and Wellington for RNZAF 81, 106
designs UPKEEP for Dams Raid 124–30
and AAD Committee 125
supported by Portal 128
meets Harris 128–9
meets Gibson 137–8
and UPKEEP trials 138–40
at Scampton and Grantham for CHASTISE 144–5, 147, 149–50, 279

Harris supports 150–1
and TALLBOY 169–70, 174, 190, 193, 202, 206
Wallis, Molly, Lady 257, 259
Walmsley, Air Marshal Sir Hugh 266
Warrender, Vice-Admiral Sir George 17
Warwick, Squadron Leader J. B. 201
Watson, Flight Lieutenant Henry 139–40
Watt, Professor Donald Cameron 255
Watts, F. C. 225
Webster, Sir Charles 253
Webster, Air Vice-Marshal Sidney 56
Westland Aircraft 54, 56, 64
White, Major 17
Whitworth, Air Commodore J. N. H. 133, 139, 140, 142, 144, 150, 151, 152, 154, 172
Wiggin, Arthur 67
Wiggin, Sir Charles 276
Wiggin, Second Lieutenant Douglas 67
Wiggin, (Caroline) Eva 67, 96
Wiggin, Eva, *later* Nisbet, Eva 67
Wiggin, Frances, *later* Scarlett, Frances 67
Wiggin, Hilda, *see* Cochrane, Hilda, Lady
Wiggin, Mary, *later* Fanshawe, Mary 67
Wiggin, Lieutenant Noel 67
Wilkes, Group Captain T. M. 79, 80, 82, 85, 245
William IV, HM King 9
Williams, Captain T. D. 28
Wilson, Flight Lieutenant Harold 136, 144, 165, 167, 168
Winterbotham, Group Captain F. W. 125, 129
Wollaston, Sir Mountford 88
Wood, Flying Officer L. G. 33–4
Worsley, Flight Lieutenant O. E. 56
Wright, Robert 254–5
Wyness, Squadron Leader D. R. C. 203

Yalta Conference 215
Yearsley, Captain Kenneth 274
Young, Squadron Leader Henry 135, 144, 145, 147, 149–50

Index II

Place Names

Aachen 111
Abberton Reservoir 141
Abbeville 173
Abbotts Ann 71
Abergavenny 240
Aboukir Bay 3
Aden 57–62, 66, 70, 72, 73, 75, 76, 112
Alexandria 35, 71
Amman 36, 37
Ancon 8
Antheor Viaduct 169, 170, 173, 175, 194
Antwerp 66, 68, 202
Aquata Scrivia 166
Archangel 201
Ardrossan 13
Arndean 237
Arnhem 213, 214
Arosa Bay 19
Aswan 66
Auchans House 2
Auckland 78, 83, 84, 86, 245, 266
Augsburg 119, 120

Baghdad 36, 38, 40, 41, 43, 63, 211, 266
Bala Lake 137
Baltimore 4
Banbury 122
Bantry Bay 17, 18
Barbados 15–16
Bardufoss 205
Barrow-in-Furness 26, 27
Basel 203
Basque Roads 7
Basra 44, 60
Beersheba 36

Belgrade 51, 55
Bentley Priory 75
Berehaven 17
Bergen 204
Berlin 54, 55, 65, 68, 114, 121, 156, 161, 162, 177–9, 180, 181, 183–4, 222, 232, 247, 276
Bermuda 16
Bever Dam 149
Bladon Castle 244, 250
Blida 158–9, 166, 171
Bochum 156
Bologna 166
Bormes-les-Mimosas 258
Boulogne 193, 200
Boulogne-Bilancourt 119
Bradbrook House 233
Bremerhaven 200
Brest 103, 114, 118, 191, 196, 200
Brindisi 71, 73
Broomhall 237, 259
Brunswick 66, 189, 191, 204
Brussels 54, 65
Buckden 95
Budapest 68
Buntingsdale Hall 76
Burford 251, 258, 260
Burnt Norton 122
Burton-on-Trent 244
Bushy Park 214, 219

Caen 196,
Cairo 32, 34, 36, 38, 41, 66, 72, 73, 211, 212, 213
Calais 192, 200

Callao 8
Camberley 49, 50, 228–9, 230
Campalto 29
Canton Island 87
Cap d'Antifer 192
Cardington 47, 48
Cattaro 51
Charlton King's 67
Cheltenham 67, 251, 259
Chequers 142
Cherbourg 19, 203
Chesapeake Bay 4
Chesil Beach 126, 127, 138
Chipping Norton 250, 251
Christchurch (New Zealand) 81, 82, 86, 245
Christmas Island 87
Ciampino 28, 29
Cirencester 66
Coln Rogers 251
Cologne 54, 65, 104, 111, 120, 156, 171
Constance, Lake 65, 158
Cook Islands 86
Corfu 71
Crawford Priory 12–14, 46, 66, 83, 88, 95, 224, 236, 249, 250
Crete 71
Croydon 51, 56
Culross 3
Cupar 11
Dardanelles, 28
Darmstadt 65, 197, 200, 201, 255
Derby 219, 242, 244
Derwent Reservoir 138, 141
Devonport 16
Dhala 58–9
Diemel Dam 142
Dieppe 192
Dijon 56
Djenovici 51
Dollar 237
Dorsten 146
Dortmund 156
Dortmund–Ems Canal 117, 167–8, 169, 193, 194, 202, 263

Douai 64
Dove, River 244
Dresden 200
Dublin 18
Dubrovnic 51
Duisburg 68, 111, 156, 191
Dülmen 146
Dundonald Castle 2
Dunedin 86
Dunfermline 237
Dunkirk 70, 117
Düsseldorf 66, 156
Dvina, River 201

East Horsley 259
Eder Dam vii, 124, 141, 147–8, 149, 150, 151, 153, 158, 164, 267
Edinburgh 54
Eifel Mountains 206
Elbe, River 119, 161
Elburz Mountains 44
El Jid 36, 41
Emden 167
Emmerich 148
Ennepe Dam 142, 149, 153
Entebbe 72
Essen 68, 111, 156
Eyebrook Reservoir 141
Exning House 104

Fairspear House 252
Ferrara 29
Field House 95–6
Fiji 86, 87
Fiume 51
Flixecourt 173
Folkestone 23
Frankfurt 54, 65, 111, 177
Friedrichshafen 65, 157–8, 162, 166, 276
Friesian Islands 144

Gallipoli 28
Gander 212
Gelsenkirchen 156

Genoa 111, 166
Gibraltar 212, 218
Giessen 204
Gilze-Rijen 149
Glane, River 167
Glebe House 251
Glenrothes 250
Gloucester 212, 213
Goose Bay 212
Grantham 121–2, 144, 145, 147, 148, 149, 150
Great Bitter Lakes 34
Great Rollright Manor 250–1
Greenwich 48–9, 50
Grove Farmhouse 251, 252, 256, 266
Guadeloupe 4
Gumley Court 246

Hadhramaut 61
Hadra 42
Halifax (Nova Scotia) 16
Hamadan 43
Hamburg 111, 112, 114, 161–2, 177
Hamm 149
Hannover 54
Harburg 204
Harrow 213, 214
Harwich 24, 29
Harz Mountains 163
Heilbronn 204
Heligoland 116
Heston 64, 66
High Wycombe 104, 123, 129, 142, 174, 180, 199, 263
Hillah 38
Holdshott House 223
Holyrood House 11, 54
Homberg 204
Howden 47
Howden Reservoir 141
Huntingdon 93, 96
Hutt Valley 88

Ijmuiden 196
Innsbruck 51

Isfahan 44, 258
Ismailia 34

Jerusalem 37
Juba 72

Kaa Fjord 201
Kano 212
Karachi 213, 215
Karnak 32
Kassel 153
Kastellorizo 34
Kasvin 43, 258
Kembs Barrage 203
Kenya, Mount 72
Kermanshah 43
Khanikin 43
Khartoum 72, 212
Khoram 42
Kiel 103, 111
Kilmarnock 2
Kingston 214
Kirkuk 39, 42, 60, 211
Kirkwall 25
Klosters 68, 258
Königsberg 197
Krefeld 111, 156
Kut-el-Amara 67

La Chapelle 189
Lagos 212
Ladysmith 9
Lahej 57, 58, 60
Lamlash Bay 18
Langton Matravers 122
La Pallice 114, 195
Larnaca 34
La Spezia 159
Lar Valley 258
Leafield 252
Le Court 246
Le Creusot 120, 132, 158
Le Havre 192, 193, 200
Leighton Buzzard 224

Leipzig 54, 65, 68, 177
Lille 191
Lincoln 134
Lister Dam 142, 153
Livingstone (Southern Rhodesia) 72
Ljubljana 51
Lorient 114, 120, 157, 195
Lübeck 54, 111
Luxor 32

Magdeburg 54
Mahon 5
Mailly-le-Camp 190, 192
Malta 7, 135, 212, 213, 220, 277
Mannheim 111, 279
Maoribank 88
Market Drayton 78
Martinique 3, 4, 5
Melton Mowbray 46
Milan 111, 166
Mimoyecques 194
Miramar 85
Mitttelland Canal 124, 153, 167, 202
Möhne Dam vii, 124, 138, 139, 141, 144, 146–7, 148, 150, 151, 152, 153, 157, 164, 267
Mönchengladbach 200
Monmouth 240
Montgomery (Alabama) 225
Montreal 212, 257
Morton Hall 180
Moscow 237, 239
Mostar 51
Mosul 39, 41–2
Much Hadham 122
Mühlheim 68
Mukalla 61
Munich 111, 156, 190, 192, 204–5

Nagasaki 246
Nairobi 72
Nant-y-Gro Dam 126
Navarino 9
Newcastle 240

New Delhi 215
New Orleans 4
Newport 238, 241
New York 257
Nice 56
Nicosia 34
Nineveh 42
Norman Leys 121
Novi Sad 51
Nuremberg 65, 114, 156, 183–4, 204

Oban 18
Oddington 91, 251
Old Hall 242–4, 249
Oléron 7
Oslo Fjord 111, 207
Osnabruck 111
Ottawa 98, 257
Oxford 91, 93, 237, 252, 253, 254, 258

Padua 55
Paisley 1, 2, 3, 27
Palermo 5
Palmerston North 84, 245
Pant-y-Goitre 240, 244
Paphos 34
Paris 51, 67, 189, 194
Peenemünde 162–3, 173, 207
Perim 59
Persepolis 44
Pilsen 157
Ploesti 159
Plymouth 4, 15
Pontevedra Bay 19
Pontresina 45
Portland 17, 19
Port Said 34, 36
Portsmouth 5, 50
Prague 65
Putney 214

Quebec 16

Rafa 36
Raglan 240

Ramadi 36, 37, 41
Ramleh 37
Reculver 138, 141, 154
Reykjavik 212
Rheydt 200
Rhine, River 54, 55, 158, 203, 213–14
Roehampton 21
Rome 28, 29, 274
Rothensee Ship Lift 167, 174
Rotorua 83
Rotterdam 202
Rügen 163
Ruhr, River 124
Ruhr Valley 68, 107, 108, 124, 140, 142, 152, 153, 154, 156, 161, 167, 183, 184, 196, 204
Rutbah 36

St Anton 65
St Leu d'Esserent 194
St Lucia 15
St Moritz 67–8
St Nazaire 114
St Vincent's Hall 121, 133, 138, 159, 164, 180
Salisbury (Southern Rhodesia) 72
Salzburg 68–9
Samarra 43
San Domingo 4
San Polo d'Enza 166
Santiago 8
Saumur Tunnel 193
Sayun 62
Scapa Flow 18, 19, 20, 21, 25–6, 274
Scheldt, River 202
Scholven 196
Schweinfurt 190
Shane's Castle 13
Sheffield 138
Shibam 61
Shinfield Park 223
Shipton-under-Wychwood 251, 252
Shiraz 44, 258
Sibenik 51

Singapore 69–70, 74, 80, 81, 219
Siracourt 194
Soissons 75
Sorpe Dam 138, 141, 148, 149, 153
Southampton 44, 58
Storrington 258
Stuttgart 65, 111, 132, 156, 177, 196
Suez Canal 34, 58

Takoradi 212
Tarim 61
Taupo 83
Teddington 126, 128, 214
Teheran 43–4, 258
Tema 237
Texel 146
Thebes 32
Timsah, Lake 34
Tonga 86, 87
Torneträsk, Lake 205–6
Toronto 4, 257
Toulouse 186–7
Tragino Aqueduct 166, 195
Travemünde 54
Trinidad 15–16
Tromsø 202, 205, 206
Trondheim 204
Troon 2
Turin 111, 135

Urft Dam 206
Usk, River 238, 240

Valdivia 8
Valparaiso 8
Venice 29, 55
Vienna 51, 65, 68
Vigo 19
Vranjska Banja 51
Vyrnwy, Lake 137

Wainfleet 141, 162
Walcheren Island 202–3, 204
Warnemünde 54

Washington D.C. 4, 103, 143, 148, 150, 225, 232
Wellington (New Zealand) 82, 83, 84, 85, 86, 88, 89, 260
Wesseling 196
Weser, River 124, 153
Weybridge 137–8, 154
Weymouth 17
Wilhelmshaven 114
Wroughton 258
Wüppertal 156

Yagodnik 201
Yeovil 54

Zagreb 51
Zell am See 69
Ziza 36–7, 38, 41
Zweizimmen 236